D0849614

Management and Industrial Relations Series

7

The debate on inflation accounting

Management and Industrial Relations Series

Editors:

DOROTHY WEDDERBURN
Principal of Bedford College, London

MICHAEL BROMWICH
Professor of Finance and Accounting, University of Reading

and

DOUGLAS BROOKS
Director, Walker Brooks and Partners

Social science research has much to contribute to the better understanding and solution of problems in the field of management and industrial relations. The difficulty, however, is that there is frequently a gap between the researcher and the practitioner who wants to use the research results. This new series is designed to make available to practitioners in the relevant fields the results of the best research which the Economic and Social Research Council (ESRC) has supported in the fields of management and industrial relations. The subjects covered and the style adopted will appeal to managers, trade unionists and administrators because there will be an emphasis upon the practical implications of research findings. But the volumes will also serve as a useful introduction to particular areas for students and teachers of management and industrial relations.

The series is published by Cambridge University Press in collaboration with the Economic and Social Research Council.

Other books in the series

The debate on inflation accounting

DAVID TWEEDIE

UK Research Partner, Thomson McLintock & Co./KMG and Visiting Professor, ICRA, University of Lancaster

and

GEOFFREY WHITTINGTON

Professor of Accounting and Finance, University of Bristol

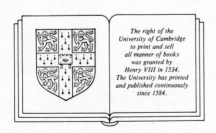

The right of the
University of Cambridge
to print and sell
all manner of books
was granted by
Henry VIII in 1534.
The University has printed
and published continuously
since 1584.

CAMBRIDGE UNIVERSITY PRESS

Cambridge

London   New York   New Rochelle

Melbourne   Sydney

Published by the Press Syndicate of the University of Cambridge
The Pitt Building, Trumpington Street, Cambridge CB2 1RP
32 East 57th Street, New York, NY 10022, USA
296 Beaconsfield Parade, Middle Park, Melbourne 3206, Australia

First published 1984

Printed in Great Britain at The Pitman Press, Bath

Library of Congress catalogue card number: 84–7683

British Library cataloguing in publication data

Tweedie, David
  The debate on inflation accounting.
  1. Inflation (Finance) and accounting
  I. Title   II. Whittington, Geoffrey
  657'.48   HF5658.5

ISBN 0 521 24586 9

PP

Contents

Contents

To Jan and Joyce

Preface

The objective of this book is to provide an historical account of the debate on inflation accounting, which has taken place more or less continuously throughout the twentieth century, but which has been particularly fierce during the past ten years when, in the wake of the oil crisis of 1973, the world economy has experienced sustained inflation at rates which, by historical standards, have been very high. We cover the whole of the twentieth century and all of those countries which have made a major contribution to the inflation accounting debate, or which have developed some significant form of inflation accounting practice. Our definition of 'inflation accounting' is eclectic, including all forms of accounting which seek to reflect the consequences of price changes, whether by means of general price indices or by reporting the market prices of specific commodities.

We have had to impose certain limitations on our study, which are discussed more fully in Chapter 1. The first of these is that we confine our attention to financial accounts, published for the use of those outside the firm, rather than management accounts. A second limitation is that we do not attempt a systematic exposition of the theory of inflation accounting, apart from a brief introductory outline in Chapter 1. This deficiency may be made good by reading the companion volume, *Inflation Accounting: An introduction to the debate*, by Geoffrey Whittington (Cambridge University Press, 1983a). A third limitation is that, despite the claims to comprehensive coverage made in the previous paragraph, we have had to give only superficial attention to some periods and some countries, in order to enable us to bring into sharper focus the countries and periods which we selected for special attention. We have concentrated on the most recent period, notably that from the early 1970s to the present time, and on the 'Anglo-Saxon' or English-speaking countries, notably the United Kingdom, which afforded us with the best opportunity to pursue original research from archives and from personal interviews.

Despite these limitations, we feel that the evolution of the theory and practice of inflation accounting, as described in the book, affords insights not only into inflation accounting and its possible future development, but also into the processes by which accounting theory and practice evolve and interact, and into the accounting standard-setting process. We spell out our interpretation of these implications in the final four chapters of the book (Chapters 11 to 14 inclusive). We stress that these conclusions depend very much on our own subjective judgement, and that our evidence is not as complete as we would wish, but we hope that our conclusions will serve as a stimulus to others to carry out further research to verify, modify or reject them. We feel that our present conclusions are at least consistent with the best evidence currently available (although the evidence may also be consistent with alternative interpretations), and we have certainly emerged from this study with a strengthened belief of the importance of this type of research.

Much of the originality of this study lies in bringing together in one place a wide variety of previously published knowledge. However, we have done some work which can claim to be entirely original in our study of the recent debate in the United Kingdom. In particular, with the permission of the then Chairman of the Accounting Standards Committee, Tom Watts, we studied the minutes of ASC and its predecessor ASSC. With the permission of the present Chairman of ASC, Ian Hay Davison, we studied a complete set of working papers of the Inflation Accounting Study Group, of which he had been a member, and we received clarification on a number of points relating to IASG from its Chairman, Sir Douglas Morpeth. We also conducted a series of interviews with leading participants in the inflation accounting standard-setting process: Professor Harold Edey, Martin Gibbs, the late Sir Edmund Parker, Professor Walter Reid, Sir Francis Sandilands and Christopher Westwick. Finally, we carried out analysis of responses to various inflation accounting exposure drafts, as reported in Chapters 4 to 6 and 13.

Apart from the interviews and assistance acknowledged in the previous paragraph, we have received helpful evidence from Professor Edward Stamp, on the evolution of ideas in *The Corporate Report* and on the early development of government thinking on inflation account-ing, and from John Foyle, who was secretary to the Hyde Committee. We have also benefited from correspondence with The Right Honour-able Mr Justice Richardson, Chairman of the New Zealand Committee of Inquiry. Others who have provided useful comments and information on overseas developments include, on The Netherlands Jan Klaassen, Jules Muis and Henk Volten, on West Germany Peter Marks, on

Preface

Sweden Hans Edenhammar, on Australia Kevin Stevenson, on New Zealand Chris Westworth, on Canada Doug Thomas and on the USA Professor Bryan Carsberg, Professor Stephen Zeff and members of the staff of the National Office of Price Waterhouse. Price Waterhouse must be accorded particular thanks for enabling one of us (Geoffrey Whittington) to visit New York, under their Faculty Fellowship scheme, in order to study American developments at first hand.

Parts of an earlier draft of our manuscript were subject to scrutiny, in relation to matters of which they have particular knowledge, by Professor Harold Edey, Sir Douglas Morpeth, Professor Walter Reid, Sir Francis Sandilands, Professor Edward Stamp, and Professor Stephen Zeff. This acknowledgement should not, however, be taken to imply their approval of our views or their responsibility for any factual errors which we have committed.

The above acknowledgements testify to the widespread encouragement and support which we have received from participants in, and observers of, the inflation accounting debate. We should like to thank many others who have helped us by providing information or critical comment or in other ways, but who are, unfortunately, too numerous to be acknowledged individually here. They include colleagues at the University of Bristol and Thomson McLintock & Co./KMG and former colleagues at the Institute of Chartered Accountants of Scotland. Responsibility for the final text does, however, rest firmly with the authors. We are joint and equal authors having shared responsibility for the original draft in roughly equal proportions and having redrafted each other's work to such extent that it would be impossible (and irrelevant) to attempt to attribute individual authorship.

Our work was made possible in the case of one of us (Geoffrey Whittington) by the award of a Social Science Research Council Research Fellowship in Inflation Accounting for 1979–81, and in the case of the other (David Tweedie) by the support of his employers, firstly the Institute of Chartered Accountants of Scotland (where he was Technical Director until December 1981) and, secondly, Thomson McLintock & Co./KMG (of which he has been a partner since January 1982 and UK Director of Accounting and Auditing Research since April 1983). The library and research facilities of the University of Bristol, the Scottish Institute and Thomson McLintock have been invaluable. Special thanks are due to Moira Hay of Thomson McLintock for administrative support. Our joint work was given considerable initial impetus by our being able to work together, during the Autumn of 1980, at the International Centre for Research in Accounting (ICRA) at the University of Lancaster. We are grateful to Professor Edward Stamp,

Preface

the Director of ICRA, for making these facilities available, and for his enthusiastic encouragement of our work.

A final but very important acknowledgement is to Val Harvey in Bristol and Ina Peace and Patricia Laing in Edinburgh, who have typed not only the final manuscript but also innumerable earlier drafts patiently and efficiently, often improving the comprehensibility of the text by adding some of the punctuation in which at least one of us is woefully deficient.

We have long envied the author of a work on rural archaeology who was able to dedicate his book to his mother for making the sandwiches which he needed on his rambles round archaeological sites. Our rambles round the ruins of abandoned inflation accounting proposals have, unfortunately, been of a purely cerebral and sedentary nature, although they have not lacked intellectual interest. However, we have still, from time to time, needed sandwiches and these have been made by our wives, who have also filled what we would like to imagine to be large gaps in the lives of our families during our enforced absences. It is, therefore, to our wives that this book is dedicated.

November 1983   GEOFFREY WHITTINGTON
                                                              Bristol

                                                        DAVID TWEEDIE
                                                          Edinburgh

Abbreviations

AAA	American Accounting Association
AARF	Australian Accounting Research Foundation
AASC	Australian Accounting Standards Committee
ACCA	Association of Certified and Corporate Accountants
AICPA	American Institute of Certified Public Accountants
APB	Accounting Principles Board (the professional standard-setting body in the USA before the FASB was created)
ARS	Accounting Research Study (by the Research Committee of the AICPA)
ASA	Australian Society of Accountants
ASC	Accounting Standards Committee
ASR	Accounting Series Release (issued by the SEC)
ASSC	Accounting Standards Steering Committee (became the ASC in 1975)
CCA	Current Cost Accounting
CCAB	Consultative Committee of Accountancy Bodies (the parent body of ASC)
CICA	Canadian Institute of Chartered Accountants
CoCoA	Continuously Contemporary Accounting
COSA	Cost of Sales Adjustment
CPP	Constant Purchasing Power
CVA	Current Value Accounting
EC	European Community
ED	Exposure Draft
EEC	European Economic Community (now EC)
FAR	Förenigen Auktoriserade Revisorer (the Swedish professional body)
FAS	Financial Accounting Standard (issued by the FASB)
FASB	Financial Accounting Standards Board (the private sector body which sets accounting standards in the USA)
HC	Historical Cost
IASC	International Accounting Standards Committee

Abbreviations

IASG	Inflation Accounting Steering Group (set up by the ASC in the UK)
ICAA	Institute of Chartered Accountants in Australia
ICAEW	Institute of Chartered Accountants in England and Wales
ICAI	Institute of Chartered Accountants in Ireland
ICAS	Institute of Chartered Accountants of Scotland
ICMA	Institute of Cost and Management Accountants (formerly ICWA)
ICWA	Institute of Cost and Works Accountants
IdW	Institut der Wirtschaftsprüfer
LIFO	Last in, first out (a method of stock valuation)
MWCA	Monetary Working Capital Adjustment
NIVRA	Nederlands Instituut van Registeraccountants (the Dutch professional body)
NRV	Net Realisable Value
NZSA	New Zealand Society of Accountants
PSSAP	Provisional Statement of Standard Accounting Practice (issued by ASSC)
PV	Present Value
RC	Replacement Cost
RRA	Reserve Recognition Accounting (as defined by SEC in the USA)
RT	Real Terms Accounting
SAP	Statement of Accounting Practice
SEC	Securities and Exchange Commission (the public sector standard-setting body in the USA)
SSAP	Statement of Standard Accounting Practice (issued by ASSC or ASC)
UK	United Kingdom
USA	United States of America

1
Introduction

1 Purpose of the book

Our intention in writing this book is to survey the historical development of inflation accounting. We are concerned with the development
both of ideas and of practice, and one of our main purposes is to trace
the interaction between ideas and practice. Also, we have attempted to
give an account of the events in the world outside accounting which have
influenced accounting thought and practice. Such factors are very
important: to take an obvious example, it is unlikely that inflation
accounting would ever have seemed to be relevant or interesting had
there been no inflation.

The motivation for this study is a desire to understand the extremely
tortuous and apparently muddled debate on inflation accounting which
has taken place during the last fifteen years or so, particularly in the
English-speaking countries, but also in continental Europe and Latin
America. It is clear from this debate that inflation accounting is not a
subject which lends itself to solution merely by the rigorous application
of logic to broadly accepted principles. In this respect, the inflation
accounting debate is merely one example of the problems facing
accounting. There is a lack of generally accepted principles because a
changing environment has made traditional principles obsolete, and the
process of evolving new principles is essentially political,[1] involving the
reconciliation of the conflicting interests of various groups of preparers
and users of accounts. Users are very diverse, including not only the
investor and creditor, who are the traditional recipients of financial
accounts, but also, for example, trade unions, for wage and employment
negotiations, and governments whose tax revenue and broader economic strategy may be affected by the form of inflation accounting.[2]

Apart from the political problems of reconciling the conflicting
interests of different parties, there has also been a degree of muddle
caused by sheer ignorance. This was due partly to the fact that theorists
had not developed fully the relevant ideas, since theoretical interest
tends to follow from practical problems rather than anticipating them,

1

but it was also due in part to the fact that many leading participants in the debate were ignorant of existing theory. Accountants are often ill-versed in the literature of their own subject, and this has been exacerbated by the shortage of time available for reading and research when committees of busy men are required to produce politically acceptable solutions to complex problems in very short periods of time. We attempt to provide evidence of this in subsequent chapters, and the theme is developed further in Chapter 13.

This combination of factors has been compounded, in our view, by adherence to the traditional view that there should be a single set of financial statements prepared on a single principle (such as the traditional historical cost method), culminating in a single profit figure (the 'bottom line' of the income statement) which encapsulates the total performance of the business entity during a period. The information needs of a variety of users might be more adequately met by reporting a variety of information. The existence of uncertainty may also provide a reason for reporting a variety of information rather than a unique measure of performance. The 'variety of information' approach does not necessarily result in a complicated report, and we illustrate our own solution to the problem in Section 4 of this chapter and in more detail in Chapter 14.

In the previous paragraphs, we have outlined the questions which were in our minds when we set out on the task of writing this book: to some extent the question asked always constrains the nature of the answer which is obtained. However, we have tried, in the subsequent chapters, to present the facts of the case as clearly as possible, making our own assumptions clear when it is necessary to make judgements.

2 Scope and limitations

Our basic method is historical, tracing, in chronological order, events in the practical world and developments in the theory of inflation accounting. We have concentrated our attention on the United Kingdom, because it was the UK debate which first kindled our interest in the subject, and the UK affords us the best access to original sources. It is therefore in the chapters relating to the UK that we have the greatest claim to originality, having interviewed leading participants in the debate and studied working papers of various committees, notably the Inflation Accounting Steering Group (IASG), as well as analysing the published submissions of various parties to the Accounting Standards Committee (ASC).

However, it is impossible to study the UK in isolation, because there has been a considerable international exchange of ideas and practices. This is most obvious within the English-speaking world, which shares many legal and professional traditions and which is united by strong economic ties. We have therefore devoted separate chapters to the USA and Australasia and part of another chapter to Canada and South Africa. Historically, continental Europe has played a very important rôle in the development of the theory of inflation accounting, and it is hoped that our historical chapters will help to rectify the common neglect of this in the English literature. In another chapter, we survey the current state of inflation accounting in continental Europe. Finally, we also trace the development of inflation accounting in Latin America, which was the first area of the world to see the successful application of fairly comprehensive systems of inflation accounting (particularly in Brazil and Chile) and provides the only contemporary examples of the application of Constant Purchasing Power (CPP) accounting.

The limitations of our study are considerable. We have already referred to our own preconceptions and interests, which necessarily constrain the analysis. Another obvious set of constraints are imposed by the vastness of the subject and the limitations of our own time, access to sources, and the length of the book. However, within these constraints, we hope that we have produced a more comprehensive account of the subject than has been available before.

One limitation which is inevitable, but which is a source of considerable regret, is that we have confined ourselves mainly to financial accounting (the published reports available to those outside the management of the firm) rather than management accounting (the internal information produced for management decisions within the firm). The wish to improve management accounting information has been a strong motivating force in the case for improved financial accounting, the assumption being that the improvement of the financial accounting base will improve that of management accounting. The Sandilands Committee Report in the UK provides a recent example (1975) of this attitude, but its origins lie in the integrated management and financial accounting systems proposed by the pioneering European business economists, such as Limperg. The reasons for our relative neglect of management accounting are twofold. Firstly, we have an enormous amount of information relating to financial accounting, which has been the subject of public debate in many countries, and this provides more than sufficient material for one book. Secondly, management accounting is, by its very nature, less well-documented publicly. Its practices are at the discretion of individual managements, and are often regarded as confidential. Thus, the task of documenting them and tracing

3

their development both historically and internationally is beyond our resources. However, it is an area which requires further research.

One other self-imposed limitation is that we made no attempt to give a systematic account of the theory of inflation accounting or to explain the importance of the subject. That task has already been undertaken in the companion volume (*Inflation Accounting: An Introduction to the Debate*, by Geoffrey Whittington, Cambridge University Press, 1983a). The reader of this book is assumed either to have read the companion volume or to be already convinced of the importance of inflation accounting and well-versed in the various techniques available. The next section (Section 3) of this chapter gives a brief résumé of these techniques, but this is intended merely as superficial revision for the already initiated, and its main purpose is to define the labels which we subsequently attach to different groups of techniques. This should avoid any confusion which might arise from the absence of any universally accepted nomenclature of inflation accounting methods, and it should also avoid the need for tedious repetition of detailed definitions later in the book. Section 4 will go on briefly to explain our own preferred solution to the current inflation accounting dilemma in the UK. This is intended to give the reader some indication of our preconceptions and prejudices, not to provide a panacea which renders all subsequent thoughts or debate nugatory. Finally, Section 5 of the chapter outlines the plan of the rest of the book.

3 Inflation accounting methods

In this book, we define 'inflation accounting' to include all methods of dealing with price changes. Inflation is usually assumed to be concerned with the declining purchasing power of the currency, i.e. with the rise in the general level of prices. If all prices move in unison, this poses no problem of definition, and a general price index, based upon the average proportionate change in the prices of a broad basket of goods, will also capture the changes in the prices of specific individual goods (indeed, when the correspondence between price changes is perfect, there is no need to calculate a general index: the price change of any specific good will suffice). However, in reality, prices of different goods change at different rates and even in opposite directions. In these circumstances, we face the choice of adjusting for price changes by a specific index (the proportionate change in the price of one good or a narrowly defined group of goods) or by a general index (the average proportionate change in the prices of a broadly defined basket of goods, chosen to reflect 'the general price level' or 'the purchasing power of money'). Much of the controversy about inflation accounting arises from this distinction: indeed, some writers would argue that only the second type of adjustment (using general indices) can deal with inflation (e.g. Myddelton, 1981) whereas others (such as the Sandilands Committee, 1975) reject entirely the concept of inflation defined in terms of the general price level.

In order to illustrate the basic techniques of inflation accounting, we shall use a simple numerical example.[3] We assume that a trading business acquires stock for £20,000 at the beginning of a period, and there is no further buying or selling during the period. There are no other sources of revenue or expense. By the end of the period, the market value of the stock had risen by 20 per cent but general inflation had occurred at only ten per cent. The opening capital consisted of a £5,000 interest-free loan and £15,000 equity capital contributed by the proprietors. The sole asset was the £20,000 stock.

The traditional method of accounting is the historical cost method, HC. This values assets at historical cost (what was originally paid for them), less a depreciation provision in the case of wasting assets. In the case of stocks, HC would conventionally be modified by the conservative principle of reporting market value when it was lower than HC. Otherwise, there is no systematic modification of HC (although occasional revaluations of fixed assets are permitted in certain countries), and there is no attempt to allow for the effects of general inflation.

The application of HC to our simple example yields the following:

HC

Closing Balance Sheet

	£		£
Equity capital	15,000	Stock (at cost)	20,000
Loan	5,000		
	20,000		20,000

Profit and Loss

	£
Operating profit	NIL

The closing balance sheet[4] reflects the single transaction, the purchase of stock, at historical cost. No subsequent transactions have occurred to incur further historical costs, and the increase in the market value of the stock precludes the operation of the 'lower market value' rule. For the

5

same reason, the profit and loss statement shows a 'no change' position, with NIL profits.

An alternative technique, which attempts to deal with the problem of general inflation is constant purchasing power accounting, CPP. This attempts to translate money units recorded at different dates into constant units measured at one date, just as we might translate different foreign currencies into a single unit, usually the domestic unit, by means of an exchange rate. In CPP accounting, the exchange rate is determined by the proportionate rise in a general price index, and the most popular unit of measurement, equivalent to the domestic currency unit in the currency translation case, is the current currency unit. Hence, the system of CPP most commonly advocated is *current* purchasing power accounting.

Applying the current version of CPP to our numerical example, and using the rise in the general index (10 per cent) as our exchange rate gives:

CPP

Closing Balance Sheet

	£		£
Equity capital (£15,000 × 1.1)	16,500	Stock (£20,000 × 1.1)	22,000
Add Gain on borrowing	500		
	17,000		
Loan	5,000		
	22,000		22,000

Profit and Loss

	£
Operating profit	NIL
Gain on borrowing	500
Total	500

Both the stock (a 'non-monetary' asset) and the equity interest (a 'non-monetary' claim) are translated into current £s by applying the general index. The loan, on the other hand, is a 'monetary' claim, i.e. it is denominated in monetary units irrespective of date. Thus, it is not translated into current £s: it now represents a claim of £ current 5,000, whereas formerly it was £ opening 5,000. The ten per cent rise in the general index represents a gain on borrowing, which is credited to the equity interest. If the firm had held 'monetary' assets, such as cash in the bank, these would give rise to an analogous but opposite (since they are assets, not claims) 'loss on monetary assets'.[5]

The obvious weakness of CPP when applied to the historical cost valuation basis, as in the above illustration, is that it might not reflect accurately the changes in the specific prices of the assets held by the firm. In this case, we have already assumed that the stock has risen in price by more than the general inflation rate and is valued, at the period end, at £24,000, rather than the £22,000 shown by our indexed historical cost.

A method of accounting which deals with the latter problem, and which avoids entirely the use of general indices, is current cost accounting, CCA, as proposed by the Sandilands Committee in the UK. Applying this system to our numerical example yields the following:

CCA (Sandilands)

Closing Balance Sheet

	£		£
Equity capital	15,000	Stock (current	
Add Capital maintenance reserve	4,000	cost)	24,000
	19,000		
Loan	5,000		
	24,000		24,000

Statement of gains

	£
Operating profit	NIL
Unrealised holding gain	4,000
Total gains	4,000

This system revalues the stock at its current market price, £24,000, and the surplus of this over the historical cost, £20,000, is recorded as an unrealised holding gain of £4,000. This is added to equity capital as a maintenance reserve, necessary to preserve the physical substance of the business, rather than being recorded as profit available for distribution to proprietors.

The measurement of current cost or current value is obviously a serious and controversial problem. One possible basis is replacement cost, RC (which itself has a number of variants) and another is net realisable value, NRV (which also has a number of variants).[6] A third possibility is the present value, PV, of the prospective services which the asset will yield in use within the firm. The basis adopted by the Sandilands Committee, and widely adopted as the basis of professional proposals throughout the English-speaking world is a compromise measure, value to the firm (sometimes called value to the owner, deprival value or opportunity value). This chooses RC or 'recoverable amount', whichever is the lower. 'Recoverable amount' is the higher of PV or NRV. One way of looking at this basis is to regard it as being the traditional HC system with RC replacing HC as the fundamental valuation principle and with 'recoverable amount' replacing market value as the conservative safeguard against over-valuation. As we shall see, the 'value to the firm' method has been a source of much controversy in the recent debate on inflation accounting.

An equally important source of controversy concerning the Sandilands method of CCA has been its lack of general index adjustment. Unlike CPP it shows no gain on borrowing or loss on holding monetary assets, because it eschews entirely the use of general indices which might capture the effect of inflation on items of fixed monetary amount. A possible solution to this problem is to combine the CCA valuation base with CPP adjustment, to produce a real terms, RT, system. This combines the CCA revaluation of individual assets with reference to specific price changes with a general index adjustment of capital, to yield the CPP gain on borrowing or loss on holding monetary assets. The RT system, applied to our numerical example, yields the following:

Real terms (RT)

Closing Balance Sheet

	£		£
Equity capital (£15,000 × 1.1)	16,500	Stock (current	
Real holding gains on stocks	2,000	cost)	24,000
Gain on borrowing	500		
	19,000		
Loan	5,000		
	24,000		24,000

Profit and Loss

	£
Operating profit	NIL
Real holding gains on stocks	2,000
Gain on borrowing	500
Total	2,500

Introduction

This system reports the real holding gain on stocks, i.e. the amount by which the rise in the value of the stocks has exceeded the rise in the general index: this is the excess of the CCA value over the original CPP value (historical cost restated by applying the general index). In addition, the system recognises the gain on borrowing which occurs because the loan is denominated in monetary units which depreciate in real purchasing power as inflation occurs. If the stock had risen in price at less than the rate of inflation, a real holding loss would have been reported. If the firm had held monetary assets, the inflationary loss on holding them would have been reported.

It seems that the RT system is capable of combining the virtues of the CPP and CCA systems. However, for a variety of reasons which we shall explore later, some standard-setting bodies, notably in the UK, have not found this solution attractive and have attempted to adapt the CCA system to show a gain on borrowing without resort to general price indices. This has been done by means of the gearing adjustment, which splits the holding gain not into 'money' and 'real', by reference to a general index, but into a capital maintenance reserve and distributable profit, by reference to the gearing ratio. The gearing ratio is the ratio of loans to total long-term capital (net worth) of the business. The gearing adjustment, when applied to our numerical example, yields the following:

CCA with gearing adjustment

Closing Balance Sheet

	£		£
Equity capital	15,000	Stock (current	
Add Capital maintenance reserve	3,000	cost)	24,000
	18,000		
Distributable profit	1,000		
	19,000		
Loan	5,000		
	24,000		24,000

Profit and Loss

	£
Operating profit	NIL
Add Geared holding gains	1,000
Distributable profit	1,000

9

The gearing ratio is $1/4$ ($= £5,000/£20,000$) and the money holding gain on stocks is £4,000 ($= £24,000 - £20,000$). The gearing adjustment regards the money holding gain on that portion of stocks financed by the loan as distributable profit, without any abatement for inflation. On the other hand, none of the gain on the portion financed by equity is regarded as profit: it must be retained in order to maintain equity's share of the substance of the business.

The gearing adjustment has been a subject of much controversy, as we shall see later. In practice, it has been modified in the UK by being applied only to *realised* holding gains: in our simple example there are no realised holding gains, so that the restricted gearing adjustment would be NIL. Another problem of the gearing adjustment is that it fails to deal with the loss on holding monetary assets, when these exceed borrowing. This has been dealt with in the current UK standard (*SSAP16*, 1980a) by adding a monetary working capital adjustment to the current cost system.[7] This is a charge against profit based upon a specific index adjustment of the net monetary working capital necessary to sustain the firm's business. In our simple example, there is no monetary working capital, so that the problem does not arise.

We have given above a brief catalogue of the basic techniques available for dealing with the inflation accounting problem. This should serve as a guide to our nomenclature for those already well versed in the theory and technique of inflation accounting and may also have provided a brief revision course, but it is not intended as an adequate guide for the beginner. Those who have found this section inadequate should turn to the companion volume (Whittington, 1983a) for guidance.

4 Our preferred solution

Our own view as to how the problem of accounting for changing prices should be solved is based upon two assumptions. Firstly, we assume that accounts are typically prepared under conditions of considerable uncertainty and in conditions of market imperfection and disequilibrium which make it unlikely that single-valued measures of the profit or net worth of a business can be arrived at with any degree of precision or objectivity. Secondly, we assume that accounts are required by a variety of users for a variety of purposes, and that not all of those needs will be met by exactly the same information. Examples of users are investors, creditors, employees, tax authorities, and public regulatory bodies concerned with price controls or restrictive practices.

Each of these assumptions points towards a variety of information, rather than, for example, focussing on a single number, such as the 'bottom line' of the profit and loss account, as being the only 'true' summary of the business entity's performance and economic condition. The former assumption (uncertainty, etc.) indicates that the accountant should aim to provide a set of information to which the user can apply his own judgement in order to assess the value of the relevant variables: too much emphasis by the accountant on summary measurement within his own constrained model of the world can lead to a serious loss of information.[8] The latter assumption (variety of users and uses), indicates that a relatively wide range of variables would be of interest, even if measurement could be precise and unambiguous, e.g. the profit measure used by the tax authorities might well be different from that used by shareholders,[9] and certain users of accounts may not be interested merely in profit (a take-over bidder may be more concerned with asset values and a creditor with the assessment of liquidity).

Of the basic methods of inflation (or price change) accounting presented in Section 3 above, the one which, in our opinion, best meets these eclectic needs is the Real Terms (RT) approach, which combines information from the CPP (general price-level changes) and CCA (specific price changes) systems. We would advocate a profit and loss statement of the type pioneered by Edwards and Bell (1961), which attempts to identify operating profit, realised and unrealised holding gains, and the effect of general inflation in reducing money gains to real gains (or losses). If the gearing adjustment is found to be useful, it is even possible to include this as one stage of such a statement, as Kennedy (1978a) has demonstrated. We have shown elsewhere how the present UK standard, *SSAP16*, could evolve in the direction of producing this type of RT income statement (Whittington, 1983b).

We would also favour publication of the balance sheet on a current cost valuation basis, as giving an important indication of the present state of the business. We would be less certain as to the precise nature of the valuation basis which should be adopted. Value to the business has the advantage of being already widely established as the basis of standard practice in the English-speaking world, and it seems to be a sensible pragmatic compromise. However, both RC and NRV have found eloquent supporters, as we shall see later in the book, and the case for value to the business in the aggregate assessment of net worth and profit has never been stated to our full satisfaction. There is some attraction in the idea of reporting multiple values for assets, on alternative bases, where the differences are material. On the other hand, there are costs to preparing additional valuations, and costs to the reader of accounts in interpreting them.

One approach to accounting for price changes which we would

certainly reject is the view that the correct solution is to eliminate inflation and return to the historical cost base. The elimination of inflation may be a desirable economic and social end (although it will also entail costs), but it will not solve our accounting problem, for two reasons. Firstly, the inflation which has occurred over the period since the Second World War, and particularly since the oil crisis of 1973, means that any historical values based on transactions occurring in that period will be permanently distorted by inflation. Secondly, even if general price inflation were eliminated, it is inconceivable that *relative* price changes could be eliminated in a healthy market economy: relative price changes are the mechanism which matches supply to demand. As we have already indicated, CCA and RT (which has a CCA valuation base) deal with changes in specific prices, and therefore capture relative price changes. RT is therefore capable of capturing information which HC does not record, even when there is no general inflation. Only CPP adjustments could be rendered redundant in the latter situation, and even they might be necessary because of the effects of past inflation.

These are our own views on price-change accounting or, more loosely, inflation accounting. We wish to emphasise that they have been stated in this summary form to give the reader a view of our preconceptions, rather than as a self-contained and convincing statement intended to persuade the reader to our point of view. However, we certainly do not object to the reader sharing our point of view, and we hope that we have stated it more fully and persuasively in Chapter 14.

5 Plan of the book

The remainder of the book falls into two distinct parts. Part I, Chapters 2 to 10 inclusive, contains the substantial body of evidence which we have collected. Chapters 2 and 3 trace the early history of ideas and practice throughout the world, up to the mid-1970s, when the acceleration of inflation rates prompted the 'CPP revolution' in the English-speaking world. Chapters 4, 5 and 6 trace the subsequent British debate, from the CPP revolution to the CCA counter-revolution and through a subsequent turbulent period of compromise and debate which has lasted until the present. Chapters 7 and 8 trace the parallel developments in the USA and Australasia, respectively, during the same period. Chapter 9 traces developments in three groups of countries elsewhere in the world: firstly, Canada and South Africa, which are the remaining countries in the Anglo-Saxon tradition; secondly, continental Europe, which has developed distinct traditions of its own which have had a significant influence on developments in the Anglo-Saxon countries; thirdly, Latin

America which, under pressure of severe inflation, has seen the establishment in practice of CPP systems. Finally, Part I ends with a summary of the present state of inflation accounting throughout the world, at the present time (mid-1983): it seems likely that this will prove to be the most ephemeral chapter in the book, since the current inflation accounting standards in both the UK and the USA are under review, as they approach the end of trial periods, and new proposals continue to appear elsewhere with undiminished regularity.

Part II, comprising Chapters 11 to 14 inclusive, is shorter and more speculative. This contains our own interpretation of the debate described in Part I. Chapter 11 discusses the competing methods of inflation accounting and how they have developed and competed with one another. Chapter 12 discusses various themes in the debate and attempts to trace the evolution of various models of capital maintenance and methods of valuation. Chapter 13 addresses the fundamental issue of why the debate has taken its particular course, and why there has been apparently so much confusion, such strong disagreements, and such erratic changes of course. The rôle and motivation of different parties to the debate are seen as crucial elements in this explanation. Finally, in Chapter 14, we consider what we can learn from our study about the future development of inflation accounting and, more generally, about the process of setting accounting standards.

PART I

The debate

2
Inflation accounting before the Second World War

1 Origins: inflation accounting before 1919

Inflation accounting is probably as old as inflation itself, since inflation clearly has important effects on accounting measurement which is based upon monetary units, and these effects are unlikely to have escaped the attention of the shrewder users of accounting information. However, we are concerned here not to trace the history of inflation accounting for purely antiquarian purposes, but rather to trace the evolution of ideas which has led to the current state of thinking on the subject. For this purpose, it is sufficient to trace the main roots of the present debate in the period of hyper-inflation, which occurred at historically unprecedented rates in parts of Europe during the period following the First World War.

There were, however, a number of important contributions to inflation accounting ideas which anticipated rather than followed the post-war inflations. Germain Boer (1966) has traced the origins of the debate on replacement cost accounting to the deflation which took place in the United States in the period 1865–96 following the Civil War. In a number of rate regulation cases relating particularly to rates charged by railways, the government agencies attempted to substitute replacement cost for historical cost as the basis of depreciation charges. In a period of deflation, this substitution would clearly lead to lower depreciation charges and higher reported profits, strengthening the case for reducing rates. The use of the 'fair value' (i.e. a current value rather than historical cost)[1] in such cases was approved by the Supreme Court in the case of Smyth v. Ames (1898). The inflation which followed, in the early years of the twentieth century, led to a reversal of positions in many cases, the regulatory agency preferring historical cost, and the regulated enterprise preferring replacement cost. This provides an early example of how self-interest can influence the selection of income measures.

Another important event which occurred before the First World War was the publication, in 1911, of Irving Fisher's *The Purchasing Power of Money*. Fisher advocated indexation as a means of overcoming the

17

inequities resulting from inflation when contracts are negotiated in money terms. This policy has subsequently been adopted in certain Latin American countries, notably in Brazil, and has received support in the 1970s from a number of economists, including Professor Milton Friedman (1974). Although Fisher did not deal specifically with the indexation of accounts (apart from pp. 108–9 of Fisher, 1925), his advocacy of the use of consumer price indices to dispel 'the money illusion' in a period of inflation clearly presages constant purchasing power (CPP accounting), and Fisher's work was cited by Middleditch (1918), one of the first writers on inflation accounting.

Thus, it could be argued that some of the basic ideas of both CCA and CPP accounting were known before 1914. However, the First World War brought high government expenditure, high inflation rates and a crop of articles on inflation accounting. The first article in English dealing explicitly with the general problem of inflation accounting (as opposed to replacement cost accounting in the context of rate regulation cases) has been credited to Livingston Middleditch Jr (1918) (see Zeff, 1976a). This was followed by an impressively clear early paper by Paton (1918), and the earliest known British comment on the subject appeared in print in the same year (Fells, 1919).[2] Paton advocated specific price adjustment: 'It is not *general* but *specific* price changes that the accounts should follow.' He advocated the separate reporting of unrealised holding gains in the income statement. Such a proposal was revolutionary, as it violated the cherished realisation principle, and Paton adopted a more conservative posture in his subsequent work.[3] This early crop of papers was a little unsure in its treatment of the distinction between general and specific price adjustment, and nowhere was there a clear case made for stabilised accounting of the CPP variety, but this deficiency was very soon made good in the response to the post-war inflations in Germany and France.

2 Inflation and stabilised accounting in the 1920s

The period following the First World War was marked by unprecedented rates of inflation in many European countries,[4] but the most remarkable of these was undoubtedly the hyper-inflation in Germany, which culminated in the complete collapse of the value of the paper-Mark in 1923.[5] The practical response of businessmen in these circumstances was to prepare additional balance sheets in gold-Mark equivalents, since the gold-Mark was a relatively stable unit of value. This pointed the way towards CPP accounting, since translation into gold-Marks involved converting historical costs (in paper-Marks) into a unit of constant value (gold-Marks). It also made clear the analogy which is commonly made between CPP accounting and currency translation: the conversion from paper-Marks to gold-Marks was literally translation into a different currency. More recent proposals for CPP are based upon translation into a common unit of measurement (such as currency units of purchasing power at a single date), but this unit can be regarded as a notional currency, and the translation procedures are the same.

It would, however, be misleading to suggest that the practice of accounting at this period was a fully developed form of CPP accounting. In fact, adjustment was usually confined to balance sheets, the balance sheet being the centre-piece of financial reporting at the time, and stabilised profit and loss accounts, or other flow data, were not usually provided. The central purpose of Schmalenbach's *Dynamische Bilanz* (Dynamic Accounting) (1919) was to advocate a change in the emphasis of financial accounting towards flow data.

On the other hand, the crisis induced by inflation did stimulate some important work by accounting theorists which was ahead of contemporary practice and did directly anticipate CPP accounting. Sweeney, the great pioneer of CPP accounting in the English-speaking world, acknowledged his debt to the German and French writers of the 1920s, particularly Mahlberg. Sweeney (1928) gives a numerical example of gold-Mark stabilisation adapted from Mahlberg (1923), which contains the essential elements of his subsequent proposals for full stabilisation of the balance sheet and profit and loss account. Much later, Sweeney (1964a) acknowledged Mahlberg as the author of 'the most logical, clear, complete and practical' of the German treatises on inflation accounting.

Mahlberg was a pupil of Schmalenbach, and both preferred the stabilisation of historical costs as a method of dealing with inflation rather than the alternative of replacement cost, although Mahlberg preferred the gold-Mark as the constant unit of measurement, whereas Schmalenbach preferred a unit based upon a general price index, such as was later used in the CPP proposals of the early 1970s. The fact that contemporary accounting practice favoured gold-based stabilisation methods (i.e. Mahlberg's method, rather than Schmalenbach's) was probably due to the fact that, in conditions of extreme hyper-inflation, this was the most practical method of dealing with the obvious problem of the collapse in value of the currency, gold being seen as the only widely accepted medium of exchange which could be relied upon to maintain its real purchasing power. However, Schmalenbach's preference for stabilised accounting of the CPP variety, based upon general indices applied to historical cost values, was based upon a consistent intellectual position as to the purposes of accounting and the methods appropriate to their achievement, and the choice of unit of stabilisation was a mere detail, relative to the principle of stabilisation, upon which Mahlberg and Schmalenbach were in agreement. For this reason, the next section will give a brief account of Schmalenbach's theoretical framework.

Neither the practice nor the theory of stabilised accounting was confined to Germany. The other country whose intellectual contribution subsequently had the greatest influence on the development of inflation accounting in the USA and Great Britain was France, in which gold-Franc balance sheet stabilisation was practised during the 1920s, although inflation there never reached the hyper-inflationary proportions experienced in Germany. Wasserman (1931) summarised much of the French literature, relating to the period 1919–27, for the benefit of an English-speaking audience. It is clear from this article that there was a lively debate in France concerning the techniques of stabilised accounting, and such writers as Leger appear to have identified most of the essential ingredients of a CPP system (Leger, 1926, summarised in Wasserman, 1931, pp. 21–2). The influence of French writers is demonstrated by the fact that in 1927 Sweeney postponed publication of his classic work, *Stabilized Accounting*, in order to take account of the French literature which was appearing at the time: '. . . the French literature, having benefited from the earlier experiments in neighbouring Germany, tended to be more mature, concrete and practical' (Sweeney, 1964a, p. xxii).

Although the emergence of gold-based stabilised accounting was perhaps the most novel response to the inflations which followed the First World War, replacement cost accounting also flourished as an alternative method of dealing with the problems of accounting in a period of inflation. This was particularly the case in the USA. The theory of replacement cost accounting also flourished in this period, particularly in the German school led by Schmidt, and the Dutch school led by Limperg. These will be discussed further in later sections of this chapter, but first we shall consider the reasoning behind the historic cost-based general index stabilisation advocated by Schmalenbach.

3 Schmalenbach

Eugen Schmalenbach (1873–1955) spent the whole of his academic career at Cologne, but by his teaching and writing he became a central figure in German business economics. His achievements as a teacher, practitioner, consultant and author in a wide range of areas, including auditing and business management, are documented in a recent biography by Forrester (1977). His main work on financial accounting, *Dynamische Bilanz* (Dynamic Accounting) was first published in 1919 and there were twelve subsequent editions, the thirteenth appearing posthumously in 1962. Fortunately, the twelfth edition is available in an English translation by Murphy and Most (1959).

The essential purpose of Schmalenbach's dynamic accounting was to shift the emphasis of accounting from the balance sheet, a static statement, to dynamic statements of changes in position, such as the profit and loss account. He rejected the 'dualist' view that it was possible to produce an articulated balance sheet and profit and loss account which would produce both a balance sheet which would serve the 'statist's' objective of giving a realistic snapshot of the entity's current assets, liabilities and net worth and the 'dynamist's' objective of measuring accurately the performance of an entity resulting from its transactions for the period. When these two objectives conflicted,[6] Schmalenbach asserted that the dynamic objective should be paramount because it was only by an accurate appraisal of the earnings that the business as a whole could be valued, this value being the capitalised value of the prospective earnings stream. He rejected the view that it is possible to appraise the value of the business by aggregating the values of the individual assets (less liabilities); even if the assets are valued at appropriate current values, there will be a difference attributable to goodwill.

Thus, Schmalenbach was revolutionary in his time, and his central objective strikes a very modern note. Recent advocates of current cost accounting have emphasised the rôle of profit measures such as 'distributable operating flow' as indicating an earnings stream which is available for shareholders and which should therefore be a starting point for estimating the future stream to be capitalised in valuing the shares (e.g. Kennedy, 1976, Sale and Scapens, 1978).[7] Schmalenbach did not, however, hope to achieve his ends by the methods of current cost accounting: indeed, he specifically rejected the replacement model proposed by his rival, Fritz Schmidt.

Schmalenbach's method was to match costs to revenues within the traditional historical cost framework, placing emphasis on the accuracy of the allocations to the profit and loss account, and regarding the balance sheet as a mere accrual sheet, recording sunk costs not yet allocated to profit and loss, rather than as a serious attempt to value the assets of the business. His justification for doing this was his historical analysis of the evolution of accounting (Schmalenbach, 1959, Chapter 1), which suggested that historical cost was a perfectly adequate basis

21

for venture accounting (a cash to cash situation, in which return on cost is unambiguously defined). The problem arose when a business continued in operation for an indefinite period. It was no longer possible to account on a venture basis, and unexpired costs had to be accrued to be written-off against future revenue, giving rise to the rôle of the balance sheet as an accrual sheet.[8] The accurate matching of costs against revenues was now essential in order to obtain an accurate measure of the performance of the business during a particular period.[9]

In Schmalenbach's view, it was important to improve the quality of the profit and loss account by emphasising the matching process.

> The statist asks whether the addition has increased the value of the fixed assets. The dynamist asks whether the addition is to be booked as expenditure in the year of purchase or manufacture, or requires division into expenditure applicable to several years, and he has in mind not only the year in which the addition is made, but also the years to come. He treats these years as his children, not wishing to favour one to the disadvantage of another. (Schmalenbach, 1959, p. 85)

Subsequent work on the allocation problem, particularly that by Thomas (1969 and 1974), suggests that the improvement of matching is an arid pursuit, since many of the allocations involved are essentially arbitrary. Equally, some of Schmalenbach's detailed arguments betray the lack of a clear theoretical basis upon which such allocations can be made.[10] He is also vague as to the precise use to which he would put the information, e.g. although he asserts that the capitalisation of *future* earnings is the correct method of valuing the business, he never discusses the relationship between *past* earnings reported in the profit and loss account, and future earnings:

> It is no part of the function of the profit and loss account to anticipate future profits or losses; this is a matter of the valuation of the business as a whole. (Schmalenbach, 1959, p. 155)

This omission is particularly regrettable, because advocates of current cost accounting have subsequently justified their own model on similar grounds, although they too might often be criticised for failure to explore adequately the assumptions necessary to move from current earnings to predictions of future earnings.

From this basic argument, Schmalenbach derives his case for historical cost as a basis for accounting. From there it was a simple step to advocate stabilisation of the measurement unit, by means of general indices, in times of inflation, and Schmalenbach illustrated the techniques of CPP stabilisation in some detail in the earlier editions of *Dynamic Accounting* (Forrester, 1977, pp. 39–40).

Apart from his direct contribution to the development of CPP accounting based on historical cost, Schmalenbach developed a whole range of ideas which have subsequently become important. He was an advocate of designing accounting information for specific uses (Schmalenbach, 1959, Chapter 9), and he was a pioneer of management accounting (as, for example, in his work on charts of accounts, described in Forrester, 1977, Chapter 6). His emphasis on the integration of management accounting with financial accounting led him to advocate the appraisal of performance using budgeted performance as a standard (Schmalenbach, 1959, Chapter 8), thus anticipating one aspect of the work of Edwards and Bell (1961). His emphasis on the importance of the full detail of the trading account rather than the simplified profit and loss account (Schmalenbach, 1959, p. 61) also anticipates an important element in the Edwards and Bell approach. It is also possible to detect the origins of funds flow and cash flow accounting in the 'dynamic' approach to accounting. Finally, although Schmalenbach insisted on the realisation principle and was an advocate of historical cost valuation of goods and services bought for consumption by the business, he was prepared to contemplate the valuation at selling price of 'speculative' assets, which are held primarily for the purpose of re-sale at a profit (Schmalenbach, 1959, p. 180).[11] All of this adds up to a formidable contribution to accounting thought, despite some of the limitations which have been exposed by subsequent developments.

4 Replacement cost in the 1920s and 1930s

The development of replacement cost accounting in the USA before the First World War has already been described briefly in the first section of this chapter. In the period following the First World War, inflation continued in the USA, although not at the rate experienced in some European countries, and replacement cost adjustments continued to be the most popular method of adjusting for the effects of inflation on accounts.[12] The relatively moderate rates of inflation experienced in the USA meant that there was not the compelling need to translate American accounts from dollars into units of standard value, so that Sweeney, the American pioneer of stabilised accounting, drew his inspiration and practical experience from continental Europe rather than from the USA. By the time Sweeney had published his major work (1936), the problems of inflation had been superseded by those of the recession, which was associated with deflation, and interest in forms of inflation accounting did not revive until the inflationary period following the Second World War.

Sweeney (1936, Chapter 3) discussed the historical background of replacement cost valuation, and he offered some astringent comments on the motives of some of the advocates and practitioners of replacement cost accounting:

> As a consequence of the rapid rise in prices during and after the recent great war, the previous high degree of solidarity existing in the opinions of accountants throughout the world became disrupted. Many then adopted the contemporaneously radical view that depreciation should be based on cost of reproduction. However, after the importance of the subject had begun substantially to wane during the subsequent periods of comparatively stable price levels, these rebels returned in large numbers to the ranks of those who had steadfastly continued to hold the old traditional views. The reproduction-cost method was, therefore, it would seem, a forward step that traversed about half the distance towards the goal of real-capital maintenance. It was doubtless a safer and more conservative plan of procedure to adopt during the inflation years than the old theory, because it gave rise to higher depreciation charges – charges probably more nearly related to those that would have resulted from attempts to preserve original, real, economic capital. (Sweeney, 1931, p. 173)

Sweeney himself preferred his stabilised accounting system to be applied to a replacement-cost valuation base rather than a historical-cost base (i.e. what we described in Chapter 1 as a 'real terms' method), but this procedure enabled him to retain a proprietary concept of capital maintenance (general purchasing power maintenance) rather than the entity concept of capital (maintenance of the specific assets held by the business) preferred by the pure replacement cost school.

Replacement cost theory was best developed on the continent of Europe in this period, although it did achieve some discussion in the USA (e.g. by Bauer, 1919, and Paton, 1920). In particular, the German school led by Fritz Schmidt and the Dutch school led by Theo Limperg produced comprehensive theories of replacement cost accounting which have directly influenced the course of the debate on inflation accounting in the 1970s. For this reason, subsequent sections will deal with the respective contributions of Limperg and Schmidt.

Before turning to these European contributions, we should, however, mention another important contribution made by American writers during the inter-war period, namely the exploration of alternative methods of current valuation. John B. Canning's *The Economics of Accountancy* (1929) provided a thorough critique of contemporary accounting practice[13] and offered alternatives which were designed to bring the accountant's practices more in line with the economist's forward-looking methods of valuation. Canning therefore preferred the discounted present value of future receipts as the ideal method of valuation, but in seeking practical surrogates for this value he was willing to use net realisable value or replacement cost, in appropriate circumstances. His justification for valuing certain fixed assets at replacement cost based upon 'opportunity differences' anticipates the idea of 'value to the owner'[14] which was subsequently adopted by the Sandilands Committee. Bonbright (1937), another American author, was responsible for the precise form of deprival value, otherwise known as 'value to the business' or 'value to the owner', which, in the notation devised by Solomons (1966a) and popularised by Parker and Harcourt (1969), found its way into the Sandilands Report. A final American work on valuation which deserves mention is MacNeal (1939), which provides powerful advocacy for market values, a case developed more recently, particularly with regard to selling prices, by Chambers (1966) and Sterling (1970).[15]

5 Schmidt

Fritz Schmidt (1882–1950) was Professor of Business Administration at the Johann-Wolfgang Goethe University, Frankfurt-am-Main. His seminal work on accounting was *Die Organische Bilanz* (1921), which may be regarded as the first major theoretical treatise on current cost accounting.[16] He wrote prolifically on this subject, his publications including two papers contributed to *The Accounting Review* (1930 and 1931, both reprinted in Zeff, 1976a), but most of his papers (including one published posthumously in 1952) appeared in *Zeitschrift für Betriebswirtschaft*, which he founded and edited. His work (surveyed by his pupil, Schwantag, in 1951) covers a much wider range than accounting, including many contributions to macro-economic theory, especially the theory of employment and the trade cycle, and his contribution to accounting can be fully understood only in the context of this work.

Schmidt's 'organic' theory of accounting was concerned with the rôle of the individual firm as part of the national economy. He was

25

concerned that the accounting practices of the firm should be conducive to an appropriate allocation of resources in the economy, and asserted that this would be the case only if profit were calculated by deducting from revenue the current replacement cost of the resources used in earning it:

> . . . if one wishes to seize the opportunity of a condition of value differences in order to make a profitable turnover, the necessary calculation must take place at the moment the resolution is made. One must therefore compare the cost value and the sale volume as of the same day and estimate how far this value could be changed between the beginning of production and the day of sale. (Schmidt, 1930, p. 236)

Apart from this concern with the allocation of resources, Schmidt was concerned with the aggravation of the trade cycle which could occur if historical cost rather than current cost profit were used in making investment and output decisions: historical cost would overstate profitability in boom periods and understate them in the slump, thus exaggerating the trade cycle (Schmidt, 1927).[17] Both the trade cycle argument and the allocation of resources argument pointed to a concept of current cost operating profit identical to that subsequently adopted by Edwards and Bell (1961), and later adopted in a number of practical accounting reforms of the current cost accounting variety.[18] Only in the case of the 1975 West German proposals for current cost accounting has there been explicit recognition of Schmidt's contribution (Coenenberg and Macharzina, 1976).

With regard to capital maintenance, Schmidt adopted the entity view, that the capital to be maintained was the specific productive capacity of the enterprise, rather than a fund of money or real purchasing power. Thus, holding gains on the fixed assets or stocks of the business would be debited to the asset account in the current value balance sheet but would be credited to a revaluation reserve rather than to the profit and loss account, the result being essentially similar to the proposals of the Sandilands Report,[19] omitting Sandilands' Statement of Gains, i.e. current cost operating profit was the final line of Schmidt's profit and loss account. Schmidt's reasoning which lay behind his choice of capital maintenance concept was based upon his 'organic' view of the business entity as part of a larger entity, the national economy:

> Some theoretical explanation of the reasons why appreciation cannot be profit is needed at this point. For this purpose we

must consider the enterprise as a part of the national production machine. It will then be clear that a maintenance of total productivity as of a certain moment will only be possible, if the productive instrumentalities of all individual enterprises concerned are preserved intact. The maintenance of productive power as a whole is not possible if accounting is based on an original value basis. The reason is that pure appreciation would then appear as profit whenever a change of value has taken place between the purchase and selling dates for the materials and wages that compose a product. (Schmidt, 1931, p. 289)

In 'the maintenance of productive power as a whole' we can see the origins of 'operating capacity', 'the substance of the business' and other recent attempts to define the capital maintenance concept underlying current cost accounting.

Later in the same paper, Schmidt (1931, p. 292) compared his capital maintenance concept with its two main competitors: money capital and real capital (i.e. money capital adjusted by an index of general purchasing power). The former (money capital) clearly fares relatively badly in periods of inflation, in which the value of monetary units declines both from the point of view of the entity (ability to purchase replacement assets) and of the proprietor (ability to purchase consumer goods and services). However, Schmidt's reasons for rejecting real capital maintenance are weaker and foreshadow a controversy which was to continue, unresolved, for the next half-century. He gives three reasons:

(1) 'In the first place, the advocates of index-accounting oppose setting up the balance sheet at current values.' As Sweeney later demonstrated, this is not necessarily true.

(2) 'Further on the use of a uniform index is made very difficult because the original costs may have arisen at very different dates.' This technical problem of stabilisation, where the basic accounting system is inadequate, surely applies equally to the application of specific price changes in current replacement cost accounting.

(3) 'Moreover, there are difficulties in defining the index correctly.' This problem is, of course, still with us, but again we may question whether, under conditions of changing demand, costs and technology, replacement cost is any less difficult to define than general purchasing power.

A final contribution by Schmidt, which is rarely attributed to him, is his statement of the basic ideas which ultimately led to the formulation of the gearing adjustment, which has recently found its way into professional standards (e.g. the recommendation of the West German Institut der Wirtschaftsprüfer, 1975, and the Hyde Guidelines, 1977, and *SSAP16*, 1980a, in the UK). He was prepared to modify his strict replacement cost basis for capital maintenance in the case of 'speculative assets' which were financed by loans. It will be recalled that 'speculative assets' were a category also used by Schmalenbach.[20]

Schmidt put the case for recognising the geared gain on speculative assets, as follows:

> Only in one case can appreciation be real profit to the businessman, viz. when he uses money credit to buy goods for speculation outside of his regular business needs. If his selling prices thereafter are higher than the money lent plus interest and costs after selling the goods, the difference will be his realized speculative gain. This kind of profit is especially high in times of rising general price levels. But this kind of private profit is no profit to the community, because the lender of money loses the same buying power on his money that the borrower gains. (Schmidt, 1931, p. 291)

Thus, in reporting the gains to proprietors, Schmidt was prepared, in this limited case, to recognise geared gains as income.

Elsewhere (Schmidt, 1930, pp. 237–8), he put this argument at greater length, and illustrated it with a numerical example. In setting up this example he explains the case for not recognising the ungeared portion of the gain on speculative assets. He makes out the case in terms of the *general* purchasing power index:

> In all speculations with personal capital one will have to consider the change in the purchasing power of money, which is on the whole nothing more than the reflection of the general price changes of goods. The measuring-rod for this change is the general index number, which, it is self-evident, will also be used when the purchasing power of money has risen. (Schmidt, 1930, p. 237)

The numerical example (in abbreviated form) is as follows:

> Let the invested capital be $10,000 and interest at 10 per cent for one year, the duration of the speculation. Expenses will be neglected. Let the general index number move once from 100 to 200 . . .. The goods or shares purchased for the speculation should rise from 100 to 180 . . ..

I   Speculation with Borrowed Capital

Investment	$10,000
Interest	1,000
Speculation profit	7,000
	$18,000
Proceeds of sale	$18,000

II   Speculation with Personal Capital

Investment	$10,000
Interest	1,000
Increase in value of initial capital from 100 to 200 to be in a value correction account	10,000
	$21,000
Proceeds of sale	$18,000
Loss	3,000
	$21,000

It will be observed that the 'speculation profit' in I comprises a gain on borrowing of $10,000, less a real loss on the asset of $3,000 (as reported in II), but Schmidt does not make this dichotomy. It is clear from this example that Schmidt had identified the essential argument for the gearing adjustment but that his approach differed from the subsequent British gearing adjustment proposals (e.g. Godley and Cripps, 1975) in at least two respects, firstly he indexed the equity ('personal capital') by a general rather than a specific index, and secondly, he confined the adjustment to 'speculative assets'. The latter feature highlights the problem of identifying which specific assets are financed by which specific sources of finance.[21]

In summary, Schmidt may be regarded as the seminal writer on current cost accounting. He identified a number of problems which are still being debated today, particularly the 'entity' view of capital maintenance and his concept of profit is a central feature of the current accounting standards which are currently in force in the USA and the UK. He also developed the basic idea of the gearing adjustment which has found favour (albeit in a very different form) in the UK, but not the USA. A notable omission from his work is a comprehensive discussion of the distinction between general price-level changes and relative price changes, and his discussion of the use of general price indices is ambivalent.

6 Limperg

Theo Limperg (1880–1962) was a professor at the University of Amsterdam and a distinguished accounting practitioner, being a founding partner in one of the leading Dutch professional accounting practices. In the period between the two world wars, he developed a system of replacement cost accounting, which was subsequently applied by Philips of Eindhoven and a number of other Dutch firms.[22] It was largely due to the force of his influence that The Netherlands became, during the period following the Second World War, the only country in which replacement cost accounting was widely practised, albeit by a minority of companies.[23]

Limperg seems to have exerted his influence mainly through his teaching and his professional activities. His collected works were published only after his death (Limperg, 1964) and none of his writings is published in English. There is also some doubt as to the extent to which he was influenced by Schmidt, whose views on replacement cost accounting were, in many important respects, similar. MacDonald (1977) writes that the replacement value theory applied by Philips 'is based on principles of business economics introduced by the German Professor Schmidt, subsequently expounded by a succession of Dutch professors, mainly from Amsterdam University', and he supports this assertion with a reference to a paper by Schmidt presented in 1926 to an international accountants' congress in Amsterdam. Mey (1966), Limperg's successor at Amsterdam, seeks to minimise the importance of Schmidt's influence, drawing attention to the different concepts of value adopted by Schmidt (who advocated replacement *cost*) and Limperg (who advocated replacement value, as explained below). Whatever the truth of the matter, it is clear that Limperg's work fits well into the tradition of German contributions such as those of Schmalenbach and Schmidt. Like these two authors, Limperg regarded accounting as only one aspect of economic activity and devised his theory of accounting as part of a wider theoretical view of business management and its rôle in the economy. He therefore shared the view of these German authors that the accounting system should be of service to management in addition to being an aid to the appraisal of the firm's overall performance. He also shared with them the basic assumption of the continuity of the business.

The difference between replacement value, used by Limperg, and replacement cost, used by Schmidt, is that Limperg was concerned with the minimum cost of replacing the factor service (i.e. assuming the economically most efficient method of replacement) not the replacement cost of the actual factor used in production (which might have been sub-optimal). Limperg also was prepared to modify replacement value, in circumstances which he regarded as exceptional, by applying a rule which is very similar to the familiar 'value to the owner' rule:

> The value of a commodity is its realisable value or its replacement value, but always the lower of the two. As to the realisable value, a distinction should be made with regard to factors of production between the direct and the indirect realisable value; of these two the higher is always relevant. (Limperg quoted in Burgert, 1972).

Direct realisable value is immediate sale value and indirect realisable value is proceeds realisable in the ordinary course of business: if this is a discounted present value, the rule becomes identical with value to the owner.

The object of Limperg's system was to provide a comprehensive set of cost information which would aid management, but the same information was deemed to be appropriate as a basis for reporting to shareholders. The balance sheet would therefore show assets at replacement value (reduced, where appropriate, to a lower realisable value) and the capital to be maintained intact when calculating profit would be defined on a similar basis, in order to show only that profit which would be distributable to shareholders after maintaining intact the productive flow of the business. This concept was modified in two ways. Firstly, decreases in value of assets held by the firm were to be charged against profit, although increases in value were not credited to profit. Secondly, a distinction was made between 'normal' stocks, which are necessary to maintain the output flow, and 'speculative' stocks, which are not required for this purpose. Limperg would recognise gains on the latter, as would Schmidt.

Clearly, Limperg's profit measure is subject to the same strictures as Schmidt's, from those who prefer a proprietary to an entity view of the firm. Limperg's adjustment for lower realisable value adds a degree of complication to the definition of what exactly is being maintained. This, and other criticisms of Limperg's system, are made by Burgert (1972). However, despite the difficulties implicit in his theoretical framework,[24] and the possible doubts as to the originality of his system, Limperg's influence must be credited with the considerable achievement of persuading a number of leading Dutch companies, notably Philips, to adopt replacement cost accounting both for managerial purposes and for financial reporting. This, in turn, has served to meet the arguments of those sceptics in other countries who have claimed that replacement cost accounting is infeasible.[25] We shall see in later chapters that the Dutch example had an important influence on the international debate.

7 Sweeney

The most important work on inflation accounting published in English during the inter-war period was undoubtedly Sweeney's *Stabilized Accounting*, which was published in 1936. This has proved to be the basic source of reference on the subject in the English language until the present day, and will probably continue to be so for some time to come, as professional standards have not yet fully absorbed Sweeney's ideas.

Henry Whitcomb Sweeney (1898–1967) wrote his major work as a doctoral dissertation for Columbia University. He was engaged on the work from 1924 to its publication in 1936, although he was, at the same time, engaged in earning his living as a teacher and (for most of the time) a member of the audit staff of a public accounting firm. He also spent some time in Germany and was strongly influenced by the German writers of the 1920s. He pursued his work with unrelenting thoroughness, studying European experience (Sweeney, 1927, 1928 and 1934) and the economics literature on capital and income (Sweeney, 1931, 1933a and 1933b) as well as the literature and practice of accounting in the USA, the latter gained at first hand as a result of his conscious policy of ensuring that any proposals which he made would above all be practical (Sweeney, 1964a, p. xix). A fascinating account of the writings of *Stabilized Accounting*, together with some astringent comments on the subsequent development of inflation accounting, will be found in Sweeney (1964a), and an appraisal of his work, together with reprints of the papers which he published to elaborate upon the theoretical background of the book, will be found in Zeff (1976a).

Sweeney's preferred system of stabilised accounting was, in essence, extremely simple. He regarded the problem of general inflation as being best dealt with by the application of general index adjustments to both the balance sheet and the profit and loss account, to yield full CPP stabilisation. He provided detailed worked examples of this system, based upon real-world examples, and his work provided the model for *Accounting Research Study No. 6* (AICPA, 1963),[26] which, in turn, has been a model for subsequent proposals for CPP adjustment in the USA (including, most recently, *FAS33*, 1979). However, unlike *ARS6*, Sweeney advocated that replacement cost rather than historical cost should, ideally, be the valuation basis to which CPP adjustment is applied. He was thus a pioneer not only of CPP, but also of real terms accounting. He believed that the capital to be maintained intact should be measured as a proprietary concept in terms of real command over goods and services in general, rather than in terms of the specific assets owned by the firm, as advocated by Schmidt or Limperg (Sweeney, 1933a). However, he did follow these authors in believing that replacement cost was the appropriate basis for valuing the assets of the firm (Sweeney, 1936, Chapter 3). His treatment of appreciation involved a distinction between realised and unrealised gains: by this means he hoped to appease the practical demands of the traditional accountant who would be unwilling to recognise unrealised gains as income. By offering a two-stage income statement, the first stage recording realised gains and the second unrealised gains, Sweeney gave the conservatively minded reader the option of ignoring the second (unrealised) section, and in this sense he was a precursor of the Edwards and Bell approach of providing building blocks rather than a single income number.[27] He was meticulous, and even a little pedantic, in drawing the line between realised and unrealised gains, even insisting that the loss on holding money, in a period of inflation, was an unrealised gain, since the money would have to be exchanged for goods in order to realise the loss.[28]

It is apparent from our survey of the work of the 1920s that few, if any, of Sweeney's proposals were original. Sweeney's unique contribution was to impose a coherent and consistent pattern upon them, to express the case for them with clarity, logical consistency and eloquence, and to demonstrate through his meticulously worked case studies that his system was feasible. A particularly important feature of his work is the clear distinction which he made between general inflation (a fall in the general purchasing power of money) and specific price changes (changes in the rate at which specific goods exchange for money, which may be due partly to inflation but which may also contain an element of relative price change, i.e. changes in the price of the specific good relative to goods in general). Earlier writers on accounting had tended to confuse this distinction[29] or to handle the relative uses of specific and general indices in a somewhat ambivalent manner. Sweeney showed clearly that general inflation and relative price changes were distinct problems but that both general and specific price changes could be accommodated within a single balance sheet or profit and loss account.

This is not to say that Sweeney's work was perfect. His income statement fell short of the level of information disclosed by the Edwards and Bell system,[30] and his cautious advocacy of replacement cost led to a common misunderstanding that his preferred system was CPP adjustment of historical cost[31] rather than replacement cost information. There are also some details of his work which are not entirely clear or well-justified.[32] Furthermore, although he studied the theory of capital and income with characteristic care, his arguments on these issues are essentially pragmatic, e.g. his preference for replacement cost over other current values is not fully explained. However, in its time, Sweeney's contribution was remarkable, and his clarification of the central issues was a contribution of lasting importance.

8 Conclusion

By the beginning of the Second World War, the lines of battle had been drawn up for the future debate on inflation accounting. Germany and France in the 1920s had provided the basic work on the CPP model, and Germany and The Netherlands had provided the CCA model. Sweeney had clarified the techniques of CPP for the benefit of an English-speaking audience and had shown the possibility of combining current valuation of assets, based on specific prices, with general purchasing power adjustment of capital, based on a general index. Apart from replacement cost, realisable values and 'value to the owner' had been advocated as alternatives to replacement cost. A number of other ideas had been aired which would subsequently become important, including the basic idea of the gearing adjustment. In the sphere of practice, there had been experience of rudimentary CCA and CPP systems. The task which remained was, however, enormous, and has not yet been completed. In the realm of theory, the grounds for choice between the competing systems required clarification, and, in the area of practice, the political problems of achieving consensus between a wide range of divergent interests would have to be overcome, in addition to the technical problems of implementation, before a method of inflation accounting would be accepted as standard accounting practice, rather than a piecemeal adjustment made on a discretionary basis to cope with a temporary difficulty.

3
Developments in inflation accounting from the Second World War to 1974

1 Introduction

The last chapter surveyed developments in the theory and practice of inflation accounting until the depression of the 1930s. The depression led to a loss of interest in inflation accounting, since it removed, at least temporarily, the problem of inflation. This explains the very limited impact of Sweeney's book on its publication in 1936 and the fact that Schmalenbach drastically shortened the treatment of inflation accounting in later editions of his book *Dynamic Accounting*. There were some isolated developments of importance during this period, such as the acceptance of LIFO inventory valuations for tax purposes in the USA in 1938, but generally the 1930s were a barren period for inflation accounting.

The Second World War did lead to a revival of economic activity and its aftermath included inflation which led to renewed discussion of inflation accounting in both the UK and the USA. During the war itself, attention was concentrated on the problems of running a planned wartime economy, and the relevance of inflation accounting methods based upon indices was, in any case, seriously diminished by the existence of suppressed inflation (excess demand appearing in the existence of queues and black markets, but not being allowed to affect official price indices), as both Schmalenbach (1959) and Sweeney (1964a) testify.

During the post-war period, interest in inflation accounting in both the USA and the UK proceeded continuously but at a level which tended to vary with the immediacy of the problem, as indicated by the rate of inflation. Mumford (1979) provides an interesting survey of the post-war inflation accounting debate in the UK interpreted in this manner.[1] There were two periods of particularly rapid inflation during the period. The first, during the period 1951–52, was associated with the Korean War and subsequently subsided, although it led to a flurry of activity in the inflation accounting field in the UK. The second was the

35

period of accelerating inflation starting in the late 1960s and continuing to accelerate until the end of the period considered in this chapter (1974), reinforced by the oil crisis following the 1973 Middle Eastern War. This inflation has continued until the present time and has become the greatest inflation experienced in either the UK or the USA during the last hundred years.

The period ends in 1974 because this saw the high point of CPP accounting based on historical cost. The urgency of the accounting problems caused by the inflation led to the issue of the first accounting Standard (albeit a provisional one) on the subject, the UK's *PSSAP7* (1974). Later in the same year, CPP proposals were issued by the FASB in the USA, and by the Canadian and Australian professional bodies. A CPP exposure draft for New Zealand appeared in 1975 and a discussion paper for South Africa in the same year. There were also important CPP developments in Brazil and Chile in 1974, and an ultimately abortive CPP proposal was made by the professional body in Mexico. Thus, by the end of this period, it might seem that CPP based upon historical cost would be at least the first stage of the accounting profession's response to inflation in the English-speaking world and in Latin America. In fact, 1974 also saw the first developments in 'the Current Cost Revolution',[2] when the Sandilands Committee started work in the UK.[3] This will be the subject of the following three chapters. Only in Latin America did CPP practice survive.

An interesting feature of the post-war debate on inflation accounting has been its self-contained nature within the English-speaking world. As will become apparent, there are remarkable parallels between developments in the USA, the UK, Australia, Canada, New Zealand and South Africa, and these are due to the international exchange of ideas and experience between these countries. Within Western Europe, other than the United Kingdom, there has been no such homogeneity. Apart from the 1975 West German recommendation (Institut der Wirschaft-sprüfer, 1975) which was substantially ignored in practice, The Netherlands was the only country to develop any form of inflation accounting by the mid-1970s, as a matter of approved practice.[4] Here, replacement cost accounting has been practised by a significant minority of listed companies, under the influence of Limperg and his followers, whose views were described in the previous chapter. The lack of developments in Europe, particularly in France and Germany, which were responsible for pioneering work in the 1920s, is probably due to the relatively low inflation rates experienced there, particularly in West Germany. It may also be due partly to the different orientation of financial reporting in these countries, which is directed more towards the fulfilment of legal requirements and less towards the provision of information for shareholders who wish to make investment decisions in the context of an active stock market. The European experience will be considered further in Chapter 9.

A distinct set of developments has taken place in Latin America during this period, and these too will be considered further in Chapter 9. In certain countries in Central and South America inflation has been experienced at very high rates comparable with those in Europe in the 1920s rather than in the post-war period.[5] This has made the problem of adjusting accounts for declining money values much more urgent than elsewhere, and, as in Europe in the 1920s, the most practical immediate remedy which has commended itself has been CPP accounting. This has been the case most notably in Brazil, and, somewhat later, in Chile, where indexation of various contracts has been adopted widely in the economy as a means of reducing the inequities which might result from incorrect anticipation of the rate of inflation. The experience of Latin America seems to have had remarkably little impact on the debate on inflation accounting elsewhere in the world, possibly because Latin American inflation rates were exceptionally high, so that the experience was not considered relevant elsewhere.

Another development of the period, which will be discussed later in this chapter, was the continuing refinement of alternative theoretical approaches to inflation accounting. This has been the work mainly of academics, especially in Australia, the UK and the USA, but these academics have had a considerable influence on the development of accounting standards and practice, e.g. they include Professor Mathews, the Chairman of the Australian Committee of Inquiry into Inflation and Taxation, whose Report (May 1975) made an important contribution to the subsequent 'Current Cost Revolution'. However, there was a significant time-lag in the adoption of these ideas: current cost accounting did not become a serious candidate for practical implementation in the English-speaking world until 1975, but it was based upon the work of academics in the 1960s and much earlier, e.g. Schmidt's work published in 1921, which was discussed in the previous chapter. The CPP model, which was the leading contender for practical implementation in the period discussed in this chapter (i.e. prior to 1975) relied mainly on theoretical work which had been done before the Second World War (notably that of Sweeney), and it is therefore appropriate to review the professional developments of the period before the development of theory, which affected later professional developments.

Part I The debate

2 Professional developments in the USA, 1945–74[6]

The post-war inflation in the USA revived the concern of many companies that the historic cost depreciation charge made in conventional accounts did not reflect adequately the replacement cost of the assets used up in the course of the period.[7] As a result of this concern, in 1947, two companies, United States Steel and Du Pont, made supplementary depreciation charges to reflect the decline in the purchasing power of money which had occurred since the (pre-war) time when historical cost had been incurred. This was rejected by the Securities and Exchange Commission, but a third company, Chrysler, managed to achieve the same result, and gain SEC approval, by making the additional charge in the form of accelerated depreciation of historical cost (a procedure analogous to the LIFO treatment of stocks). In the same year (1947), the Committee on Accounting Procedure of the American Institute of Accountants issued *Accounting Research Bulletin No. 33*, which recommended against the adjustment of depreciation to allow for price-level changes, but in 1948 it modified this position by recommending experimentation with supplementary price-level adjustment statements.

It had become clear that there was fundamental disagreement amongst members of the accounting profession as to how business income should be measured, and 1947 saw the setting up of the Study Group on Business Income, chaired by George O. May and sponsored jointly by the American Institute of Accountants and the Rockefeller Foundation.

The Study Group on Business Income worked for five years. Its final report (1952) was drafted under the direction of the Chairman, George O. May, and is largely consistent with his own views (May, 1949),[8] but is rather cautiously worded, reflecting no doubt, the disparity of views amongst the membership, as indicated in the notes of dissent at the end of the Report. The Report recognised the problem of changing price levels, and its tentative conclusion on this issue was as follows:

> . . . it would seem that in the longer view methods could, and should, be developed whereby the framework of accounting would be expanded so that the results of activities, measured in units of equal purchasing power, and the effects of changes in value of the monetary unit would be reflected separately in an integrated presentation which would also produce statements of financial position more broadly meaningful than the orthodox balance sheet of today.

and

> For the present, it may well be that primary statements of
> income should continue to be made on bases now commonly
> accepted. But corporations whose ownership is widely
> distributed should be encouraged to furnish information that
> will facilitate the determination of income measured in units of
> approximately equal purchasing power, and to provide such
> information wherever it is practicable to do so as part of the
> material upon which the independent accountant expresses his
> opinion. (Study Group on Business Income, 1952, p. 105)

Thus, the Study Group clearly pointed the way towards CPP accounting, albeit in a cautious and evolutionary manner. The Group's membership included a number of senior and highly respected members of
the accounting profession as well as economists and businessmen, so
that its conclusions were likely to carry weight in the subsequent debate
on inflation accounting. Its other publications also made an important
contribution to the development of ideas, notably *Five Monographs on
Business Income* (1950), and particularly the essay by Alexander, which
later provided the inspiration for an influential paper by Solomons
(1961).

The overall impression left by the work of the Study Group is,
however, one of lack of urgency, and the reason for this is not difficult to
find: inflation was not very rapid at the time. After rising 30 per cent
between 1945 and 1948 the US consumer price index levelled out and,
despite a brief revival of sharp inflation in 1950–51, the picture was
generally one of steady but slow inflation until the late 1960s. Thus, the
most notable events of the 1950s came from an academic body, the
American Accounting Association. In 1951 an AAA committee gave
support for supplementary financial statements showing the effects of
changes in the general price level, and in 1957 this was revised to include
the possibility of adjusting for specific price changes. In the period
1955–56, the AAA published three influential studies of general price-
level adjustment (Jones, 1955 and 1956; Mason, 1956). Jones' work was
an extension of his earlier work (Jones, 1935 and 1949): it included case
studies which demonstrated both the materiality and the practicality of
general price-level adjustment, and his later work gave added force to
this by providing general algebraic formulae for such items as the
depreciation shortfall which would arise from charging historic cost
depreciation in a period of inflation. Mason's study provided a concise
manual of the technique of general price-level adjustment. Both Jones

and Mason confined their analysis to general price-level adjustment, and neither followed Sweeney in recognising the gain or loss on monetary items in the profit and loss statement:[9] both preferred rather to make the adjustment direct to the equity section of the balance sheet. There was also an increasing volume of work in this field by other academics at this time.

In 1960, the American Institute of Certified Public Accountants (formerly the American Institute of Accountants) appointed Maurice Moonitz as its Research Director, and two studies were set in hand which had an important effect on the subsequent debate on inflation accounting: indeed, they could be said to represent the two strands of thought which the current US Standard, *FAS33*, is somewhat uneasily attempting to reconcile. Firstly, in 1962, Accounting Research Study No. 3, *A Tentative Set of Broad Accounting Principles for Business Enterprises*, by Sprouse and Moonitz, advocated current value accounting. Their proposals were in the spirit of Canning (whose work was described in the previous chapter), being based on the assumption that the accountant should adopt the forward-looking valuation procedures favoured by economists. In particular, Sprouse and Moonitz advocated that stocks should be valued on a net realisable value basis and fixed assets should be revalued periodically on a replacement cost basis, using index adjustments to interpolate between revaluations. They did not make detailed proposals for dealing with the general price-level problem, which was dealt with in *ARS6, Reporting the Financial Effects of Price-Level Changes*, published in 1963.

ARS6 treated the problem of inflation, expressed in general price-level changes, as being entirely distinct from the problem of changes in the relative prices of specific assets. This general price-level problem was a problem of a fluctuating unit of measurement and should be dealt with by producing supplementary financial statements, expressed in units of constant purchasing power by general price index adjustment. These supplementary statements could be derived from a historical cost base, although a current value base was not ruled out. The controversial gain or loss on monetary items was to be reported in the stabilised profit and loss statement as a separate item, in contrast with its treatment in the AAA studies of 1955–56. This amounted virtually to a proposal that Sweeney's (1936) system should, at last, be adopted, and Sweeney himself (1964b) wrote an enthusiastic review of *ARS6*, although, perfectionist that he was, he did not approve of all the details and was particularly critical of the failure to distinguish between realised and unrealised gains on monetary assets:

The main flaw in the Study is its indecisive and unrealistic handling of an inescapable and substantial element in nearly all practical stabilization procedure, to wit, money-value gain and loss . . ..
The Study's treatment of money-value gain is, first, indecisive because it fails to furnish a clear understanding of whether that common and substantial form of profit and loss ought to be treated as income in nature or as capital in nature. And, second, its treatment is unrealistic because it ignores the vital distinction between realized and unrealized income.
(Sweeney, 1964b, p. xxxiii)

The Study did recognise that the treatment of monetary gains and losses was a controversial area and devoted a whole section (Appendix C, pp. 137–65) to it, including an alternative proposal (by M. M. Deupree, pp. 153–65) which advocated '. . . that inflation losses on monetary assets required by the business should be charged to current income, and that inflation gains on the net monetary liability (total liabilities less monetary assets in excess of operating requirements) should be associated with the operating assets and taken into income as those assets are charged to operations' (p. 159). There is a similarity between this proposal and the version of current cost accounting now in operation in the UK (*SSAP16*, 1980a), which embodies a monetary working capital adjustment (relating to 'monetary assets required by the business') and a gearing adjustment (which enables 'gains on net monetary liability' to be 'associated with the operating assets and taken into income as those assets are charged to operations'). However, this proposal did not find favour and did not reappear in the subsequent proposals which were based on *ARS6*.

Other features of *ARS6* which are worthy of note are the appendices which deal with index numbers (Appendix A), examples of 'Disclosing Effects of Price-Level Changes' taken from published accounts in the USA and elsewhere (Appendix D) and the 'Annotated Bibliography of Cases' (Appendix E) which summarises the findings of various case studies of price-level adjustment which had been carried out mainly by academics (e.g. the work by Sweeney (1936), and Jones (1949 and 1955) referred to earlier). These appendices represented the main contribution of *ARS6* to the advancement of knowledge. The demonstrations of stabilisation technique in *ARS6* were not an advance on the work of Sweeney (1936) or Mason (1956) or material which had appeared in various editions of Paton's text books (see Zeff, 1979a).

The theory was also rather narrowly developed in *ARS6*, concentrating on the unit of measurement argument (i.e. the dollar is an unsatisfactory unit of measurement because its purchasing power fluctuates) rather than discussing the fundamental issues of income measurement which lie behind the choice between the stabilised historic cost approach and the current cost approach. '. . . the Study's corpus . . . is shallow as a theoretical essay . . .. Any dissertation that endeavors to assay the merits of general price-level adjusted financial statements must probe the depths of the theory of asset valuation-income determination' (Zeff, 1964). Sweeney also objected to the brevity of the theoretical content of the Study, but in different terms: 'This abbreviated exposition, only a summary in reality, is good, although much too concise for all except advanced students' (Sweeney, 1964b, p. xxxiv). The assumption implicit in Sweeney's judgement, that stabilisation of the 'rubber dollar' was a self-evident requirement, irrespective of the basis of the underlying reports, has been an important factor in polarising the debate between CPP and the alternatives, notably CCA in later years.

There was also an interesting contrast between Sweeney and Zeff in their prognostications for the future. Sweeney saw the fact that the report emanated from a professional body (albeit as a research study rather than a recommendation) as a hopeful sign for the future: 'It may provide the final impetus that raises stabilised accounting from the underworld of accounting to the upperworld.' Zeff, on the other hand, was pessimistic:

> In this writer's view, the United States public accounting profession . . . is not likely to endorse price-level accounting of any sort unless the intensity of inflation increases. And even then, the most probable action would be to augment conventionally-stated merchandise expense and depreciation expense by amounts based on a formula that mixes general and specific price changes. (Zeff, 1964, p. 333)

In the event, the first part of Zeff's prediction was correct, but not the second. The endorsement of price-level accounting was delayed until inflation became more rapid, but when it came, it took the form of supplementary stabilised statements, so that, in the long term, Sweeney's prediction was correct. It was the intervention of the Securities and Exchange Commission in 1975 which led to a revival of interest in specific price changes.

The next important event in the USA was the publication in June 1969 of the Accounting Principles Board's recommendation *APB3*,

Financial Statements Restated for General Price-Level Changes. This recommended supplementary statements which were adjusted by a general price index, using the model proposed in *ARS6*, including the reporting of the gain or loss on monetary items as a part of the profit and loss statement. It relied heavily on *ARS6* and added nothing new to the debate. It took the form of a recommendation, rather than an opinion as to good accounting practice, and it was not necessary for auditors to remark, in their reports, on any departure from it. Its authority was derived from Accounting Research Bulletin No. 43 (1953) which merely reiterated the 1948 statement, encouraging the use of supplementary schedules to 'explain the need for retention of earnings in the face of rising general price levels' (*APB3* p. 1). Effectively, *APB3* was merely an elaboration of a practice which was already permitted but not widely followed. It is therefore not surprising that it had virtually no impact on practice: only one company, the Indiana Telephone Corporation, followed it, and this company had been producing price-level adjusted data before *APB3* was issued.[10]

However, inflation continued at an accelerating pace, particularly following the 1973 oil crisis. The Financial Accounting Standards Board, which began work in 1973, placed inflation accounting high on its agenda and in February 1974 issued a discussion memorandum: *Reporting the Effects of General Price-Level Changes in Financial Statements*. This followed *ARS6* and *APB3* in discussing a proposal for supplementary reports showing the effects of general price-level changes. After consideration of comments on the discussion memorandum, an exposure draft, *Financial Reporting in Units of General Purchasing Power*, was issued on 31 December 1974, with a nine-month exposure period. This too reiterated the proposals of *APB3* and acknowledged its debt to this earlier proposal (footnote to p. 1). It also emphasised that the proposal for general index adjustment of historical cost did not preclude the future introduction of current value base, an issue which would fall within the scope of the Board's Conceptual Framework project. Thus, on a conceptual level, the FASB by the end of 1974 had not advanced beyond *ARS6* and *APB3* which had been issued more than ten years earlier.

On the other hand, it might be considered that the 1974 Exposure Draft was a great advance, because CPP accounting was possibly less than one year away from becoming standard accounting practice. However, even here there was cause for disquiet. The Exposure Draft had been prepared very quickly, probably without the careful consultation and political persuasion necessary to ensure the support of such crucial bodies as the SEC,[11] and already the SEC Chief Accountant,

John C. Burton (1974), had expressed his opposition to the historical cost-based CPP system embodied in *ARS6*. This opposition was soon to take a more practical form, with the SEC's intervention of 1975, which is discussed in Chapter 7. However, before considering this, we must review events elsewhere, and especially in the United Kingdom, where also 1974 was an important year for CPP accounting.

3 Professional developments in the United Kingdom, 1945–74

For most of this period, developments in the United Kingdom ran parallel with those in the USA.[12] Until the period after the publication of *APB3* (1969), the UK was generally behind the USA in the pace and intensity of consideration of inflation accounting, but in January 1973 it issued a CPP exposure draft (*ED8*) nearly two years before its US counterpart, and in 1974 CPP was embodied in a UK accounting standard (*PSSAP7*, 1974) albeit a provisional one which was subsequently withdrawn.

In the three years immediately following the Second World War, the UK, like the USA, experienced one of the sharpest inflations within living memory (as it was at that time). This naturally led to agitation from business and from others, such as academics, for reconsideration of the traditional historical cost methods of accounting. The response of the Institute of Chartered Accountants in England and Wales was to issue its *Recommendations on Accounting Principles*, *N12*, 'Rising Price Levels in Relation to Accounts', in January 1949. This rejected any form of inflation accounting whether by replacement cost or by general index methods and reaffirmed that historical cost should be the basis of published accounts. Any allocation made to compensate for the effects of inflation should be a transfer to reserves, not a charge against profits. It thus followed the earlier example of the American Institute of Accountants (1947). The rate of inflation had, by 1949, slackened, and the leaders of the profession no doubt hoped that the problem of inflation would become a purely academic issue, of no material importance for the practitioner.

An interesting illustration of professional attitudes at the time is provided by the following anecdote by Professor William Baxter, concerning his pioneering paper on inflation accounting (Baxter, 1949):

> I read my 1949 paper on inflation accounting to a meeting of the
> Manchester Statistical Society. As I left the hall, I overheard
> the talk of two men in front of me. Obviously one was a
> member of the society, and the other his guest; the latter's dress

and bearing proclaimed him an accountant of some note. The member asked nervously whether the discussion of inflation accounting had proved interesting. 'Interesting, yes' came the judicial reply '. . . but of no practical importance'. At the time, this was reasonable enough. But mounting inflation was soon to show up the absurdities of the historical cost system, and led financial journalists to poke fun at the defenders of orthodoxy. (Baxter, 1978a, pp. 19–20)

The 'mounting inflation' to which Professor Baxter refers accelerated during 1950–52, due to the rise in demand associated with the Korean War. Even before then, the legacy of the 1945–48 inflation became apparent when the Millard Tucker Committee[13] was appointed in 1949 to enquire into the taxation of profits. The evidence to this committee revealed considerable disagreement within the accounting profession as to the appropriate definition of profits. The Institute of Chartered Accountants in England and Wales found itself in the difficult position of defending its *N12* recommendation of historical cost for reporting purposes but maintaining that some allowance for inflation might be appropriate in assessing profits for tax purposes. This position is potentially defensible (or, in Watts and Zimmerman's terms, an appropriate set of excuses could be found)[14] but the Institute did not manage to produce a convincing defence of it at the time. In the event, the Committee was unwilling to recommend any changes in the tax base to allow for inflation,[15] and the problem was passed on to the Royal Commission on the Taxation of Profits and Income which, in its *Final Report* (1955), made the basic assumption '. . . that there will not be any marked decrease or increase in the purchasing power of money in the United Kingdom' (p. 6, para. 23).

The Royal Commission reported in 1955, by which time the rate of inflation had once more declined. In the meantime, however, the inflation of 1950–52 and the disagreements within the accounting profession which were apparent in evidence to the Millard Tucker Committee had led to a flurry of activity, culminating in the issue of a new Recommendation, *N15*, by the ICAEW in May 1952. This followed the publication of two reports, one by the Research and Technical Committee of the Institute of Cost and Works Accountants (1952), and one by the Taxation and Research Committee of the Association of Certified and Corporate Accountants (1952), both of which proposed systems of replacement cost accounting. Both proposed replacement cost valuation systems with corresponding, entity-based replacement cost capital maintenance concepts. As might be expected, the ICWA document was oriented towards management decisions and that of the ACCA towards financial accounting and taxation, the latter being a particularly important issue in the UK where, unlike the USA, LIFO stock valuation was not allowed for tax purposes.

The ICAEW's *N15*, 'Accounting in Relation to Changes in the Purchasing Power of Money' was a response to these revolutionary proposals. This reiterated the belief, previously expressed in *N12*, that historical cost should continue to be the basis of published accounts. It readily admitted the deficiencies of such accounts, particularly in periods during which the monetary unit fluctuates in value, and recommended that the effects of inflation should be quantified in the directors' report, rather than in the accounts. It recommended appropriations of profits to reserves, rather than charges against profit, as a means of recognising in the accounts the excess of reported profits over inflation-adjusted profits.

There was considerable controversy between the professional bodies concerning these diverse proposals (see Mumford, 1979), e.g. in 1954 the Scottish Institute advocated experimentation with supplementary statements reflecting price changes but, ultimately, the conservative views of the ICAEW prevailed, partly perhaps because of the predominant position of this body in the practising profession, but also no doubt because the rate of inflation had fallen, permitting such optimistic assumptions as to future price stability as those made by the Royal Commission on Taxation (quoted above). Inflation continued at a modest rate through the remainder of the 1950s and most of the 1960s. The rates of inflation experienced during this period (ending in 1968) were at the lower end of what has been described as 'the discussion range' (Burton, 1975), i.e. they were sufficient to stimulate discussion of the problem by academics and thoughtful practitioners, but not significantly high to create urgent demands for reform from companies or users of financial statements. It should be noted that the distortions caused by inflation are not merely a function of the current annual rate of inflation but also of the cumulative inflation since acquisition (when historical cost was established) of the assets and liabilities of the firm. Thus, although inflation was at modest annual rates during the period from 1952 to 1968, the cumulative effect of this on such items as historical cost depreciation was potentially serious.

It was considerations such as these which led one thoughtful practitioner, Mr (later Sir) W. E. Parker, to write *Accounting for Stewardship in a Period of Inflation*, which was 'prepared under the aegis of the Research Committee' of the ICAEW and published in August 1968. The anonymity of the author was due to the fact that he was, at the time of writing the paper, the President of the ICAEW and it was considered important that the paper be regarded as a discussion document rather than a statement of Institute policy. *Accounting for Stewardship* advocated supplementary statements incorporating CPP adjustments of historical cost. Like the American *APB3*, which appeared in the following year, it advocated that the gain or loss on monetary assets and liabilities should be reported in the profit and loss account, as a separate item. Its approach was evolutionary, pointing out (para. 1, p.1) that Recommendation *N15* had stressed the deficiencies of the monetary units of measurement in a period of inflation and had advocated quantification of the impact of these deficiencies on reported profit. However, *N15* had stopped far short of specifying exactly how the effects of inflation should be calculated and had confined adjustments of the accounts to appropriations of profit to an Inflation Reserve, whereas *Accounting for Stewardship* was prepared to contemplate that 'ultimately one might look forward to the converted accounts taking the place of the conventional accounts as a basis for reporting on stewardship . . .' (para. 40, pp. 22–3).

The inspiration for *Accounting for Stewardship* came partly from the USA.[16] The author, a partner (later senior partner in the UK) in Price Waterhouse had, in his early days with the firm, worked for a time in the New York Office as an assistant to George O. May. He was always in contact with American thinking on the subject and was familiar with Perry Mason's (1956) AAA pamphlet and with *ARS6* (1963). Another influence was the analogy of currency translation, which had, of course, been influential in the development of stabilised accounting in the 1920s, and which is very clearly drawn in the second and third sections of *Accounting for Stewardship*, 'An exercise in currency conversion' (paras. 6–10) and 'The establishment of "rates of exchange"' (paras. 11–14). The author had been interested in inflation accounting over a long period (he made some interesting observations on the subject in a talk given in 1952 to the 1949 Discussion Group, the text of which we have seen) and had published an article on the subject based upon a paper which he presented to the Eighth International Congress of Accountants in New York in September 1962 (Parker, 1962), well ahead of serious interest in the subject by the Council of the ICAEW. The publication of the 1968 research paper[17] was an attempt to stimulate serious discussion of the subject within the profession (and particularly the ICAEW) before the problem of inflation accounting became too urgent to allow such a discussion.

In the event, the author's hopes for *Accounting for Stewardship* were not fulfilled in the short term. The initial discussion was negligible.

However, a powerful ally was at hand in the form of an accelerating inflation rate. The formation, in 1969, of the Accounting Standards Steering Committee, gave a new impetus to professional standard-setting, and inflation accounting was one of the first items to be put on the programme of the new body, in 1970. In May 1971, the ASSC held a special plenary meeting 'to discuss the problems of accounting under inflationary conditions' and to investigate 'the possibility of establishing an accounting standard requiring finanancial statements to disclose the effects of changes in the purchasing power of money' (ICAEW Press Release dated 7 May 1971). The final phrase suggests that CPP was already the favoured solution. Present at the plenary meeting were 'representatives of the Confederation of British Industry, the Stock Exchange, the Take-over Panel, Investment Analysts and other accountancy bodies' (the ASSC at the time, embraced only the Chartered bodies). A further plenary meeting was held in July 1971, after which a paper, prepared for these meetings by the Technical Department of the English Institute, was published by *Accountancy*.[18]

This paper, 'Inflation and Accounts', became known as 'the Tombstone document', because of the design of its cover, rather than its contents. It outlined a method of CPP accounting similar in all essential respects to the 1968 research paper, *Accounting for Stewardship*. The body of the paper presented the case for adopting such a system as supplementary to historical cost accounts, and appendices dealt with implementation problems, provided a worked example, and gave factual detail as to inflation rates, their impact on profits, and inflation accounting practice in the UK and abroad. Although the paper was issued for discussion, with a disclaimer as to its representation of the views of ASSC, it presented the case for a CPP solution rather than giving equal weight to the case for some form of CCA. Furthermore, in the event, the system presented in 'the Tombstone document' was that which was eventually proposed by ASSC in *ED8* in January 1973.

In view of this, it is worth reviewing the reasons given in 'the Tombstone document' (p. 3) for preferring a CPP solution. These were:
(a) The proposed system would adapt 'conventional published accounts' to 'reflect the effects of changes in the purchasing power of money'.
(b) CPP accounts would retain the advantage of the historical cost basis 'that cost is an ascertainable, objective fact' whereas 'alternative solutions, such as "replacement cost" or "fair value" accounting would introduce factors other than pure price-level changes'.
(c) 'All companies would be in the same boat' in having to produce CPP accounts. This would overcome the reluctance of preparers 'to

break new radical paths in the field of accounting, particulary when it would produce an apparently less favourite [*sic*] position or result'.

(d) Some confusion might be caused by the publication of figures on two bases (HC and CPP), but this risk was considered to be outweighed by 'the advantages of the possession of the more useful information obtainable from the CPP figures'.

(e) The extra burden of calculating CPP figures would also be compensated by 'the advantage of having more relevant and meaningful information'.

This amounts to a rather weak case for CPP. Each of the 'advantages' listed above is contentious. (a) is merely an assertion which does not explain why CPP confers an advantage on the user. (b) is formally incorrect, in that HC does not necessarily deal with 'ascertainable, objective fact', e.g. when assessing depreciation charges. Furthermore, the possibility that the greater subjectivity of current value might be compensated by the greater user-relevance of the information, is not considered. (c) would apply to a uniform application of *any* system, not merely CPP. Furthermore, although the system would be common to all companies, its impact would vary from company to company, depending on such factors as the age of the fixed assets and the net monetary position. (d) is asserted as a matter of subjective judgement, upon which the ASSC and its successor, the ASC have singularly failed to carry out any serious empirical investigation. A similar assertion could be made with equal authority (in the absence of empirical evidence) about any competing system, such as replacement cost or current cost accounting. (e) is equally an untested assertion and, again, it is possible that the greater additional work involved in current cost accounting might be compensated by the even greater benefits of the information provided.

Thus, the theoretical case for CPP in 'the Tombstone document' was decidedly weak. It relied essentially on the earlier evolutionary arguments of *Accounting for Stewardship*, and its plea for dealing with the problem of the fluctuating unit of measurement as a distinct problem from that of valuation. This case for historical cost-based CPP adjustment rested on its evolutionary advantages as a simple and apparently objective adjustment of the traditional system, which could be implemented without tackling the difficult problem of introducing current values in accounts.

The 'Tombstone' also briefly outlined the possible repercussions of its proposals (p. 4) for investment analysts, management, taxation, prices, wages and dividends. This outline was brief, speculative and unsupported by research. It was sufficient to show that the proposals had important consequences beyond the conventional ambit of the accounting profession.

The object of these comments on the 'Tombstone' is not to criticise its authors,[19] who did a competent job in producing a discussion document in a short time, but to demonstrate how little thought or preparation lay behind the professional proposals as of August 1971. With the aid of hindsight it is possible to see here some of the seeds of subsequent problems, e.g. the brief discussion of the economic repercussions of the system was quite likely to alert the Government to the need for a wider consideration of these issues, and the terms of reference of the Sandilands Committee did, in fact, refer to each of the items listed in the 'Tombstone's' 'Repercussions'. These deficiencies became important because of subsequent events: instead of its being merely a discussion paper, the Exposure Draft, *ED8* issued in January 1973, contained the same set of CPP proposals.

This is not to say that the ASSC did not take care to consult all interested parties. The impressive range of representation at the plenary meetings has already been indicated. The Government was also asked if it wished to set up an enquiry to which ASSC would make representations, but in December 1971 the Government declined to do so for the time being, whilst reserving its future position. The ICAEW Summer School in 1971 (reported in *The Accountant*, 16 September 1971, pp. 382–6) was devoted to the topic 'Inflation – the accounting and social implications', and heard a variety of views, although the Chairman and final speaker was Mr W. E. Parker, who gave an eloquent presentation of the case for CPP.[20] The Confederation of British Industry set up its own enquiry, the Barran Committee, which supported the CPP solution (Confederation of British Industry, 1973). It is fair to say that, in the period which elapsed between the issue of the 'Tombstone' (August 1971) and the publication of *ED8* (January 1973), no strong objections were raised against the CPP solution. The ASSC had certainly shown partiality for the CPP approach, but whether this amounted to 'stage-managing' the debate, or whether it was merely the exercise of responsible leadership is a matter for individual judgement.[21]

The ASSC also initiated a programme of field-testing to assess the practical difficulties and the materiality of CPP adjustments (Cutler and Westwick, 1973), and it produced a working manual to illustrate the techniques of CPP. Thus, it directed its limited research resources to the technical aspects of CPP rather than researching the wider issues of the choice between CPP, current cost and other methods, and their relative merits in meeting the needs of users of accounting information. With hindsight, it is easy to criticise this policy, but, at the time, given the increased urgency of the inflation accounting problem (due to the accelerating rate of inflation), the simplicity and convenience of CPP from the point of view of the accounting profession, the apparent agreement of other users to this solution, and the limited availability of resources for research, the policy probably seemed to be the most effective means of making progress.

The contents of *ED8*, published in January 1973, reflected this approach. Quoted companies would be required (and others recommended) to produce supplementary CPP-adjusted data (the valuation base remaining historical cost, and the CPP up-dating being subject to the 'cost or market value, whichever is the lower' constraint). The gain or loss on monetary items was to appear as a separate item in the stabilised profit and loss account. The basic system was therefore the same as that of *Accounting for Stewardship*, *ARS6* and *APB3*.[22] The exposure period was to end in July 1973, and the earliest date of application would be for accounting periods starting in January 1974.

The issue of *ED8* marked the high point of CPP in the UK debate. The UK had overtaken the USA in its progress towards CPP accounting. However, the UK also became a leader in the Current Cost Revolution when, in July 1973, one week before the exposure period for *ED8* was due to expire, the Government intervened by announcing its intention to appoint an independent committee of enquiry, which, after some delay, began work in January 1974 under the charmanship of Mr (later Sir) Francis Sandilands. The appointment and work of this committee will be discussed in the following two chapters.

In view of the delay which was likely to elapse before the Sandilands Committee reported and the continuing urgency of the problem due to an accelerating inflation rate, the ASSC issued its Provisional Standard *PSSAP7*, in May 1974. The proposals were, for practical purposes, the same as those of *ED8* but relatively more attention was given, in the text of *PSSAP7*, to the relationship of the proposals to replacement cost accounting (emphasising that the two systems were complementary rather than competitive with one another). This may partly have reflected the ASSC's response to the submissions which it had received on *ED8* (analysed in the next chapter), but it may also have represented an attempt to anticipate and compromise with the likely conclusions of the Sandilands Committee. There would, after all, have been little point in appointing the Sandilands Committee had the Government and the members of the Committee been convinced in advance of the merits of CPP, as embodied in *ED8*.

Thus, in the United Kingdom, as in the United States, 1974 saw important professional moves towards CPP, but potentially more important signs that governments were not satisfied with this solution.

4 The development of theory (1945–74)

Earlier sections of this chapter have concentrated on professional developments, within standard-setting bodies and other professional organisations, culminating in the proposals for the implementation of CPP in 1973 and 1974. The latter proposals did not represent an advance on the ideas put forward by Sweeney (1936), so it was not necessary to allude to any developments in theory during the post-war period. However, it would be grossly misleading to suggest that no theoretical developments took place during this period: in fact, the theoretical debate, mainly amongst academics but also involving practitioners, was more vigorous during this period than in the pre-war period, within the English-speaking world. Furthermore, although the professional developments of the period did not reflect contemporary theoretical developments, it seems possible that there might be a lag between the development of theory and its implementation in practice, so that the theoretical developments of this period might be a leading indicator of practical developments in the following period.

With these considerations in mind, this section briefly sketches some of the developments of the period. The selection is necessarily subjective and the treatment superficial, because the 1960s in particular were a period of great activity in accounting theory, as is evidenced by the high proportion of the literature referred to in the companion volume (Whittington, 1983a) which was published in this period. Useful surveys of the development of accounting theory are provided by Moonitz and Nelson (1960) and by Nelson (1973). A preliminary evaluation of the present state of the theory of inflation accounting was given in the final chapter of Whittington (1983a) and certain themes will be developed further in later chapters. Here it is hoped to give a brief outline of the main developments.

The immediate post-war period of the late 1940s was characterised mainly by a more detailed working out of ideas which were already available. There was a debate on the merits of replacement cost accounting (much of which is summarised in Prest, 1950) and the case for CPP accounting was also clarified and discussed (e.g. by Baxter, 1949, in the UK). The work of the Study Group on Business Income in the USA has already been referred to. Its outstanding contribution to theory was probably the monograph by Alexander (1950), which explored the concept of income thoroughly from the economist's standpoint,[23] emphasising the problem of uncertainty and concluding that there are three crucial issues in income measurement:

> . . . the real versus the money measure, inclusion versus exclusion of capital gains, and accrual versus realisation as the criterion for timing of a gain or loss . . .. But income is used for so many different purposes that a set of decisions on the three major issues appropriate to one use of a measure of income may well be inappropriate to another. (Alexander, 1950, p. 94)

This recognition that income is not an objective, single-valued number, but should be defined in relation to the purpose for which it is used pervades the theoretical development of the subject throughout the period and up to the present time.

Some of the work of the 1950s, such as that by Jones (1956) and Mason (1956) has already been referred to. There was a considerable amount of academic work in this mould, essentially filling out the CPP framework defined by Sweeney, who was himself (Sweeney, 1964a) contemptuous of much of the work of the period (although not that of the authors referred to here). In the area of replacement cost accounting, equally it could be said that there was no obvious advance on the work of Schmidt or Limperg, although there were some useful elaborations of their ideas. For example, one piece of work, which deserves special emphasis because of the subsequent contributions of one of its authors, is Mathews and Grant (1958), an application of replacement cost accounting to Australian companies, which lays particular emphasis on the implications of the results for the trade cycle (originally suggested by Schmidt, 1927).[24] It also attempts to justify replacement cost accounting (specifically, the adjustment of historical cost accounting by making additional charges for replacement cost of goods sold and depreciation), on the grounds that the resulting income measure is an appropriate basis for the dividend decision and for taxation.[25]

It was, however, the 1960s which saw the burgeoning of theoretical work in accounting. Nelson (1973), describes it as 'a golden age in the history of *a priori* research in accounting', although he then proceeds to explore the deficiencies of the work of the period. The main feature of the work of the period was the proposal of a number of alternative models for financial accounting in a much more precise and comprehensive form and supported by much more rigorous theoretical arguments than previously. The limitation of this approach (as expounded at greater length by Nelson) was a neglect of empirical evidence to support assumptions and lack of concern for deriving empirically testable conclusions. The result was a vigorous theoretical debate, which clarified the assumptions and theoretical properties of alternative models but which offered no means of deciding which model would best meet the practical requirements of the real world. It is also possible to criticise the work of this period for its failure to derive the accounting model from users' information needs: a more common practice was to define a 'grand model' and then attempt to justify it in terms of its ability to meet the needs of users.[26] There was a tendency for authors to attempt to defend their models against all possible alternatives in all possible uses, i.e. as general purpose information.

The latter deficiency was exhibited least in the work of Edwards and Bell (1961) and it may be for this reason that their book was probably the most influential single work of the period. Edwards and Bell set out to construct an accounting system which would be suitable for *ex post* evaluation of a firm's performance during a particular period. They avoid the difficulties of valuing subjective goodwill by confining their system to the use of current market values of assets. Their system involves three important dichotomies: between operating gains (due to the firm's manufacturing and trading activities) and holding gains (the gains in asset values due to price changes which take place during the time in which the assets are held); between nominal gains (measured in terms of monetary units which fluctuate in value) and real gains (measured in units of constant purchasing power); and between realised gains (resulting from a transaction in the open market) and unrealised gains[27] (resulting from changes in market prices, but not confirmed by market transactions).[28] By implementing these three dichotomies, Edwards and Bell proposed, within a single set of accounting statements, to show a variety of information which they considered to be relevant to the evaluation of a firm's activities for different purposes. The important result of this approach is to draw attention to the multiple dimensions of a firm's performance and to de-emphasise the 'bottom line' of the income statement. Such an approach has recently been adopted by the FASB in the United States, in its inflation accounting standard (*FAS33*, 1979b) and in its conceptual framework (FASB, 1981b).

Edwards and Bell might be criticised for failure to show in a precise manner how any particular user would or should make use of the data provided by their system. Equally, their dichotomies might be criticised: that between holding gains and operating gains being particularly controversial (Drake and Dopuch, 1965).[29] However, the most controversial aspect of their system was their choice of valuation base. They demonstrated the potential relevance of a variety of valuation bases and presented a choice between two, one based on net realisable values and one based on replacement costs. They then indicated a preference for replacement cost, on the ground, essentially, that replacement is generally more relevant to a business which will continue its operations over the foreseeable future. Their choice was made on somewhat pragmatic grounds: they believed that reporting a variety of valuation bases was infeasible so that it was necessary to make a choice between bases, recognising that this involved rejecting information which might potentially be relevant. As a pragmatic judgement, it is difficult to quarrel with this. The authors themselves have since amended it: Edwards (1975) concedes that selling prices ('exit values') are probably more useful than replacement costs ('entry values') in the case of goods held for re-sale, and Bell and Johnson (1979) are also willing to use a mixture of entry values and exit values, on the basis of an adaptation of 'deprival value' reasoning. As we shall see in subsequent chapters, this type of approach to valuation has been favoured by the majority of those standard-setting bodies which have proposed forms of current cost accounting during the past decade.

After the publication of their original work (1961), Edwards and Bell were the subject of a vigorous attack by Chambers (1965), who became the leading advocate of accounting based on net realisable values. His book, *Accounting Evaluation and Economic Behavior* (1966) was his main statement, although he was probably the most prolific writer on accounting theory in the 1960s and has since amended his views on certain matters of detail.[30] Chambers' essential message is that: *'Opportunity costs (market resale prices) are relevant to the firm always.'* (Chambers, 1965, author's own emphasis.) From his view that selling prices are always relevant (representing one opportunity which is available) he somewhat uncompromisingly rejects alternative valuation bases (which may also be relevant in certain important situations). His approach is very much that of a valuer, concerned with the balance sheet, and, in the income statement, with increase in command over assets (a Hicks No. 1 or No. 2 income measure) rather than with an operating profit which maintains the earning capacity of the business (a Hicks No. 3 measure). He also proposes the use of a general index for the measurement of capital to be maintained, i.e. he supports the maintenance of real proprietary capital in measuring income. Some of his views were discussed in the companion volume to this book (Whittington, 1983a), and it is not possible to consider his work in detail here. It should, however, be noted that, although the use of market values in accounts had long been advocated (e.g. by Canning, 1929, and MacNeal, 1939), Chambers' theoretical arguments were much more sophisticated than those of his predecessors, arguing from a closely

55

Part I The debate

defined set of assumptions about the desirable properties of accounting data[31] and his system was much more rigorously defined in terms of realisable values.[32] However, his work provides a good example of the weakness as well as the strength of the work of the 1960s, in his dogged and perhaps even dogmatic defence of a single global model to the exclusion of all others.

Another important writer of the period whose views support a net realisable value basis for accounts is Arthur L. Thomas (1969 and 1974), whose elegant exploration of the allocation problem leads him to conclude that the traditional accrual method of accounting involves time allocations (accruals) which are essentially arbitrary. To overcome this problem, he advocates recourse to current market values of assets, and net realisable values in particular. Replacement values would also be acceptable, were they current market values, but replacement cost systems, such as the current cost accounting systems incorporated in UK and USA accounting standards, often involve arbitrary allocations in the assessment of depreciation. This is an example of an issue raised by theorists which is likely to become of practical importance with the implementation of current cost accounting.

Chambers' proposals did not go unchallenged in the 1960s, and one of the strongest challenges came from 'deprival value' (or 'value to the owner') advocates, whose views subsequently have prevailed, in the sense that their version of current value has been incorporated in the current cost standards of the UK and the USA. Solomons (1966b) and Baxter (1967) both reviewed Chambers' valuation basis critically, advocating value to the owner as an alternative, and Solomons stated the precise rules for deprival value in the now familiar inequality form in another paper (Solomons, 1966a).[33] Subsequently, Baxter (1975) presented a complete system of inflation accounting, with value to the owner as the valuation base, but with real capital (i.e. real general purchasing power of capital) as the capital maintenance concept to be used in measuring income. The case for value to the owner, as presented by Baxter, is essentially pragmatic:[34] given the need to report only a single value for each asset, the value to the owner rules provide a means of choosing what seems to be the most important of the alternative values in the particular circumstances.[35] An even more pragmatic extension of the principle is to resort entirely to replacement cost, on the ground that this is the value which will most commonly emerge as value to the owner in practice (Gee and Peasnell, 1976).

The advocates of both the Edwards and Bell and the opportunity value approaches to replacement cost were somewhat pragmatic in their arguments and prepared to concede the potential virtues of alternative

56

methods of valuation. They also typically adopted a general index-adjusted real capital maintenance concept in periods of inflation.[36] However, replacement cost did not lack advocates of a more fundamental kind during the period under review. Gynther (1966) was cleary influenced by his study of the Dutch replacement cost system and proposed a replacement cost system with an entity concept of capital maintenance, very much in the spirit of Limperg and Schmidt. He was perhaps the clearest and most eloquent advocate of the entity approach during this period. Mathews also continued to advocate a replacement cost system, and his highly critical review (1965) of *ARS6* (containing the description 'useless information' in the title), provided ample testimony to his opposition to stabilised accounting of the CPP variety. To anyone acquainted with this paper (and the author's other work such as Mathews and Grant, 1958), the contents of the Mathews Report (1975), which will be discussed at length in Chapter 8, would contain no surprises. Another study of replacement cost which deserves mention is that of Revsine (1973), a scholarly exploration of the theoretical properties of replacement cost accounting, particularly in relation to the surrogate hypothesis (that accounting values, such as replacement costs, can be surrogates for economic values, i.e. discounted present values of future receipts). This has served to define the limitations of the replacement cost model rather than to strengthen the case for its use in practice (Revsine, 1976).

The developments described above were all essentially evolutionary, dealing with balance sheets and profit and loss accounts and with alternative models of valuation and measurement which had been available for some time. There were, however, more revolutionary developments, such as the lively discussion of cash flow reporting (Lawson, 1971; Staubus, 1971 and Lee, 1972). Even these had origins which could be traced back to such writers as Schmalenbach, but the readiness of theorists to abandon completely the traditional forms was a novelty. There was also concern with novel areas such as human asset accounting, and with reporting to users outside the traditional providers of finance (shareholders and creditors). The quickening pace of practical developments suggests that some of these ideas may move from theory to practice at a much greater pace than past history might lead us to expect.[37] If this occurs, new problems may be posed by the need to adjust new forms of report for the effects of inflation, but certain new forms may not require such adjustments. Indeed, this may be one of their attractions relative to more traditional accounting. For example, this might be the case with cash flow reporting, which was seriously considered (although not at great length) by the Sandilands Committee.

This concludes our discussion of the theoretical developments in the broad area of inflation accounting which have taken place between 1945 and the early 1970s. Since that time, theoretical work has continued to refine various aspects of the alternative 'grand models' proposed in the 1960s. Attention has focussed more on specific problem areas, with more limited but possibly more realistic aims. There has also been a welcome increase in the amount of empirical research, some of which was surveyed in the companion volume (Whittington, 1983a). The present state of theory is well-represented in the recent book edited by Sterling and Thomas (1979), which includes contributions from many of the leading current contributors to financial accounting theory and focusses on the problem of accounting for a simplified firm owning depreciable assets. A wide variety of valuation bases is supported by the various authors, each employing arguments more sophisticated than would have been the case a decade or more earlier, but there is little or no consensus as to those models which can be ruled out as practical possibilities. Even historical cost and CPP adjustment on an historical cost base have received support from some leading theorists in recent years (notably Ijiri, 1971 and 1976). However, this type of basis has received support only from a small minority, and the majority of theoretical writing in recent years has been concerned with the precise form which current value reporting should take, rather than with the (generally accepted) principle that some form of current values should be reported. In this sense, our review of the theoretical work of the period matches that of the review of professional developments earlier in the chapter: the apparent ascendancy of CPP accounting based on historical cost in 1974 was likely to prove at best a temporary stage in the evolution of current value accounting on a real terms basis and at worst a false dawn, the retreat from which would lead to more confusion than if this stage had never occurred.

The most recent theoretical development which deserves mention is the recognition that under realistic conditions of uncertainty and market incompleteness, income or profit can be strictly indeterminate, and so cannot be represented by a single number. This idea, derived from economic theory, was introduced into the accounting literature in an explicit and rigorous form by Beaver and Demski (1979), who infer from this that the accountant should attempt to provide the reader of accounts with a set of what they describe as 'fuzzy information', rather than a precise income number. The same idea was expressed more informally by Bromwich (1977) and Peasnell (1977). This line of argument lends powerful support to the Edwards and Bell 'information set' approach.

5 Conclusion

Earlier sections of this chapter traced the evolution of inflation accounting in the USA and the UK to the end of 1974. In both countries, 1974 saw pronouncements by professional standard-setting bodies in favour of CPP adjustments of traditional historical cost data. However, in both countries also, there were signs that government intervention might lead to a rejection of this approach to the problem of inflation accounting. In the USA, the chief accountant of the SEC, the government agency with authority to specify the contents of publicly filed accounting reports, had expressed a clear preference for replacement cost accounting, and in the UK the Government had appointed the Sandilands Committee, presumably because, in its view, the professional CPP solution might not be adequate. Our review of the theoretical work of the period also suggested that support for the professional approach was very limited: most theorists were advocates of some form of current value accounting, although there was considerable diversity of view as to the precise form which this should take.

The period 1974–75 saw parallel developments in the rest of the English-speaking world. Australia, Canada, New Zealand and South Africa all produced exposure drafts or discussion papers on CPP accounting similar to the UK's *ED8* and the USA's *APB3* (and the subsequent 1974 FASB Exposure Draft). None of these advanced beyond the Exposure Draft stage, and in two of these countries this was attributable to the appointment of government committees of enquiry (the Mathews enquiry in Australia and the Richardson Committee in New Zealand), the reports of which advocated current cost accounting. The course of this 'Current Cost Revolution' is traced in the following chapters.

4

The contemporary British debate I: the watershed of the CPP experiment, 1973

1 Introduction: an over-view of the debate, 1973–80

This chapter and the two chapters following continue the analysis of the British[1] debate on inflation accounting begun in Section 3 of the last chapter. The main purpose of this chapter is to examine in detail the events of the crucial year 1973, a year which could be deemed to have been a watershed in the UK debate, marking as it did the beginning of the end of the British experiment with constant purchasing power (CPP) accounting. The following two chapters deal with the advent of the United Kingdom's current cost (CCA) proposals, and in particular with the Sandilands Report, and the ensuing CCA pronouncements of the Accounting Standards Committee (ASC).

1973 began with the issue of the ASSC's CPP Exposure Draft, *ED8*, and ended with the Government being about to announce the members and terms of reference of a Committee of Enquiry into Inflation Accounting (subsequently the Sandilands Committee). The responses to the ASSC's *ED8* proposals had been divided. While, in general, professional accountants supported the ASSC's Exposure Draft, strong opposition came from industrial preparers and from users of financial statements, many of whom advocated current value methods of accounting. Just as *ED8*'s exposure period was ending and before the ASSC had time to consider its future course of action, the Government intervened in the debate and shocked the profession by announcing its intention to appoint a Committee of Enquiry into Inflation Accounting.

The next chapter deals with the period 1974–75, which saw the publication of the Sandilands Report. Although the ASSC published a provisional CPP standard (*PSSAP7*) based on *ED8* in May 1974 it was obvious that the inflation accounting debate in the UK would stagnate until the publication of the Sandilands Report. The Report, duly published in September 1975, advocated sweeping changes in the UK's method of financial reporting. The Committee's main conclusion was that the best form of accounting in a period of inflation is current cost accounting (CCA), which reflects the changes in the prices of the specific assets owned and used by the firm. The Committee rejected entirely the use of general purchasing power indices, thus polarising the debate by expressing outright opposition to the CPP system favoured by the professional standard-setters. Moreover, it was proposed that CCA would be the basis of the main published accounts, not merely supplementary statements.

The period 1976–80, described in Chapter 6, saw the professional standard-setters working to produce an acceptable system on the basis of the Sandilands Report, but taking account of the views of the profession which, in its response to the Sandilands Report (CCAB, 1975), had favoured combining CCA with CPP in a 'real terms' solution. The work of devising the new system fell to the Inflation Accounting Steering Group (IASG), chaired throughout the period by Mr (now Sir) Douglas Morpeth.[2] Not surprisingly, in view of the importance and controversial nature of its task, the IASG encountered difficulties and setbacks, but it finally produced the first British inflation accounting Standard, *SSAP16*, which was introduced in 1980 with a view to revision after a three-year trial period.

The main landmarks of the period 1976–80 were *ED18*, published in 1976, the Hyde Guidelines of 1977, *ED24* published in 1979, and, finally, *SSAP16*, 1980.

ED18, published in 1976, was the first British current cost exposure draft. Like the Sandilands Report, it proposed that the main accounts should be on a current cost basis, which was elaborated in considerable detail. General price-level adjustments were to be banished from the main accounts and to appear only in a supplementary statement. These revolutionary proposals proved to be unacceptable to the profession, partly because of the requirement that the main accounts be on the new basis, and partly because it was clearly intended that the new system would eventually apply to all companies, irrespective of size. The failure of the new system to reconcile Sandilands with the CPP system, to produce a satisfactory treatment of monetary assets and liabilities, also played a part, as did the apparent complexity of the *ED18* proposals. The outcome was that *ED18* was rejected by a resolution of a special meeting of the Institute of Chartered Accountants in England and Wales, in July 1977.

The response of the ASC was to set up a small working party, under the chairmanship of Mr William Hyde, which produced the *Interim Recommendation on Inflation Accounting*, popularly known as the Hyde Guidelines, in November 1977. These were extremely simple, concerned only with providing supplementary profit and loss information, and confined to leading companies. Thus, most of the pitfalls of *ED18* were avoided, whilst the technical detail of *ED18* provided useful background for implementation and enabled the Guidelines to be brief and apparently simple. There were three adjustments to the profit and loss account. The first two, the cost of sales adjustment and the depreciation adjustment showed the additional cost of goods sold and depreciation charges arising from the use of a current cost rather than an historical cost basis. The third adjustment, the gearing adjustment, introduced an adjustment for the gain on long-term borrowing which used specific prices, rather than the general indices used by the CPP method. The first two adjustments (for cost of sales and depreciation) were abated by the ratio of long-term debt to total net worth (the gearing ratio). Thus, realised holding gains on stocks (cost of sales adjustment) and fixed assets (depreciation adjustment) were recognised to the extent that they were financed by long-term borrowing (gearing). This provided an ingenious means of reconciling the Sandilands approach with some recognition of the gain on borrowing and proved to be an effective means of gaining consensus, even if it was theoretically an impure solution.[3]

The Hyde Guidelines were not mandatory but were followed by enough leading companies to provide useful experience of CCA, as a background to the next full Exposure Draft, *ED24* (1979) which, without amendment of its essential features, became the first British current cost accounting Standard (*SSAP16*) in 1980. *SSAP16* retains two essential features of the Hyde approach, the gearing adjustment and supplementary disclosure for leading companies only, as the minimum requirement (although current cost is *permitted* as the basis of the main accounts). The Hyde principle of simplicity has also been retained, e.g. in encouraging the use of specific price indices where revaluation is difficult or expensive. To the Hyde framework, *SSAP16* adds a full current cost balance sheet, and the Hyde gearing adjustment has been amended by the separate treatment of monetary working capital, the maintenance of which is now allowed for by a monetary working capital adjustment. This is a charge for the additional cost of maintaining monetary working capital, calculated in a similar manner (also using specific price indices) to the cost of sales adjustment, which reflects the additional cost of maintaining stocks, the non-monetary component of working capital.

Thus the present British current cost accounting Standard is the result of a long period of negotiation and inevitably bears the mark of compromise. The polarisation of the debate was epitomised by the Sandilands Committee's stark rejection of CPP in favour of CCA, and the spirit of compromise was epitomised in the Hyde Guidelines, which pointed the way to a practical solution, albeit one which will require future development.

Thus the debate in the UK drew to a temporary close in 1980. The remainder of this chapter considers in greater detail than hitherto one of the crucial years of this controversial period, 1973, and the aftermath of the issue of *ED8*, when the control of the UK inflation accounting debate passed from the accountancy profession to the State.

2 Exposure Draft 8 (ED8): Accounting for Changes in the Purchasing Power of Money

ED8 was published in January 1973. The background to its publication was described in Section 3 of the previous chapter. Here we shall merely review the main features of the document itself.

The *ED8* proposals were for a supplementary inflation-adjusted statement to be published by listed companies. The historical cost convention would remain the basis of the main accounts and would also be the basis to which the CPP adjustments were applied: historical costs of non-monetary assets and equity claims would be converted into current £s by applying the change in the general price index which had occurred since their acquisition. Where CPP-restated historical cost exceeded current value of assets, the conservative 'cost or value, whichever is the lower', rule would apply. Occasional revaluations of fixed assets would still be permitted, but essentially the valuation system would be historical cost restated in current £s. This was similar to the system proposed earlier in Britain in the ICAEW research paper *Accounting for Stewardship in a Period of Inflation* (1968) and by the United States Accounting Principles Board in 1969 (*APB3*).

The advantage of this system was that it was relatively objective, relying mainly on the application of published price indices. It therefore imposed little additional burden on accountants or auditors. It had three obvious deficiencies. Firstly, although it was in principle a very simple system, in substance it looked complicated to the layman, and the concept of a constant purchasing power unit did not have immediate intuitive appeal. Secondly, the valuation basis did not, in general, take account of the market values of the specific assets held and used by the individual firm, so that industry tended to regard it as unrealistic. Thirdly, it was proposed to regard the gain on long-term borrowing as part of profit. This is, of course, typically an unrealised gain, and its treatment is one of the most controversial aspects of CPP systems whenever they are discussed. Firms which were suffering from rising replacement costs, low profit margins and high interest rates, at the time when *ED8* was issued, found it difficult to believe that they could be making a profit because of the erosion of their long-term borrowing by inflation. They may have been wrong in this attitude, confusing profit with cash flow, but nevertheless this particular feature of *ED8* undoubtedly provoked considerable opposition.

Since *ED8* was the first Exposure Draft on inflation accounting in Britain, the responses to it provide the first publicly available evidence of the attitudes to inflation accounting of a wide cross-section of preparers and users of accounts. We present our own analysis of these responses in Table 4.1.

3 The responses to ED8

In all, 113 comments on *ED8* were received by the ASSC. This level of response was only slightly higher than the typical response to exposure drafts issued by 1973 and indeed was lower than the response to *ED1* (Associated Companies – 152 responses) and *ED6* (Stocks and Work in Progress – 150 responses).

It is possible that the level of submissions to the ASSC on the current purchasing power Exposure Draft may have been indicative of accountants' unfamiliarity with a subject affecting the general nature of accounting measurement, in contrast to their knowledge of the more specific subjects encompassed by *ED1* and *ED6*. The latter Exposure Drafts were concerned with subjects of obvious interest to the respondents: companies already had accounting policies to deal with the problems of associated companies and stocks and would be aware of the potential effect of the Exposure Drafts' recommendations. Few companies and reporting accountants, however, would necessarily be familiar with the application of accounting for changing price levels and many may have believed that inflation would affect all companies equally. It is notable that the companies which did respond to *ED8* included a number who were in the small minority which *had* formulated an approach to inflation accounting (see note 6).

If a lack of understanding of the significance of the Exposure Draft's proposals were to be the reason for the low level of response, then it would seem that more should have been done to bring the ramifications of the new system of accounting to the attention of those concerned with financial reporting. In early 1973 it seemed likely that a CPP accounting system would slip into effect almost without critical assessment by the vast majority of the UK's accountants.[4]

Many of those who did submit comments on the Exposure Draft to

Table 4.1. *Support for and opposition to the ED8 proposals*

Group	No.	Support %	Opposition %	Neutral/no comment/ no applicability %
Representative bodies – accountancy bodies	7	86	14	—
Technical advisory committees of ICAEW	17	71	6	23
Representative bodies – preparers of accounts	8	63	—	37
Practising firms of accountants	13	62	38	—
Representative bodies – users and non-preparers	4	50	25	25
Individuals (excluding academics)	26	46	42	12
Academics	11	36	64	—
Companies and corporations	27	26	74	—
Total	113	49	41	10

the ASSC did, however, appear to be well aware of the potential effects of the ASSC's proposals and expressed views ranging from firm support to outright opposition to the standard-setting body's conclusions, although the vast majority was in favour of some form of accounting for the effects of price-level changes.

Analysis of the responses by the present authors showed that only 49 per cent of all submissions were in favour of the current purchasing power method proposed in *ED8*: 41 per cent of the submissions indicated opposition to the proposals, generally because of a view that other systems of accounting were considered to be preferable to the ASSC's recommendations.

These figures differ from those given by Westwick (1980, p. 359) who reproduces the analysis based on 93 responses prepared by him, as a member of the ICAEW's secretariat, for the ASSC in 1973. Our figures, based on an analysis of all 113 responses are less favourable to *ED8* than Westwick's. There is no suggestion, however, that there was any attempt to hide the true picture from the ASSC; our own analysis convinced us of the difficulty of determining the view each respondent was attempting to communicate. Many responses were internally inconsistent; several (especially from committees or representative bodies) attempted to reconcile differing viewpoints with the result that the reader was left confused and uncertain as to the respondents' intentions.[5] There is an obvious lesson to be learned here: standard-setters can neither be assisted in their task, nor can respondents justifiably complain that their points have been overlooked, if the response in question is not consistently argued or its thrust clearly expressed!

Table 4.1 reveals that the support for *ED8* came mainly from professional accountants: from accountancy bodies, practising firms and district advisory committees of the Institute of Chartered Accountants in England and Wales. The opposition came mainly from users and industrial preparers of financial information: from companies, corporations and private individuals.

Even the support for *ED8* could not be interpreted as being solid. Analysing the responses favourable to *ED8* into explicit and qualified support (Table 4.2) it can be seen that the apparent backing for the Exposure Draft shown in Westwick's figures was not firm: only one in five of the respondents was apparently committed to *ED8*'s proposals.

Even among the accountancy bodies themselves, doubts about the viability of the Exposure Draft's proposals were obvious. While only one accountancy body (the Dutch Institute, NIVRA) actually opposed *ED8*, three UK accountancy bodies (ICAI, ICAS and ICMA) only gave

Table 4.2. *Depth of support for the ED8 proposals*

Group	No.	Explicit support %	Qualified support %	Total support as per Table 4.1 %
Representative bodies – accountancy bodies	7	14	72	86
Technical advisory committees of ICAEW	17	30	41	71
Representative bodies – preparers of accounts	8	13	50	63
Practising firms of accountants	13	23	39	62
Representative bodies – users and non-preparers	4	25	25	50
Individuals (excluding academics)	26	23	23	46
Academics	11	9	27	36
Companies and corporations	27	15	11	26
Total	113	19	30	49

it lukewarm support, arguing that the proposals could only be considered to be a short-term solution. For example:

> . . . [The Institute's Committee] does not believe, however,
> that [the CPP approach] is the ultimate word on the subject and
> would like the whole field reviewed when a standard has been in
> force for two or three years. *Institute of Chartered Accountants
> of Scotland*
> . . . full support is given to CPP accounting on the grounds of its
> practicability as possibly an interim measure in the
> improvement of financial reporting. It is nevertheless essential
> that consideration be given to permitting the use of more
> refined concepts, either in parallel with or, in the longer term,
> instead of the CPP method. *Institute of Cost and Management
> Accountants*

The opposition to the Exposure Draft was led by many companies and corporations and in particular by the influential Society of Investment Analysts which had previously supported the ICAEW's CPP Discussion Paper. Now the Society rejected CPP and argued in favour of an income measure based on an entity system of capital maintenance involving the maintenance of monetary as well as physical assets – a concept which would not be proposed officially in the UK until the advent of the Hyde Guidelines some four years later:

> We accept that CPP accounting is conceptually logical but does
> it give the users of Company Accounts an answer that has any
> particular relevance? We would prefer the use of replacement
> cost accounting as used by Philips, but perhaps with the
> difference that its application would supplement rather than
> replace historical cost accounting. Although RCA may not have
> been conceived to show the effects of inflation, we believe it
> does in fact provide the best answer and approaches more
> closely internal management accounts that may be used to show
> quite specifically what part of the profits are required by a
> company to maintain its assets and its working capital at current
> prices.

The Society's views on replacement cost were shared by several companies, some being more critical of the Exposure Draft than others.[6]

> . . . The different make-up of particular companies must be
> taken into account when assessing the overall effects of
> inflation. It is our view that the overall effect of changes in the

purchasing power of money on individual companies can be assessed only by taking into account the price changes relating to the actual physical assets they employ . . ... We consider that the proposed method (*ED8*) is only an arithmetical exercise which has no real meaning. *Pilkington*

As regards emphasis we consider that to view the problem solely from the standpoint of the shareholder or potential investor fails to cover the equally or possibly more important objective of ensuring that day-to-day management decisions are soundly based.[7] The exposure draft completely ignores the responsibility of accountants in this respect. The former category would, we are convinced, also prefer that this was done. The application of the replacement theory of accounting as used by us does, we maintain, overcome all the disadvantages mentioned. As a first step, *ED8* is a move in the right direction, but we strongly recommend that considerably more thought should be given to the problem. In any event, we submit that where companies implement an alternative approach which goes further than the proposed then at least they should be released from any obligation to publish supplementary information. *Philips Industries*

In all just over one-quarter of the 113 respondents, almost all of whom expressed opposition to *ED8*, stated some preference for the incorporation of replacement cost or current values in financial statements. Apart from the valuation system proposed, other particular aspects of the Exposure Draft attracted criticism. For example, about one-fifth of the submissions mentioned their authors' concern about the inclusion of the gain on borrowing in profit. Additionally, several others, mainly from companies, warned that the novelty of the CPP statements or the fact that such statements were to be issued in tandem with the HC statements could result in the reader of financial reports becoming confused, either by the concept of purchasing power units being used in place of the familiar money units, or by the production of two profit figures.

In summarising the overall impression given by the comments received by the ASSC, it could be said that while the standard-setting body may well have received slightly more submissions supporting rather than opposing its proposals, the support was not enthusiastic and came mainly from representative bodies of accountants or from professional accountancy firms. Opposition, at times strong, came from private individuals and, more importantly, from the corporate sector.

Those concerned with financial reporting were clearly divided on the issue of accounting for price-level changes and divided in a way that would make it difficult for the accountancy profession's own standard-setting body, the ASSC, to produce a standard acceptable equally to the profession and to industry and users of financial statements.

Table 4.3 reveals the magnitude of the split between the two groups. While 70 per cent of the group of respondents which consisted of representative bodies and practising firms of accountants appeared to support a standard based on the principles of *ED8*, only 39 per cent of the larger group, comprising users and industrial preparers of financial statements appeared to give similar support. Indeed, a majority (52 per cent) of the latter group seemed to be opposed to the Exposure Draft's recommendations: only 19 per cent of the accountancy bodies and firms appeared to hold a similar view.

While Table 4.3 reveals that an overwhelming majority of the responses from the accountancy firms and representative bodies of accountants supported the *ED8* proposals, the table also shows that the largest proportion of this group appeared to accept (rather than actively support) *ED8* or looked upon the Exposure Draft as an evolutionary measure which would eventually be supplemented by some other recommendation. Loyalty to the profession may well have prevented some of these respondents from opposing the ASSC's proposals, a loyalty probably reinforced by the belief that there was little prospect of achieving enforcement, in the short term, of any radical departure from the historical cost convention (Westwick, 1980, p. 356).

Another, more positive, explanation for the overall support given to the *ED8* proposals by practising accountants could, however, lie in the obvious advantages accruing to the practising accountant in his rôle of auditor in the implementation of a CPP system of accounting for inflation. The testing of current purchasing power financial statements would not involve a great deal of work additional to the verification of HC accounts. Additionally, the application to verifiable historical cost figures of a general index produced by the Central Statistical Office would mean that no subjectivity on the part of management would enter into the adjustments to the historical cost figures, apart from the occasional application of the 'lower of adjusted cost and market value' rule.

To the practising accountant therefore a CPP system would probably be perceived as but a small step away from historical cost accounts. A measure based on units of purchasing power may well have appeared to him to be a simple, inexpensive, objective, and therefore easily audited,

Table 4.3. *Summary of support for ED8*

Group	No.	Explicit support %	Qualified support %	Qualified opposition %	Outright opposition %	Neutral %
Representative bodies and committees of accountants/ practising firms of accountants	37	24	46	8	11	11
Other respondents – mainly users and industrial preparers of financial statements	76	17	22	15	37	9
Total	113	19	30	13	28	10

adjustment to the traditional financial statements. Current value accounting, on the other hand, possibly raised anxieties about an erosion both of objectivity and of the principles of realisation and conservatism.

While the practising accountants may have been supporting what they saw as an alternative to an accounting revolution, to the opponents of *ED8*, a current purchasing power system could equally have been considered revolutionary. The proponents and opponents of *ED8* appear to have approached the problem of accounting for price-level changes from two quite different standpoints, each of which could well have appeared to the other side as leading to fundamental changes in the existing system. The polarity of these views was later clarified by the Sandilands Report (1975). The two sides, however, were seeking to achieve different objectives. Many of the opponents of *ED8* were more concerned with opportunity values rather than original cost and preferred an entirely new system of accounting. The supporters of the CPP system were attempting to retain a stabilised HC system but in doing so assumed that an individual could think in terms of purchasing power units and that this somewhat artificial construct would be preferable to obliging an individual to attempt to deflate money values by his own perception of the depreciation of the currency.[8] The purchasing power unit proposed on *ED8* was to be used to stabilise accounts in terms of a fixed basket of goods and services in general demand. This would result in assessing the effect of price-level changes caused by a popular measure of inflation (the Consumer Price Index) based on a general expenditure pattern, not necessarily related to that of the reporting company. This may have been acceptable for assessing the effect of inflation on shareholders' capital, but it undoubtedly moved valuation of the firm's assets and costs away from the market place. Therefore, for those interested in the specific expenditures of a company, namely management and users of accounts, CPP financial statements could be seen as producing 'fictitious' income and value measurements, which reflected neither potential future operating profit nor values representing the 'worth' of assets to the firm. The CPP measures were probably perceived as blurring the true impact of price changes on a company, and as intuitively unreal and irrelevant to the enterprise concerned. This group of opponents of the CPP system favoured the retention of a normal money unit system and was concerned more with the specific effects of inflationary conditions as they affected the performance of a particular enterprise.

Some anecdotal evidence supporting the above view of the probable attitude of corporate management and users of accounts was provided by McRae and Dobbins[9] (1974). The management accountant, they concluded, prefers specific indices to enable him to monitor efficiently the operations of the many sub-systems making up the business. As inflation potentially affects each of these sub-systems in a different way, management would prefer to use specific indices to obtain a more realistic picture of the movement of prices in each system. Additionally, the manager would have more control of the detailed indices applied within the firm. The imposition of an externally calculated index was viewed with some alarm as a loss of control.

McRae and Dobbins also observed that every industrial firm involved in their research had, in introducing inflation accounting procedures, ignored the gain resulting from the reduced value of debt. They attributed this to the desire of companies to minimise reported profits for tax purposes: although the gain on borrowing was not part of the corporation tax base at the time, there was clearly a danger that it would be made so if companies reported substantial gains on borrowing. Certainly, concern about the corporation tax base was an important factor in subsequent support for current cost accounting, as will be apparent from the developments of the 1974–75 period, described in the following chapter. Thus, McRae and Dobbins' observation is consistent with later developments, and points to another reason why the *ED8* 'gain on borrowing' was opposed by companies.

Turning from the industrial preparers of accounts to the users, McRae and Dobbins found that financial analysts did not want the accountants to come between the analysts and the historical description of the cash flows. In view of the comments of the analysts on *ED8*, specific indexation presumably would not, in their view, mask cash flows as much as the use of a general index.

By mid-1973, the ASSC's difficulties were obvious. The Committee was faced with deeply divided views at a time when inflation was beginning to rise and there was pressure for an answer to the problem of accounting for price-level changes to be found. One possible solution was suggested to the ASSC by Westwick (1980, p. 359), namely to require companies to produce inflation accounts but to allow them to choose their own methods of accounting for inflation. This advice was apparently rejected on the grounds that an accounting standard should lay down only one method and that CPP was a clearly described system (in *ED8* and elsewhere), whilst RC accounting was a family of systems and poorly documented. The ASSC therefore, in opting for a policy restricting experimentation (a policy which has generally persisted throughout the UK debate), was obviously adopting a strategy risking the alienation of one group of respondents to *ED8*.

4 The Government's intervention

The dispute which could possibly have developed between the ASSC and the users and industrial preparers of financial statements was, however, averted. Six days before the end of the six-month period allowed for comment on *ED8* the Government shook the accounting profession when Mr Walker, Secretary of State for Trade and Industry, announced in Parliament on 25 July 1973 that the Government was to set up an independent committee of enquiry into the case for adjusting company accounts to allow for the effects of inflation.

In response to a Parliamentary question about the Government's reaction to the ASSC's CPP accounting proposals, Mr. Walker said:

> Proposals that company accounts should reflect changes in costs and prices raise important issues, with implications for *inter alia* the efficiency of company management; the allocation of resources; investment decision taking; industrial competitiveness; corporate taxation; and counter-inflationary policy. In view of the wide range of national interests affected by the subject, the Chancellor of the Exchequer and I have decided to set up a small independent committee to consider the various methods of adjusting company accounts and whether, and if so how, company accounts should allow for changes in costs and prices, and to make recommendations.

The ASSC was probably more shocked by the timing of the announcement than by the fact that the Government intended to explore the problem through a public inquiry. At an earlier meeting (1971), which included representatives of the Department of Trade and Industry, the Committee had been warned by civil servants that accounting standards were not merely a professional exercise of limited interest, as the financial effects of standards had wide repercussions and obviously affected the Government. The Committee was reminded that the Government needed assurance that problems were being dealt with in an orderly manner and with reasonable dispatch. Shortly afterwards, however, the ASSC received an indication from government sources that a suggestion that the Government should be asked to set up a Committee of Enquiry into the subject of accounting for price-level changes was unlikely to be favourably received. The ASSC understandably was anxious to know the Government's intentions and asked the Department of Trade and Industry for clarification. Until the Government's views were known, the ASSC decided to hold back from its own examination of the issue but, in the interim period, issued a highly focussed paper (discussed earlier in Chapter 3) on *Inflation and Accounts*, which advocated current purchasing power accounting.

Later in 1971, the then Secretary of State (for Trade and Industry), Mr Davies, had stated in a speech that, although the Government had a close interest in the subject of accounting for price-level changes, it was not prepared at that stage to do more than maintain a watch over the work which the accounting profession proposed to undertake. This was confirmed by the Department of Trade and Industry which, significantly as it transpired, stated that, while the Government's opinion was that accountants and other interested parties should be left to pursue the matter at that time, possible future action was not ruled out. A further comment by a representative of the Department of Trade and Industry immediately prior to the issue of *ED8* indicated that the Department would wait and see what the reaction to the Exposure Draft would be. With hindsight, therefore, it can be seen that the Government kept its options open. Nevertheless, the timing of the announcement of the Committee of Enquiry immediately before the end of *ED8*'s exposure period caused considerable surprise, appearing to the profession to be a delaying tactic to prevent the ASSC from producing a standard based on the Exposure Draft. (The membership and the terms of reference of the Committtee of Enquiry were not announced until 21 January 1974.)

Why then had the Government decided to act when it did? From the evidence presented to us (much of it from Professor Edward Stamp, at the time Chief Accounting Adviser to the Treasury) it was obvious that, well before the end of the exposure period, the Government and the Civil Service were seriously concerned by the implications of *ED8* becoming a Standard and were considering setting up a Committee of Enquiry. Three major problems were obvious to the Government:
(1) The need for government support for an inflation accounting standard.

The ASSC had apparently told the Government on an informal basis that its support would be required if an inflation accounting standard were to be fully effective. Given the Government's responsibility for the Companies Act requirement that accounts should show a true and fair view, some civil servants believed that the Government could not stand on the sidelines but had to decide whether or not a true and fair view could be shown, if the effects of price-level changes were not reflected in published financial statements. If inflation accounting were deemed to be necessary for the purposes of the Acts, then it was believed the Government would have to decide whether the *ED8* approach or some other method was the best means of meeting the true and fair view objective.

(2) The need to ensure that the method of reporting changes in price levels was acceptable to the financial community as a whole, and not simply to a particular section of it.

The Government's prime interest in the form and content of published accounts was perceived to be two-fold:

(a) to protect investors and creditors;[10] and

(b) to promote the efficient allocation of economic resources.

It was clear from the responses of many large companies that they did not believe that *ED8* would result in accounts fairly reflecting their performance and financial position – a situation which could have consequential adverse effects upon the efficient operation of the capital markets. Despite the opposition, however, it seemed likely that the accountancy profession would impose its own preferred solution on the financial community. While, in a letter to the authors, Mr Walker stated that he did not remember receiving any representations from industry, these, he wrote, may well have been made to the Department of Trade and Industry. Mr (later Sir) Douglas Morpeth (then Vice Chairman of the ASSC) was more positive on this point. He wrote, in a letter to one of the authors, that there were indications that the Government had been lobbied by a number of companies which opposed the introduction of a CPP standard.

Our evidence indicates that the Civil Service had been following the debate, and was concerned about the fears of many managers, being aware not only of the view of some management accountants that *ED8* was too heavily biased towards the 'stewardship' function of accounts and of little use in management decision-making, but also of the lack of discussion of alternative methods such as replacement cost accounting. The Civil Service was certainly aware of proposals other than CPP. Professor Stamp informed us that, during the early period of his appointment as Chief Accounting Adviser to the Treasury, he discussed the current value proposals expressed in his 1971 paper (Stamp, 1971) with senior civil servants and was involved in planning the introduction of these proposals in nationalised industries and in government trading organisations.[11] Indeed, in the Spring of 1973, officials in the Department of Trade and Industry noted that the acceptance of a partial method of inflation accounting, such as applying replacement cost to fixed assets and stocks, would underline the need to maintain a company's real capital investment and would cause less of an upheaval than CPP accounting. Some thirty months later the Sandilands Committee came to similar conclusions.

(3) The implications for the Counter Inflationary Policy and Taxation. In mid-1973 the Government maintained control over pay, prices and

dividends. To the extent that the *ED8* proposals would lower conventional profits, obvious problems would arise for the price control policy, since profit margins were an important element of the control regulations. In some respects, however, lower recorded profits could have advantages. The apparent need to retain funds to maintain real capital could have made dividend control more palatable to shareholders, and, additionally, the pressure for pay increases might have eased if the lower profits were perceived as being a fair measure of economic performance.

On the other hand, the acceptance by the Government of an accounting method which required continuous adjustment of revenues, costs, assets and liabilities could have been seen as amounting to a general and public recognition of the instability of money as a unit of account. This could have some adverse effects on government policies. Firstly, the government sector, as the major borrower (through the national debt), had been the major beneficiary of the then recent inflation in the UK; for example, the real return on government debt was negative during 1974 and the return on National Savings was particularly bad.[12] Secondly, inflationary expectations and pressures could well have been aroused by indexation. (Interestingly the Government embarked on its ill-fated 'threshold' pay policy in October 1973, allowing additional pay increases during the period of the policy for every 1 per cent the RPI rose above 7 per cent.) Thirdly, taxation policy could have been seriously affected.

The Inland Revenue had two concerns about the adoption of inflation accounting:

(1) there almost certainly would be pressure for the adjusted (and generally lower) profits to be used as the basis for company taxation; and

(2) the adjustment of business income to reflect the effects of inflation would undoubtedly lead to pressure to ensure that allowances for price-level changes were incorporated in personal taxation policy.

At the time of *ED8* the Government benefited through the well-known phenomenon of fiscal drag – in the personal sector by higher money incomes being subjected to higher marginal tax rates, and in the corporate sector by corporation tax becoming partly a capital levy through the failure to allow replacement cost of all assets for tax purposes. (This was later substantially relieved by the addition of stock relief to the capital allowance system.)

As a consequence of the 1977 Finance Act (the so-called Rooker–Wise Amendment), the Government now has explicitly to refuse to increase certain personal taxation reliefs by an amount less than the percentage increase in the retail price index applied to the previous year's allowance. In 1973, however, deflationary measures such as raising the level of taxes could have been effected simply by failing to change personal allowances, enabling the Government's policy to be obscured by the money illusion.

The indexation of published financial statements could therefore have been a major milestone on the way to an economy in which the money illusion was dispelled – a 'real terms' as opposed to a money unit economic system, in which the rate of inflation could no longer be used as a safety valve for the reconciliation of competing claims on the real resources of the economy. The fear existed that indexation by removing some of the unpleasant consequences of inflation, might institutionalise it.[13]

The above reasons for the Government's actions were confirmed in part by an Assistant Secretary at the Department of Trade and Industry who informed a plenary meeting of the ASSC in September 1973 that, while the Government had been glad to see the accountants 'grasping the nettle' of inflation accounting, the pace of inflation had grown and the need to abate it had become a matter of overriding national importance. Both because of the pressure on the Government to recognise inflation accounting for taxation and other purposes, and because a significant minority appeared to prefer methods other than those advocated in *ED8*, it was felt that there was a need for an independent enquiry. The problem was now too important to be left to the accountants alone to come forward with a solution.

A few months later, the publication of the terms of reference of the Committee of Enquiry reiterated the Government's view of the wide-ranging nature of the problem and expanded upon the Secretary of State's initial comments to the House of Commons by requiring the Committee to consider its eventual recommendations for accounting for the effects of price-level changes in the light of:

(1) the effects upon investment and other management decisions, and upon the efficiency of companies generally (this point was made by several companies and the Society of Investment Analysts in their comments on *ED8*);

(2) the effect on the efficient allocation of resources through the capital market (a point of undoubted interest to both the Government and investors who would wish to be able to assess the reality of a company's relative performance and financial position);

(3) the need to restrain inflation in the United Kingdom (a major objective of the Government);

(4) the requirements of investors, creditors, employees, Government

and the public for information (a demand to consider *user* needs);
(5) any implications for taxation of the profit and capital gains of companies, the assumption being that the share of the total direct tax burden borne by the company sector remained unchanged (the Government being concerned with a fair allocation of the taxation burden among companies but unwilling to contemplate a reduction in tax revenues from the corporate sector);
(6) the repercussions on the accounts of other corporate bodies (obviously, if an acceptable method of accounting for price-level changes could be found, its application would have benefits beyond the company sector, particularly in the nationalised industries); and
(7) the procedures in other countries, particularly the EEC. (Major developments were about to take place in Australia and the USA, although the proposed changes were almost certainly unknown at the time the terms of reference were determined. Among the EEC countries only The Netherlands was then actively interested in discovering a means of accounting for inflation.)

The basic question posed to the Committee ensured that it considered the views of the significant minority opposed to the methodology of *ED8*. The Committee was required 'to consider whether, and if so how, company accounts should allow for changes (*including relative changes*) in costs and prices, having regard to established accounting conventions based on historic costs, the proposal for current general purchasing power accounting put forward by the Accounting Standards Steering Committee, and other possible accounting methods of allowing for price changes, and to make recommendations'. (Emphasis added.)

The responses of industry and users of financial statements to *ED8*, the Government's concern to ensure that a new system of financial reporting was not adopted without examining in depth alternative approaches and its fears about the dangers of institutionalised inflation would appear to have persuaded the Government to institute the Committee of Enquiry before the ASSC upgraded its CPP Exposure Draft to the status of an accounting standard, thereby presenting the Government with a *fait accompli*.

Having decided to stop, at least temporarily, the profession's solution to the problem of accounting for inflation, the Government obviously had to select the Committee so that the viewpoint of those opposing the profession's view could be heard. The terms of reference (mentioned above) clearly referred to current value systems. The Government now ensured that such systems would be considered by the Committee of Enquiry by including among the Committee's members[14] Lord Caldecote, the Chairman of Delta Metal, the financial director of which had submitted comments on *ED8* favouring the use of a replacement cost method; A. J. W. S. Leonard, the Group Treasurer of Shell who had, most probably, been exposed to Dutch ideas on replacement accounting; and Michael Inwards, the financial controller of the Pye Group (a subsidiary of Philips Industries whose accounts had been produced in terms of replacement costs for many years).[15] Mr Inwards was one of three accountants on the Committee, only one of whom was in practice. No member of the Committee of Enquiry had been involved in the process of drafting *ED8*. The UK accountancy bodies at this stage had lost control of the debate on inflation accounting.

The next chapter considers the profession's response to this situation and goes on to consider the work of the Sandilands Committee in the light of the constraints imposed by its membership and terms of reference, as well as the evidence available to it, the continuing public debate on inflation accounting, and the persistence of inflationary pressures in the economy.

5

The contemporary British debate II: the Sandilands Committee and its Report (1974–75)

1 Introduction

In the previous chapter, we traced developments in the United Kingdom up to the announcement of the terms of reference and membership of the Sandilands Committee, in January 1974. In this chapter, we shall consider the work of the Sandilands Committee, its Report, published in September 1975, and the initial reactions to the Report, which culminated in the establishment of the Inflation Accounting Study Group late in 1975, its first meeting being held on 6 January 1976. We shall also discuss developments during this period in the accounting profession, in the public debate on inflation accounting, and in the economy, because these had an important bearing both on the deliberations of the Sandilands Committee and on the future developments of inflation accounting standards.

2 PSSAP7 – the Current Purchasing Power Standard

The Government's announcement, in July 1973, that it was to establish a Committee of Enquiry (the Sandilands Committee) left the Accounting Standards Steering Committee (ASSC) with the problem of what should be done about its current purchasing power (CPP) Exposure Draft, *ED8*. Given the dichotomy of views – the professional accountants generally favouring CPP accounting and a majority of other commentators on *ED8* showing a preference for some form of current value accounting (usually replacement cost) – it appeared that the ASSC had three basic options in producing any future pronouncement on accounting for the effects of inflation:

(1) to continue with the advocacy of CPP accounting and produce a standard based on *ED8*. This course of action could have led to some major companies failing to implement the Standard thereby casting doubt on the efficacy of the whole standard-setting process,

unless the Standard were subsequently endorsed by the Sandilands Committee;

(2) to switch to a replacement cost system instead of one based on a general price index. While this approach would have indicated that the ASSC was prepared to listen to critics of its proposals it ran the risk of antagonising those who had supported the thrust of *ED8* (something which subsequently happened in the response to *ED18*, in 1976) and of appearing to pre-empt the decision of the Sandilands Committee;

(3) to allow the choice of either general price-level accounting or current value accounting. This would presumably have satisfied most of the proponents and opponents of *ED8* and also those who preferred a flexible approach to inflation accounting until further research on the subject had defined more clearly the problems and had resulted in an agreed solution, but it would have disappointed those who looked to ASSC for firm guidance.

The ASSC eventually decided on a subtle variation of option (1). It would continue to support the CPP method and publish what was to be a Provisional Standard based on *ED8*. It was presumed that a *Provisional* Standard would be persuasive in effect in encouraging companies to follow the Standard: failure to observe the ASSC's pronouncement, however, would not lead to mention in the auditor's report. The decision to opt for a Provisional Standard was not a difficult one to make in the circumstances: the ASSC's reluctance to publish a mandatory standard on the subject resulted from a warning from the Department of Trade and Industry that such a step would be regarded as a confrontation with the Government.[1]

PSSAP7, the Provisional Standard published in May 1974, advocated identical accounting practices to those proposed in *ED8*.[2] A statement supplementary to the historical cost financial statements would show the historical cost accounts converted by the application of a general price index. An Appendix to the Provisional Standard attempted to allay much of the criticism directed at *ED8*, by outlining the differences between current purchasing power accounting and replacement cost accounting. It argued the case for CPP on the grounds that such a system considered the capital of the undertaking as being the purchasing power invested in the enterprise by its owner. Replacement cost accounting, according to the Appendix, was more of a management tool. However, in an apparent attempt to increase acceptance of the draft standard, the Appendix indicated that fixed assets could still be revalued under CPP[3] and additionally suggested that, where it was considered to be relevant to shareholders, a replacement cost supplementary accounting statement, additional to, and separate from, the CPP supplementary statement, could be produced. Again, to allay criticism, another contentious aspect of *ED8*, the gain on borrowing, was considered explicitly in *PSSAP7*. In defence of the suggested policy of including the gain on borrowing in profits, *PSSAP7* argued, firstly, that profitability should not be confused with liquidity, and, secondly, that it is inconsistent to exclude gains when profit has been charged with the cost of borrowing. The gain on borrowing continued to be an area of dispute throughout the 1970s in the USA as well as in the UK. The next committee to consider the problem was, however, not the ASSC but the Government's Committee of Enquiry.

3 The working of the Sandilands Committee[4]

The membership of the Sandilands Committee was finally determined in January 1974 and the Report was published in September 1975. This was a remarkable achievement in view of the facts that the membership of the Committee was part-time and that few of its members had been deeply involved in inflation accounting prior to their appointment.[5] Even its severest critics have not questioned the industry of the Sandilands Committee.

The input into the Committee's deliberations came from the following sources:
(1) the terms of reference laid down by the Government;
(2) the background and prior experience of the members of the Committee;
(3) the research undertaken by the Committee;
(4) the evidence submitted to the Committee;
(5) the economic environment of the period and the public debate on inflation accounting which arose from it.
We shall consider each of these factors in turn. Their interaction provides a good illustration of the way in which practical decisions about accounting are shaped by the environment in which they are made.

(1) The terms of reference

The terms of reference were determined by the ministers who appointed the Committee, the Chancellor of the Exchequer and the Secretary of State for Trade. They were:

> To consider whether, and if so how, company accounts should allow for changes (including relative changes) in costs and

prices, having regard to established accounting conventions based on historic costs, the proposal for current general purchasing power accounting put forward by the Accounting Standards Steering Committee, and other possible accounting methods of allowing for price changes, and to make recommendations. In considering the question the following matters, *inter alia*, should be taken into account:

  (i) the effects upon investment and other management decisions, and upon the efficiency of companies generally;

 (ii) the effect on the efficient allocation of resources through the capital market;

(iii) the need to restrain inflation in the United Kingdom;

(iv) the requirements of investors, creditors, employees, government and the public for information;

 (v) any implications for the taxation of the profits and capital gains of companies, the assumption being that the share of the total direct burden borne by the company sector remains unchanged;

 (vi) the repercussions on the accounts of other corporate bodies;

(vii) procedures in other countries, particularly EEC.

It is clear that these terms of reference left all options open to the Committee, by referring to the extant CPP proposals as well as to 'other possible accounting methods'. However, it is equally clear that CPP was to be given no particular priority, and the emphasis on 'price changes' rather than 'inflation' or 'changes in the general price level' left the way open for the Sandilands Committee's complete rejection of the use of general purchasing power indices. Furthermore, the list of matters which should be taken into account contains a number of items which might reasonably have been expected to point in the direction of some form of current cost accounting. In particular, item (i) refers to management accounting, and even the ASSC conceded (in *PSSAP7*) that replacement cost accounting was relevant to management accounting.[6] Items (ii) and (iv) both imply information about the economic performance of the individual company, which clearly raises the question of the changing prices of the specific assets held and used by the company. The profession had justified CPP in terms of fulfilling the stewardship requirement, rather than measuring economic performance (ICAEW, 1968). Furthermore, items (iii) and (v) raise the important public policy issues of restraining inflation and of the tax base, both of which imply objections to CPP accounting, as a form of indexation which might lead to the institutionalisation of inflation and the erosion of the tax base. Thus, the terms of reference, whilst allowing freedom to the Sandilands Committee, did require it to consider some important objections to CPP accounting.

(2) The background of the Sandilands Committee members

This was discussed briefly in the previous chapter. Whereas the ASSC was a professional accounting body, with strong representation from the practising arm of the profession, the twelve members of the Sandilands Committee included only three qualified accountants, of whom only one was in public practice. The remaining representatives had wide experience of industry, commerce, finance, the law, trade unions, economics and public affairs. They were clearly chosen as being appropriate to the consideration of the wide range of matters which they were required to take into account.

It is obviously impossible to know the precise attitudes to inflation accounting of each member of the Committee at the time of appointment, but it is clear that a Committee of this composition was much more likely to favour alternatives to CPP than a professionally-oriented body such as ASSC. The opposition to CPP had been expressed by industry and commerce and, to a lesser extent, by the financial community, and these groups were well-represented on the Committee. Moreover, of the three qualified accountants, one, Mr Inwards, was employed by a member of the Philips group, which was already deeply committed to replacement cost accounting, and another, Professor Reid, had a special interest in management accounting, an area in which even the ASSC was prepared to concede that replacement cost accounting was relevant. However, it would be wrong to suggest that CPP views were likely to be entirely unrepresented: individuals do not necessarily adopt the attitudes of their peers, and at least one member of the Committee, the practising accountant, Mr Chilvers, had partners who had been active in the process leading to the adoption of CPP by the ASSC.[7]

(3) The research undertaken by the Sandilands Committee

The most authoritative account of the work of the Committee is in the Chairman's Preface to the Report (pp. xiv–xvi). It is clear that, in the seventeen months which elapsed between its first meeting (21 January 1974) and the signing of the Report (25 June 1975) there was no time for research of a fundamental nature. The Committee's research took the form of abstracting the available literature, receiving evidence, studying practice in other countries, and surveying the attitudes and practices of

UK companies. In this work, the Committee was supported by a secretariat, provided by the Civil Service, and by a number of commissioned reports by outside consultants.

The studies of the available literature would not have led the Committee in any particular direction, as the literature dealt with a wide variety of alternatives. The evidence is discussed in the following section. The studies of practice in other countries included visits by Working Parties to the United States and Holland. The former established contact with the Securities and Exchange Commission, which was, at the time (October 1974), evolving its own requirements for replacement cost disclosure (announced in June 1975),[8] and the visit to Holland left the Committee impressed by the successful application of replacement cost accounting by certain large firms, and by the support for replacement cost accounting in the Dutch professional body (NIVRA). Contact was also made with the Mathews Committee in Australia, which was also working towards a replacement cost recommendation. Other countries also were studied. It is perhaps indicative of the strength of the replacement cost (or current cost) view which seems to have evolved in the Committee, that it managed to interpret the Brazilian system as a simplified replacement cost system, rather than a special form of CPP system (using a wholesale rather than a retail price index).[9]

The survey of attitudes and practices with respect to inflation accounting in UK companies is of some interest. Its results were generally favourable to the ASSC's CPP approach, but there was enough diversity of opinion to accommodate the Committee's contrary conclusion. In particular, there was widespread anxiety about including the gain on borrowing in profit: a source of continued controversy whenever CPP proposals are discussed. Furthermore, the survey was carried out early in the Committee's work (April and May 1974), and the Preface to the Report refers to the fact that its validity was qualified by the fact that 'thinking on this subject has moved so rapidly during the year', a clear reference to the events described in (5) below.

(4) The evidence submitted to the Sandilands Committee

The evidence presented to the Sandilands Committee was never published. Some submissions were, however, publicised by their authors and others are referred to in the Report, and from these it would seem that the Committee of Enquiry was faced with the same conflicting viewpoints as the ASSC in considering the comments on *ED8*.

Not unexpectedly, five of the major UK accountancy bodies[10] made a joint submission to the Committee defending the CPP method proposed in *ED8* and *PSSAP7*. The argument was on by now familiar lines. Replacement cost accounting was criticised as being mainly of use to management for decision-making purposes, being concerned with maintaining a given level of physical assets, generally disregarding the gain to equity as a result of the effects of inflation on borrowed money, and being more complex and subjective than CPP. CPP was stated to provide an immediate and practical method of reporting during a period of inflation which could be applied to all companies for the information of investors, creditors and employees.[11]

One of the major opponents of *ED8* – the Society of Investment Analysts, which had earlier supported CPP, presented to the Committee of Enquiry an alternative view to that of the professional accountancy bodies. In a press release accompanying their submission the Society summarised their argument:

> Since companies are normally assumed to be run on a going concern basis, the principal purpose of inflation adjustments should be to show whether or not a company is maintaining its physical capital. If this aim is accepted, the most appropriate method will be some form of replacement cost accounting. The current purchasing power method proposed by the Institute of Chartered Accountants appears to be designed to show if shareholders' capital is maintaining its purchasing power. The Society feels that this is a misplaced concern which will lead to results of doubtful usefulness. It may give rise to misleading comparisons between companies and may still leave some companies making inadequate provisions for the maintenance of capital. Although more difficult to apply, the replacement cost method makes use of specific price data and gives information which will be of more practical use to both management and shareholders.

The Society's evidence supported the comments in the press release by attempting to meet criticisms of RC and recommending principles to be used in a replacement cost system. Additionally, the submission attacked CPP on the grounds that such a system failed to maintain physical capital; failed to take account of specific price movements and thereby failed to reflect the effect of price changes on contrasting companies; used a general index which did not cover capital goods, raw materials or semi-manufactures; and probably failed to produce figures of use to management.[12]

Many of the other critics of *ED8* – especially from industry –

presumably gave similar evidence to the Committee. The Society of Investment Analysts' submission has been reported here to give the probable flavour of such critiques of the CPP approach and because the Society's rôle as a professional body dealing with the provision of advice to investors made it uniquely qualified as an informed and impartial commentator on the requirements of investors and of the capital market, which the Committee's terms of reference required it to consider.

(5) The economic environment and the public debate on inflation accounting

The economic environment during the period in which the Sandilands Committee was sitting was one of hitherto unprecedented inflation in the United Kingdom. Table 5.1 shows that retail prices were generally sixteen per cent higher in 1974 (the first year of the Committee's work) than in 1973. In 1975 (the final year of the Committee's work) they were 24.3 per cent higher than in 1974. Moreover, the quarterly figures show a steady increase in the annual inflation rate, culminating in a peak in the third quarter of 1975, which saw the publication of the Sandilands Report (it having been submitted to the Government at the end of the previous quarter). It was thus inevitable that the need to restrain inflation (item (iii) of the terms of reference) would be one of the matters considered urgently by the Committee.

There was, however, another striking feature of price changes at the time which probably had at least as important an influence on the Sandilands Committee's deliberations. As Table 5.1 clearly demonstrates, the *relative* prices of different groups of commodities changed dramatically. In the aftermath of the Middle East War of 1973 the retail price index had become seriously out of line with the wholesale price index of materials and fuel. While in the four years 1970–74 the retail price index had risen by 48 per cent and the index of wholesale prices had risen 51 per cent, the index of the wholesale prices of materials and fuel had risen by no less than 113 per cent. The squeeze on the profits of manufacturing industry dependent on raw materials was therefore likely to be considerable. Certainly, adjustments to profit based on the retail price index were unlikely to reflect the true effect of inflation on companies where manufacturing processes required large quantitites of raw materials.

Not only did these striking changes in relative prices point to the failure of CPP's general index approach as a reflection of the economic position of the individual firm, thus reinforcing industry's already expressed

Table 5.1. *Prices 1970–78, 1970 = 100*

	Wholesale prices index				Index of retail prices	
	Materials and fuels purchased by manufacturing industry		Output of all manufactured goods – home sales			
Year	Index	% Change on previous year	Index	% Change on previous year	Index	% Change on previous year
1970	100	5.2	100	7.1	100	6.4
1971	104.4	4.4	109	9.0	109.4	9.4
1972	109.1	4.5	114.8	5.3	117.2	7.1
1973	144.5	32.4	123.3	7.4	127.9	9.1
1974	213.3	47.6	151.2	22.7	148.4	16.0
1975	245.7	15.2	184.8	22.2	184.4	24.3
1976	312.0	27.0	216.8	17.3	214.9	16.5
1977	357.7	14.6	259.7	19.8	248.9	15.8
1978	355.3	(0.1)	283.3	9.1	269.6	8.3

Source: Economic Trends

doubts about CPP, but the fact that costs were rising more rapidly than retail price led to the so-called 'profits crisis' of 1974, which was the subject of a public debate. This public debate was followed closely by the Sandilands Committee. The central concern of this debate was the immediate problem of taxation, and, in particular, the tax treatment of stocks, rather than the wider problems of financial reporting, although there was some concern about the appropriate measure of profit for the purposes of price control, dividend distribution and wage restriction, all of which posed difficulties in the context of the Government's counter-inflationary policy. The purposes for which profit was being measured were never really clearly defined by any participant in the debate: the broad assumption seems to have been that a single 'correct' measure of profit will serve all purposes.[13]

This debate had wider implications than its effect on the Sandilands Committee. In the short term, it helped to focus the complaints of industry about the effects of the 'profits crisis' and was therefore instrumental in persuading the Chancellor of the Exchequer to introduce Stock Relief for corporation tax purposes in November 1974, and in the longer term, the debate led to the proposal of the gearing adjustment, which subsequently became adopted in the current cost accounting Standard, *SSAP16* (1980a). It is therefore worth reporting the debate in some detail.

4 The debate on the profits crisis and inflation accounting, Autumn 1974

The debate was initiated by Merrett and Sykes' article, published in the *Financial Times* on 30 September 1974. They argued that the reported profits of UK companies, based upon the conventional historical cost accounts, were exaggerated by the inclusion of stock appreciation and the failure to charge replacement cost depreciation. These deficiencies were particularly serious in a period of rapid inflation, in which the nominal value of a constant amount or real stocks would rise rapidly, and the gap between the historical cost and the replacement cost of fixed assets would be large. Merrett and Sykes alleged that the consequent over-statement of reported profits was masking a 'profits crisis', in which firms would be unable to maintain their real physical assets, because the high cost of replacement needed to be funded at high interest rates with the prospect of very poor future returns (due to high production costs, selling prices held down by government policy, and high taxation).

The Merrett and Sykes analysis made an important contribution in helping to identify the difficulties facing the company sector at the time. There are two valid strands to their argument. Firstly, the *ex ante* rate of return on replacement investment may well have looked unattractive at the time, due to high interest rates and taxation, rising costs and depressed selling prices. Secondly, many firms may have faced a *liquidity* crisis (rather than a profits crisis) due to the depressed state of financial markets producing a situation of capital rationing at a time when high replacement costs were creating exceptional demands for new capital funds.

The more contentious aspect of Merrett and Sykes' analysis was their conclusion for the measurement of *ex post* profit. They advocated (with taxation and price policy particularly in mind) that profit should be measured after charging the replacement cost of goods sold and depreciation. Thus, their measure of profit was very similar to the Operating Profit subsequently advocated in the Sandilands Report,[14] with the exception that they advocated replacement cost rather than 'value to the firm'. They excluded all holding gains from profit, whether on holding physical assets or on debt. Their capital maintenance concept was thus concerned with the maintenance of the physical assets of the entity and paid no attention to the impact of general inflation. This was also a characteristic of the subsequent Sandilands Report and led to a polarisation of the CCA and CPP views.

The contemporary British debate II

A simple illustration of the Merrett and Sykes approach (based upon the example used by Godley and Wood, 1974), is as follows. Suppose a firm starts a period with stock valued at £100, financed solely by equity:

Opening Balance Sheet

	£		£
Equity interest	100	Stock (at cost)	100

Suppose that it sells the stock for £130, but then replaces it at an increased cost of £130. Merrett and Sykes would then show a NIL profit:

Profit and Loss Account

	£
Sales	130
Less Replacement cost of goods sold	130
Profit	0

However, the balance sheet value of equity interest has risen:

Closing Balance Sheet

	£		£
Equity interest	130	Stock (at cost)	130

The reason why this increase in the equity interest, £30, is not shown as profit (as it would be if we charged historical cost, of £100, against profit) is that it is regarded as necessary for the maintenance of capital. Merrett and Sykes adopt an *entity* approach to capital maintenance, i.e. they believe that the maintenance of the *specific* assets of the firm must be provided for before a profit is recognised. There are two obvious alternatives, money capital maintenance, which is implicit in the historical cost approach and which does not allow for inflation, and real capital maintenance, i.e. maintaining the general purchasing power of capital, as in CPP. The latter approach would coincide with Merrett and Sykes' if general inflation was at the same rate as the specific price change of the firm's assets, 30 per cent in the example. Otherwise, the real capital approach would not coincide with the entity approach and a real profit or loss would appear, e.g. if general inflation were only ten per cent, the capital to be maintained would be only £110 and there would be a real profit of £20, whereas if general inflation were 50 per cent, the capital to be maintained would be £150 and there would be a real loss of £20.

The distinction between the three approaches to capital maintenance was not made clear in Merrett and Sykes' original article, or in the subsequent debate, which led to the evolution of the gearing adjustment, which is a hybrid of the money capital maintenance concept (for the geared portion of the company) and the entity approach (for the equity-financed portion of the company). However, the distinction was and is of much more than purely academic interest, particularly in its implications for the treatment of changing stock values. For example, at the time when Merrett and Sykes' article was published, oil prices had risen more rapidly than prices in general (i.e. more in line with column 1 than column 3 of Table 5.1), so that oil companies had received substantial real holding gains on their stocks. Merrett and Sykes' 'entity approach' would not regard these gains as part of profits for the purposes of taxation or price control, whereas the 'real terms' approach *would* treat them as profits.[15]

The most significant immediate response to Merrett and Sykes came from Godley and Wood (1974). Whereas Merrett and Sykes' article sought to defend business interests against what they saw as excessive taxation and oppressive price controls, Godley and Wood approached the problem as economists sceptical of these complaints. It would not be unreasonable, therefore, to describe the motivation of the conflicting parties as partly political, in the sense that one group (Merrett and Sykes) were 'pro-business' and the other group (Godley and Wood) were, if not 'anti-business', at least sceptical of what they saw as special pleading for the business community to be insulated against inflation when the rest of the community was not afforded such protection.

The Godley and Wood argument was based upon an example of a firm which was entirely loan-financed. It was argued that, if such a firm were able to sell at a constant mark-up on historical cost, it could distribute its stock appreciation as profit and finance the replacement by further borrowing:

Opening Balance Sheet

	£		£
Loan	100	Stock (at cost)	100

Profit and Loss Account

	£
Sales	130
Less Historical cost of goods sold	100
Profit	30

If this profit is paid out as dividend and taxes, and replacement stock is bought (as in the previous example) for £130, the additional cost being financed by a loan, we have:

Closing Balance Sheet

	£		£
Loan	130	Stock (at cost)	130

Godley and Wood therefore concluded that, at least to the extent that a firm was loan-financed, historical cost provided an appropriate measure of profit. It should be noted that they based their analysis upon two assumptions, firstly that the firm could borrow and secondly that the prospective return would justify the replacement investment, both of which were contrary to Merrett and Sykes' view.

The most influential counter-attack, made by Day (1974), did not make this last point but instead claimed that Godley and Wood's analysis did not apply to an equity-financed firm. Day's variant of the numerical example was as follows:

Opening Balance Sheet

	£		£
Equity	100	Stock (at cost)	100

Profit and Loss Account

	£
Sales	130
Less Replacement cost of goods sold	130
Profit	0

Closing Balance Sheet

	£		£
Equity	100	Stock (at cost)	130
Loan	30		
	130		130

Day argued that an equity-financed firm would have to raise a loan in order to pay the £30 dividend which could have been paid in the Godley–Wood loan-financed example. Thus, the equity shareholders would end the period owning only 100/130 of the company, whereas they owned it all at the beginning of the period.

This argument was Day's most important contribution to the debate, because it appears to have been accepted by at least one of the authors of the Godley–Wood paper, whose response in the Godley–Cripps paper one year later (October 1975) was to propose the gearing adjustment: the holding gain on the geared (loan-financed) portion of the firm's capital would be regarded as profit, and that on the equity-financed portion would be regarded as being necessary to maintain the ungeared (equity) capital. This, in turn, was an important contribution to the debate because the gearing adjustment, albeit in a modified form, was adopted by the Hyde Committee (1977) and subsequently was a feature of the first current cost accounting standard in the UK, *SSAP16* (1980a).

Another objection to the Godley–Wood analysis, raised by Day, was that Godley and Wood had made no provision for interest payments on the loans, a burden which Merrett and Sykes had emphasised. Day conceded that this could easily have been refuted by Godley and Wood, on the ground that their cost-plus pricing assumption meant that all costs, including interest payments, could be passed on to the consumer. Indeed, as Meeks (1974) pointed out, they could use this same argument to demonstrate that a firm could also always earn a satisfactory return on equity in a period of rising prices. However, as Meeks suggests, this would have been a dangerous line of defence, because it would have pointed to the crucial nature of their contentious assumption of cost-plus pricing. Merrett and Sykes' central point was that firms at the time were suffering a profits crisis because they were unable to pass on increased costs and taxes in this manner, so that their *ex ante* estimates of income were inadequate to justify replacement investment.

The valid part of the Godley–Wood argument was that they identified an element of double counting in Merrett and Sykes' estimates of real *ex post* income.[16] It is not legitimate to charge *money* interest, which includes an allowance for inflation, as well as deducting depreciation and stock appreciation adjustments, which are also designed to show the additional burden imposed by price rises. This amounts to double counting: we should either deduct money interest from a money profit figure or real interest from a real profit figure. Godley and Wood failed to point out that a similar argument should be applied to equity. Equity profits may have looked poor at the time, after charging replacement cost of goods sold and depreciation, but the real rate of interest was also low at the time.

Another weakness of the Godley–Wood analysis, and indeed of the original Merrett–Sykes article, was the failure to consider the use of general indices to adjust the capital to be maintained. Both pairs of authors accepted (or failed to reject) the entity approach to the maintenance of equity capital, i.e. it was the specific assets of the firm rather than a fund of general purchasing power which was to be maintained. Thus, in the case of oil companies' inventory values rising more rapidly than inflation, the real holding gain would not be recognised as profit to the extent that it was equity financed. To the extent that it was debt financed, Godley and Wood recognised the *total* gain in money terms, but failed to dichotomise this gain into the two components identified by the 'real terms' approach: the gain on borrowing (due to the decline in real purchasing power of debt fixed in depreciating money units) and the real gain on assets (due to the asset rising in value more rapidly than the rise in the general price level). This early omission of general price-level considerations in this influential public debate led naturally to the development of the Godley–Cripps gearing adjustment one year later and its ultimate adoption by the ASC in the Hyde Guidelines as a means of overcoming the problem of dealing with monetary assets and liabilities within a current cost framework which (following the Sandilands Report) rejected the use of general purchasing power indices for measuring gains and losses on monetary assets and liabilities.

In the shorter term, the Merrett and Sykes argument triumphed, partly, no doubt, because there clearly was a liquidity crisis and a crisis of confidence (i.e. low *ex ante* expectations of profitability) in British industry, which required immediate relief. This took the form of Stock Relief, which was introduced in November 1974.

5 Stock Relief

The Stock Relief was introduced less than two months after Merrett and Sykes' article was published. It allowed companies relief against taxable profits on *all* the increase in value of their stocks above a certain level (determined as a percentage of profits). It therefore gave relief for marginal increases in stock values which were due to *volume* changes as well as price changes, i.e. the additional value could be due to the accumulation of additional stocks at constant prices rather than the maintenance of existing stocks at increased prices. It thus went beyond what Merrett and Sykes had asked for and gave companies an easy method of tax avoidance, by increasing the volume of stocks held.[17] It was intended as a temporary measure, but in fact was not modified seriously (to remove the effect of volume changes) until 1981.

The introduction of Stock Relief had two implications for the subsequent development of inflation accounting.

Firstly, by giving companies tax relief at least as generous[18] as that which they could expect from a tax based on replacement cost accounting (as advocated by Merrett and Sykes), the advent of Stock Relief reduced the possible tax advantages to companies of pressing for this type of reform. Companies had been a source of criticism of the CPP proposals of *ED8*, but it was now possible that some of them would see the maintenance of historical cost accounting as their preferred alternative rather than (as previously) the untried and possibly expensive replacement cost system. Moreover, once the tax base had been clearly separated from reported profits, there was less incentive to report low profits (as would occur on a replacement cost basis). This incentive would remain for price control and wage negotiations, but for raising new capital in financial markets there was an incentive to paint a more optimistic picture.

Secondly, the Stock Relief provided some indication of the thinking of the Sandilands Committee in the Autumn of 1974, as its Chairman had been consulted by the Chancellor of the Exchequer prior to the introduction of the new relief. Clearly, the price-change element of Stock Relief was based upon changes in specific prices rather than a general index.[19] Thus, it seems that the Sandilands Committee had been impressed by the contribution of Merrett and Sykes to the public debate. Their final recommendations are consistent with this view.

6 The Sandilands Report

Having considered the evidence, the Sandilands Committee finished its Report in June 1975 and it was published in the following September. It reached three main conclusions: firstly, that it was essential that accounts allowed for changes in costs and prices; secondly, that existing accounting conventions did not do so adequately and tended to present the affairs of companies in a misleading way; and, thirdly, that the most fruitful line of development in inflation accounting was a system based on the principles of current value accounting, which showed the specific effect of price changes on individual companies. The new current cost accounting system was to be implemented in the main accounts of companies, not merely published as supplementary information.[20]

In the balance sheet, fixed assets and stock were to be valued at 'value to the business' which the Committee attributed to Bonbright (1937, p. 71), adopting the familiar formula:

> The value of an asset to a company is its written down current replacement cost (current purchase price), except in situations

where the written down current replacement cost is higher than both the 'economic value' and the net realisable value in which case the value of the asset to the company is the 'economic value' or the net realisable value, whichever is the higher.

In practice, this meant that replacement cost would be the valuation basis in the typical situation, in which the firm holds assets for future use within the business.[21] This same valuation method was to be used for calculating depreciation and the cost of goods sold, charged against profit.

Thus, the Sandilands Committee was proposing a revolution in accounting practice, by changing its valuation base from the traditional form of historical cost to the new current value basis. Moreover, the Committee set itself in direct opposition to the ASC's recent advocacy of CPP (in *PSSAP7*) by flatly rejecting the use of general price-level indices and questioning the usefulness of the idea of a general price level.

The only adjustments which the Report advocated with respect to monetary assets and liabilities were those which might reflect specific price changes. No adjustment was to be made to monetary assets which were deemed to be shown at their 'value to the business' without alteration. Liabilities were to be left at their historical cost values but further research was suggested into the practical problems of requiring that certain liabilities (for example, debentures traded in the market) should be shown at their value to the business. In the short term, however, the Committee proposed that the concept of prudence should predominate and traded liabilities should not be shown at less than their face value, thus precluding the recording of any holding gains arising from the decline in market price, below par, of traded loan stocks.

Two adjustments were to be made to the profit and loss account. The charge for 'cost of sales' in the income statement was to reflect the 'value to the business' of stock consumed during the year (usually replacement cost) and the depreciation charge was to be calculated on the basis of the assets' current 'value to the business' at the end of the year.[22] Profit, after charging all expenses on a current cost basis and after deducting interest payments, was described as current cost profit.

The revaluation of assets on a current cost basis would lead to holding gains or losses. These were not included in operating profit, but were to be added to reserves. They were to be recorded in a Statement of Gains, a new financial statement. This statement recorded current cost profit, after tax, and to this was added any extraordinary gain and each type of holding gain for the year (losses being deducted). The total comprised the 'total gain for the year after tax', i.e. the increase in net worth attributable to shareholders, on a current value basis, after tax but before dividends. The form of the statement was reminiscent of some of the proposals of Edwards and Bell (1961), and owed something to the pioneering work of these authors, although their proposals were more comprehensive and sophisticated than the Sandilands proposals, embracing the identification of real holding gains, a concept which the Sandilands Committee rejected.

Another new statement proposed by the Sandilands Committee was the Flow of Funds Statement, which was designed to highlight the liquidity of the firm, in terms of its recent funds flows. This became part of standard accounting practice (*SSAP16*) the month following the signing of the Report, but is not directly relevant to inflation accounting, except that the Sandilands Committee's support for it indicates that the Committee was fully aware of the distinction between profitability and liquidity, a distinction which was not made entirely clear in the 1974 debate on the profits crisis and which became even less clear in the subsequent debate on gearing and monetary working capital.

The general spirit of the Sandilands proposals was therefore one of providing a useful set of information, rather than focussing on a single number such as the bottom line of the profit and loss account. This was apparent in the Committee's lack of clear recommendations on the appropriate basis for corporation tax. Although taxation was listed in the terms of reference, the Report came to no clear conclusions on the subject and recommended a further enquiry into the taxation implications of current cost accounting. This was a rational and sensible decision: the Committee had not had sufficient time to explore all of the items in its terms of reference, and there was no reason to assume that a measure (or set of measures) of performance suitable for managers or investors necessarily provided a good tax base. However, seen in retrospect, the fact that the Sandilands Report offered no obvious tax advantage to industry may have helped to reduce industry's enthusiasm for current cost accounting, increasing the subsequent difficulties of the Inflation Accounting Study Group.

In summary, the Sandilands Report was a formidable piece of work, prepared under great time pressure with slender resources. It proposed a revolution in the valuation basis of accounting and flatly rejected the general index approach to inflation accounting (CPP) which had hitherto been favoured by the professional standard-setters (the ASSC). It also left a number of technical matters to be dealt with, and, by being non-committed on the subject of the tax base, offered no tax advantages over the system then in force (which combined 100 per cent initial allowances on certain types of investment with a similar tax relief on incremental investment in stocks). All of these problems were left in the hands of the Inflation Accounting Steering Group (IASG), which was jointly sponsored by the Government and the ASSC, in accordance with the suggestion of the Sandilands Report (Chapter 12, para. 552). In retrospect, it is not entirely surprising that the IASG's progress was far from smooth.

7 Sandilands and general purchasing power

One feature of the Sandilands Report which deserves special mention is its complete rejection of the general purchasing power approach, because it meant that the UK accountancy bodies now found their previous proposals (*ED8* and *PSSAP7*) completely overturned. The Sandilands Committee had specifically compared the utility and comprehensibility of the two competing units of measurement (monetary or purchasing power) underlying the whole basis of accounting measurement and had rejected the purchasing power system.

The criteria for the choice of the measurement unit were outlined by the Committee (para. 149) as follows:

> The monetary unit has been used for centuries as the basis of accounting and it is clear that a new unit of measurement should be adopted only after serious consideration and if it can be demonstrated that it has significant advantages over the monetary unit. Proposals have been made to us involving a departure from the monetary unit as the unit of measurement without detailed consideration being given to the qualifications required of a unit of measurement. We suggest that the following are the principal criteria for a unit of measurement underlying an accounting system:
>
> (1) The unit should be equally useful to all users of accounts.
> (2) The unit should not change from year to year.
> (3) The unit should be the same for all enterprises presenting financial statements.
> (4) The unit should preferably be a physical object which could be exchanged by the users of accounts.
> (5) The unit should present a constant 'value' through time.

These criteria do not, however, lead automatically to an obvious choice. Criterion (2) is ambiguous: it does not specify which properties of the unit should not change. Criteria (1) and (3) are, at first sight, neutral as far as the choice between money and purchasing power units is concerned, both measurement units can satisfy criterion (3) while criterion (1) would require empirical testing to ascertain which of the alternatives would be of most utility to all users although a nominal monetary unit and a unit measuring the general command over goods would both appear to have possible uses. Criterion (4) (the physical object) obviously points to the use of a money unit while criterion (5) necessitates the use of a purchasing power unit although the Committee argued (para. 409) that while the movements of the RPI might be indicative of changes in the 'purchasing power' of money held by individual shareholders they are unlikely to be indicative of changes in the 'purchasing power' of money held by institutional shareholders, companies or other organisations which make use of the annual accounts of companies.

The selected criteria were not, therefore, sufficient to indicate a clear choice between the competing measurement units. On the basis that the purchasing power unit could not be demonstrated to have significant advantages over the monetary unit in that it did not meet all five criteria laid down,[23] the Committee decided to retain the traditional money unit as the basis of accounting measurement, leaving readers of accounting statements to make their own intuitive assumptions about the effects of price changes upon the figures shown.

The Committee's fundamental objection to the use of the constant purchasing power unit were summarised in Chapter 2 of the Report (para. 28) as follows:

> A general index of price changes or of the 'purchasing power' of money is of little practical use and the concept of 'general price changes' and its converse, 'the general purchasing power of money', are unquantifiable. The term inflation describes a situation where the movement in the average price level of goods and services in a period is upward. However, the average movement of prices and the rate of inflation will vary for different individuals and entities in the country according to the selection of goods and services which they buy. It is incorrect to assume that a wide-ranging index such as the Retail Price Index can be a measure of the rate of inflation equally appropriate to all individuals and entities.

This is, of course, an extreme view. For example, the bald statement 'are unquantifiable' is entirely unsupported by argument or evidence: these concepts may not be *precisely* quantifiable, but this is true of many concepts in accounting, not least in current cost accounting. Moreover, general indices are used for a wide range of purposes in practice, and in some Latin American countries, notably Brazil, were used in accounts even at the time of the Sandilands Report. This is *prima facie* evidence that these indices are found useful.[24]

However, whatever the merits of the argument, the Sandilands Committee was clearly persuaded that general indices had no place in inflation accounting. The Committee was also of the opinion that the CPP method as a whole was complicated, was liable to mislead and, conceptually, was the most difficult method of inflation accounting suggested to the Committee in evidence. The Committee concluded that if UK company accounts were to show more adequately the effects of changes in prices, accounting practices must change – not the unit of measurement in which the accounts are expressed. The Report concluded that its own current cost accounting proposals would deal adequately with inflation:

> In our opinion Current Cost Accounting is a fully
> comprehensive method of accounting for inflation, and we do
> not consider that any useful purpose would be served by
> combining it with the current purchasing power method.
> (Chapter 1, para. 13)

This complete rejection of the CPP approach polarised the difference between the ASSC's original approach and the Sandilands approach which the IASG was now required to implement, thus adding to the difficulties facing the IASG in persuading the profession to accept the new system. Sandilands' parallel rejection of adjustments for the gain on borrowing or loss on holding monetary assets led subsequently to the adoption of the gearing and monetary working capital adjustments as methods of dealing with monetary assets and liabilities without having recourse to general indices. Subsequently, Sir Francis Sandilands himself stated publicly (Sandilands, 1978) that he favoured the gearing approach and that he felt that his Committee had been wrong to neglect the gain on borrowing arising from rising prices.

The reasons for the Sandilands Committee's strong opposition to the use of general indices and the CPP approach were probably:
(1) The CPP method as advocated by the ASSC had used CPP-adjusted historical cost to value fixed assets and measure depreciation. It was felt that the use of specific indices or prices was the only means of reflecting realistically the state of the individual firm.
(2) It was recognised that a CPP approach could be applied to a CCA valuation base, but it was felt that this would add a large amount of complexity to the new system, which would not be matched by

additional information content: the Committee's view was that the individual was the best judge of how inflation affected him:

> We believe that little useful information would be presented to a user of accounts by such a procedure and the effect would be to confuse him and to make the annual statements too complex. (para. 546)

(3) In accordance with its terms of references, which required it to look at the wider implications of inflation accounting for the economy, the Committee felt that the use of general indices would have bad effects in helping to institutionalise inflation. CPP methods had been evolved during the German hyper-inflation of the early 1920s and were, at the time of the Sandilands Committee's investigations, used in practice only in certain Latin American countries, notably Brazil[25] and Chile (see Chapter 9), where inflation had reached very high levels. Sir Francis Sandilands, in an interview with one of the present authors, referred to the fact that there was now no interest in CPP methods in the Federal Republic of Germany because of its unfortunate associations with inflation in the 1920s.

It was left to a Steering Group to produce a workable accounting standard on the basis of the Sandilands Report (Chapter 14), but before that group (the IASG) started work, the ASSC produced an important discussion paper, *The Corporate Report*, which had implications for inflation accounting, and there were a number of public reactions to the Sandilands Report.

8 The Corporate Report

The Corporate Report was a discussion paper produced by an ASSC working party on the scope and aims of financial reporting. It was published a few weeks before the Sandilands Report, and it is of considerable interest because it advocated further study of the value to the firm concept, adopted by Sandilands as its valuation base:

> Value to the firm has the advantage that it is designed to exploit the best features of the various current value systems. This flexibility gives it merit. Relying on multiple bases of accounting, the system is subtle in concept and requires accounting and management resources not always readily available at present in many of the entities of the economic size with which we are concerned. But the theoretical merits of the basis are undeniable and its possibilities as a practical system have been demonstrated by a number of companies.

This suggests that the ideas proposed by Sandilands would not be entirely without support in ASSC circles (although the Report was a discussion paper rather than a firm statement of opinion). However, the scope and aims working party also suggested work on other approaches to current value reporting, particularly multi-column reporting (i.e. reporting alternative valuation bases in different columns), and it took a different view from the Sandilands Committee of the immediate future. The former suggested that *PSSAP7* should be retained in the short term but that the CPP statement should be accorded equal status to the historical cost accounts. Beyond that, however, the scope and aims working party believed that current value methods of measurement, accompanied by the use of a general index adjustment would in time prove to offer superior means of measuring financial performance and position. A practically-orientated programme of research and testing was recommended to develop a workable and standardised system of current value accounting capable of general application. In contrast to this, the Sandilands Committee, as mentioned earlier, rejected the CPP measuring unit and also recommended that a Steering Group with a permanent staff should be set up to prepare an initial standard of Current Cost Accounting for issue by the professional accountancy bodies in time for it to apply to accounts for periods commencing after 24 December 1977. In the meantime the Sandilands Committee stated that companies should wherever possible adopt the essential features of CCA before it became mandatory.

Thus, the Sandilands Committee was more extreme than the scope and aims working party in its criticisms of CPP and was in favour of immediate action rather than the further research favoured by the working party.

9 The accountancy profession's Initial Reactions to Sandilands

In the light of these conflicting views the accountancy bodies issued their *Initial Reactions* to the Sandilands Report (CCAB, 1975). As the Government was anxious to have the profession's reaction to the Report before the new Parliamentary Session began (November) a detailed examination of the Report was not made. Instead the accountancy bodies concentrated on the Committee's central recommendations (excluding the taxation effects) with a view to setting out as unequivocably as possible the profession's initial response.

The response, submitted to the Government at the end of October 1975, welcomed the Report's conclusions as a major step towards the objective of more relevant and informative reporting and accepted that, provided requisite indices were made available, the CCA system could be an acceptable and practicable method of accounting for non-monetary assets at their current values. The accountancy bodies, however, disputed the claim made in the Report that CCA was a fully comprehensive system of accounting for inflation since the proposed system failed to deal with, or dealt inadequately with, the decrease in the value of monetary assets, the decrease in the value of liabilities, the whole effect of inflation on proprietary capital, the difference between monetary and real holding gains, and comparability between accounts over a period of time.

The method for dealing with these problems, illustrated in the ASSC document, was the 'real terms' approach, using a current value base, such as the value to the firm method advocated by Sandilands, but combining this with a general purchasing power (CPP) adjustment to the capital to be maintained intact. This would identify the real gain on borrowing, the real loss on holding monetary assets, the difference between monetary and real holding gains, and profit after maintaining real proprietary capital (in CPP terms) intact. Translation of previous years' figures into current £s (again using a general purchasing power index) would improve comparability between years. Essentially, this was the system rejected in para. 546 of the Sandilands Report. The accountancy bodies agreed, however, that work should start forthwith on the development of a new accounting standard based on the Report's proposals but which would, in addition (as suggested by *The Corporate Report*), require information on the basis of current purchasing power. If the current cost financial statements were not to be fully stabilised in terms of a general purchasing power index then the accountancy bodies proposed that reporting entities should at least compare the change in the capital invested, as measured by the Report's proposals, with the change required to maintain the purchasing power of equity capital. In others words, the maintenance of the physical asset base would be compared to the maintenance of proprietors' capital in real terms. This minimum concession to the CPP approach was later embodied in the supplementary Statement of Change in the Shareholders' Equity Interest contained in the IASG's first Exposure Draft (*ED18*, 1976).

A statement issued a few weeks later by the accountancy bodies dealt with the problem of reporting in the period until the publication of an accounting standard based on the Sandilands CCA proposals. Companies were encouraged to use HC for their statutory accounts until details of the CCA method had been considered in greater depth. A supplementary statement was also recommended to adjust the results and financial position of the company for the effects of specific and/or general price-level changes. To re-emphasise their view outlined in the *Initial Reactions* the accountancy bodies recommended the use of the stabilised CCA method as amplified in that document, or alternatively either the Sandilands CCA method or the CPP method based on HC as set out in *PSSAP7*.

10 Conclusion

In many ways the statement by the accountancy bodies was a face-saving device for the profession. The Secretary of State for Trade, in making a statement on the Sandilands Report in the House of Commons at the end of November 1975, had endorsed the recommendation of the Committee of Enquiry that current cost accounting should become the future basis for company accounts. Consequently, having virtually been ordered by the Government to produce a current cost solution to the problem of accounting for inflation the best the profession could hope for was to modify the proposals of the Committee of Enquiry to safeguard, in the form of supplementary statements attached to the main current cost accounts, what it considered to be the crucial aspects of the proprietary based CPP system outlined in *PSSAP7*. Indeed, two days before the statement on the interim period was issued the UK accountancy bodies in consultation with the ASSC had announced the establishment of a Steering Group with the main task of preparing an exposure draft on CCA.

Thus, the background against which the Steering Group started work was not propitious. The Government had intervened by appointing the Sandilands Committee. This, in turn, had further polarised the debate by its hostility to all vestiges of the CPP system, and the 'real terms' compromise offered in the CCAB's *Initial Reactions* had not found favour in government circles. The most obvious weakness of the Sandilands Committee approach was in its treatment of monetary assets and liabilities. This had already been revealed by the public debate which followed the publication of the Sandilands Report, and which is reviewed in the following chapter.

6
The contemporary British debate III: ED18 to SSAP 16 (1976–83)

1 Introduction

The previous chapter dealt with the Government's intervention in the UK inflation accounting debate. This had resulted in the profession's CPP proposals being rejected by the Government's Committee of Enquiry into Inflation Accounting (the Sandilands Committee), which had proposed a current cost solution to the problem of accounting for changing prices. The CCAB's *Initial Reactions* to the Sandilands proposals, advocating a 'real terms' approach attempting to bridge the gap between current purchasing power and current cost accounting systems, had failed to persuade the Government that the way forward should not be based solely on a current cost approach. The ASC's Inflation Accounting Steering Group (IASG) was therefore left with no alternative but to draft an internally consistent CCA exposure draft based on a specific model – in this case the proposals of the Sandilands Committee.

An attempt to reconcile the polarised CCA and CPP factions in the debate was nevertheless evident in the Steering Group's terms of reference which required it to take account of the CCAB's *Initial Reactions* to the Sandilands Report and to attempt to assuage some of the profession's fears of CCA, namely the problems of its implementation and its inherent subjectivity, both by carrying out research on the practical application of CCA and by keeping in mind the potential difficulties auditors might face if there were to be a diminution in available objective audit evidence.

The terms of reference (which had been agreed with the Secretary of State for Trade) were *inter alia*:

(1) to take account of the *comments* that had been made on the Sandilands Report, in particular those of the Consultative Committee of Accountancy Bodies;

(2) to carry out such research as it considered necessary;

(3) to consider those matters identified in the Sandilands Report as requiring further study, in particular:
  (a) the practical application of the Committee's recommendations for the valuation of fixed assets, stock and work in progress, including the use of published indices, in relation to companies in various classes of business and of various sizes; and
  (b) the need for objective verification of CC accounts, bearing in mind the requirements of auditors in this respect; and
(4) to test the practicability of draft proposals by 'field tests' on a suitable selection of companies.

At the end of November 1976, a little over one year after the Sandilands Committee had reported, the ASC published the results of the IASG's deliberations – the UK's first CCA Exposure Draft, *ED18*. In retrospect, four fundamental decisions, two of which had been taken by the Sandilands Committee and two by the IASG, almost guaranteed that the Exposure Draft would be met by considerable opposition.

(1) Current Cost Accounts were to become a company's main accounts in place of the traditional historical cost financial statements (a Sandilands recommendation). To minimise both the work load of companies and the possible confusion inherent in the production of two sets of financial statements, it was proposed in the Exposure Draft (para. 273) that the period of parallel running of historical cost and current cost accounts should be kept as short as possible – a period of two years was suggested.[1]

(2) The time scale for the introduction of the CCA system was to be very short. Listed companies and other large entities were to apply the eventual CCA standard to periods beginning on or after 1 July 1978 (six months behind the proposed Sandilands schedule). For other companies whose turnover or assets exceeded £100,000, the latest relevant period for application of the CCA proposals was that beginning on or after 1 January 1980. No commencing date had been fixed for smaller companies.

These two recommendations of the Sandilands Committee, now made operational by the IASG, meant that for all but small companies, a major change in accounting practices was imminent – a change which would result in the disappearance of the traditional historical cost accounts six years after the issue of the Exposure Draft (in periods commencing on or after 1 January 1982).

Two other major decisions (taken by the IASG) compounded the anxieties of preparers and auditors of financial statements.

(3) The IASG interpreted the task of introducing a CCA exposure draft as one of rewriting accounting conventions and, consequently,

instead of dealing with a single topic the Steering Group became involved in taking a position on many contentious accounting problems including leasing and deferred taxation – issues on which the ASC had, at that time, still to arrive at a settled policy for historical cost accounts.

(4) No single capital maintenance system was proposed. The Steering Group believed that the maintenance of the capital should involve more than the Sandilands physical assets capital maintenance system. It could not however agree on an alternative system and ultimately gave directors the discretion to determine the method appropriate for their company.

These two decisions of the IASG were heavily criticised in the responses to the Exposure Draft: the first because the comprehensive nature of *ED18* was considered to be too complex; the second because the appropriation of profit to compensate for inflation was to be left to the directors. The discretionary nature of this appropriation was widely perceived as leading to a lack of definition of profit.

The complexity of the Exposure Draft was undoubtedly a tactical mistake and was not repeated by the ASC as it progressed towards the CCA standard. The lack of a definition of profit, however, was far more understandable and probably few of those who criticised the Exposure Draft on these grounds would have been satisfied if the IASG had plumped for one of the many versions of CCA profit proposed in the public debate during 1975 and 1976. To expect the IASG to produce a universally acceptable profit measure at that time was to expect the virtually unattainable – a point to which we shall return below.

The principal changes to the existing historical cost financial reporting system proposed by the Exposure Draft were:

(1) non-monetary assets would be shown in the balance sheet at their value to the business (deprival value – as recommended by the Sandilands Report)

(2) revenue would be charged with depreciation calculated on the value to the business of the assets concerned, and with the cost of sales calculated (generally) at the replacement cost of the goods consumed (recommendations of the Sandilands Committee)

(3) two new statements would feature in the annual report:

    (a) the appropriation account (a substitute for the Sandilands' Summary of Total Gains) in which would be shown the current cost profit, the revaluation surpluses of the period, the dividends to be paid to the proprietors and the amount which the directors considered should be retained within the business having regard to their assessment of its needs; and

(b) the (supplementary) statement showing the effect of the change in the value of money (as proposed by the CCAB in its *Initial Reactions* to the Sandilands Report) which would reveal how the shareholders' stake in the company had altered in real terms by showing the real gain or loss on holding the company's portfolio of non-monetary and monetary assets, i.e. the opening equity interest (after allowing for changes in capital during the year) adjusted for changes in the RPI would be compared to the closing CCA equity.

The core of the Exposure Draft was therefore derived (as was intended) from the Sandilands proposals and in that respect posed a few novel conceptual problems for the IASG – the two adjusted charges against revenue (depreciation and cost of sales) and the asset valuation system were taken directly from the proposals of the Committee of Enquiry.

The details of fixed asset valuation were, however, different from those of Sandilands and eventually led to problems in the implementation of the Exposure Draft.[2] For example, unlike the Sandilands proposals which advocated the use of industry-based fixed asset indices to determine the current replacement cost of plant and machinery, *ED18* required suppliers' prices, or replacement cost estimates or the company's own index based on its purchasing expenditure, in preference to an authorised external index. It was interesting to note, however, that where an external index had to be used, the IASG, possibly responding to the work of Peasnell and Skerratt (1976) and Bourn, Stoney and Wynn (1976), preferred asset-specific indices to the industry-specific indices advocated by the Sandilands Report.[3] Like the Sandilands Report, *ED18* proposed that valuation of land and buildings should be undertaken by professionally qualified valuers. Such valuations were to be undertaken at intervals of not more than five years, and more frequently if the assets represented a major proportion of the company's gross assets or if there had been considerable market variations or major changes in the property assets since the previous professional valuation. These proposals did not prove to be popular with the corporate sector and many commentators on the Exposure Draft were to object to the cost of such valuations.

Having considered briefly the main proposals of *ED18*, we now turn the clock back slightly to consider the early work of the IASG, the creation of its first CCA exposure draft (*ED18*) and the adverse reaction to it. The chapter then continues by examining the hasty revisions to the IASG's plans following the traumatic rejection of CCA by the members of the English Institute in July 1977; namely the Steering Group's simplified proposals embodied in the Hyde Guidelines (1977) which ultimately led, via a second CCA exposure draft (*ED24*), to the production of a CCA Standard (*SSAP16*) issued in March 1980 – some four and a half years after the publication of the Sandilands proposals.

2 The IASG – its members and initial difficulties

The IASG, under the chairmanship of Douglas Morpeth, was a sub-committee of the ASC but because of the perceived national importance of the issue the Government contributed one-third of its costs, the remainder being supplied by the profession, industry and commerce. The composition of the Steering Group reflected the interest of several different parties in the outcome of the inflation accounting debate. The Group consisted of three accountants in public practice, five qualified accountants with industrial and commercial experience, two civil servants (one of whom was a qualified accountant), an academic accountant and a stockbroker who was a member of the Stock Exchange Council.

To expedite the Steering Group's deliberation a list of 25 'problem areas'[4] was drawn up early in 1976 and allocated for consideration to various outside experts and to six main working parties which included members of the IASG.[5] This policy of dealing initially with many different problems was a function of the time pressure on the IASG, the relatively large secretariat made available by the cash resources of the Steering Group and the willingness of many very eminent accountants to become involved in the important work of the Steering Group. With the benefit of hindsight the resources available to the IASG may have been a disadvantage. The segmented approach and the eagerness evident from the beginning of the Steering Group's work to tackle most of the identifiable problems connected with the introduction of a new system of accounting ensured that the resulting Exposure Draft was bound to be lengthy and complicated. A further result of this approach was that related subjects would be considered as separate problems and were considered initially by different working parties – the work of one obviously impinging on that of another. For example, the capital maintenance issue was considered by two working parties – that concerned with the legal implications of CCA examined the concept of the Statement of Total Gains, while another group considered the treatment of monetary items. The conceptual core of the new Exposure Draft, therefore, did not appear to be considered explicitly at the outset of the operation. Instead, it seemed that the pressure of a deadline for completion of the work led initially to a haste to tackle individually the identified issues, although the main committee did attempt to review progress on a regular basis. However, in the event, the Exposure Draft simply took shape as time passed, fundamental questions being resolved on a piecemeal basis.

As mentioned earlier it could be said that the initial decision on the mode of tackling the work of the Steering Group played an important part in the Exposure Draft's ultimate rejection. As we shall see later several members of the IASG became alarmed at the nature of the Exposure Draft being created and their fears of a reaction against its complexity once issued was borne out by events.

Given the comprehensive nature of *ED18*, it would be impossible to deal in this chapter with all the problems tackled by the IASG during 1976. Instead we shall concentrate on its major difficulties – the treatments of holding gains and monetary items and the related question of the capital maintenance system to be adopted.

Most of the Sandilands proposals were accepted with relatively little debate. The theoretical merits of the asset valuation proposals of the Committee of Enquiry had already been recognised and further study of the system suggested in the ASSC's own discussion paper *The Corporate Report*, issued one month before the Sandilands Report. The depreciation and cost of sales adjustments were not matters of serious contention although simpler methods of calculating the current cost of sales (e.g. LIFO) were discussed. The main difficulties arose from the view of the Committee of Enquiry that a summary statement of total gains and losses for the year should be shown in the accounts since, for certain types of company, holding gains may be of greater importance than 'operating profits' (Sandilands, para. 540) and from the need to attempt to reconcile the CCAB's view on the treatment of monetary items outlined in the *Initial Reactions* with that expressed by Sandilands (para. 537) namely:

> Because we are recommending that accounts should continue to be drawn up in terms of monetary units (pounds), it follows that no gains or losses in terms of money can arise solely through holding monetary items when prices are changing. The question of whether such gains should be classed as profit does not therefore arise as it does when accounts are drawn up in terms of current purchasing power units.

On the outcome of the debate on these two issues hung the question of the capital maintenance system to be chosen by the IASG. This was undoubtedly the most difficult conceptual problem faced by the IASG: an issue which was to be at the heart of the UK debate during the next

111

few years. The CCAB's reaction to Sandilands, arguing for information on the basis of current purchasing power (a reaction which the IASG's terms of reference forced it to consider) caused immense difficulties for the IASG. As it transpired, the Steering Group was unable to come to an agreed position.

Due to the importance of this matter we have concentrated on this aspect of the IASG's debate on the proposed *ED18*. As a guide to the way the debate progressed, we have examined the issues, as did the IASG, in two parts, looking firstly at the Sandilands Statement of Total Gains proposal and, secondly, at the issue of the treatment of monetary items.

(i) *The summary statement of total gains*

The Sandilands summary statement of total gains or losses received little support from the IASG working party considering the issue. Ultimately despite the appreciation of the working party that holding gains and losses were important in assessing the overall position of a company, the statement was rejected for four main reasons:

(1) it would probably have been produced in the form of a supplementary statement as it did not articulate (as a connecting statement) with either the balance sheet or the profit and loss account. (It could, however, have formed a link between the two statements in a manner similar to that of the eventual solution – *ED18*'s appropriation account.)

A supplementary statement was not considered appropriate for two reasons. Firstly, if the supplementary statement proposed by the CCAB in its *Initial Reactions* were to be recommended in the Exposure Draft there was a danger of too many statements being required; and, secondly, much of the information given in the summary statement of total gains or losses would be available elsewhere in the financial statements;

(2) the statement did not reveal the surplus for the year available for distribution, but could possibly be interpreted as doing so;

(3) the statement departed from long-established terminology and therefore users of accounts, and particularly unsophisticated users, might find it difficult to understand;

(4) the statement did not fit in with the form of accounts set out in the draft EEC (Fourth and Seventh) Directives.

The objections are interesting and, to a certain extent, reveal the rigidity of the thinking of the IASG. The first objection indicates a fear of information overload yet fails to consider whether a statement of total gains would be more useful than other data then supplied to those reading the accounts. The third objection failed to recognise that most unsophisticated users had difficulty in understanding the 'long-established terminology' used in financial accounts and that accounting jargon could be clarified with benefit to many users of accounts.[6] The fourth objection, while true, is irrelevant – a supplementary statement would have been permissible under the Directives' articles.

Objection (2) encompassed two fears of the IASG. Firstly there was a concern about the restrictions created by the Sandilands 'physical assets' capital maintenance concept and a belief that the total gains for the period did not adequately reflect the gains available for distribution after maintaining the substance of the business at the required level. (There was, as shown below, to be considerable dispute in the IASG about the definition of the substance of business.) Secondly, some members of the IASG appeared concerned about the classification of unrealised gains as part of the total gain for the year, seemingly believing that the objective of an income statement or statement of gains was not to portray the overall performance of a company during a period but instead was to reflect distributable income.[7]

(ii) *Monetary items*

The working party dealing with monetary items under the chairmanship of Professor Edey very quickly realised that it would have difficulty in reaching agreement on the treatment of monetary gains and losses. One view was that the Sandilands operating profit should not be changed, other members of the working party believed that some adjustment to reflect the gain and losses on monetary items in a time of inflation would have to be recorded. Some three months after starting work the working party's discussion centred round a paper outlining six different treatments of monetary items.[8]

The proposals could be divided into three groups:

A *The 'entity' proposals*, namely
  1 The Sandilands system
  2 The Philips system
B *The 'proprietary' proposals*, namely
  3 The CCAB 'ideal' system
  4 The CCAB 'compromise' system
C *The 'proprietorial/entity' or 'gearing' proposals*
  5 The Godley system
  6 The Gibbs system

Each of the above systems assumed a current cost base for the valuation of assets. A brief description of, and the views of the IASG on, each system is given below.

1 The Sandilands system

The Sandilands proposals outlined in the last chapter envisaged the maintenance of the physical non-monetary assets of a company – namely fixed assets and stocks. Revenue, consequently, would be charged with the depreciation of fixed assets and cost of sales both measured on a current cost (value to the business) basis. Holding gains or losses on fixed assets and stocks would not form part of profit but would be taken to reserve.

While the Sandilands proposals were relatively uncomplicated, the Steering Group was well aware that the proposals had already been criticised by the CCAB on two counts; firstly in maintaining the operating capacity only of the entity's physical assets the effect of rising prices on the relation of monetary assets and liabilities to the level of business activity had been ignored; and secondly, in reporting the effect of operations on the proprietors' interest in the business, profit was treated in money terms and no attempt was made to reflect the effect of changes in the general purchasing power of money.

2 The Philips system

The other entity system considered by IASG was that employed by Philips – one of the most elaborate replacement cost systems in operation and one which, in general, was broadly based on Limperg's theoretical model. Profit was charged with the replacement cost of depreciating assets and stock consumed – the revaluation adjustment was taken to reserve. Theoretically, general purchasing power gains and losses on monetary items were also recognised in income. In practice, however, profit was charged with the loss in the purchasing power (as measured by the cost-of-living index) of the stockholders' equity invested in net monetary assets. The argument for the latter charge was that 'part of the stockholders' equity is invested in . . . monetary assets (and consequently) the purchasing power of that part (of the equity) will diminish in the case of a decrease in value of currency of the country'.[9]

The system was lopsided in that no gain on net liabilities was ever shown – although there was provision for adding to profit gains on net monetary assets if purchasing power rose but only to the extent of any reserve for losses in purchasing power. Conservatism prevailed over consistency in the Philips system. This system has since been changed – see Chapter 9.

The system was ultimately rejected by the Steering Group as a possible model because of both its lopsided nature and its failure to show the effect of operations on the purchasing power of owners' capital. Of more interest to the IASG were variants of the CCAB's own 'real terms' model.

3 The CCAB 'ideal' system

A 'real terms' current value system, forms of which had earlier been developed in the USA by Sweeney (1936) and Edwards and Bell (1961) and propagated in the UK by Stamp (1971) and Baxter (1952 and 1975), would have met the CCAB's main objections to the Sandilands proposals. Baxter, a colleague of Edey, had just published a book on the subject through the medium of the Research Committee of the ICAEW. Not surprisingly, therefore, Baxter's proposals were seriously considered by the IASG. Baxter advocated that profit should consist of the Sandilands operating profit plus adjustments for the gain in the general purchasing power of current liabilities less the general purchasing power loss incurred in holding monetary assets.[10] Gains on long-term liabilities were to be shown separately. (Doubt existed whether or not such gains should be taken to profit in whole or in part before the liabilities were repaid or kept as a reserve until repayment.)

Realised real gains or losses[11] on holding assets were also included in income. (Whether or not unrealised real holding gains should be included in profit remained an open question.) At this stage, assuming gains or losses on all liabilities were to be included in profit, ideal income would be identical to profit on a CPP basis. The system was, therefore, not designed to maintain a company's specific assets and as such was a departure from the Sandilands entity philosophy. Possibly for this reason, the system's relative complexity, and because the response to *ED8* indicated that views on stabilised accounts were divided, the Steering Group decided not to adopt this method but instead turned their attention to the simpler proposal originally outlined in the CCAB's *Initial Reactions* to the Sandilands Report.

4 The CCAB 'compromise' system

While the CCAB may have preferred the ideal system, its *Initial Reactions* to the Sandilands recommendations outlined a compromise if a fully stabilised system were not to be acceptable. The compromise proposed involved a supplementary statement which compared the closing net assets valued on the Sandilands basis with opening assets valued on the same basis and expressed in terms of £s at the period end. This would show whether the change in the stated value of closing net assets had been sufficient to maintain the purchasing power of opening net assets. Excluding capital injections and repayments, the differences would be due to two reasons – the gain or loss on monetary items (not reflected in the Sandilands proposals) and the difference between the movement in the general index and specific price changes affecting non-monetary assets. While the proposal would have met the CCAB's major objections to the Sandilands proposals it obviously suffered from the disadvantage of appearing to introduce a statement of less apparent importance than the main CC accounts.

In addition to examining the conclusions of the Committee of Enquiry, the Philips method and the CCAB's two proposals, the IASG considered two other systems being actively discussed in the press while the Steering Group was deliberating.

5 The Godley system
In their 1974 paper (discussed in Chapter 5) Godley and Wood had attempted to demonstrate how under certain extreme assumptions – including the financing of stock entirely by borrowing – the whole of stock appreciation could be counted as profit denominated in money terms. As we mentioned in Chapter 5, Godley and Cripps argued in a later paper (1975) that the Sandilands proposals were equally extreme in that it was assumed only equity financing was used and that no investment was financed by borrowing. Godley and Cripps concluded that an intermediate position was appropriate and that the portion of stock appreciation and holding gains on fixed assets financed by borrowing should be included in profit. The distributable surplus would then maintain fixed and working capital (in the form of stocks) intact while also retaining the initial ratio of debt to shareholders' funds. This was the beginning of the debate about the gearing adjustment in the UK – although, two years earlier, Vermeulen of the Philips company had suggested a similar adjustment in his submission to ASC on *ED8*. (Interestingly, in view of Martin Gibbs' interest in the gearing adjustment, the submission had previously been given as a paper at a seminar organised by his firm, Phillips and Drew.)

The Godley–Cripps system is outlined briefly below.

Opening Balance Sheet

	£		£
Equity	60	Stock (at cost)	100
Loans	40		
	100		100

Closing Balance Sheet (Sandilands)

	£		£
Equity	60	Stock (at cost)	130
Profit	—		
Revaluation reserve[12]	30		
Loan	40		
	130		130

At the beginning of the period it is assumed that the price of stock rises 30 per cent. If the business sold its opening stock for £130 and then replaced it for £130, historical cost profit would be £30, and Sandilands profit would be NIL. Godley and Cripps argued, however, that the proportion of the holding gain on stock financed by borrowing could be distributed and replaced by additional borrowing, i.e. £12 could be distributed, because the gearing ratio (debt:equity) would be maintained at 40:60 by borrowing the £12 distributed.

Closing Balance Sheet
(after dividends and additional borrowing)

	£		£
Equity	60	Stock (at cost)	130
Revaluation reserve	18		
Loan	52		
	130		130

It should be noted that the assumption of additional borrowing is an illustration of the system not a determinant of income. The increase in wealth occurs at the moment the asset rises in value not when the additional borrowing is raised, i.e. even if there were to be no increased borrowing the holders of equity would be better off. Nevertheless, the gearing adjustment stimulated the confusion between liquidity and profitability which has bedevilled the inflation accounting debate in the UK.

The Godley–Cripps system still treated profit in money unit terms[13] and only took account of the effect of rising prices to the extent that the firm was financed by liabilities and the price rises affected the specific assets held by the firm. Additionally, it failed to consider the problem of the effect of price rises on monetary assets. The proposal, however, was not at this stage fully developed; for example it was not concerned with the detailed calculation of the gearing ratio (e.g. whether borrowing should be considered to consist of all liabilities or simply long-term liabilities) but it gave others insights into a possible means of accounting for the effects of price changes on liabilities within a monetary unit accounting system. The proposal was developed further by Gibbs while the IASG was still considering the problem of monetary items, and consequently the more primitive, yet seminal, Godley–Cripps system was rejected by the Steering Group.

6 The Gibbs system

Gibbs (1976) developed the argument of Godley and Cripps in an article published in *The Times*, February 1976 and, with other authors, in a booklet published in April of the same year. He attacked the Sandilands system on the grounds that, whereas an appreciation in the money value of a constant volume of stocks would be considered to be a holding gain, a similar increase in the money value of a constant volume of debtors would be considered to be profit. In neither case, he argued, could taxes or dividends be paid without borrowing new money or reducing the real assets employed in the business. This inconsistency, he stated, would mean that the profits of financial institutions and other organisations holding a large proportion of their assets in monetary form would be overstated while the profits of other entities whose liabilities exceeded their monetary assets would be understated. Gibbs was, in effect, arguing that the Sandilands physical assets operating capacity maintenance concept should be extended to ensure that an entity's net working capital was also maintained (i.e. the operating capacity of fixed assets and stock, and debtors less creditors should be maintained).

Accordingly, Gibbs believed that account should be taken of the loss incurred in holding certain monetary assets financed by the owners of an enterprise. Similarly he believed that not all the holding gains on stocks should be charged against profit – instead he argued the proportion financed by short-term creditors should be considered to be a gain accruing to the shareholders as profit.

The inclusion of holding gains in income had already been attacked by Merrett and Sykes (1974b) as being imprudent given that there was no guarantee that the gain would turn up in cash without increasing the borrowing. Interest on this additional borrowing might not then be offset by a proportionate increase in sales revenue and consequently while the balance sheet gearing would have been maintained, income gearing (interest as a percentage of profits before interest) could well arise. Gibbs, however, argued that if stocks are financed by creditors it could be assumed that creditors would be prepared to finance a constant

volume of stocks and accordingly an increase in the cost of stock held
would only lead to a drain on a company's financial resources to the
extent that the stocks were financed by the company itself and not by
creditors.

> We could get a definition of 'operating profits' which more
> accurately reflected the company's inflow and outflow of cash if
> we deducted *working capital appreciation* (the increased cost of
> stock plus debtors less creditors) rather than stock
> appreciation.[14]

Banks and similar organisations were to include cash in working
capital on the grounds that such entities have to keep a proportion of
their assets in liquid form.

The system defined above obviously suffered from the defect that it
appeared to be more of a cash flow rather than an income measure, as it
ignored the effects of inflation on both long-term liabilities and (for most
companies) on cash itself. As the system was developed, Gibbs *et al.*
introduced a further adjustment to profit to take account of the gain to
equity resulting from financing a proportion of the enterprise's assets by
borrowings. Whereas creditors could be expected to increase in line
with the money value of the goods supplied, it was argued that
longer-term borrowing and bank overdrafts could only be increased if
the lenders were prepared to permit such an increase. Using the
Godley–Cripps argument. Gibbs *et al.* pointed out that in times of
inflation if the dividends of a company not growing in real terms were to
be restricted to the Sandilands operating profits, its debt:equity ratio
would be reduced progressively to zero as the revaluation reserves
increased the equity stake in the business. Such a policy pursued over
the long term was in the authors' opinion 'taking financial conservatism
to ridiculous levels'. It was argued, therefore, 'that provided additional
borrowing facilities were available, it would be perfectly acceptable to
distribute some of the holding gains in addition to the operating profits'.
The *theoretical* limit to this distribution would be the point at which the
debt:equity ratio was maintained at the level ruling at the beginning of
the year.[15]

The Gibbs CCA system undoubtedly had its attractions for some
members of the Steering Group (*ED24*'s operating profit measure was
based on the Gibbs proposals) and ultimately convinced Sandilands
himself that adjustments to reflect the effect of price-level changes on
monetary items were probably necessary (Sandilands, 1978). It offered a
distributable profit measure taking account of liquidity considerations
which could well have been appealing for industrialists who preferred a

measure of actual flows of funds not 'theoretical' purchasing power gains or losses. It had, however, several disadvantages:

(1) it made no allowance for the real loss companies suffered in holding cash – it seemed that banks and similar organisations had to hold cash but other entities did not;

(2) it did not give a clear dividing line between short-term and long-term borrowings (if a company financed stock by means of an overdraft it would have a higher charge against operating profit through the medium of the working capital adjustment but a higher proportion of holding gains added back in the gearing adjustment than a company whose stocks were financed by creditors);

(3) it did not stabilise the accounts in real terms; and

(4) its income measure broke with then established rules. The measure seemed to be attempting to indicate the maximum distribution possible while maintaining the assets employed in the business financed by the shareholder (generally with the exception of the purchasing power of cash holdings). This then was neither a pure proprietary nor a pure entity approach but a hybrid proprietorial entity measure which gave the impression that the emphasis should be placed on cash flow rather than income. Initially income was determined after maintaining a form of net operating capability, but ultimately the requirement that the debt:equity ratio should be preserved, resulted in the maintenance of only the portion of operating capacity financed by shareholders.

The IASG working party was, however, not the only group assessing the various possibilities for accounting for the effect of price-level changes on monetary items. A shadow committee (the Government Steering Group on Accounting for Inflation) was formed internally by the Government to examine the IASG's proposals as they developed and to brief the government-appointed members of the Steering Group on the Government's likely reactions to the Steering Group's views. It was evident that the shadow committee was not enthusiastic about the prospect of the IASG going beyond the Sandilands operating profit notion and proposing the introduction of a 'third figure' (as the shadow committee termed it) to divide holding gains into real and monetary components and, in particular, to report the real gain on borrowing and the real loss on holding monetary assets which occur in a period of inflation. Concern was expressed that the IASG, without guidance from the Government, would not take account of the wider implications of the measurement of profit (e.g. the effect on dividends, wages, taxation and price control) but would be concerned more with solving a major accounting problem. Ultimately, it was feared that the IASG's proposals could have been unacceptable to the Government and a clash between the Government and the accountancy profession would then have been inevitable.

Papers circulated by government officials at an early stage in the debate attacked the two main proposals then being debated – the Godley method and the CCAB compromise method. Godley's system was criticised as it did not deal with companies which were holders of net monetary assets and was based on the hypothesis that the maintenance of the company's gearing ratio was an appropriate benchmark against which to measure performance. The CCAB method came in for even stronger criticism mainly on the grounds that:

(1) the Sandilands Report had argued that general inflation was not a meaningful concept in the context of an on-going business;

(2) the fact that the asset values rose faster than inflation was irrelevant if the assets had to be retained in the business;

(3) maintaining the purchasing power of the shareholders' interest was of no consequence when deciding how much of the profit could be distributed without enfeebling the company; and

(4) using indexation in company accounts could lead to pressure for indexation in other areas.

These arguments may well have led the Government to oppose the insertion of a 'third figure' in the profit and loss account. In May 1976, a Treasury paper was sent to the IASG's working party dealing with monetary items, stating that its officials considered that 'the Government is likely to be able to accept a recommendation that, for the immediate future, the accounting standard should be based on the Sandilands profit concept but that a supplementary statement (should) be annexed on the general lines indicated in the CCAB *Initial Reactions*'.

These comments, coupled with the lack of agreement on the issue in the IASG, were probably decisive. The Steering Group, however, despite the reservations of government officials who were anxious that the Sandilands operating profit concept should have a prominent position in the accounts, were reluctant to ignore the effect of price-level changes on monetary items in the profit and loss account.

Accounting for the effect of price-level changes on monetary items – the decision

Given the CCAB's firm belief, expressed in the *Initial Reactions*, that the Sandilands proposals were flawed by their limited physical 'capital maintenace' objective which failed to reflect the effect of inflation on monetary items, the Sandilands system could not be accepted un-amended. The inconsistent nature of the Philips approach and the novelty of the untried Godley and Gibbs systems probably ensured that they would not be incorporated as a compulsory part of the CCA system in the forthcoming Exposure Draft. Of the two remaining (CCAB) proposals, the 'compromise' method was probably chosen by the Steering Group because of its supplementary nature (which did not obstruct the effective trial of the new CCA system), its relative simplicity, possible opposition to a stabilised accounting system (a feature of the 'ideal' method) and the knowledge that the Government would accept this proposal. The CCAB 'compromise' method therefore appeared in *ED18* as a statement supplementary to the main CC accounts, thereby helping to maintain the profession's apparent prefer-ence for the proprietary approach advocated in *ED8* and *PSSAP7* and overturned by Sandilands.

While the supplementary statement ensure that the IASG complied with its remit to take account of the CCAB's comments on Sandilands, the IASG was still determined that the Sandilands proposals of main-taining only the physical assets of the business could not be allowed to emerge unscathed in the main CC accounts. The Steering Group was of the opinion that the 'substance of the business' which had to be maintained before income was determined was broader than that envisaged by Sandilands and should probably incorporate monetary items. The problem lay in defining which assets should be maintained.

The IASG appeared to be hopelessly divided. Draft 8 of *ED18* (21 September 1976) provided for a discretionary transfer out of current cost operating profit plus revaluation surpluses to what was then termed the 'Capital Maintenance Reserve'. The discretionary nature of the transfer had become necessary because members of the Steering Group simply could not agree on the definition of the substance of the business and consequently the amount of profit which could prudently be distributed. The discretionary transfer was, therefore, simply a com-promise solution to the problem.

Draft 10 of *ED18* (18 October 1976) in which the IASG's ultimate solution – the Appropriation Account – was first introduced[16] tacitly admitted the failure to agree on the substance of the business by changing the title of the former Capital Maintenance Reserve to the Revaluation Reserve and by introducing an appendix to guide directors in making transfers to or from the reserve.

The IASG made no attempt to hide its difficulties over *ED18*'s capital maintenance model. The introduction to the Exposure Draft stated that there existed a lack of consensus on the definition of the substance of the business and consequently the proposed solution was but an interim palliative until a greater degree of agreement became evident.[17] The initial presumption was that the surplus on the revaluation of assets should be retained in the business. An amount greater or less than the surplus could, however, be taken to the revaluation reserve by the directors based on their assessment of the 'needs of the business' (para. 137). The guidance given to the directors (*ED18* – Appendix 2) on this matter reflected the conflicting solutions evident in the public debate at the time the IASG was deliberating.

Inter alia, directors could, if they wished, appropriate amounts greater than the net surplus on the revaluation of assets by:

(1) maintaining monetary assets by adjusting for net monetary working assets as well as stock (i.e. stock + debtors – creditors). Banks and other financial institutions could, in addition, seek to maintain cash resources (as in the Gibbs proposals);

(2) providing for backlog depreciation if the replacement cycle of the relevant assets led to the amounts set aside by depreciation being insufficient for their replacement (an area of dispute within standard-setting bodies at the time);[18]

(3) maintaining shareholders' equity[19], i.e. abandon the Sandilands, Philips, Godley and Gibbs entity-style approach and revert to proprietary capital maintenance originally preferred by the CCAB.

Amounts less than the net revaluation surplus could be taken to the revaluation reserve at the directors' discretion when:

(1) stocks were effectively financed by trade creditors so that the stock revaluation adjustment was in excess of that required to replace stock (as in the Gibbs proposals);

(2) assets were replaced by the use of long-term and/or short-term borrowings – i.e. where directors were able and intended to finance the purchase of replacement assets by such borrowings while maintaining a 'reasonable debt : equity ratio' (as in the Godley and Gibbs proposals).

The Exposure Draft was, therefore, attempting to discover if a consensus could be found. Directors were required to explain the basis and reasons for the amounts appropriated to or from revaluation reserve. In many respects a standard based on the proposals of *ED18* would have resulted in a referendum being taken – the popular policies would have been identified. In practice, however, savage assaults were launched against this aspect of *ED18* and led in part to its rejection.

The IASG was not unaware of the potential reaction to the Exposure Draft. Two months before the publication of *ED18*, the Steering Group debated whether or not the developing Exposure Draft should be drastically simplified and whether its publication should be delayed. Some members of the Group had become exceedingly alarmed at possible resistance to the detailed proposals arising from their complexity, subjectivity, the problems on which the Group still could not reach agreement and the additional work load involved in implementing the proposals. The Group's dilemma was whether it should attempt to deflect possible criticism by expressing its doubts on its own proposals – stressing that these were in the nature of compromise solutions and thereby possibly weakening the drive to implement CCA – or whether it should ignore the misgivings of some of its members risking (as one of these members wrote in a letter to its Chairman) 'the Steering Group's recommendations being rejected leaving us back where we started with all the disadvantages of historic cost accounts and our work branded as a failure'.

In the event, the Steering Group elected to proceed with the publication of *ED18*, possibly encouraged by favourable responses from the limited number of companies used to field-test the IASG's emerging proposals – responses which later Westwick (1980) reported were favourably biased and untypical of what turned out to be the view of industry as a whole. It was probably inevitable that only companies which were really interested in the subject of inflation accounting would be willing to act as field testers.[20] There is therefore an obvious lesson for standard-setters here: field testing should be confined to testing the feasibility of proposals rather than used to assess attitudes.

The IASG was, by now, however, alerted to the possibility of problems with *ED18*'s general acceptability and to the necessity to develop a simpler fall-back position in the event of a hostile reception to the Exposure Draft.[21] As it transpired, the fears expressed by some members of the Group were well-founded.

The reaction to ED18

(i) The responses to ED18

The Steering Group received a total of 746 submissions on *ED18*; 666 letters of comment and 80 questionnaires returned by field test companies – the number of comments far exceeding the responses to any exposure draft issued by the ASC either prior to or since the publication of *ED18*. In the following analysis, where the IASG's own internal data has been used, multiple submissions have been combined revealing that 694 separate respondents (about one-half of whom were from the corporate sector) submitted their views on the Exposure Draft – 56 commenting only through the medium of a field test questionnaire

Table 6.1. *Commentators' reactions to the proposals for the introduction of CCA – based on the form in which CCA should be introduced*

	%	
Support for CCA		
CCA should be the main accounts* from commencement	29	
CCA should be the main accounts after an introductory period during which CCA is presented in a supplementary statement, or as footnotes to HC accounts, or in a restricted form	5	
CCA should be presented as a restricted form of main accounts (e.g. CCA profit and loss account only) from commencement	11	
CCA should be presented as a restricted form of main accounts after an introductory period as a supplementary statement or as footnotes to HC accounts	1	
Other comments – apparently in favour of CCA	12	58
		—
Neutral		
Other comments – no general view expressed		5
Opposition to CCA		
CCA information should be presented only as a supplementary statement or as footnotes to HC accounts	16	
Another form of inflation accounting preferred (mainly CPP)	7	
Other comments – apparently opposed to CCA	7	
HC information only should be published	7	37
		—
No. = 694		100

*i.e. at least with fixed assets on a current value basis in the balance sheet and the consumption of both stock and fixed assets charged to profit and loss account at current value.
Source: IASG internal document

and 638 submitting letters or both letters and field test questionnaires.

Table 6.1 reveals that a majority of those commenting on the Exposure Draft agreed with the IASG's proposal that current cost information should be included in a company's financial statements. Only about one-third of the respondents, however, supported the Steering Group's view that current cost accounts should supersede the historical cost financial statements as the entity's main accounts.

Support for this proposal was strongest in industry, i.e. among those who would prepare the current cost information (39 per cent), among user groups (39 per cent), and practising accountants (34 per cent) and weakest among individual respondents (23 per cent). Interestingly, merely 5 per cent of the respondents from industry proposed that only historical cost information should be shown in a company's financial statements. While a substantial minority appeared to be willing to accept the change from HC to CC main accounts the IASG was under no illusions that these respondents were supporters of *ED18* in its entirety. Only about 9 per cent of those commenting appeared to be reasonably satisfied with the general thrust of the Exposure Draft. That only a small proportion of respondents were satisfied was corroborated by the present authors' own analysis of a sample of the respondents.

Our aim in drawing this sample was threefold: firstly to check the IASG's own analysis; secondly, to obtain the views of those respondents who could be termed opinion leaders at the time, i.e. those whose views would probably been considered carefully by the IASG;[22] and thirdly to obtain a flavour of the opinions expressed. Consequently, we examined the responses of: the six accountancy bodies comprising the CCAB; the ten largest accountancy firms; major companies which were known to be pioneers in the field of inflation accounting (e.g. ICI, Philips, Pilkington and Tesco); and all major representative groups of users and preparers of accounts. A random ten per cent sample of the remaining responses was then drawn. In all, some 142 responses were examined and 133 included in the following analysis – the remaining nine responses being eliminated either because they were concerned purely with one specialist aspect of the Exposure Draft (e.g. the submissions from the Royal Institution of Chartered Surveyors and the Insolvency Practitioners Association) or because the respondent, while supplying splendid entertainment, did not deal with the subject at issue.[23]

It must be admitted that the results of our analysis[24] presented below do not necessarily reflect accurately the overall response. Our informal sample, however, enabled us to ascertain the general style of the responses which does appear to be broadly similar to that perceived by the ASC.

Table 6.2 reveals the general reaction of the sample respondents to the Exposure Draft. As revealed by the IASG's own analysis very few respondents appeared willing to accept *ED18*'s proposals without amendment.

A large majority – about three out of every four respondents examined – called for major changes to the ASC's proposals. Just over half of this group (40 per cent of the sample), while suggesting

Table 6.2. *Adjustments required to* ED18

Group	No.	No adjustments/ adjustments of a minor nature/ neutral %	Substantial adjustments %	Outright opposition to *ED18* %
CCAB bodies	6	—	100	—
Representative bodies – accountancy bodies	14	7	72	21
Practising firms of accountants	19	5	58	37
Representative bodies – preparers of accounts	38	5	82	13
Companies and corporations	39	3	82	15
Representative bodies – users of accounts	7	29	71	—
Individuals	10	—	60	40
Total	133	5	76	19

alterations, indicated that they disapproved of the overall principles on which the Exposure Draft was based – these respondents were classified (Table 6.3) as voicing qualified opposition to *ED18*. 36 per cent of the sample were deemed to have given qualified support to the proposals – these respondents, while proposing major changes, had not attacked the idea of inflation accounting or CCA or the basis of the method of accounting for price-level changes proposed in *ED18*.

Overall, while about two in every five respondents appeared to be sympathetic to the broad thrust of *ED18*, a majority (59 per cent) were generally opposed to the Exposure Draft. Indeed, one respondent in every five was totally opposed to its proposals. Only two categories of respondent sampled appeared to be in favour of the Exposure Draft. Six of the seven user groups seemed to be generally supportive of the ASC's paper the only other category revealing a majority in favour of the proposals in principle being the accountancy bodies representing the CCAB – four out of the six expressing qualified (often heavily qualified)

Table 6.3. *Depth of support for and opposition to the ED18 proposals*

Group	No.	Explicit support %	Qualified support %	Qualified opposition %	Outright opposition %	Neutral %
CCAB bodies	6	—	67	33	—	—
Representative bodies – accountancy bodies	14	7	29	43	21	—
Practising firms of accountants	19	—	16	42	37	5
Representative bodies – preparers of accounts	38	—	42	40	13	5
Companies and corporations	39	3	38	44	15	—
Representative bodies – users of accounts	7	29	57	14	—	—
Individuals	10	—	20	40	40	—
Total	133	3	36	40	19	2

Table 6.4. *Main criticisms of* ED18 *(This analysis excludes comments from those submitting only field test questionnaires.)*

ED18 approach is too complex	49%
ED18 approach is too subjective	33%
ED18 approach is too costly	28%
Concern about how smaller companies could implement *ED18*	18%
ED18 timetable is too rapid because there is a need for international harmonisation	15%
Need for acceptance for tax purposes prior to the introduction of CCA	11%
CCA is not useful	10%
ED18 timetable is too rapid because there is insufficient knowledge of CCA techniques and the effects of CCA	8%
CCA will be inflationary	6%
Need for acceptance for price control purposes prior to the introduction of CCA	4%
No. = 638	

Source: IASG internal document

support. Other representative bodies of accountants were in the main opposed to the Exposure Draft as was a majority of the professional accountancy firms (including eight of the nine small firms included in the sample). The accountancy profession consequently appeared to be divided between its leaders and the grass roots – and even the leaders of the profession may have been swayed by considerations of loyalty to the ASC.

The main criticisms directed against *ED18* are outlined in Table 6.4 which is based on IASG's own analysis of the responses to the Exposure Draft. The analysis of our sample of responses (Table 6.5) reveals similar complaints. It can be seen from the table that the fears of some of the Steering Group's members, prior to the issue of the Exposure Draft, were borne out by the reaction of a large proportion of the respondents. The complexity, subjectivity, implementation problems and costs of preparing the current cost information clearly alarmed many respondents.

Table 6.5. *Aspects of ED18 criticised*

Aspects of ED18	Total bodies %	CCAB bodies %	Representative bodies – accountancy bodies %	Practising firms of accountants %	Representative bodies – preparers of accounts %	Companies and corporations %	Representative bodies – users of accounts %	Individuals %
Complexity	59	67	71	79	61	54	29	40
Subjectivity	44	33	21	63	37	51	29	50
Speed of implementation	41	50	43	47	47	36	29	30
Expense	41	33	50	37	45	49	—	30
Historical cost abandonment	38	50	36	53	37	36	14	40
Range of enterprises affected	26	50	50	42	24	18	—	—
CCA statements as main accounts	23	17	7	42	18	31	—	10
Total No.	133	6	14	19	38	39	7	10

The most common complaint evident was the complexity of the proposals – mentioned most frequently by all major groups of respondents whether preparers, users or auditors.[25] Next came the subjectivity inherent in the Exposure Draft's proposals – of particular concern to practising firms of accountants which doubtless could foresee arguments with their clients if management were to be allowed considerable discretion in the measurement of asset values and in the determination of profit. This attitude is, of course, entirely consistent with the practising accountants' support for the more 'objective' CPP proposals of *ED18*, the auditing of which would have been a relatively simple extension of the work done on historical cost accounts. Indeed, it is interesting to note that over half of the practising firms of accountants were concerned about *ED18*'s proposed eventual abandonment of historical cost – 53 per cent of them mentioned this aspect of *ED18* as a cause of concern.

Two other major criticisms of the Exposure Draft were made by two out of every five of the respondents sampled. The proposed speed of implementation of the Exposure Draft's proposals (entities with a turnover or total assets in excess of £100,000 and whose financial statements were intended to give a true and fair view were expected to comply with the Standard based on *ED18* in periods commencing 1 January 1980 – some three years after the publication of the Exposure Draft) was of particular concern to practising accountants and representative bodies of both accountants and preparers of accounts. Expense too was a major worry – particularly to representative bodies of accountants, to companies and to the smaller practising accountancy firms (who possibly feared fee resistance from their clients). Interestingly, none of the user groups objected to the Exposure Draft's proposals on the grounds of expense – they would receive the benefits of the additional information without incurring the direct cost of its preparation.

A problem mentioned mainly by the corporate sector was the question of the international harmonisation of inflation accounting proposals. Companies were concerned about this question on two grounds. Firstly there was a danger, particularly for multi-national corporations, that differing international proposals would lead to major difficulties and expense in the preparation of their financial reports. Secondly, there was a concern that, if the United Kingdom moved too far ahead of the rest of the world in advocating current cost accounting, corporate CCA results might be misinterpreted by overseas investors with consequential effects on investment in the UK when unfavourable comparisons were drawn with HC results in other countries.

Turning to the specific technical proposals of the Exposure Draft, Table 6.6 shows that three recommendations were believed to be bound to create problems, by two out of every five of the respondents. The valuation of fixed assets was of major concern to preparers of accounts mainly on the grounds of complexity and expense. The appropriation account was attacked by three of the six accountancy bodies comprising the CCAB (five of these bodies were also concerned about the vague profit concept of *ED18*). The absence of a definite treatment for monetary items was also a major point of concern – particularly to accountants, who some four years after the *ED8* proposals may have been coming to accept that a system of accounting for price-level changes was incomplete unless it incorporated a method of accounting for the effect of inflation on monetary assets and liabilities.

Taking an overview of the objections to *ED18*, it could be said, that, in many ways, self interest lay behind many of the criticisms of the Exposure Draft's proposals. The desire of practising accountants for objectivity and a precise definition of income in current cost accounts, in addition to their reluctance to abandon historical cost accounts, reflected their concern with the difficulties of auditing the proposed CC financial statements. On the other hand, perhaps not unnaturally, preparers of accounts did not appear to be as worried as auditors about either the prospect of the increased element of judgement involved in the preparation of their accounts or the greater discretion given to directors in the determination of income. The expense of implementation was of more relative importance to this group.[26]

As mentioned above, many of the doubts about *ED18* were shared by the professional accountancy societies. Indeed, four of the CCAB accountancy bodies proposed alternative CCA schemes – the Institute of Chartered Accountants in Ireland backing its view that fundamental changes in *ED18* were necessary before a CCA standard could be produced, with the threat that, unless some of the major difficulties perceived by the Institute were adequately overcome, the Institute would find it difficult to give support to a standard based on *ED18*. This was a significant warning since if one of the ASC's governing bodies opposed the introduction of a standard it could not be issued.

Two of the accountancy bodies (ICAS and ICMA) advocated a return to the Sandilands operating profit concept. The Scottish Institute proposed that current cost depreciation and cost of sales adjustments should be included in the main (historical cost) accounts. The Institute of Cost and Management Accountants proposed a similar treatment but were undecided whether the adjustments should appear in the main historical cost accounts or in a supplementary CCA statement.

Table 6.6. Objections to the various proposals

Treatment	Total bodies %	CCAB bodies %	Representative bodies – accountancy bodies %	Practising firms of accounts %	Representative bodies – preparers of accountants %	Companies and corporations %	Representative bodies – users of accounts %	Individuals %
Valuation of fixed assets	41	17	21	32	50	59	—	30
Appropriation account	41	50	36	47	39	36	43	50
Monetary items	39	50	36	53	39	28	57	40
Measurement of profit	32	83	36	58	32	10	29	30
Cost of sales adjustment	19	33	—	32	13	23	14	20
Total No.	133	6	14	19	38	39	7	10

While these two Institutes believed that ultimately a working capital adjustment might also be necessary, the ICAEW had no doubts about the need for such an adjustment.

> . . . any system of current cost accounting which does not allow for the maintenance of net monetary working capital is inadequate.

Following the views of Gibbs, the ICAEW argued that a net monetary working capital adjustment should cover any monetary items 'which are inherent in the operation of the business[27] but should exclude any items which can be regarded as part of the financing arrangements of the business'. It was accepted by the Institute that shareholders gained from long-term as well as short-term borrowing but that the former gain was different in nature from the benefit accruing from the finance of working capital. No method was suggested to reflect the gain on long-term liabilities – this was (rather illogically) to be left to the future. An adjustment for monetary working capital was, however, considered to be essential to ensure that the resulting CCA standard was concerned with the maintenance of what was deemed to be all net operating assets.

One Institute (ICAI), however, had no qualms about including gains on all borrowings in income. Additionally, the Irish Institute proposed that real gains on assets should be included in profit. Its proposal involved firstly an adjustment being made to the HC profit to account for the current cost depreciation (no adjustment to account for the current cost of sales was proposed), secondly the inclusion in income of revaluation surpluses on fixed assets and stock and thirdly the deduction of a capital maintenance adjustment to preserve equity capital in current (CPP) terms.[28]

The differing view of the Institutes reflected the magnitude of the IASG's task in producing an acceptable definition of income. The Institutes, however, were bound to have a great influence on the ASC and it was not surprising to see the ASC move in the direction suggested by them – a slower speed for implementation, less complexity and, ultimately, an adjustment to take account of the effect of inflation on monetary working capital.

The IASG were certainly aware of most of the potential objections to *ED18.* In many respects the Steering Group had been, as one member of its staff put it to the present authors, 'painted into a corner by Sandilands'. Much of the criticism directed at the Steering Group undoubtedly was aimed at the wrong target – the Steering Group had been asked to implement the Sandilands Report taking into account the comments of the CCAB.[29] While the final result may have been over-elaborate in some aspects and vague in others – especially, as far as imprecision is concerned, in its income concept (in large part due to the veto the Sandilands Report had imposed on adjustments for the effects of inflation on monetary items), the Steering Group had met its terms of reference in a remarkably short time.

Certainty in the measurement of income is unattainable. Respondents to the Exposure Draft failed to agree among themselves yet criticised the Steering Group for failing to produce an acceptable method of measuring income. In some respects, however, the Steering Group could perhaps have gone further than they did. Their views on income measurement appeared to have been frozen at the time of Sandilands yet the debate had moved on – Gibbs, Godley and Kennedy were all advocating adjustments to reflect the effect of price changes on monetary items. *ED18*'s appropriation account, as we have discussed, opened the door to the experimental use of any one of the differing income theories in vogue but gave no hint of the future direction the ASC might take.

(ii) The revolt against ED18

The IASG had not initially intended to issue a further exposure draft on CCA but expected, since 'the subject (was) too important and too urgent for the process of debate which (had) been going on since at least 1971 to be prolonged further',[30] to proceed straight to the publication of a statement of standard accounting practice. The Steering Group, however, conceded that changes had to be made if the eventual Standard were to be acceptable and in a statement issued at the end of May 1977 agreed to consider especially: means of simplifying the proposals; the problems of implementation found by smaller businesses; slowing down the introduction of CC statements as the main accounts; and finally the need to deal with the effects of price changes on monetary items. By then, however, it was too late.

Before the IASG could put its proposals into effect, a groundswell of opposition to *ED18* resulted in two members of the Institute of Chartered Accountants in England and Wales (Messrs Keymer and Haslam) succeeding having convened a Special Meeting of the Institute in July 1977 to consider the resolution, 'that the members of the Institute of Chartered Accountants in England and Wales do not wish any system of Current Cost Accounting to be made compulsory'.

In a message to the members of the Institute Keymer and Haslam argued that the system of CCA recommended both by The Sandilands Report and by *ED18* involved the eventual abolition of HC accounts. They considered that this was so fundamentally wrong that only a motion such as the one to be put to the Special Meeting could halt such a system being imposed. They argued against being forced to introduce CCA statements suggesting instead that there should be a recommendation of 'best accounting practice' proposing that a CCA statement should be supplementary to the HC accounts of certain types of companies.

Statements sent to the Institute's members from its Council and its President put the case for CCA. These statements emphasised the 'inadequate' and 'misleading' nature of HC accounts, arguing that a voluntary system of CCA would not be sufficient to ensure that industry and commerce received the information they required and therefore the Institute must take a lead in ensuring that CCA eventually became the main system of accounting. Additionally, the President's message reiterated the need for the changes in *ED18* already under review – to no avail. The resolution was passed by 46 per cent of the members of the Institute voting by 15,512 votes to 13,184. Interestingly, it is worth noting in passing that many commentators have interpreted this vote as a rebellion against the Institute and the profession's establishment, yet it is a striking feature of the responses that none of the CCAB bodies gave *ED18* unqualified support. Substantial changes to *ED18*'s proposals would undoubtedly have come whether or not the Special Meeting had taken place. In any event, the post-Sandilands rush towards a comprehensive CCA system in the UK was checked; a gradualist approach now appeared to be the only acceptable way forward.

Immediately after the Special meeting, the Council of the ICAEW issued a statement reaffirming its view that the introduction of an acceptable system of accounting in the face of inflation was urgently needed. The Council also recognised, however, that there should be a re-appraisal of the approach to accounting for price-level changes following further consultations with representatives of finance, commerce, industry and the Government. This statement was supported in the House of Commons the following day by the Secretary of State for Trade, who reaffirmed the Government's desire 'that current cost accounting should become the basis for the preparation of company accounts as soon as practicable'.[31]

The ASC itself issued a 'Statement of Intent' later the same month. Considering both the resolutions passed at the Special Meeting of the English Institute and the comments received on *ED18*, the Committee came to the conclusion that there was an obvious unreadiness to accept a standard based on *ED18* without substantial simplification and modification of the proposals of the Exposure Draft. The ASC commented, however, that the submissions and the Special Meeting demonstrated that a wide recognition existed both of the distortion in historical cost accounts caused by inflation and of the urgent need to indicate the extent of this distortion. Given this need for action, the ASC considered that it should, as a longer-term objective, continue the work of producing an acceptable and workable system of price-level accounting for promulgation as an accounting standard or standards – this would involve the careful analysis of the comments on *ED18*. In the short term, however, as an indication of the effects of inflation on HC accounts was urgently required, it was proposed that, in conjunction with the IASG, simple guidelines should be prepared for supplementing HC accounts with information in respect of both depreciation of fixed assets and the cost of sales in terms of current costs and, additionally, with an adjustment to take account of the effects of gearing. The aim was to publish the Guidelines in time for companies to produce the CCA information to supplement their HC financial statements for the year to 31 December 1977. Speed, therefore, was of the essence.

3 The Hyde Guidelines

The proposed Guidelines had to be acceptable. They would therefore have to eliminate most of the controversial and complex aspects of *ED18* – this was not to be a comprehensive system of CCA dealing with deferred tax, leasing or complicated valuation methods. Instead the Guidelines were intended to apply on a voluntary basis only to quoted companies and would require these companies to produce a supple-mentary profit and loss account showing relatively simple adjustments to the HC profit or loss account. No published balance sheet was required, thereby removing the corporate sector's concern with the complexity and expense of valuing fixed assets.

A Committee which included three members of the IASG was set up under William Hyde, a member of the ASC, and quickly got down to work. In many respects – as was obvious from the ASC's statement of intent – the major decisions had already been taken. (In fact, the Committee never met – its work was undertaken by post or telephone.) In examining the submissions on *ED18* it had become clear to the IASG that the current cost charges for depreciation of fixed assets and cost of sales were relatively uncontroversial and had already been largely accepted by the ASC's governing bodies. These two adjustments were, therefore, incorporated in the new proposal but, in the interests of simplicity, without any specific guidance on the more complicated situations. The need to remove *ED18*'s controversial appropriation account but to give recognition to the gain or loss on monetary liabilities was, however, a more complex problem.

During *ED18*'s exposure period the IASG had been wrestling with this difficulty. In April 1977 the Steering Group was actively considering the eventual adoption of a gearing adjustment and was examining, among others, adaptations of the 1976 New Zealand (Richardson) adjustment and an adjustment which the Steering Group identified as being very similar to that proposed by the West German Institute in 1975. While the Steering Group believed that both a monetary working capital adjustment and a gearing adjustment were necessary in the long term, by July 1977 the former adjustment had been abandoned on the grounds of simplicity in the short term and the IASG was working on versions of what was called the 'Ford' gearing adjustment. Ford[32] in their 1976 accounts had produced a version of *ED18* current cost accounts but based on the Godley and Cripps philosophy in which income was charged with current cost depreciation and cost of sales adjustments and then credited with the portion of the revaluation surplus relating to assets financed by borrowings. The adjustment was, however, amended by the IASG and the final version ('Ford Mark III' as it was called) had two adaptations.

Firstly, the adjustment was extended to the case where there was an excess of net monetary assets – in such a case an additional charge against income would be made by applying an appropriate index to the excess. Secondly, in the case where liabilities exceeded monetary assets there was a conservative reluctance on the part of the IASG to include (as Ford had done) unrealised holding gains in income. The gearing adjustment instead would abate the current cost adjustments for depreciation and cost of sales by adding back to profit that portion of the additional charges for the use of these assets financed by borrowing, i.e. income was to be charged with the additional cost of maintaining the operating capacity financed by shareholders.

John Foyle, the secretary of the Hyde Committee informed the present authors that neither the West German gearing adjustment which was similar in many respects to the eventual Hyde adjustment nor the well-publicised submission of the London Society of Chartered Accountants on *ED18* had materially influenced the IASG's thinking. In the case of the former the fact that the West German Institute's proposals had not been put into effect led to the proposal being discounted (although it could not be denied that knowledge of the proposal may have subconsciously affected the thinking of key members of the Hyde Committee or IASG). By the time the influential London Society of Chartered Accountants published its submission on *ED18*, which recommended a gearing adjustment restricted to realised gains (the realised cost-saving approach), the IASG was apparently already coming to a similar conclusion[33] – the favourable reaction to the Society's proposals, however, helped to confirm the IASG in its view.

While several commentators on *ED18* would probably have preferred two separate adjustments for monetary items – a monetary working capital adjustment *and* a gearing adjustment – the Hyde Committee followed the ASC's July 1977 statement of intent ensuring that the Guidelines were relatively simple and only involved one adjustment for monetary items in addition to the generally accepted current cost charges for fixed assets and cost of sales. The essential task as seen by ASC was to produce an acceptable document – CCA was at its nadir in the UK at the time and another failure by the ASC to produce a workable set of rules for CCA would have cast serious doubts on the Committee's ability to produce effective accounting standards. The Hyde Guidelines were in the nature of a tactical move to ensure that progress continued towards an eventual CCA standard. Consequently, the Guidelines were the antithesis of *ED18*; they were short whereas *ED18* was long; they were simple whereas *ED18* was complex;[34] they applied only to a few companies whereas *ED18* applied to many.

There was obvious pressure on the ASC's governing bodies to accept the ASC's Guidelines and to a large extent they did. The Institute of Chartered Accountants of Scotland, however, was concerned that the gearing adjustment might be rejected for two reasons. Firstly the Institute believed that the compromise monetary working capital/gearing adjustment was inconsistent[35] in form leading to entirely different treatments depending upon whether an excess of liabilities or monetary assets existed. Secondly, it was aware that certain companies had used other means of portraying the overall effect of gearing and effects of price-level changes on monetary assets when implementing *ED18* and might wish to continue the experiments with these other treatments. The impasse was eventually broken when the draft Guidelines were altered to allow companies to use their own methods of accounting for the effects of gearing provided these were disclosed in a note to the CCA statement.

The Guidelines, which were officially styled *Inflation Accounting – An Interim Recommendation by the Accounting Standards Committee*, duly appeared at the beginning of November 1977 recommending that listed companies include in their financial statements a supplementary statement showing the three adjustments to historical cost profit foreshadowed in the ASC's July 1977 statement of intent. Operating profit was struck after charging the HC profit with current cost depreciation and current cost of sales adjustments. The incorporation of the gearing adjustment then resulted in the determination of the profit attributable to shareholders – a new term in the UK at the time which probably had been taken from the Richardson Report proposals in New Zealand (1976). While the gearing adjustment was regarded in certain quarters with some misgivings, on the whole the ASC's gamble in issuing the Guidelines was successful. The emotional climate surrounding the introduction of CCA was changed and in introducing an adjustment to take account of the gain or loss on monetary items, the IASG paved the way for a more comprehensive CCA pronouncement which would introduce two separate adjustments for monetary items – the monetary working capital and gearing adjustments.

4 ED24 – the second CCA Exposure Draft

The Hyde Guidelines were accepted reasonably well by industry. In the year to June 1979 47 per cent of the 300 large industrial and commercial companies (all taken from the top 500 companies in *The Times* 1000) whose accounts were examined in the ICAEW's *Survey of Published Accounts 1979* (Skerratt, 1980) had provided supplementary information on the lines suggested by the ASC's voluntary *Interim Recommendations*. In all, some 56 per cent of the companies produced some form of price-level adjusted data and a further 12 per cent stated that they were awaiting firm proposals before disclosing such information.

The first indication of more substantial proposals had come in a statement of intent issued by the ASC in July 1978 indicating that a new CCA exposure draft would be produced evolving from the Hyde Guidelines and taking into account comments made on *ED18*. At this time, one year after the ICAEW's Special Meeting on *ED18*, the ASC were still only too well aware of the need to secure support for any new CCA pronouncement and, consequently, the statement of intent attempted to defuse three of the major objections to *ED18*.

It was proposed that the new Exposure Draft:

(1) would recommend that the CCA profit and loss account and balance sheet should be supplementary to the historical cost accounts. No suggestion of the new statements supplanting the HC accounts was made – indeed, like the Hyde Guidelines, the new CCA profit and loss account was to commence with HC profit before interest and taxation;[36]

(2) would apply only to listed companies and other large undertakings – smaller companies would be given guidance on simpler methods of following the principles on a voluntary basis;

(3) would be confined to principles and objectives – guidance notes of a non-compulsory nature would outline methods of implementing the proposals of the Exposure Draft thereby keeping the Exposure Draft relatively simple and free from detail.

The new Exposure Draft – *ED24, Current Cost Accounting* – published in April 1979 generally conformed to the statement of intent. One significant (albeit ambiguous) departure, however, could have implied that CC and HC accounts were of equivalent status. For those companies to which the Exposure Draft applied, the current cost accounts were to be included in the annual financial statements 'in addition' and not necessarily 'supplementary' to the historical cost accounts.

Apart from meeting most of the commitments in the statement of intent, the proposed standard attempted to remove other criticisms of the earlier CCA Exposure Draft. Firstly, many of the pronouncement's potential critics were probably disarmed both by the ASC's admission, in introducing the Exposure Draft, that no agreed solution on the price-level accounting system to replace the traditional historical cost system had been reached in any part of the world, and by its declaration that the aim of the Exposure Draft was to propose a practical and workable standard which would be a move forward in the evolution of the subject. The impression that the ASC did not regard the Exposure Draft as its final thinking on the subject was clear. Many of the commentators on the Exposure Draft expressed their approval of this approach and encouraged flexibility and experimentation.

Secondly, the asset valuation method in *ED24* was far less complex than the *ED18* proposal, the controversial and complex deprival concept being excluded and the simpler 1976 Australian proposals adopted. Value to the business was now defined as net replacement cost or, if a permanent diminution in the value of the asset to below net replacement cost had been recognised, the greater of the net realisable value of the asset and, where applicable, the amount recoverable from its further use.

Thirdly, the new Exposure Draft had a clearly defined income concept. (*ED18*, it will be remembered, had been severely criticised for the lack of an explicit definition of income.) The proposed income measure was not, however, without its problem and most of the criticisms of *ED24* concerned its measure of profit. Current cost operating profit was deemed (para. 5) to be 'the surplus after allowing for the impact of price changes on the funds needed to continue the existing business and maintain its operating capability'. Operating capability was broadly defined as the 'quantum of goods and services that the business is currently able to supply with its existing resources'. In other words, the *ED24* proposals appeared to seek to maintain a *fund* of wealth for investment in a changing portfolio of assets – an approach seemingly closer to a proprietary view of invested (shareholder's) funds than to a rigid interpretation of the entity concept with its more static view of corporate asset holding.

The basic method of maintaining operating capability had been agreed by the IASG (which produced the Exposure Draft for the ASC) at an early stage in its deliberations. The financial statements prepared under the *ED24* proposals would, like the Hyde Guidelines, present both current cost operating profit and the profit attributable to shareholders. Since, however, opinion on the question of monetary items had 'hardened and become clearer' since the days of *ED18*'s Appropriation Account (Background Papers to *ED24*, para. 17) the 'Hyde' gearing adjustment was split in the manner earlier proposed by Gibbs and considered by the IASG during the preparation of *ED18*. The adjustments for monetary items now consisted of a monetary working capital adjustment (the MWCA, which, together with the by now familiar depreciation and cost of sales adjustments, was charged against operating profit) and a gearing adjustment which reduced the three current cost charges against operating profit by the proportion of long-term borrowings to total long-term financing[37] to arrive at CC profit attributable to the shareholders – a profit deemed to allow 'for the effect of price changes on that proportion of the net operating assets which has been financed by the shareholders' (*ED24*, para. 16).

At this stage it would appear that the ASC had, at least for the time being, abandoned CPP accounting. Real terms accounting was considered to be 'an additional complication' which was 'not generally acceptable' (Background Papers, para. 21). Even *ED18*'s supplementary statement of change in shareholders' net equity interest after allowing for the change in the value of money was not re-introduced in the new Exposure Draft.

While the new proposals took account of the post-Sandilands debate on gearing, the Gibbs method of bringing into profit the realised and unrealised holding gains financed by borrowing was, after considerable discussion, not considered to be sufficiently prudent and was consequently rejected.[38] The Hyde system of adding back only the appropriate proportion of the current cost adjustments to HC profit was retained. This followed 'the long standing convention that major unrealised capital value increases are not shown as part of the annual profit' (Background Papers, para. 103). New ground was not to be broken here.

The Gibbs proposals on the monetary working capital adjustment intended to allow for the effect of price changes in the monetary working capital needed to support the operating capacity of the entity were, however, accepted.[39] In order 'to limit the subjectivity involved' (*ED24*, para. 12) monetary working capital was to be considered to be trade debtors less trade creditors. While consideration was given to defining monetary working capital in terms of 'the net total of current assets and liabilities' (presumably with the exception of stock) it was decided that such a definition 'could take the result too far from the basic concept and in particular could allow the inclusion of overdrafts that in effect represented quasi-permanent finance' (Background Papers, para. 100). Consequently, overdrafts and cash balances were ultimately excluded from the MWCA for businesses other than financial institutions except where it could be shown that their exclusion was misleading.

The MWCA probably caused the IASG and the ASC more problems than any other aspects of the Exposure Draft. The presumption that cash balances and bank overdrafts would be excluded from monetary working capital resulted in two anomalies. Firstly, the MWCA could obviously be manipulated if companies switched the financing of their stocks from trade creditors to the bank. Secondly, the proposal that cash and similar assets excluded from the monetary working capital adjustment should be deducted from long-term liabilities before the gearing adjustment was calculated could, on occasion, result in a surplus of monetary assets over liabilities. Such a surplus was considered to represent funds that were not part of the operating assets and which, consequently, were surplus to requirements or held for investment in operating assets that would ultimately extend the entity's present operating capacity (Morpeth, 1981). Therefore, despite the fact that cash holdings would undoubtedly be losing value in times of rising prices, no adjustment was to be made.

Not surprisingly, the two adjustments for monetary items attracted some adverse comment in the submissions to the ASC on *ED24*. In general, however, it appeared that the major companies, professional accounting firms and the six accountancy bodies which were represented on the ASC were favourably disposed towards the Exposure Draft. Table 6.7 which shows the response of a sample of the 248 replies to *ED24* received by the ASC (i.e. those responses of preparers and auditors of accounts most likely to be affected by an accounting standard based on the *ED24* proposals) reveals that 83 per cent of our sample broadly supported the Exposure Draft: 78 per cent of the 32 companies listed in the first 100 of *The Times* 1000[40] and eight of the top ten accounting firms were supportive (albeit with some reservations).

Table 6.7. *Depth of support for and opposition to the* ED24 *proposals*

	No.	Explicit support %	Qualified support %	Qualified opposition %	Explicit opposition %
CCAB bodies	6	33	67	—	—
Top ten practising firms of accountants	10	40	40	20	—
Top '100' companies	32	31	47	13	9
Representative bodies	5	100	—	—	—
Total	53	40	43	11	6

Support was also forthcoming from all five of the influential representative bodies sampled, namely the CBI, the three major finance directors' groups[41] and the Society of Investment Analysts.

As mentioned above, adverse reaction was, however, evident with regard to the two adjustments for monetary items – the monetary working capital (MWCA) and gearing adjustments. In all six of the top ten accountancy firms, three of the six accountancy bodies comprising the CCAB and thirteen of the 32 of the top 100 companies made adverse comments about the monetary working capital adjustment, while five of the accounting firms, three of the CCAB bodies and thirteen companies seemed to dislike the proposed gearing adjustment.

The dispute over the MWCA centred on the definition of monetary working capital. The omission of bank overdrafts (opposed by five of the top ten accounting firms, three of the accountancy bodies comprising the CCAB and nine of the companies) and cash (opposed by six of the accountancy firms, three of the accountancy bodies and ten of the companies) from the definition was opposed on both practical and theoretical grounds. Some of the respondents also attacked the failure to take account of the loss on holding 'surplus cash' during a period of inflation when no gearing adjustment was made as a result of cash holdings exceeding long-term liabilities.

The gearing adjustment itself was also criticised on conceptual grounds. Two of the accountancy bodies, seven companies and two of the accountancy firms called for further consideration of the proposal to base the adjustment on the full revaluation surpluses and not merely on the depreciation, cost of sales and monetary working capital adjustments. Other critics called either for the abandonment of the adjustment or for a more flexible approach until a consensus on the type of adjustment was reached.

Apart from the debate on the two adjustments for monetary items, the Exposure Draft was relatively uncontroversial. There was, however, a certain element of unease at the divergence between the entity-based proposals of the ASC and the more proprietary-orientated draft standard of the FASB (1978b). Several companies called for the need for international harmonisation on the subject; two of the top ten UK accounting firms called for further research on the proprietary *v.* entity capital maintenance argument, while one accountancy firm and two major companies (Distillers and Shell) called for the maintenance of shareholders' capital as opposed to the maintenance of a company's operating capability.

The opposition to the Exposure Draft was, however, relatively muted in comparison to that evident on the publication of *ED18*. While differences in approach were preferred by many commentators the opponents of the proposed system were neither so numerous nor so vociferous as in the past. The scene was finally set for the UK's first CCA standard.

5 The UK's first CCA Standard – SSAP16

The statement of standard accounting practice resulting from *ED24* – *SSAP16, Current Cost Accounting* (March 1980) – closely followed the thrust of its preceding exposure draft. As before, the scope of the Standard was limited to listed and other large companies and *ED24*'s four adjustments to HC profit re-appeared albeit with certain amendments. A major alteration, however, was the elucidation of the ambiguously worded proposal in the Exposure Draft that the CCA statements should be issued *in addition to* (presumably meaning either 'supplementary to' or 'as the equivalent of') HC statements. The Standard now gave companies the option to choose either CCA accounts or HC accounts as their main financial statements.[42]

Three of the major criticisms of *ED24* were examined by the IASG and the ASC in producing the Standard although in only one instance did the standard setters move their position. Firstly, the argument that bank overdrafts and cash balances should be included in working capital was partially accepted.[43] The Standard now required that the portion of overdrafts and cash arising from fluctuations in the volume of debtors, stocks and creditors was to be considered part of monetary working capital.

While the change of emphasis was undoubtedly welcome there were those who argued that it would lead to disputes between auditors and companies over the fluctuating portions of bank overdraft or cash while others argued that in times of inflation the loss on holding any cash balances whether held for day-to-day operations or for precautionary or speculative purposes should be included in operating profits.

The latter viewpoint was considered in the second change from *ED24*. Where no gearing adjustment was made because cash balances not included in monetary working capital were in excess of long-term liabilities, entities were encouraged to include in the notes to their CCA statements information on any changes in the value to the business of such 'excess' cash and in its effective purchasing power. No adjustment to profit was, however, to be made. In explanation *SSAP16* stated that such excess monetary assets were not part of the net operating assets for the purposes of the Standard and were not covered by 'the current cost framework' being more in the nature of assets held for investment. The problem, while identified, had not been solved – largely because the ASC had not had the opportunity to re-expose a proposed solution to the 'complex issues' (as it termed them) raised. In this area at least the inflation accounting debate in the UK will continue.

The third area of criticism explicitly considered by the ASC was the gearing adjustment. Here the ASC held fast to its original solution. Two counter proposals were suggested to the ASC:

(1) that the adjustment should be based on the year's revaluation surpluses whether realised or unrealised (the realisable holding gain approach); and

(2) that companies should be allowed to use whatever version of the gearing adjustment they regarded as being appropriate – this viewpoint being reinforced by the argument that other contentious aspects of the Standard encouraged a certain element of discretion (e.g. the MWCA) whereas the gearing adjustment proposed allowed no flexibility.

At the height of the argument support for the ASC position came in the form of the December 1979 CICA Exposure Draft *Current Cost Accounting* which adopted a gearing adjustment (termed a financing adjustment in the CICA Draft) similar to that of the ASC – previously the Canadian proposal had been expected by many in the UK to endorse the realisable holding gain approach but the prospect of introducing into the financial statements 'a significant element of income that is based on amounts that are unrealised and (are) perhaps subject to a significant degree of uncertainty' (CICA, 1979, para. B.42) proved too much for the CICA. A further weapon – the need for international harmonisation (albeit still not with the USA) – was now added to the ASC armoury and helped the Committee to overcome its critics.

Despite further pressure from the Technical Committees of both the English and Scottish Institutes the ASC reiterated its belief;

(1) that the cash flow approach, the prudence concept and the EEC Fourth Directive all demanded that a credit should not be taken to profit until it was realised (thereby preventing the realisable holding gain approach with its unrealised revaluation surpluses being adopted); and

(2) that comparability demanded that companies should use the same basic adjustment and that no major deviations from the prescribed treatment should be permitted. (A minor concession was made of suggesting that different gearing adjustments, with accompanying explanations, could be shown in the notes to the accounts.)

Another optional note to the accounts suggested in *SSAP16* highlighted a difference between *SSAP16* and its predecessor *ED24*. While the Exposure Draft had dismissed Real Terms accounting, *SSAP16* (para. 36) proposed the disclosure of a statement of the change in shareholders' equity interest after allowing for the change in the general purchasing power of money; a statement similar to both the CCAB's 'Initial Reactions' to the Sandilands Report and to *ED18*'s statement of change in shareholders' net equity interest. Such a statement, it was believed, would be of interest to some users, particularly in situations where excess monetary assets deemed not to be part of the operating assets of the enterprise existed or where part of a group of companies had investment activities exempt from the requirements of the Standard. It appeared, therefore, that a recognition was growing that the limitations of the operating capacity capital maintenance concept might require the disclosure of other methods of accounting for the effect of price-level changes.

When *SSAP16* was issued the ASC stated that it accepted that *SSAP16* was not the final answer to the problem of accounting for inflation and that the Standard would need careful monitoring resulting in appropriate revisions – the need for revision being balanced against the need for reasonable stability: three years being believed to be appropriate. In the event the experiment with *SSAP16* came close to ending prematurely. In July 1982 history almost repeated itself. Keymer and Haslam, the instigators of the ICAEW's 1979 Special Meeting which spelt the demise of *ED18* had called another Special General Meeting of the ICAEW at which was put the motion 'that members of the ICAEW deplore the introduction of *SSAP16* and call for its immediate withdrawal.' On this occasion the motion was narrowly defeated (by 15,745 votes to 14,812).[44]

An analysis of those voting would prove to be an interesting research project. Many would not have had to produce CCA accounts, some may not have been fully aware of the substance of *SSAP16*, some may simply have been registering a protest against the accounting establishment. Nevertheless, at the time of the voting it appeared that a great deal of opposition still existed both to aspects of *SSAP16* and more probably still to the concept of inflation accounting itself. This is not unduly surprising. The CCA debate has led to several different recommendations being proposed within a brief period – a fear may well exist that the profession is unable to produce an acceptable means of accounting for inflation in the short term and that yet more changes may be on the way. Additionally, the usefulness of CCA may seem to many to have lessened. For example, the annual inflation rate as measured by the retail price index had fallen from over 26 per cent p.a. in September 1975 (the date of the publication of the Sandilands Report), to under 9 per cent p.a. at the time of the 1982 Special Meeting. More importantly, the Government was showing no inclination to base corporate taxation on CC accounts – a major inducement to change in the post-Sandilands era.[45] Neither, with the abolition of price controls by the Conservative Government, was there an obvious need for CC information to enable companies to obtain price increases. For the preparer of CC accounts the cost factor may well have appeared to outweigh the benefits. For the user it was probable that the accounts were still a novelty and their value relatively obscure.

6 Recent developments

At this point the debate in the UK rested. Having (if the Sandilands Report is included) seen a different inflation accounting proposal in every year between 1973 and 1980 with the sole exception of 1978, the UK profession appeared to be determined to leave *SSAP16* virtually unchanged until at least 1984 (although it was proposed, but never implemented, that additional CCA standards dealing with subjects such as comparative figures and with entities excluded from the scope of *SSAP16* should be introduced before then).[46] The aim was to give preparers and users an opportunity to gain experience in dealing with the practical problems posed by *SSAP16* and in interpreting the information provided.

A working party, latterly under the chairmanship of Tom Neville, Finance Director of Vickers, was set up in November 1980 and consulted a wide range of users, preparers and auditors of *SSAP16* accounts. Much later a series of research projects sponsored by the ICAEW and under the direction of Professor Carsberg was commissioned to assess the usefulness of CCA in terms of its cost and benefits.

The interim report of the Neville working party was published in April 1983 (The Final Report published September 1983 had similar conclusions and recommendations) and concluded *inter alia* that:

most people believe that pure historical cost accounts are unsatisfactory at a time of significant price changes;

only a small number of preparers and auditors believed that *SSAP16* should be left substantially unamended;

although a majority of users would be content to let *SSAP16* stand for some years without major amendment, they, in fact, made little use of *SSAP16* information (a small minority of users made substantial use of CCA information);

there was no consensus among those who were unhappy with both *SSAP16* and pure HC accounts as to what should follow *SSAP16*;

the inclusion of two sets of accounts in the annual report was widely regarded as confusing and bringing the profession into discredit (although many thought the provision of supplementary information was unavoidable for the foreseeable future in the absence of a consensus on accounting for price-level changes);

the depreciation and cost of sales adjustments were nearest to commanding general support in principle – the monetary working capital and gearing adjustments commanded less support;

a CCA balance sheet was regarded by many people as misleading; and

small businesses appeared to be almost unanimously opposed to any extension of *SSAP16* to them.

In the absence of the results of the ICAEW research studies, not due until later in 1983, the ASC Sub-Committee responsible for drafting the successor to *SSAP16* (the Inflation Accounting Sub-Committee)[47] was greatly influenced by the recommendations of the Neville working party, by an inflation rate low by recent standards, and by the fear that opposition to CCA might force yet another Special Meeting of the ICAEW and end the CCA experiment in the UK.

The main recommendations of the Neville Working Party were:

the new inflation accounting Standard should apply to *all* entities whose accounts were intended to give a true and fair view;

the Standard should require accounts to show the effects of changing prices when these effects were material;

different methods of calculating changing prices should be allowed; and

a price-level adjusted balance sheet should not be required.

The ASC's Inflation Accounting Sub-Committee was divided in its view on one of these recommendations. A majority agreed with the view of the Neville Working Party that *SSAP16*'s successor should apply to all companies. A minority (among whom was one of the present authors) opposed the principle of 'universality', as it had been termed, on the grounds that a standard applying to *all* companies would have to be of a low basic level to encourage general compliance and would not advance the experiment in the UK but it could even end it.

Three main arguments lay behind this view. Firstly, larger companies, faced with a freedom to account for price-level changes as they wished, could ignore the complexities of accounting for price-level changes by adopting simplistic methods; secondly, as complaints from users and auditors grew about the discretion allowed (a major objection, it will be remembered to *ED18*'s appropriation account) the proposed standard could be rejected. For comparative purposes, users would have to be content with the lowest common denominator of diverse voluntary approaches. Thirdly, further research into the benefits of CCA for users of the accounts of smaller companies (especially those with few share-holders) was required before such companies were encouraged to meet the costs of implementing a system of price-level accounting, however simple.

Despite these views, the successor to *SSAP16* began to develop on the lines of the Neville Report. Initially, it was proposed that a single adjustment, which could be the aggregate of several different adjust-ments, should be made to the HC profit and loss account with a corresponding entry in the balance sheet. The composition of the adjustment was to be explained in the notes. The proposal, however, ran into difficulties with the provisions of the 1981 Companies Act which did not allow unrealised gains to be included in income and could therefore have prevented certain companies, had they so wished, from showing the real gains on their assets in their income statement or, indeed, could have prohibited the use of a gearing adjustment based on realisable holding gains of the type proposed by Godley and Cripps. (The Act would, however, have allowed note disclosure of unrealised gains.)

Latterly, the proposed standard has become even more flexible. Companies are simply required to account for price-level changes if the effect of inflation is material, and to disclose the method of accounting for the changes. While the proposal has at the time of writing still to be ratified by the ASC, the immediate future of the inflation accounting experiment in the UK is uncertain.

The long-term difficulties, as we discuss further in Chapter 14, do, however, remain. These problems, the disputes over basic concepts and the growing quest for international harmonisation (especially between the UK's entity and the USA's proprietary approaches), almost certainly mean that the debate in the UK is far from over – whatever form the successor to *SSAP16* takes.

Appendix to Chapter 6: inflation accounting steering group problem areas

Preliminary list – 6 January 1976

1   Relevance of CCA and CCA/CPP to the users of published accounts as identified by *The Corporate Report*
2   Scope – which organisations should be covered
3   Valuation of assets
4   Calculation of depreciation
5   Valuation of stock
6   Calculation of cost of sales adjustment
7   Distributable profit: need to define?
8   Legal implications
9   Valuation of liabilities
10 Valuation of marketable and unquoted securities
11 Associates
12 Subsidiaries
13 Overseas assets and operations
14 Problems of special groups
15 Liquidity – should companies publish a statement on the adequacy of cash resources?
16 Goodwill and other intangibles
17 Format of CCA
18 Comparative figures
19 Publication of interim statements
20 Calculation of deferred tax
21 Treatment of realised holding gains
22 Audit implications of proposed standard on CCA
23 Retention of historical cost figures
24 Compatibility of CCA/CPP with:
    (a) 4th Directive (draft)
    (b) IASC
    (c) ED/SSAP of overseas accountancy bodies
    (d) Overseas legislation

(e) UK Stock Exchange requirements
(f) Overseas Stock Exchange requirements
25 Impact of proposed SSAP on CCA on other standards issued by ASSC

7

Inflation accounting in the USA (1975–80)

1 Introduction and over-view

In Chapter 3, we traced the history of inflation accounting in the USA from the end of the Second World War to the end of 1974, when an exposure draft by the Financial Accounting Standards Board proposed a CPP system based on historical cost. However, it was also pointed out that the Chief Accountant of the Securities and Exchange Commission had expressed a preference for a replacement cost system, so that the seeds of the American contribution to the 'Current Cost Revolution' had already been sown. In August 1975, the SEC took the crucial step of announcing its intention of requiring certain replacement cost data as supplementary disclosures to the published accounts of large listed companies. This was duly enforced for accounting periods ending on or after 25 December 1976.

The result of the SEC's action was to delay the FASB's plans for CPP accounting. Although the SEC had maintained its neutrality with respect to the merits of CPP, the effort of implementing the SEC's replacement cost requirements was likely to prevent the implementation of CPP, and, in addition, it was necessary to consider how the new information should (if at all) be related to the CPP proposal, which had been conceived in relation to the traditional historical cost system. It should be noted that the FASB is in a weak position in any possible disagreement with the SEC, since, as the independent, privately sponsored standard-setting body, it derives its authority ultimately from the acceptance of its pronouncements by the government agency, the SEC, which has the power, under the Securities Acts of 1933 and 1934, to determine the content of financial statements issued to investors by corporations subject to its jurisdiction (about 10,000 of the leading corporations in the USA).

The FASB continued with its field tests of the CPP proposals, publishing the results in May 1977. On a conceptual basis, the fundamental issue of measurement was examined in a Discussion Memor-

154

andum, *Conceptual Framework for Financial Accounting and Reporting: Elements of Financial Statements and Their Measurement*, published in December 1976. This was followed, in December 1978, by a new exposure draft, *Financial Reporting and Changing Prices*, with an exposure period ending in May 1979. This compromised between the FASB position of 1974 and the SEC position of 1975 by allowing each enterprise to choose between presenting supplementary statements on either a CPP basis (the FASB's original position) or on a current cost basis (partly similar to the SEC requirements, but with an important technical difference between replacement cost and current cost which will be discussed later). This was followed, in March 1979, by a Supplement on *Constant Dollar Accounting*, which amended the CPP system proposed in the 1974 Exposure Draft, incorporating some of the lessons learned from the field study.

After receiving written comments and the preliminary reports of six special industry task groups, and holding a conference and public hearing on the Exposure Drafts, the FASB published *Statement of Financial Accounting Standards No. 33, Financial Reporting and Changing Prices* (commonly referred to as *FAS33*) in September 1979. This abandoned the 'either, or' approach of the 1978 Exposure Draft and instead required unaudited supplementary information on *both* a CPP and a CCA basis, but stopped short of requiring that the two bases should be combined in a 'real terms' solution. This was the first mandatory accounting Standard dealing with inflation accounting in the English-speaking world (*APB Statement No. 3* having been only a recommendation and the UK's *PSSAP7* having been only provisional) but it contained the seeds of further change.

In the short term, there was the problem of specialised assets, such as oil and mineral reserves, which did not lend themselves easily to the current cost system proposed in *FAS33* and were the subject of a further exposure draft, *Financial Reporting and Changing Prices: Specialized Assets*, April 1980 and the issue, later in the same year, of three additional standards, *FAS39*, *FAS40*, and *FAS41*. The SEC had once more intervened by insisting on its own requirements (SEC, 1978) for 'reserve recognition accounting' (RRA), an attempt to estimate economic value for oil and gas reserves (it had, on the other hand, agreed to waive its replacement cost requirements for those companies complying with the current cost requirements of *FAS33*). The subsequent discussion of the relative merits of RRA and current cost revealed a certain degree of ambivalence in the FASB's interpretation of its own current cost system, although the SEC has subsequently moderated its advocacy of RRA.

155

The specialised assets issue revealed one of the longer-term developments implicit in *FAS33*, namely the clarification and possible extension and amendment of the current cost valuation base. On a conceptual level, this is likely to be affected by the future developments of the FASB's conceptual framework project. On a practical level, it will be affected by future attitudes of the SEC, and also by the experience of preparers and users of accounts prepared under the *FAS33* conventions. The FASB has embarked upon a major research project to evaluate this experience (FASB, 1981a). Another issue which must inevitably arise is the relationship between CPP and CCA. At present, these are required as alternatives, although experimentation with combinations of the 'real terms' variety is encouraged. After a period of experimentation, a 'real terms' solution might emerge, but alternatively a choice might be made between CPP and CCA. Present indications (as of 1983) are that a current cost/constant dollar system (a real terms system) would be preferred to a historical cost/constant dollar system were such a choice to be made (Freeman, 1983), and a pure CCA system is unlikely to be favoured in view of the FASB's preference for a real financial measure of capital (FASB, 1981b).

The remainder of this chapter will review these developments in more detail, particularly with respect to the theoretical arguments supporting them, in the hope of obtaining a greater insight into both the present state of practice and the possible future developments. Firstly, we shall consider the SEC intervention requiring replacement cost; then, successively, we shall review the current state of affairs, and the likely future developments implicit in the FASB's conceptual framework project and the SEC's current attitude.

2 The SEC replacement cost requirements, 1975–76

In a speech given on 30 May 1974 (and subsequently published in February 1975) the Chief Accountant of the SEC, John C. Burton, outlined his preference for a replacement cost approach to the problem of accounting for inflation. Although this speech carried the customary disclaimer that it did not necessarily represent the views of the SEC, its arguments were entirely consistent with the replacement cost requirements which were subsequently proposed by the SEC (2 August 1975), and it is therefore worth some attention. A similar set of arguments had been advanced by the Chief Accountant in a paper published in November 1974 (Burton, 1974).

The central objective of financial accounting was assumed to be that stated in the Trueblood Report (1973), to provide users with information relating to 'earning power . . . defined as the enterprise's cash generating ability' (Burton, 1975). Thus, the centre-piece of financial reporting was the income statement rather than the balance sheet. The income statement should be based on the matching principle, the central object of matching being to provide a good indication of current 'cash generating ability'. There is an obvious similarity here to Schmalenbach's much earlier pleas for 'dynamic accounting'. However, the Chief Accountant did not share Schmalenbach's view that this end would be well-served by historical cost accounting, adjusted, in times of inflation, by CPP methods. His view was that inflation distorts costs: 'matching historical monetary costs against current revenues will not give a good approximation of the long-run average net cash inflows at current activity levels . . .'. Costs were to be viewed as specific to the firm, so that historical cost adjusted to CPP units (called PuPU, or Purchasing Power Units by the Chief Accountant) were not adequate. Reference was made to the recent (1973–74) increase in oil prices, at a rate much more rapid than that of the general price level, to illustrate the potential inadequacy of CPP-adjusted historical cost as an indication of the current costs of a specific firm whose input costs did not follow the pattern of the general price index. The Philips system was quoted as a working example of a replacement cost system which matched current revenues to current costs. The only use envisaged for CPP (or PuPU) measurement was in the case of dividends, in which CPP measurement might be useful in giving the investor a view as to how well his dividend income has maintained its real purchasing power. Finally, although the balance sheet was not a central concern, and replacement cost in the balance sheet was not a measure of the value of the enterprise's assets, replacement cost could be used as an approximation to economic value and was probably better for this purpose than historical cost or CPP-adjusted historical cost.

This argument has the virtue of at least attempting a theoretical justification of the replacement cost method, based upon the objectives stated in what, at the time, was the most recent and authoritative professional statement on the subject (Trueblood Report, 1973). However, the conclusions are assertions rather than inferences logically derived from the assumptions. For example, 'long-run average cash flows at current activity levels' is a concept which needs precise definition to give it real meaning and a much more tight set of assumptions for it to be obtained from a replacement cost system. Specific issues requiring clarification are whether 'cash flows' are defined in nominal terms or in units of constant purchasing power (presumably the former), whether inflation is expected to continue (if it is, maintenance of current cash flows measured in nominal terms would be an inadequate bench-mark) and if so, at what rate, and what is the anticipated relationship between the firm's future costs and future prices (if prices will rise in proportion to costs, the current cash flow might be regarded as a 'real terms' cash flow in the sense that it will increase in the future in proportion to inflation). It should, of course, be recognised that the Chief Accountant's speech and articles (Burton, 1974 and 1975) were for a fairly broad audience and such precise analysis might be inappropriate in this particular context. However, it would have been reassuring if he had been able to refer to work which did justify his conclusions, but this was not the case. Nor did the subsequent SEC proposals or the discussion of them lead to any such work. The academic work available, such as that by Revsine (1973) and Kennedy (1976), suggests that the Chief Accountant's arguments were, in fact, of much narrower validity than their confident pronouncement suggested since they depended upon restrictive assumptions about future price changes.

At the end of June 1975 an official announcement was made (*Journal of Accountancy*, June 1975, p. 3) that the SEC intended to release a proposal requiring certain companies to disclose supplementary replacement cost data. The detailed proposals were released on 21 August 1975, only a few days before the publication of the Sandilands Report in the UK (5 September), with a comment period expiring on 31 January 1976. They became the basis of *Accounting Series Release No. 190*, issued on 23 March 1976.

The essential proposals in the August 1975 Release were as follows. Certain replacement cost data were required to be disclosed by way of footnote. The disclosure was to be required (initially at least) only of large firms (who could more easily bear the cost) and it was to be unaudited (as a concession to the 'soft' nature of replacement cost data). The essential data required were current replacement costs of inventories (disclosing the excess of market value over replacement cost, where this was material) and fixed assets appearing in the balance sheet, and the current replacement cost equivalent of cost of goods sold and depreciation charges shown in the income statement. Replacement cost data were not required for land (which does not depreciate) or for assets which were not necessary for the continuing operations of the business.

The wording of the release indicated some anxiety concerning the relationship of the SEC's replacement cost approach to the CPP approach favoured by the FASB. Reference was made to the fact that *Accounting Series Release No. 151*, in January 1974, had urged the supplemental disclosure of profits on holding inventories but had met with little response. By pointing out that this Release had indicated the SEC's preference for replacement cost disclosure nearly a year before the FASB issued its CPP Exposure Draft, it was possibly hoping to disarm the possible criticism that it was now (August 1975) effectively countermanding the FASB's proposed solution to the inflation accounting problem. This wish to avoid overt conflict with the FASB is apparent in the SEC's emphasis on the partial nature of the replacement cost data required, and the statement that consideration of a change to a comprehensive system of replacement cost accounting must await the results of the FASB's conceptual framework project. The SEC was also careful to emphasise the fact that a CPP system, such as that favoured by the FASB, could be applied to a replacement cost base just as easily as to an historical cost base.

The reasons given for the proposals in the SEC's August 1975 release were entirely consistent with the views of its Chief Accountant, discussed earlier. The 'objective . . . is to improve investment decision-making, it . . . will also be useful to managers for internal purposes and to macro-economic decision makers'. In the latter context, the possible uses of replacement cost for tax purposes was mentioned, and reference was made to The Mathews Report, in Australia, which had recently advocated a replacement cost basis for measuring taxable income. It was claimed that the central purpose of accounts was 'to give investors information about the current economics of business operations rather than the value of business assets'. Thus, replacement cost was required to give an accurate picture of the 'cost of maintaining the operating capability' of the firm, to be charged to the profit and loss account;[1] any benefits in the form of improved balance sheet valuations were of secondary importance.

After considering 350 letters of comment on the August Release, the SEC issued *Accounting Series Release No. 190* on 23 March 1976. This enacted all of the basic proposals made earlier, effective for financial statements for fiscal years ending on or after 25 December 1976. Three concessions were made. The size qualification, which had previously been left undefined, was set at a level which made the new disclosures apply to only the very largest companies, for whom the cost of disclosure was alleged to be small relative to the potential benefits, SEC registrants with 'inventories and gross property, plant and equipment which aggregate more than $100 million and which comprise more than ten per cent of total assets'. Secondly, a 'safe harbor' rule was proposed to protect preparers of replacement cost data who had exercised 'reasonable care' and 'good faith' against possible legal penalties resulting from its inaccuracies. This made some allowance for the 'soft' nature of replacement cost data. A third concession to criticism was a delay of one year in the application of the rule to mineral resources and certain foreign assets. An advisory committee was set up to assist in implementation, and the experimental nature of the new disclosures was emphasised, considerable flexibility being permitted.

The theoretical arguments of *ASR190* were those rehearsed earlier:

> Its primary objective, as articulated in the adopted rule, is to provide investors with meaningful additional information not otherwise available about the current economics of a business as a supplement to historical cost data. A secondary objective is to provide data about the current cost of inventories and productive capacity at the balance sheet date. These are the principal operating assets of many businesses. It is recognized that replacement cost does not always measure the current economic values of such assets, but in most cases it is a reasonable approximation.

No evidence was offered for the *ex cathedra* statement in the final sentence.

The next paragraph contains a statement which, with hindsight, was portentous:

> The Commission views its rule as *a first step in a process of providing more meaningful disclosure* about current economic costs and values to investors. It believes that the rule will encourage meaningful experimentation with the various approaches to providing such information and . . . it will assist the FASB in addressing the broad conceptual and practical issues involved. (Our emphasis)

Although the SEC was clearly anxious to be seen to be encouraging the work of the FASB (*ASR190* repeats the previous arguments that its proposals were not in conflict with the FASB's CPP Exposure Draft of 1974), it was also clearly willing to force change in directions which it considered appropriate when the FASB did not seem to be acting quickly enough.

A most important question about the SEC's intervention is why it happened. The SEC claimed to be acting in the interests of investors and there was a clear need from the investor's standpoint, to reflect the effects of inflation on the individual firm by the reporting of specific price changes. As the SEC pronouncements of the period make clear, there is no necessary contradiction between replacement cost accounting, or other systems based on specific prices, and CPP. The SEC was not, therefore, overrruling the FASB's proposals, but it was changing the order of priorities, since it was unlikely that companies could cope with *ASR190* and a new CPP Standard at the same time, so that CPP would have to be deferred. However, current value accounting had been on the agenda of professional standard-setting bodies since the late 1940s and its importance had been underlined by the Sprouse and Moonitz study of 1962, but it seemed to be no nearer to implementation or even experimentation. CPP had also been on the agenda for many years and had emerged for serious professional consideration in 1963 (in *ARS6*), but it had come much closer to professional implementation (recommended by *APB3* in 1969, and promulgated as an FASB Exposure Draft in 1974), admittedly with little development or serious discussion. It is likely that CPP, in its objective but somewhat mechanical use of general indices, was seen by SEC as the system which was easiest for the accounting profession but perhaps the least relevant to the investor: *ASR190* points out that 'the effect of inflation on monetary assets and liabilities can be approximated from data now publicly available'.

The view that CPP was seen as a proposal which suited the accounting profession but not other interested parties, is supported by the fact that only a minority of companies, the preparers of accounts, appear to have preferred CPP. Watts and Zimmerman (1978) report that only eighteen of 53 submissions by companies on the FASB Exposure Draft favoured CPP. This is very similar to the minority supporting the *ED8* proposals for CPP in the UK. Much research remains to be done on the public records of the FASB and the SEC to establish the nature and source of the opposition to the CPP solution, but, on the basis of the evidence currently available, it seems likely that only professional accountants were definitely in favour of CPP, and even within the profession there were some distinguished dissenters (e.g. Arthur Andersen & Co. and Touche Ross & Co. stated publicly that they were in favour of current value accounting in the USA). Thus, SEC had ample support for its intervention in *ASR190*.

The weight of the current academic writing in favour of current value accounting must also have had some influence with SEC (whose Chief Accountant came to SEC from an academic post), and the developments in Australia (whose Mathews Report is specifically referred to in *ASR190*) and the UK (whose Sandilands Report was available in draft when the SEC's intervention was announced) must also have lent support to the replacement cost proposals. Equally, the Trueblood Report (1973) in the USA had pointed the way to forward-looking, value-oriented accounting.

However, the strongest influence on the SEC possibly came from political quarters within the USA. The SEC is ultimately responsible to Congress, and is therefore subject to political pressure from that source. The 1970s saw a steady increase in the SEC's activity in relation to financial reporting.[2] Previously its attitude had been relatively passive, delegating to professional bodies most of the work of setting standards. This change of attitude may partly reflect the changing characters of SEC Chief Accountants, but it also reflects (as does the choice of Chief Accountant) the increasing concern of government and politicians. Clear evidence of this concern was provided in 1975 by a vote of Congress which required SEC to determine by December 1977 a set of accounting practices for crude oil and natural gas companies: the SEC was encouraged to rely on relevant standards developed by FASB, but if FASB failed to act, the SEC would clearly have to take the initiative. In 1976, the pressures from Congress became even more obvious. A Congressional sub-committee chaired by Rep. John E. Moss criticised FASB and recommended that SEC prescribe uniform accounting principles. Another sub-committee, chaired by Senator Metcalf, criticised the accounting profession and questioned its independence. In the light of this type of pressure,[3] the SEC's intervention in *ASR190*, and its subsequent interventions relating to inflation accounting (described below) may be seen as restrained attempts to prompt the FASB to take action which was essential if direct action by Congress was to be avoided.

Thus, the SEC's intervention in 1975–76 can be viewed as being consistent with the 'Current Cost Revolution' elsewhere in the English-speaking world. As in the other countries, a form of current cost accounting (replacement cost in the case of the USA) supplanted the CPP/historical cost solution preferred earlier by the accounting profession. Equally, the change was due to the direct intervention of the Government (through the SEC), as was also the case in the UK (the Sandilands Committee), Australia (the Mathews Committee) and New Zealand (the Richardson Committee). The motivation behind government intervention requires further investigation, but all of these countries were facing similar problems of inflation at the time and it seems that there were probably common factors influencing governments, e.g. a distaste for CPP as a basis of taxation. Furthermore, in both the UK and the USA, there are indications that there was little support for CPP outside the accounting profession, so that government intervention may have been seen as being in the interests of the community, simply as a means of providing users with financial reports which they considered to be relevant to their needs. Of course, the international parallels are by no means perfect, e.g. the SEC's requirements were for partial supplementary replacement cost data for very large companies only, whereas the Sandilands Report proposed that the main accounts of all companies be on a current cost basis. However, the international parallels are more striking than the differences.

3 The FASB response: development of the conceptual framework to December 1976

In November 1975, the FASB deferred a final Statement on CPP accounting, pending the analysis of the results of the field tests which it was conducting (finally published in May 1977), based on the 1974 Exposure Draft.

> In June 1976, the Board deferred action on its Exposure Draft on general purchasing power accounting pending further progress on its project on a conceptual framework for accounting and reporting. The Board concludes that general purchasing power information was not sufficiently understood by preparers and users, and the need for it was not sufficiently demonstrated to justify imposing the cost of implementation upon all preparers of financial statements at that time. Another consideration was the effort required at that time of many of the largest corporations in providing the current replacement cost data required by the SEC. (FASB Exposure Draft, *Financial Reporting and Changing Prices*, 28 December 1978, para. 47, p. 29)

Thus, the FASB bowed to the pressure exerted by SEC, and deferred a decision on accounting for changing prices until the conceptual framework project could shed some light on the matter. This was, of course, the direction indicated by SEC in *ASR190*.

The next significant action by the FASB was the publication, on 2 December 1976, as part of the conceptual framework project, of three documents, *Scope and Implications of the Conceptual Framework Project, Tentative Conclusions on Objectives of Financial Statements of Business Enterprises*, and a Discussion Memorandum, *Conceptual Framework for Financial Accounting and Reporting: Elements of Financial Statements and Their Measurement*. The Discussion Memorandum was the most important from the point of view of accounting for changing prices, as it dealt directly with measurement issues and the written comment and public hearings held upon it in 1977 were subsequently used as background to the Exposure Draft of December 1978.

The 'Elements and Measurement' Discussion Memorandum makes a fundamental distinction between two conceptual views of earnings: 'the asset and liability view' and 'the revenue and expense view'. The former measures earnings in terms of changes in the net economic resources of the enterprise, and therefore regards the measurement of assets and liabilities as fundamental. The latter measures earnings as the difference between revenues and expenses, and the measurement and matching of these two elements becomes critical, so that it is acceptable to accrue deferred charges as assets even when they do not represent economic resources which would command a value in the market place. A third view is that the balance sheet and income statement should not necessarily articulate, so that there is no necessary conflict between a current value balance sheet and the 'revenue and expense view' of income. The Discussion Memorandum offers a variety of definitions of the various elements of financial statements (assets, liabilities, revenues and earnings) based upon one or other of these fundamental concepts of earnings, but without attempting to express a preference. It also deals with alternative concepts of capital maintenance, making the fundamental distinction between financial capital maintenance (maintaining a sum of money value or purchasing power) and physical capital maintenance (maintaining the physical assets or operating capacity of the business).

After brief consideration of the qualitative characteristics of financial information, in Part II, with emphasis on the trade-off between relevance and reliability, the Discussion Memorandum, in Part III, goes on to present alternative measurement systems. The crucial question of the measurement unit is discussed, CPP accounting being based on units of general purchasing power, in contrast to the nominal unit of money used traditionally. Finally, five measurement systems are discussed:

(1) historical cost;
(2) current cost;
(3) current exit value in orderly liquidation;
(4) expected exit value in due course of business;
(5) present value of expected cash inflows.

Although no attempt is made to choose between these alternative systems, the discussion being confined to the enumeration of their merits and deficiencies, it will be observed that four of the five are current value systems. Furthermore, the discussion of basic earnings concepts had emphasised that the 'asset and liability view' of earnings would tend to be associated with a preference for current value systems of measurement. Thus, the possibility of current value accounting emerges clearly from the Discussion Memorandum, although no recommendation is made. The case for current value was strengthened in 1977 by the issue of an exposure draft (FASB, 1977b), subsequently revised, which took the 'asset and liability view' of earnings.[4]

The 'Tentative Conclusions on Objectives' document also had a bearing on the evolution of the FASB's attitude to accounting for changing prices. This was the outcome of the response to the FASB's 1974 Discussion Memorandum (FASB, 1974b), which threw open for discussion the objectives of financial statements suggested by the Trueblood Committee (1973). The 1976 'Tentative Conclusions on Objectives' adopted the general approach adopted by Trueblood, the main conclusions being:

(1) That 'financial statements of business enterprises should provide information . . . that is useful to present and potential investors and creditors in making rational investment and credit decisions'. (para. 8).
(2) 'Financial statements should provide information that helps investors and creditors assess the enterprise's prospects of obtaining net cash inflows through its earning and financing activities' (para. 14), since this will, in turn, enable the investor or creditor to assess the prospective returns to his investment.
(3) 'Financial statements . . . should provide information about the economic resources of an enterprise, which are sources of prospective cash inflows; its obligations to transfer economic resources to others, which are causes of prospective cash outflows; and its earnings, which are the financial results of its operations and other events and conditions that affect the enterprise.' (para. 16).

These objectives of financial statements were subsequently reiterated in *Statement of Financial Accounting Concepts No. 1, Objectives of Financial Reporting by Business Enterprises*, November 1978. Although no direct conclusion for valuation is drawn from these objectives, they clearly point to a forward-looking, economic decision-oriented system of accounting which seems more likely to encompass current values than the traditional historical cost system.

4 The 1978 Exposure Draft

In December 1978, the FASB issued its Exposure Draft, *Financial Reporting and Changing Prices*. This was the FASB's first pronouncement on the subject since the SEC issued *ASR190*, and it bore the marks of a compromise between the FASB's earlier (1974) CPP position and the SEC's obvious determination to insist upon some form of current cost accounting. In fact, the compromise was not a very subtle one: large, publicly-held enterprises[5] were to be required to provide supplementary information about the effects of changing prices on income from continuing operations, but were to be given a choice of providing this *either* on a CPP basis *or* on a current cost basis. Those choosing the current cost basis would also be required to present information on holding gains or losses, net of inflation (thus introducing an element of 'real terms' accounting), and a statement of the current cost of inventory, property, plant and equipment at the end of the accounting period (thus providing partial balance sheet information on a current cost basis). Each enterprise would also be required to disclose separately the inflation gain or loss on net monetary items and the gain or loss on foreign exchange. A five-year summary of selected financial data would also be required. Current cost methods were to be encouraged whenever current cost adjustments had a material effect on income. The current cost information would be shown at current or 'lower appropriate value', where 'appropriate value' was net realisable value when the asset was about to be sold, or value in use if the asset was to be retained for use in the business. Current cost itself was defined as the cost of the asset actually held, not the cost of another asset which might be an appropriate current replacement. A supplement (discussed in the next section) elaborated on the apppropriate methods of CPP adjustment. The exposure period expired on 1 May 1979, and implementation was proposed for fiscal periods ending on or after 25 December 1979.

The essential reason given for the Board's position was that, in accordance with the objectives of financial reporting adopted as part of its conceptual framework, 'the Board believes that supplementary information on the effect of changes in specific prices is likely to provide an improved basis for the assessment of future cash flows' (p. iii). However, the information should be supplementary because 'recently, something close to a consensus has emerged in the United States on two matters: no major changes should be made in the financial statements at this time, but something must be done to augment the typical content of financial reports so as to provide more information about the effect of price changes' (p. iii). The evidence for this 'consensus' was presumably the written and oral submissions received concerning the December 1976 conceptual framework publications. Despite the fact that 'all enterprises' were 'encouraged' to present current cost data (para. 25, p. 9), this was not mandatory, the choice of current cost of CPP being left to the preparers of financial statements. The reason given for this (para.

58, pp. 33–4) was 'the general lack of experience with constant dollar accounting and with the methods involved in the measurement of current costs'. The proposals of the Exposure Draft were intended to initiate a process of experimentation as to the feasibility and usefulness of alternative methods of reporting the effects of changing prices. This, in turn, was expected to lead to further developments in accounting standards, and the possibility of supplanting the traditional historical cost methods in the main accounts was not excluded (para. 57, p. 33).

One issue upon which the Exposure Draft did reach a firm conclusion was the concept of capital maintenance: 'The Board has concluded that the financial capital concept is the more useful, and it is adopted in this Statement' (para. 6, p. 3). Thus, 'the physical productive capacity concept of capital' was rejected, and it became possible, under the financial capital concept, to recognise holding gains as part of income. The requirement that holding gains be measured in real (CPP) terms as well as in money terms, implied a preference for the real financial capital concept, expressed in CPP units rather than nominal monetary units whose real value would decline in a period of inflation (para. 75, pp. 45–6). This preference for a financial concept of capital and for dealing with the effects of inflation by applying a general index, implied that the USA would diverge from those other countries, such as the UK, which had preferred a current cost solution, with a physical capital maintenance concept and no form of general index adjustment. These latter countries attempted to introduce the gain on borrowing by means of a gearing adjustment, and this type of adjustment has not been considered as a serious possibility in the USA, because it is alien to the financial capital maintenance concept. In *FAS33* (1979b), the FASB softened its opposition to the physical capital concept, but more recently (FASB, 1981b), it has returned to a position of clear preference for the financial rather than the physical concept.

The selection and definition of the current cost concept was of considerable interest, because the FASB's concept was different from that proposed by the SEC in *ASR190*. Whereas the SEC concept had embraced the replacement cost of the productive capacity in its most economical currently available form, the FASB concept was based upon the current replacement cost of the specific asset used up. The SEC concept, therefore, might require a further adjustment to make it suitable for incorporation in an income statement which reported current expenditure on labour and other factors of production, since this expenditure would, presumably, change due to substitution between factors of production if the assets actually used were replaced by their most economic currently available substitutes (item (e) of rule 3.17 of

ASR190). The FASB proposal, on the other hand, was suitable for application in an income statement which included other currently used productive factors. Current cost was modified to be 'value to the business' by being reduced to value in use, for assets retained for use, or resale value, for assets to be sold, when these values were lower than replacement cost. It was alleged (paras. 77 and 78, pp. 47–8) that this modification improved the usefulness of current cost as an indication of the 'cash flow potential of an asset'. This use of current 'value to the business' as an indication of cash flow potential was presumably intended as a justification for its usefulness in the balance sheet. The use of current values in the profit and loss account was justified (para. 70, pp. 41 and 43) as a means of achieving 'current matching': 'Current measurements provide useful information about the amount of operating income earned by an enterprise from continuing operations.' The precise reasoning behind this (i.e. why the information is useful) was not spelled out, but presumably has its roots in the ability of current operating income to provide a guide to future cash flow potential.

In summary, the Exposure Draft made several important innovations. Its explicit preference for current cost on a 'value to the business' basis was the first pronouncement from a US standard-setting body, other than the SEC, in favour of current value accounting. The clear preference for financial rather than physical capital maintenance put the USA on a path different from that preferred at the time by the UK and a number of other countries. The advocacy of experimentation[6] was sensible in the circumstances and pointed the way to further evolution. The potential weaknesses of the Exposure Draft were the piecemeal nature of the data required (e.g. a fully adjusted supplementary balance sheet was not required), and the large amount of latitude allowed in choosing between the current cost and the CPP methods. This entailed the danger that preparers would choose their method in order to present their affairs in a favourable light. It also meant that one, and possibly both, of the alternative methods might not be given a fair trial.

5 The field study and the Supplement on Constant Dollar Accounting

On 2 March 1979, the FASB published its Supplement to the December 1974 Exposure Draft, *Constant Dollar Accounting.* This provided the modifications and elaborations of the 1974 CPP Exposure Draft which were considered necessary in the light of the FASB's field study, which had been published in May 1977.

The Field Test was based on restating the accounts of 101 companies in CPP terms, as specified in the 1974 Exposure Draft, for the fiscal

years 1972, 1973 and 1974. It had three objectives: to discover conceptual difficulties, implementation problems, and the materiality of the
adjustments. Three areas of conceptual difficulty were identified: the
classification of deferred income taxes as a non-monetary item (more
than half of the field-test companies queried this); the classification of
items denominated in foreign currency as non-monetary items (35 of the
101 companies raised this issue); and the recognition in income of the
purchasing power gain or loss from monetary items (the main objection
being to the inclusion in income of gains on long-term debt). The
implementation problems were mainly concerned with the dating
('aging') of the acquisition of assets held, a problem which is particularly
important when a CPP system is initially established, and with the
construction of appropriate short-cut methods of estimating the relevant
information (based on various averaging procedures). The results of the
Field Test adjustments served amply to demonstrate the materiality of
the adjustments: the apparent performance of individual firms or
industrial groups was, in many cases, changed drastically, as a result of
substituting the adjusted data. A variety of accounting measures was
used to demonstrate this result, including net income, gain or loss on
monetary items, rate of return on equity, dividend payout ratio,
debt/equity ratio, book income tax rate, and depreciation.

The Supplement to the 1974 Exposure Draft incorporated the Board's
response to the field tests and the submissions received. The main
amendments to the 1974 proposals were:
(1) The index to be used for constant dollar accounting would be the
Consumer Price Index for All Urban Consumers (CPI-U). Previously, the GNP Implicit Price Deflator had been advocated. The
main reason for the substitution was that the CPI-U was published
more frequently (monthly instead of quarterly), as is the case in the
UK, where the retail price index was selected for the *PSSAP7*
adjustments.
(2) Claims denominated in terms of foreign currency should now be
classified as monetary items. This was one of the issues raised by the
field study, although the Board's adoption of the new proposal was
less than enthusiastic:

> Although the nonmonetary classification may be technically
> preferable, and result in somewhat different disclosures, as a
> practical matter the monetary classification produces essentially
> the same net effect on aggregate disclosure as restating those
> foreign currency items as nonmonetary and then reducing them
> to their net realizable value. The monetary classification

169

obviates that two-step procedure and is more understandable. (para. 4, p. 2)

(3) Deferred income taxes were to be classified as monetary items. This was also an issue raised by the Field Test, and again the Board's support for the change was qualified, the non-monetary classification being 'technically preferable', but

> the monetary classification provides a more practical solution and identifies the effect of inflation with the period the inflation occurs, rather than with the period the deferred tax item is reversed. (para. 5, p. 3)

There were a number of proposals of a more technical nature, to implement the terms of the 1978 Exposure Draft on *Financial Reporting and Changing Prices*. In particular, comprehensive restatement (as proposed in the 1974 Exposure Draft) was no longer required, constant dollar disclosure being confined to the income statement. The requirement for gains and losses on monetary items to be stated separately from operating income (as in the 1978 Exposure Draft) dealt with the final conceptual objection raised in the field study, that such gains and losses should not be regarded as part of income.

In summary, the 1979 Supplement at least broke the tradition of blindly copying the *ARS6* proposals (as had been done by *APB3* and by the 1974 Exposure Draft), but it did not produce any cogent arguments for the changes which it proposed, these being justified mainly on pragmatic grounds.

6 FAS33

In addition to issuing the two Exposure Drafts (December 1978 and March 1979), the FASB set up six special industry task groups for banking and thrift institutions, forest products, insurance, mining, oil and gas, and real estate, in order to establish the particular problems of measurement and disclosure which might be faced by these industries, in the application of the proposals for reporting the effects of changing prices. These groups held public hearings and issued Preliminary Reports, early in 1979. Public commment was invited on the Preliminary Reports and on the two Exposure Drafts, and 450 written comments were received. A Conference on Financial Reporting and Changing Prices was held in New York City on 31 May 1979 and, in the following month, public hearings were held on the Exposure Draft. Discussions took place between the FASB and the SEC, concerning the relationship

between the FASB's planned proposals and the SEC's *ASR190* requirements and the SEC's Reserve Recognition Accounting (RRA) requirements for oil and gas companies.[7] Out of all this activity emerged, in
September 1979, the USA's first Standard[8] on *Financial Reporting and
Changing Prices, FAS33*. This also had the distinction of being the first
effective Standard on the subject in the English-speaking world, since
the UK's *PSSAP7* (1974) and the 1976 Australian current cost standard
had only been provisional and were subsequently withdrawn, and the
Hyde Guidelines (1977) were merely 'an interim recommendation'.
SSAP16 was not issued in the UK until March 1980, six months after
FAS33.

The contents of *FAS33* represented a number of important changes of
the proposals of the December 1978 Exposure Draft. The most important of these was the removal of the choice of basis for the supplementary statement: *both* current cost *and* CPP data were now
required. As a result of the deliberation of the special industry task
groups, companies engaged primarily in the exploitation of natural
resources or the ownership of income-producing real estate property,
were exempt from the current cost requirements of *FAS33* but were
subject to special requirements published in 1980. These are the subject
of a later section of this chapter. The gain or loss on items denominated
in foreign currencies was no longer required to be reported separately
but was aggregated with other 'monetary' gains and losses.

Otherwise, the supplementary disclosure requirements of *FAS33*
followed substantially those of the December 1978 Exposure Draft. The
CPP information did not require comprehensive restatement and, in
particular, did not require a stabilised balance sheet: a restated income
statement was required, with the gain or loss on net monetary assets
shown separately. The current cost adjustments were confined to inventory, property, plant and equipment used in the operations of the
business. Statements were required of income from continuing operations on a current cost basis, the current cost amounts of inventory,
property, plant and equipment at the end of the fiscal year, and changes
during the year in the current cost amounts of these items, net of
inflation. The current cost concept was, as in the Exposure Draft, based
upon replacement cost of the actual assets held and used, modified to
'value to the firm' by applying what was now called 'recoverable
amount' (net realisable value of items to be sold or net present value of
items to be retained) when this was less than replacement cost. The use
of specific indices was permitted in the calculation of current cost, and a
statement was required of the basis of the current cost calculations,
together with a brief comment on their interpretation. Flexibility and

171

experimentation in presentation was still encouraged, and a volume of examples of illustrative disclosures and their interpretations was published separately (December 1979). A five-year summary of selected financial data would be required. The effective date was for fiscal years ended on or after 25 December 1979 (as in the Exposure Draft), although publication of current cost data could be delayed for one year.

A review of the Standard was promised within five years of its publication. The current cost proposals were made subject to the SEC rescinding its *ASR190* requirements for replacement cost (para. 18, p. 7), and the SEC subsequently complied with this requirement. The requirements of the Standard were restricted to large, publicly-held companies (as defined in the Exposure Draft), although other companies were encouraged to comply on a voluntary basis. *FAS33* was supported by five of the seven members of FASB. Of the two dissenting members, one was in favour of current cost disclosure but not CPP, whereas the other was in favour of CPP disclosure but not current cost. This demonstrates the division of opinion which led the Board to require disclosure of both current cost and CPP information.

FAS33 is accompanied by an exceptionally long statement of the 'Basis for Conclusions' (Appendix C, paras. 87–207, pp. 43–100). On a theoretical level, the argument starts (para. 95) from the three basic objectives stated in December 1976 (quoted earlier) and reiterated in *Concepts Statement 1*. From these, it derives (para. 94) the view that the information required by *FAS33* will be useful in four ways:

'a.   Assessment of future cash flows.' Current cost data are alleged to be useful in this context.

'b.   Assessment of erosion of operating capability.' Current costs are also alleged to be useful in this context.

'c.   Assessment of financial performance.' Disclosure of the effects of price changes is alleged to be useful here in showing the 'result of holding assets while their prices increase' and 'may provide an improved basis for assessing the worth of the enterprise'.

'd.   Assessment of the erosion of general purchasing power.' Here, general purchasing power adjustments may be useful to the investor by providing 'an improved basis for assessing whether an enterprise has maintained the purchasing power of its capital'.

A notable retreat by the Board on the theoretical front is its abandonment of its previously stated preference for the financial concept of capital:

> In the Exposure Draft, the Board expressed its conclusion that the financial capital maintenance concept is more useful than

the physical capital maintenance concept. It has subsequently concluded that it should express no preference for either concept at this time and that enterprises should present information that would enable users to assess the amount of income under both concepts. (para. 104, p. 53)

However, the Board's preference for the financial concept has since been reaffirmed by the 1981 conceptual framework Exposure Draft (FASB, 1981b).

Several arguments are advanced for not permitting choice between current cost and CPP. These include the need for both types of information to be available for comparative purposes if their relative usefulness is to be evaluated, the reduction in the burden of producing current costs data if it is compensated by exemption from the SEC's *ASR190* requirements, and the fact that the two types of information are complementary rather than competitive (it should be noted that this is inconsistent with the view that a choice should be made between the two). Another important practical factor was the deep division of opinion amongst the FASB's constituency, users tending to prefer current cost, but many preparers and public accounting firms supporting a CPP solution (para. 112, p. 56); there is an obvious parallel between these attitudes and those of respondents to *ED8* in the UK, which were reported in Chapter 4.

The essential principle upon which *FAS33* is based is that there is a deep division amongst preparers and users as to the appropriate method of reporting the effects of changing prices, and that this division will be best resolved by experimentation and the consequent accumulation of experience of both the preparation and the use of different types of information. The prognosis for the success of this experiment is made more favourable by the requirements that both CCA and CPP information should be produced, as a supplement to the traditional historical cost statements: this is a distinct improvement on the original Exposure Draft (1978) proposal that a choice should be allowed.

However, the supplementary disclosures required by *FAS33* may not have been well conceived as a basis for experimentation. The partial nature of both the CCA and the CPP requirements, and, in particular, the confinement of CCA to a restricted range of assets and the lack of a CPP balance sheet, might be thought to give neither system a proper trial. Equally, *FAS33* contains the essential components of a 'real terms' income measure, which might seem to be the obvious means of reconciling CPP with CCA, rather than regarding the two systems as competitive, but the permissive nature of the *FAS33* format for pre-

173

sentation means that it is unlikely, in many cases, that a figure for 'real terms' income can be derived easily from the statement. A format which would permit this is allowed, and even encouraged, but is not mandatory. Whether this matters or not depends on the sophistication of users of financial statements but such studies as are available (e.g. Lee and Tweedie, 1981) suggest that even institutional investors may require help in interpreting financial statements, especially novel ones which deal with reporting the effects of changing prices.

The theoretical arguments advanced by FASB in support of *FAS33* (Appendix C) may also be unhelpful in encouraging the debate towards a clear judgement as to the best available method of reporting the effects of changing prices. A variety of arguments is recited in support of a variety of measures, and these are used to illustrate the deep division of opinion amongst users and preparers, and to bolster up the case for experimentation rather than a firm decision. However, more might have been done to evaluate the alternatives and perhaps to indicate those which, on *a priori* grounds, seem less likely to be useful: in this respect the abandonment of the Exposure Draft's clear preference for financial capital maintenance might be regarded as a step backwards. Although there clearly was a deep division of opinion, and the cooperation of users and preparers is important, it might be hoped that the FASB would make a more positive attempt to provide normative guidance as to the methods which should be given most attention. One possible interpretation of the FASB's position is that it is moving towards the Edwards and Bell approach of providing a variety of useful measures, expressed in both real and nominal measurement units. This would be a theoretically defensible position, but if that were the true position of the FASB, it might be expected that *FAS33* would give more attention to integrated supplementary statements, reconciling alternative measures (on the lines of Kennedy's, 1978a, appropriation statement), and a much fuller treatment of the use of the 'real terms' approach to reconcile CPP with CCA. Furthermore, the 'Basis for Conclusions' could have been made much more cohesive by using such a framework.

Nevertheless, *FAS33* is undoubtedly an important advance in reporting the effects of price changes, and it contains the seeds of further progress. The first results of the *FAS33* system (as analysed, for example, by Price Waterhouse & Co., 1980) show that a variety of measures of financial performance are drastically different under traditional accounting, CCA and CPP. Thus, the materiality of the new disclosures is not in doubt. Their relevance may be a more difficult matter to establish, especially in view of the bewildering variety of information now available. However, the FASB is carrying out a programme of systematic research to evaluate the results, and this may be expected to make an important contribution to knowledge, as well as to the practicalities of setting future standards in this field (FASB, 1981a).

The future development of inflation accounting in the USA will not, however, depend solely on the empirical evaluation of the results of implementation of *FAS33*. Two important additional influences are likely to be the development of the FASB's conceptual framework, which will set the normative criteria to be adopted in setting and evaluating standards, and the future posture of the SEC, which has made its presence felt on the specialised assets question by its RRA experiment for the oil and gas producing industry, but which has more recently adopted a policy of less intervention. For this reason, the next two sections will consider the conceptual framework and the specialised assets question.

7 The conceptual framework, FAS33 and the future

The FASB describes its conceptual framework as 'a coherent system of interrelated objectives and concepts that is expected to lead to consistent financial sandards. It prescribes the nature, function and limits of financial reporting'. Clearly, the future development of accounting for changing prices must be consistent with this framework.

When *FAS33* was published (September 1979), the conceptual framework was defined by *Statement of Financial Accounting Concepts No. 1: Objectives of Financial Reporting by Business Enterprises* (published November 1978), the Exposure Draft (published August 1979) which preceded *Statement of Financial Accounting Concepts No. 2: Qualitative Characteristics of Accounting Information* (published May 1980), and the revised Exposure Draft, *Elements of Financial Statements of Business Enterprises* (published December 1979, a revision of an Exposure Draft issued in 1977). These may be summarised as follows:

(1) The *objective* of financial reporting (stated in *Concepts Statement No. 1*) is 'directed towards the common interests of many users in the ability of an enterprise to generate favorable cash flows'. Thus information should be directed towards the assessment of future cash flows and the current economic resource of the enterprise.

(2) The *elements* of financial statements to provide such information, defined in the December 1979 Exposure Draft (and subsequently confirmed in *Concepts Statements No. 3*, 1980) include:
    (a) Assets are defined as sources of future economic benefit.
    (b) Comprehensive income is defined as encompassing both operat-

ing income (revenue, less expenses), and other gains or losses (such as holding gains).

(c) 'Earnings' is defined as 'a significant intermediate measure or component that is part of comprehensive income'.

(3) The *qualitative characteristics* of accounting information defined as important in *Concepts Statement No. 2* are primarily relevance and reliability, subject to the constraint that the perceived benefit to the user must exceed the costs of providing the information.

The objectives had not changed notably from those stated in December 1976 (discussed earlier) but the shift to comprehensive income in the elements statement was an important new development, signalling an eclectic approach by FASB, embracing a number of alternative income measures (such as the new 'earnings' concept).

The influence of the conceptual framework can be seen clearly in *FAS33*. It is most obvious in *FAS33*'s statement of objectives (paras. 2–5, pp. 1–2), which quotes the objectives set out in *Concepts Statement No. 1*. Four specific uses of the FAS33 information are stated:

(1) Assessment of future cash flows. 'When prices are changing, measurements that reflect current prices are likely to provide useful information for the assessment of future cash flows.'

(2) Assessment of enterprise performance. 'Measurements that reflect current prices can provide a basis for assessing the extent to which past decisions on the acquisition of assets have created opportunities for earning future cash flows.' The growth in value of assets held (holding gain) is to be regarded as 'one aspect of performance even though it may be distinguished from operating performance'. This clearly points to a measurement of 'comprehensive income', as defined in the *Elements* Exposure Draft, and 'operating performance' could be measured by the 'earnings' concept.

(3) Assessment of the erosion of operating capability. 'Information on the current prices of resources that are used to generate revenues can help users to assess the extent to which and the manner in which operating capability has been maintained.' This concedes the potential usefulness of a physical capital maintenance concept.

(4) Assessment of the erosion of general purchasing power. 'Investors typically are concerned with assessing whether an enterprise has maintained the purchasing power of its capital.'

As was pointed out earlier in this chapter, the first three of these uses point to a current cost or current value accounting system, whereas the fourth points to general price-level adjustment (CPP). However, it does not necessarily point to general price-level adjustment of traditional historical cost accounts: if the case for a current valuation basis were accepted, CPP adjustments could be made to CCA data to produce a measure of 'real terms' income, within the comprehensive income framework.

One reason why *FAS33* stopped short of complete fulfilment of its objectives within the comprehensive income framework may be found in another part of the conceptual framework, the qualitative characteristics of accounting information defined in *Concepts Statement No. 2.* Current cost information has high relevance to the objectives, but lacks reliability, especially in view of the limited experience of its application. This trade-off between relevance and reliability is used to justify both the supplementary nature of the *FAS33* disclosures, and their experimental nature (paras. 6–15, pp. 3–6).

This reasoning carries with it the implication that the accumulation of experience in preparing and using the supplementary information may lead ultimately to current cost supplanting the traditional historical cost basis of the main accounts. In order to do this, current cost must pass the tests of relevance and reliability. Of these, reliability is the more obvious but also the one which is more likely to be overcome by the accumulation of experience: for example, there are signs that the experience of producing information to satisfy the SEC's *ASR190* has eased the problems of complying with the current cost requirements of *FAS33*.

The problem of relevance may ultimately prove to be more serious. The essential problem is whether current *cost* adequately reflects changing *prices* or meets the stated objectives, which often seem to imply current *values*, e.g. if 'future economic benefit is the essence of an asset' (*Elements* Exposure Draft, para. 104). *FAS33* argues for 'value to the firm' rather than a strict current cost concept, and argues that in the cases in which current replacement cost (rather than the 'recoverable amount') is 'value to the firm', replacement cost is a good surrogate for economic value. Thus it is claimed that the *FAS33* disclosures are relevant as value measures, although the theoretical literature on the surrogate hypothesis does support this view only under very restrictive circumstances. A separate use of the current cost disclosures is in measuring operating profit (what Schmalenbach would have called a dynamic measure aimed at measuring maintainable flows, as opposed to the static value measure, aimed at measuring assets). *FAS33* discreetly drops the discussion of 'current matching' which was in the earlier (1978) Exposure Draft on *Financial Reporting and Changing Prices*, but the concept is still implicitly present in objectives (1) and (3) above. There are difficult conceptual problems here, some of which were brought out in the Board's discussion (August 1980) of specialised assets. Several Board members asserted strongly that current cost accounting was not a system of value accounting, but merely a method of up-dating costs, yet their own conceptual framework (and part of the arguments in *FAS33*) seems to imply that assets should reflect economic value, not cost, where there is a difference between the two. Furthermore, the FASB concurred, without overt criticism, in SEC's proposal for RRA for oil and gas companies (discussed in the next section of this chapter), which was clearly an attempt at economic valuation of reserves. This confusion over basic concepts must be resolved before current cost, or any other alternative, can supplant historical cost as the basis of the main financial reports.

Another development implicit in the conceptual framework, and capable of more immediate implementation than the supplanting of historical cost, is the development of an integrated statement of 'comprehensive income'. Such an approach would allow the various specific price and general price-level adjustments to be made within the same income statement, together with the holding gains and losses which are, at present, left as isolated items of information. This is already encouraged in the 'reconciliation method' demonstrated in *FAS33* and its supporting illustrative booklet. The exact form of the comprehensive income statement might depend partly on the response of preparers and users to the *FAS33* experiment, but the de-emphasis of the 'bottom line', which is the essence of the comprehensive income approach, might make agreement on form more easy than in a system which attempts to define a single 'correct' earnings figure in the bottom line. The FASB's ongoing conceptual framework study of earnings may also be expected to be relevant to the future form of the income statement. The Exposure Draft, *Reporting Income, Cash Flows and Financial Position of Business Enterprises*, published in 1981, reaffirmed the FASB's view of the importance of comprehensive income. It also saw the reaffirmation of the FASB's support for the financial rather than the physical view of capital: support which had seemed to waver in some of the proposals of *FAS33*.

Further developments are implicit in the FASB's conceptual framework paper, *Invitation to Comment, Financial Statements and Other Means of Financial Reporting*, May 1980. This reasserts the primacy of relevance and reliability, subject to the constraint of costliness. It also discusses three important questions:
(1) What should be reported?
(2) Who should report?
(3) Where should it be reported?
Its reasoning provides justification for *FAS33*'s confinement of its

disclosure requirements to larger companies (answer to question (2)) and to supplementary statements (question (3)). However, should the reliability problem and the costliness be reduced by the accumulation of experience, it is possible that the answer should change and that *FAS33* should apply to smaller companies (perhaps all listed companies, as envisaged by the 1974 CPP Exposure Draft). If relevance were also established, the *FAS33* disclosures might ultimately be made in the main accounts rather than supplementary statements, although this would put greater responsibility on auditors, who, at present (under *Statements on Auditing Standards* Nos. 27 and 28) are required to carry out only 'limited procedures' to check apparent compliance with the supplementary requirements.

8 Specialised assets and reserve recognition accounting

FAS33 exempted from its current cost provisions certain industries which owned so-called 'specialized assets'. Originally six special industry task groups had been set up to consider the implications of the 1978 Exposure Draft, but two industries, banking and insurance, were brought within the provisions of *FAS33*, on the grounds that 'the general provisions of that Statement are useful and applicable' in these industries, the main issue being the materiality of current cost in these cases, rather than its relevance. The remaining four industries, forest products, mining, oil and gas, and real estate were adjudged to present special problems for current cost accounting and were the subject of a supplementary Exposure Draft, *Financial Reporting and Changing Prices: Specialized Assets*, published in April 1980, and, subsequently, of three supplementary Statements, *FAS39, FAS40* and *FAS41*, published in October and November 1980.

The specialised assets question is of interest from two distinct points of view. Firstly, it provided a rigorous test of the FASB's conceptual thinking in *FAS33*, since it dealt with a particularly difficult set of cases. The process of arguing out these cases revealed differing opinions among Board members and provided revealing case studies of the type of thinking which influenced the Board's decisions. Secondly, the oil and gas industry was already subject to special accounting requirements by the SEC, and the SEC's attitude to the FASB's deliberations showed its continuing determination to guide and, if necessary, to direct the FASB towards providing current value information which the SEC perceived as being in the interests of users of accounts.

The SEC's intervention in requiring special accounting information

179

concerning oil and gas reserves originated in the Energy Policy and Conservation Act of 1975, which mandated the SEC to prescribe accounting practices to be used in the preparation of financial information by oil and gas producers. In August 1978, the SEC decided to consider a new method of accounting, reserve recognition accounting (RRA) for oil and gas reserves. This was implemented, as a result of a decision made in December 1978, with effect for fiscal years ending after 25 December 1978. The most important feature of RRA, for our present purposes, is that it requires disclosure of the present value of future net revenues from estimated production of proved oil and gas reserves. The 'soft' nature of net present values is alleviated to some extent by the disclosure of various physical production, reserve and discovery data, and by closely prescribing the method by which present value is to be calculated, e.g. the rate of discount is prescribed, and no allowance is to be made for future price changes. In September 1979, the RRA system was extended, with effect for fiscal years ended on or after 25 December 1979, from being a mere reserve disclosure system, to being the basis of supplementary operating statements for oil and gas producing activities. There was to be a three-year experimental period, during which 'the information generated and the experience gained from the presentation of this supplemental summary will provide much of the basis for an eventual decision by the Commission as to whether RRA should be required as the accounting method for the primary financial statements of oil and gas producers' (SEC *Annual Report*, 1979, p. 28). The introduction of net present values into financial statements was a bold experiment which could only have been initiated by a body like SEC, with authority conferred by the Government, rather than one like FASB which has to earn its authority by gaining the consent of a wide constituency of interested parties, including the accounting profession.

The FASB's Exposure Draft on specialised assets (April 1980) concluded that the general guidelines of *FAS33* on current cost accounting were applicable to specialised assets. However, it conceded that the balance of relevance and reliability might be different in the case of certain specialised assets. In particular, current cost might be very difficult to establish (and therefore less reliable than in the case of other assets) and also might not represent an option which the firm would realistically consider (making it less relevant), since natural resources tend to be unique and not strictly replaceable in their present form. To overcome this difficulty, the FASB Exposure Draft developed a concept of 'fair value':

> Fair value is the exchange price that could be reasonably
> expected in an arms-length transaction between a willing buyer
> and a willing seller. (para. 25, p. 11)

Fair value was to be used to supplement current cost data in the cases of specialised assets for which it was thought to be relatively reliable and relevant.

In the case of oil and gas producers, current cost data were still required, despite the obvious difficulty of calculating them, as illustrated by the 'full cost *v.* successful efforts' controversy.[9] Segmental data for oil and gas production were also required, on both current cost and on the basis used in the main financial statements, but the most important new proposal was for the disclosure of the 'fair value' of reserves, and changes in fair value during the fiscal year. The FASB also expressed its intention to work with the SEC to obtain agreement on disclosures relating to oil and gas reserves. However, the 'fair value' proposals were based upon current market values, not upon discounting expected future net receipts, so that there was a distinct difference between the SEC and FASB approaches.

Fair values were also to be disclosed for growing timber and income-producing real estate, but mining companies were not required to provide fair value data, on the ground that the technical reliability of mineral-reserve data was low. Instead, mining companies were to provide production and price data, and estimated quantities of reserves. All of these types of companies were to provide current cost data, despite their unreliability (e.g. growing timber takes many years to reach maturity, and this raises the problem of adding interest charges to accumulated costs) and possibly low relevance (natural resources are rarely replaced by very similar assets).

The 'Basis for Conclusions', Appendix C of the Exposure Draft, recites the measurement problems of current cost in each industry and fails to establish the relevance of current cost to the achievement of the objectives of Statement 33 (assessment, respectively, of future cash flows, maintenance of operating capability, financial performance, and maintenance of general purchasing power). It is therefore not surprising that some members dissented from the Exposure Draft's proposals for current cost disclosure, preferring to regard fair value as a substitute for current cost, rather than a complement to it.

The FASB received written comments on the specialised assets Exposure Draft and held public hearings in New York City in July 1980. The clear message emerging from the public hearings was, with the exception of the valuation of real estate, a general anxiety about fair value and particularly its 'soft' nature, emphasis being put on its subjectivity, its sensitivity to volatile market conditions, and possible misunderstanding by users. Several commentators preferred the disclosure of basic data which was relevant to the calculation of fair value, rather than the publication of a single estimate of fair value which might be misleading. There was also a natural reluctance, particularly on the part of preparers, to contemplate fair value for oil and gas reserves at the same time as the SEC's RRA experiment was being conducted. The deficiencies of current cost measurement for specialised assets were also widely recognised, several commentators remarking that some form of indexed historical cost was probably the only feasible method.

The FASB discussed the specialised assets Exposure Draft, in the light of these comments, in August 1980. It was apparent that the SEC had indicated that it was not willing to abandon its RRA experiment for oil and gas companies, in favour of the FASB's proposals (current cost and fair value) and this was a material factor in the FASB's deliberations. It was decided to abandon the fair value disclosures for oil and gas producers, on the ground that fair value fails the reliability test in this industry, as in mining. The burden of the SEC's RRA experiment was also taken into consideration. The current cost disclosures were to be retained, despite their difficulties, as were the segmental data on oil and gas production. The Exposure Draft's proposals for mining (current cost, quantity of reserves, and price data) were also adopted. These proposals for oil and gas and mining were implemented in *FAS39*, issued later in October 1980.

Subsequently (February 1981), the SEC moderated its RRA stance by announcing that it did not see a future rôle for RRA in primary (as opposed to supplementary) statements and would support an FASB initiative to devise an integrated reporting package for oil and gas enterprises. The FASB then issued *FAS69* in December 1982. This modified the *FAS39* requirement by allowing historical cost/constant dollar adjustment as an alternative to current cost valuation of oil and gas reserves, but required supplementary disclosures about the volume of reserves and an estimate of the present value of future cash flows from the reserves (which had been the essence of the RRA method). Three Board members (including the Deputy Chairman) dissented from *FAS69*, mainly because the proposed disclosures involved highly subjective estimates and were a clear departure from the valuation principle of *FAS33*. It remains to be seen whether the SEC will now abandon its own RRA requirements, although this seems likely.

Inflation accounting in the USA (1975–80)

The main difficulties in the FASB's earlier (1980) discussions had related to forestry and real estate. In the case of forest products, the FASB research team proposed that current cost should be abandoned, in view of the unresolved difficulties surrounding interest charges. The Exposure Draft had recommended that current costs of growing timber should ignore interest charges on the specious grounds that the asset was usually equity financed. In practice, since the essence of timber production is that it involves growth over a long time period, during which the passage of time adds to the physical quantity of reserves, it would seem appropriate to include interest charges in the current cost valuation: certainly a replacement purchase in the open market would have to compensate the seller for his interest in the same way as for other costs.[10] This point was made by several commentators on the Exposure Draft. It might be thought that the use of fair values would circumvent this difficulty, and avoid the problem of deciding what interest rate was appropriate. However, the FASB research team proposed that fair values should be encouraged but not made mandatory, for forestry reserves, because of their lack of reliability (e.g. recovery costs vary greatly with location). The Board members were anxious about the apparent inconsistency in abandoning current cost for forestry but not for oil and gas and mining, which also faced problems, and it was finally decided to retain the current cost requirement for forestry, whilst adopting the proposal to reduce fair value to an optional experimental disclosure. The Standard which was issued in November 1980 (*FAS40*) provided relief from the burden of estimating current cost by allowing a choice of current cost or CPP in forestry.

The greatest controversy was that concerning real estate. The research staff proposed that investment properties should not be subject to the current cost disclosure requirements of *FAS33* (although development activities would still be subject to these requirements). In its place, fair value would be required as being both relevant and reliable for this particular industry. A number of Board members expressed strong opposition to the abandonment of current cost in this industry, for two broad reasons. Firstly, there was an understandable anxiety that, by abandoning current cost for this industry, FASB would seem to be giving way to a particular industrial pressure group and would encourage further pressure from other industries which had unsuccessfully sought special treatment. Secondly, and much more important from a conceptual point of view, there was a strong belief that the adoption of fair value to the total exclusion of current cost would be fundamentally inconsistent with the *FAS33* model. It was asserted that the *FAS33* system was an updated cost approach (perhaps implying the 'current matching' interpretation, discussed earlier), whereas fair value is a method of value accounting. In fact, *FAS33* does contain an important value element, because it values assets at recoverable amount when this is less than current cost. It could be argued that, for many investment properties, fair value is likely to be close to the figure which would arise from the strict application of the *FAS33* valuation rules. This discussion of the valuation of investment properties provided a clear demonstration that the Board members were not unanimous in their reasons for supporting *FAS33* or their interpretation of its implications. As a result of the discussion, it was resolved to retain the *FAS33* current cost disclosures with fair value as an additional requirement in the case of investment properties. As with forestry, the Standard (*FAS41*) which was issued later in 1980 allowed a choice *either* of current cost *or* of CPP data for real estate.

Two other specialised assets amendments were subsequently made to *FAS33*, in March 1981 and January 1982. The first of these (*FAS46*) exempted motion picture films from the current cost requirements, allowing historical cost/constant dollar valuation as an alternative, on the ground that the specific replacement cost of a film is difficult to estimate and of dubious relevance. The second (*FAS54*) exempted investment companies from the disclosures required by *FAS33*, on the ground that the 'fair value' disclosures which they already make are more relevant to the appraisal of their activities. Another amendment to *FAS33* was made by *FAS70* (December 1982), which exempted those enterprises measuring a significant part of their operations in currencies other than the US dollar. This was a consequence of the FASB's new proposals for currency translation.

The discussion of the specialised assets provides a good demonstration of FASB's thinking. The fundamental problems of applying current cost to specialised assets were mainly ones of allocation, e.g. the forestry problem of whether to add accumulated interest to the current cost of growing timber is a time allocation problem, and the oil and gas problem of deciding on a successful efforts or full cost allocation basis is a problem of allocation between different activities. However, Thomas' classic work on the allocation problem was not referred to in the FASB's official pronouncements: the discussion was in more pragmatic terms of weighing relevance against reliability. The solution to the allocation dilemma suggested by Thomas is resort to market values, and fair value could have been justified in these terms although, of course, certain assets are unique and do not have easily ascertainable market values. In this sense, the Board's retreat from fair value and its insistence on allocation-dependent current cost or historical cost/constant dollar methods in all situations (with the exception of investment companies) was a retrograde step.

There is, however, a second important aspect of the specialised assets issue which was discussed at the beginning of this section, namely the rôle of the SEC. The FASB's retreat from fair value in the important oil and gas industry was made inevitable by the SEC's insistence on carrying through its RRA experiment. The SEC clearly intended that its RRA initiative should not be an isolated experiment but should be part of a sustained programme to make financial reporting future-oriented. For example, in commenting on the development of the FASB's conceptual framework project, the 1979 SEC *Annual Report* stated (p. 29):

> The current status of financial reporting of oil and gas producing companies reflects the nature of these issues. The Commission's efforts to develop a more useful method of accounting would benefit from the existence of a conceptual framework. It should be recognised that in developing the concept of reserve recognition accounting, the Commission will, of necessity, have to deal with issues relating to the conceptual framework if they have not, by then, been resolved.

Elsewhere in the same report, there is an indication of the direction in which the SEC felt that concepts and practice should develop, in its section (p. 19) entitled 'Projections of Future Economic Performance', which refers to the Commission's 'new policy of encouraging disclosure of earnings forecasts and other forward-looking information'. Thus, RRA may be viewed as part of a comprehensive policy for achieving future-oriented reporting. This could be much more revolutionary than the current value system which some members of FASB at present regard as too radical. However, the potential pressure from SEC has since been reduced by national political factors. The election of the Republican President Reagan saw the resignation of SEC Chairman Harold M. Williams (March 1981) and his replacement by John S. R. Shad, who was more favourably disposed to self-regulation by the private sector. Since then, the SEC's public posture has been more passive and the recent observations by its Chief Accountant on the *FAS33* experiment reflect this attitude:

> Experience to date with the use of the data hasn't been a resounding success, but the lack of usefulness must be carefully examined lest it be concluded too early that changing prices data isn't needed . . .. Perhaps one thing to be learned from the

Statement No. 33 experiment is that users want data they can readily comprehend. (Sampson, 1983)

Coming from the pen which drafted the RRA proposals, this somewhat tepid support for price-change adjustments suggests a significant change of heart.

9 Conclusion

The recent history of 'inflation accounting' in the USA has seen the subject transform into 'accounting for changing prices', i.e. a form of current cost accounting has been adopted, as has been the case in the rest of the English-speaking world. As has happened elsewhere, government intervention (through the SEC in the USA) has played an important part, but current cost has also received some support from many users and a number of corporate preparers of financial statements. The US position is distinct from that in the UK and some other countries, insofar as CPP has not been abandoned, but is being used as an alternative and, in some respects, as a complement, to CCA. As a result of this, the gearing adjustment and the monetary working capital adjustment have not been discussed seriously in the USA, and seem unlikely to be considered in the future if the FASB maintains its current preference for the financial rather than the physical view of capital (FASB, 1981b).

FAS33 is an experimental proposal, and, when the results have been evaluated, certain changes may be anticipated. Particular changes which seem possible are:

(1) A choice between current cost or CPP or a reconciliation of the two in the form of 'real terms' accounting. At present, the FASB's evaluation project seems to be yielding results which would favour the 'real terms' (current cost/constant dollar) solution (Freeman, 1983).

(2) Development of the valuation basis of the current cost disclosures, possibly to include greater use of current values of the 'fair value' variety or possibly, under the influence of SEC experiment, incorporating estimated present values of the RRA variety. 'Fair value' has now been accepted for investment companies (*FAS54*) and estimated present value for oil and gas (*FAS69*).

(3) Refinement of the capital maintenance concepts, possibly involving a choice between the physical and the financial concept. The most recent published pronouncement of the conceptual framework project (the Exposure Draft, 1981b) suggests a preference for the financial concept, although it also embraces the comprehensive

income approach which can allow the coexistence of alternative concepts.

(4) Less emphasis on the 'bottom line' of the income statement, in line with the comprehensive income concept, which aims to present a variety of useful information about gains during the period, leaving the user of the information freedom to interpret it. This is supported by the 1981 conceptual framework Exposure Draft (FASB, 1981b).

(5) More emphasis on alternative financial statements, such as the funds statement, which is currently part of the FASB's programme. This could be regarded as a natural extension of the comprehensive income approach, and is seen as such by the 1981 Exposure Draft.

(6) Extension of the application of the *FAS33* disclosures or their modified forms to apply to a wider range of companies and possibly to form the main accounts. Such extensions might be justified by the accumulation of experience in preparing the new types of data. This process should reduce the cost, making it economic to provide the new data for smaller companies, and it might also increase the reliability of the data, making them suitable for inclusion in the main accounts, which are subject fo full audit, rather than the superficial audit review required for the present supplementary data.

Thus, the present state of affairs in the United States has substantial further changes implicit in it. The exact course of future events will depend upon the complex interactions of the results of the *FAS33* experiment, the reactions and attitudes of preparers and users of financial statements, the development of the FASB's conceptual framework, and the SEC, whose continuing rôle as guardian of the investor's interests and, equally important but less clearly defined, as agent of the political will of Congress, provides a force for change which is unique to the American situation. The account of the recent history of inflation accounting in the USA, given in this chapter, has, of necessity, been brief and superficial, but it should serve to demonstrate the importance of the SEC as an agent of change during the mid- and late 1970s. The future direction of SEC's influence will depend upon the national political situation and upon national economic factors, notably the rate of inflation. Much important research remains to be done on the precise factors influencing the FASB and the SEC, e.g. analysis of submissions made to both bodies as a result of requests for public comment.

One other factor which is likely to influence developments in the USA

187

is the course of events in other countries, particularly those, such as the UK and Canada, which have close trading links and important cross-country holdings by multinational subsidiaries: international compatibility of accounts for the purposes of consolidation is an important factor in the cost of new forms of financial reporting. The USA has tended to be a world leader in inflation accounting (or, after the current cost revolution, accounting for changing prices), having been a pioneer of CPP (in *ARS6*, 1963, and *APB3*, 1969) and the first country to have a full standard requiring CCA data (*FAS33*, 1979b), but it has also been influenced by events elsewhere. Thus, the SEC, in requiring replacement cost data, quoted overseas developments, such as the Mathews Report in Australia, and the FASB made similar references when it changed its position to include endorsement of current cost (in the 1978 Exposure Draft). It should also be noted that experience gained elsewhere may be transferable to the USA, because accounting is an international profession, and many of its clients are multinational companies. By the same token, events in the USA are likely to influence those in the rest of the world, and the impending appraisal of the five-year *FAS33* experiment suggests that this influence is likely to be significant.

One feature which the development of standards in the USA shares with that elsewhere in the world (such as the UK, reviewed in the previous chapters) is the essentially pragmatic nature of developments and the unsophisticated theoretical level of the discussion in the published pronouncements of the FASB and the SEC. Superficially, this might seem to demote the rôle of the theorist to that of an apologist, supplying what Watts and Zimmerman (1979) describe as 'excuses' for practical men. However, this would be a very cynical view of events. The level of discussion is the result of the problems of practical implementation in an uncertain and imperfect world, with many users and uses of information but limited capacity to provide and digest it. There is certainly a political process taking place, involving reconciliation of the conflicting interests of various preparers and users, but this does not mean that bodies such as the FASB ignore theoretical argument or logical consistency in their reasoning. To some extent, the fact that theory has made only a limited contribution supports the view that more theoretical work should be done to provide insights which are relevant to standard-setting bodies, and the FASB's conceptual framework project can be viewed as an attempt to define a framework for such developments. However, it is also true that some existing theoretical work of potential relevance has failed to find its way into the published pronouncements of the FASB (or, indeed, of the SEC) and this may be due to the short-term preoccupation with practical implementation problems and with reconciling conflicting interests, which are inevitable pressures on standard-setting bodies such as the FASB, which operate on the basis of the consent of preparers and users of accounts. We shall return to these important issues later.

8
Inflation accounting in Australasia

1 Introduction

The main purpose of this chapter is to trace the development of inflation accounting in Australia and New Zealand from 1974 onwards. These have been closely related to developments in the United Kingdom, and in several instances, notably in aspects of the Mathews Report (1975) in Australia and the Richardson Report (1976) in New Zealand, Australasian proposals have been followed subsequently in the United Kingdom.

Before embarking upon an account of these developments it is worth exploring the background to them. A striking feature of the development of accounting in Australasia is the relative strength of academic accounting there, both in research and in education, and the work of academics (most obviously R. L. Mathews, but also several others) has been a strong influence on the development of new ideas in inflation accounting. In the 1960s, Australia had an exceptionally strong array of leaders in the debate on accounting for changing prices.

As long ago as 1958 R. L. Mathews (in co-authorship with the economist J. McB. Grant) had written an important empirical and theoretical study of the effects of inflation on company accounts, advocating the measurement of income after charging replacement cost depreciation, on similar lines to the methods used by economists in National Income accounting. A later paper by Mathews (1965) attacked the American *Accounting Research Study No.6*, which advocated CPP adjustment of historical cost, as providing 'useless information'. It can therefore have been no surprise to those who subsequently appointed Professor Mathews to chair an official committee of inquiry that his Report (1975) advocated replacement cost accounting with an 'entity' (specific price-adjusted) form of capital maintenance, and no rôle for general price indices.

Another influential Australian supporter of replacement cost accounting is Professor R. S. Gynther, whose book *Accounting for Price-Level Changes: Theory and Procedures* (1966) and many other

190

writings, advocate a strong entity approach to accounting, with replacement cost as the basis both of valuation of assets and of measurement of capital to be maintained. Gynther's work was strongly influenced by his study of the Dutch application of replacement cost accounting, particularly the Philips system, and he went further than Mathews in applying the system not only to physical assets, but also to monetary assets, advocating a form of monetary working capital adjustment in his 1966 book. Gynther has had considerable influence on recent developments in current cost accounting in Australia,[1] and, as in the case of Mathews, his earlier published work points to the direction of his subsequent influence.

However, not all leading Australian academics have espoused the replacement cost form of current value accounting. Professor R. J. Chambers, of the University of Sydney, although an advocate of replacement cost accounting early in his career, has subsequently became the world's leading advocate of Continuously Contemporary Accounting (CoCoA), valuing assets at selling prices and measuring capital on a proprietary basis, adjusted by a general price index to allow for inflation. His classic statement, *Accounting, Evaluation and Economic Behavior* was published in 1966, but he has since amplified and amended his system in a remarkable number of cogently argued papers (many of which are usefully summarised in his *Autobibliography*, 1977). The fact that he has apparently had much less impact on the practical developments of the last decade than his competitors stands as a warning that we should not view practical developments merely as the outcome of an academic debate: ideas are well-received when the environment is favourable to them, not merely when they find an eloquent advocate.

Australia has also produced at least one pioneer of the eclectic valuation approach which is the basis of current cost accounting in the form which has found favour with standard-setting bodies throughout the English-speaking world. F. K. Wright (1964) derived a set of rules for 'opportunity value' and only later discovered the same system, 'value to the owner', in the work of Bonbright (1937). The same rules, described as 'value to the firm', were subsequently adopted by the Sandilands Committee in the United Kingdom. Another Australasian advocate of 'value to the firm' was Professor Edward Stamp, who held a Chair at Wellington, New Zealand, in the mid-1960s, and whose 1971 paper, advocating this valuation basis, was one of the sources quoted in the Sandilands Report. Moreover, Stamp's modification of the value to the owner rules (to avoid the reporting of net present values) was similar (but not identical) to the approaches which subsequently entered

191

standard-setters' deliberations in Australasia and, later, New Zealand and the United Kingdom.

This sample of leading Australasian contributors to the early debate on inflation accounting[2] should suffice to demonstrate that, in terms of ideas, Australasia was at least as well-prepared as the United Kingdom for the debates of the 1970s, so that it is not surprising that both Australia and New Zealand made distinctive contributions to those debates. However, it is also true that there were remarkable parallels between developments in these countries and those in the United Kingdom. Given the close business and professional ties, as well as the similar inflationary experience of the three countries, these parallels are hardly surprising. Table 8.1 provides evidence of the parallel inflation rates, and the next two sections discuss developments in Australia and New Zealand respectively.

2 Australia

(i) The first stage: CPP

Prior to 1974 many Australian companies, like their British counterparts, adopted *ad hoc* practices to reflect the impact of inflation upon their financial affairs. Some companies revalued major assets. The revaluations were, however, not for fiscal advantage, since the resulting increases in depreciation were not allowable deductions for taxation purposes but were purely in the interests of informative reporting.[3] Other Australian companies set aside a proportion of their profits or made increased charges for depreciation to provide for the increased cost of replacing assets (principally fixed assets) even though the assets themselves were not revalued – a practice which had also been adoped by many British companies (Scapens, 1973 and 1975).

In 1974, however, a more comprehensive system for accounting for price-level changes based on the CPP systems was suggested by the AASC[4] – the preliminary Exposure Draft, *Accounting for Changes in the Purchasing Power of Money* (December, 1974) being derived from the UK's *PSSAP7*. (To facilitate comparison, the paragraph numbers of the UK statement were retained notwithstanding that certain paragraphs were omitted since they were inapplicable in the Australian context.) A major difference between the UK and Australian proposals, however, was the Australian choice of the gross domestic product (GDP) implicit deflator as the indicator of purchasing power. This index encompassed not only personal consumption expenditure but also fixed capital expenditure and expenditure by financial enterprises and public

Inflation accounting in Australasia

Table 8.1. *Annual inflation rates (%)* in Australia, New Zealand and the United Kingdom 1960–80*

Year	Australia %	New Zealand %	United Kingdom %
1960	3.9	1.0	1.1
1961	2.5	1.6	2.7
1962	− 0.4	2.8	4.0
1963	0.6	1.8	2.0
1964	2.2	3.5	3.2
1965	4.2	3.4	4.6
1966	2.8	2.7	3.9
1967	3.3	6.2	2.7
1968	2.5	4.4	4.8
1969	3.0	4.9	5.4
1970	3.9	6.2	6.3
1971	6.0	10.6	9.4
1972	6.0	6.9	7.3
1973	9.4	8.1	9.1
1974	15.1	11.3	16.0
1975	15.1	14.4	24.2
1976	13.5	17.1	16.5
1977	12.3	14.3	15.9
1978	7.9	11.9	8.3
1979	9.1	13.6	13.4
1980	10.2	17.2	18.0

Source: International Monetary Fund, *International Financial Statistics, Supplement on Price Statistics*, 1981, pp. 4–5.

*per cent increase in the consumer price index over that of the previous year.

authorities in addition to taking account of exports and imports. In the UK this type of index was specifically rejected, the belief being that changes in purchasing power was 'more often conceived in relation to the purchasing power of money spent by individuals on the goods and services purchased for their own personal use' (*PSSAP7*, para. 24) – hence the ASC's ultimate choice of the Retail Price Index.

From the outset it seemed, therefore, that the Australian standard-setters did not conceive of purchasing power as being that of the private individual but were anxious to reflect the changes in purchasing power of a broad sector of the economy by including the expenditure of industry and public authorities in the scope of the index used. This policy obviously reflected doubts about the use of a CPP index based on shareholder purchasing power. The doubts of the AASC about CPP accounting were, however, fundamental, being expressed in a note on the status of the CPP Exposure Draft:

> The AASC is not yet convinced that CPP accounting should be recommended as the preferred solution to the problems associated with accounting for changes in prices and/or the general price level, but as an initial step, has prepared a preliminary exposure draft describing the CPP accounting method. Other methods of accounting for changes in prices and/or the general price level are being investigated.

The doubts of the standard-setters about the CPP method were also revealed by the aspects of the preliminary Exposure Draft on which comments would be particularly appreciated, namely the index to be used; the application of the index to paid-in capital; and other methods of accounting for price changes.

These doubts were understandable. In many respects, the preliminary Exposure Draft was issued to keep Australia in line with several other countries whose professions had, as the AASC put it, 'advocated [CPP] as a practical measure'.[5] Additionally, the month before the preliminary Exposure Draft was published, the Australian Government had announced that it would be appointing a Committee of Inquiry into Inflation and Taxation to report, by May 1975, on questions relating to the effects of inflation on taxation paid by persons and companies. As far as companies were concerned the Committee was required to examine the effects of rapid inflation on taxation paid by companies and other enterprises and this was bound to have some implications for the form of financial reporting which companies would favour in the future.

(ii) The Mathews Report

In the event the Committee of Inquiry's Report, popularly known as the Mathews Report, did have a considerable impact on the inflation accounting debate. The terms of reference set by the Australian Government in appointing the Committee were clearly oriented towards the effects of inflation on taxation, whereas the British Government's terms of reference for the Sandilands Committee, whose appointment had been announced earlier in the same year, were much wider.[6] The Australian committee was required, with respect to business:

(1) to examine the various choices available to taxpayers under the provisions of the income tax law relating to the valuation of trading stock and to assess the advantages and disadvantages of providing other bases of stock valuation for income tax purposes;
(2) to consider the advantages and disadvantages of alternative methods of providing allowance for income tax purposes for depreciation of plant and equipment, including allowance of deductions for depreciation calculated at flexible or accelerated annual rates;
(3) to make recommendations in relation to these matters.

The choice of Professor R. L. Mathews as Chairman ensured that the notion of replacement cost in place of historical cost would be considered by the four-man Committee of Inquiry, and, in the event, a current value concept of taxable income was recommended in the Report which was published in May 1975, some four months before the UK's Sandilands Report. CPP accounting was discussed by the Committee, but was rejected for various reasons, including its inclusion of unrealised gains on borrowing in profit, its irrelevance for investment, pricing and managerial decision-making, and its potential inability to maintain a company's operating capacity.

The Mathews Report proposed two simple adjustments to traditional historical cost income, a cost of sales adjustment and a depreciation adjustment, which would reflect the replacement cost of the physical assets used in the period. The cost of sales adjustment was calculated by deducting opening stocks valued at actual prices from opening stocks valued at the same prices as closing stocks. Historical cost depreciation was to be indexed to reflect the current replacement cost of the assets to which it related.[7] In calculating the stock adjustment, actual stock schedules and price lists were to be used, but, for the purpose of the depreciation adjustment, the Mathews Report suggested the use of a single index of capital goods prices.

Like the UK's Sandilands Report, the Mathews Committee's proposals appeared to be concerned with maintaining the physical operating capacity of a business. Realised holding gains on fixed assets and stock would be excluded from income 'at least until such time as they cease to be needed to finance the holding of non-monetary assets as a result of the assets being sold and not replaced' (Mathews Report, p. 599). Unlike the Sandilands Report, the Mathews Report was not intended to have a direct effect on financial reporting, although it must have had an important influence upon the debate within the standard-setting body, which, as we have already seen, was not firmly resolved to adopt a CPP solution. Certainly, the next move by the standard-setting body was

195

towards a system of reporting consistent with the Mathews Report's definition of taxable income.

(iii) The early development of CCA

One month after the publication of the Mathews Report, a second Preliminary Exposure Draft was published by AASC entitled, *A Method of 'Current Value Accounting'*. The draft probably owed as much to the well-known Australian academic preference for current value accounting systems (e.g. in addition to Mathews himself, Barton (1974), Gynther (1966) and Wright (1964) as to the terms of reference and conclusions of the Mathews Report).[8] The AASC reminded readers of the Exposure Draft that it had not been convinced that the CPP method outlined in the earlier (1974) Exposure Draft should be recommended as the preferred solution to the problem of accounting for the effects of changes in the prices of goods and services. It asked for comments on both Exposure Drafts to help determine the future direction of financial reporting in Australia.

The current value Exposure Draft advocated an income measure based on the maintenance of the operating capability of the entity – such operating capability being defined in terms of the volume of goods and services produced. It was stated that such a capital maintenance proposal would be more appropriate for organisations concerned with the purchase of a limited range of specific goods and services, the prices of which would vary relative to the prices of other goods and services, than a capital maintenance concept based on the concept of maintaining the purchasing power of shareholders' equity in terms of a general basket of goods and services.

For asset valuation, a form of deprival value was proposed. The method, however, was adapted from that of Bonbright and excluded the necessity to calculate the present value of the cash flows generated by an asset. Present value was dismissed on the grounds of: (1) the subjectivity involved in management's expectations of future events; and (2) the difficulty of determining with any accuracy the cash flow produced by an individual fixed asset. Instead only replacement cost or net realisable value were to be reported, the choice between them being determined by the expected rôle of the particular assets in the operations of the business. If the enterprise were to be deprived of assets *which were not essential to the continuance of operations*, the loss to the entity would be no more than their realisable value. Consequently, in cases where the use of an asset had been terminated, net realisable value would be used as the valuation basis. *Assets which were essential to the continuance of the entity's operations* were worth no more than the cost of the replacement of the operating capacity provided by the asset, and consequently, replacement cost would be their valuation basis.

Turning from the valuation of assets to income measurement, the Exposure Draft defined operating profit in a manner similar to the Mathews Report by charging against revenue the cost of stocks and depreciation based on the current cost of assets consumed. This method, therefore, like that of the Mathews Report, sought to maintain only the operating capability of physical (non-monetary) assets.

Monetary items presented the AASC with a difficult problem. Views were divided about the treatment to be accorded to such items at the time when the Exposure Draft was produced. Given this diversity of view, the AASC postponed a decision on the matter, claiming that further study was required before any firm recommendations could be made on the subject of the treatment of monetary items in times of changing price levels.

Two hundred and forty-two comments were received in response to the two Exposure Drafts,[9] a majority of them being in favour of a current value system. At this stage it appeared that the accounting profession and the industrial and financial sectors of the economy could well have accepted without undue protest a CVA standard restricted to the adjustments already exposed.

Accordingly, in October 1976, a Provisional Accounting Standard, *Current Cost Accounting*, was issued by the Institute of Chartered Accountants in Australia (ICAA) and the Australian Society of Accountants (ASA) with the recommendation that it should be used for the preparation of financial statements for any accounting period commencing on or after 1 July 1977. The provisional nature of the Standard ensured that its requirements were not mandatory, but entities were encouraged to provide supplementary CCA information in accordance with the Provisional Standard if full CCA financial statements were not prepared.

It was stated by the Institute and the Society that they intended to issue a full statement applying to periods commencing on or after 1 July 1978, eventually resulting in the substitution of CCA for HC. (This intention was later relaxed when the Provisional Standard was issued in a slightly amended form in August 1978. Following adverse reaction to the timetable suggested, the two accountancy bodies now 'strongly recommended' that, for accounting periods commencing on or after 1 July 1978, major entities should supply certain CCA information (similar to that required by the SEC's *ASR190*)[10] on a memorandum basis.)

Three reasons were given in the 1976 Provisional Standard for the choice of CCA and the rejection of other systems (namely CPP and Chambers' CoCoA system):

(1) The most significant aspect of changing prices was seen to be changes in the specific prices relevant to the operations of a particular entity;

(2) the purposes of financial statements (prepared for an entity as a going concern) appeared to be fulfilled better if specific prices were determined by reference to market buying prices rather than to market selling prices;

(3) CPP accounting was not considered to provide, by itself, meaningful financial information.[11]

The Provisional Standard was very similar to the 1975 Exposure Draft. The operating capacity of physical assets was to be maintained by charging the current cost of sales, and depreciation based on current values, against revenue. The asset valuation system was, however, changed and was to set a precedent for later pronouncements in the UK. It was resolved that the former *essential to the continuance of the entity's operations* criterion was flawed, in that an asset which would not be sold in the short term, and which would therefore, under the previous criterion, be valued at replacement cost, could be carried in the balance sheet at an amount greater than that which could be recovered from its use and eventual sale. The concept of prudence traditionally dictated that no assets, whether in historical or current cost accounts, should be carried at an amount greater than that recoverable from their use and ultimate sale, and accordingly the asset valuation criterion in the 1975 Exposure Draft was amended in the Standard to accommodate this element of conservatism.

In effect two questions were to be asked about each asset, namely:

(1) Is the asset *to continue in use*?

If yes – ask question (2)

If no – value at net realisable value.

(2) Can the asset's current cost (or in the case of a depreciable asset written down current cost) be expected to be recovered

(a) through charges against the revenues from the continued use of the asset, and/or

(b) by its sale?

If yes – value at replacement cost (or written down replacement cost)

if no – value at the amount of replacement cost that can be recovered (the recoverable amount).

The objections to the anticipation of cash flows outlined in the 1975 Exposure Draft appeared to have been forgotten by the Australian profession. The 'recoverable amount' and the economic value concepts are similar in that the former still requires the estimation of future cash flows relating to the individual assets and as such suffers from many of the objections raised against the economic value concept. Indeed, it could be said that the only difference between the economic value and recoverable amount concepts is the omission in the latter of a discount factor for cash flows.

All adjustments restating assets in terms of current costs were to be taken to a current cost adjustment account. Where a non-monetary asset was written down to its recoverable amount, however, the amount of the write-down was to be brought into account in the profit and loss account to maintain the previously existing level of operating capability.

Monetary assets and liabilities were normally to be shown 'at the amount at which they were initially brought to account'. Gains and losses in purchasing power arising from the holding of monetary items in times of inflation were considered by those drafting the Standard, and three viewpoints distinguished:

(1) that such gains or losses should be completely ignored;
(2) that all such gains or losses should be brought to account;
(3) that such gains or losses should be brought to account to the extent that they related to monetary assets and liabilities forming part of the working capital of the entity.

The Standard provided a hint of future developments by stating that it could be argued that the capital maintenance system underlying CCA should be concerned with the maintenance of the operating capability of 'the entity's working capital pool', but further research, including adequate field testing, was considered to be necessary before any decision could be made. For the purposes of the Standard, the initial changes from the historical cost basis were to be limited to aspects on which there was a reasonable consensus.

At this point the first stage of CCA's technical development in Australia was completed. Although a full standard had not been issued it appeared likely that the adjustments concerning fixed assets and stock – the assets usually of prime importance for the assessment of profit determination and the asset base of an enterprise – were acceptable to users and preparers of financial statements alike.

(iv) The monetary items debate

The second stage in the development of CCA began with the issue of an exposure draft *The Recognition of Gains and Losses on Holding Monetary Resources in the Context of Current Cost Accounting* by the Australian Accounting Research Foundation (AARF) on behalf of the ICAA and the ASA in July 1978. As implied by its title, this pronouncement extended the proposals of the 1976 Provisional Standard into the area of accounting for the effects of inflation on monetary items.[12]

The thrust of the paper was heavily dependent on the earlier writings of Gynther who indeed was involved in the preparation of the Exposure Draft. Capital was considered to be the operating capability provided by the *assets* (resources) of the entity. Gains or losses would only be recorded if operating capability was enhanced or impaired. It was argued with respect to monetary items that gains or losses could only occur in relation to monetary assets (resources) and could not occur in relation to funds which financed them.

Monetary working capital was considered to be the monetary resource with which an entity conducted its day-to-day business and was deemed to be a pool of funds consisting, broadly, of cash and debtors less creditors. Gains or losses in terms of specific prices would be based on this fluctuating working pool. (By way of contrast to the proposals of the Richardson Committee in New Zealand, gains or losses on net long-term monetary assets were also to be recorded.) No gains or losses, however, were to be shown on loan capital. Long-term liabilities were to be considered part of the permanent capital of the entity and, consequently, similar to the amounts contributed by shareholders. Calculating gains on such liabilities would, according to Gynther (1966, p. 149), be as illogical, in times of rising prices, as calculating gains on funds received from shareholders. Following this line of reasoning, the Exposure Draft argued that a gain on such borrowing would be illusory in that operating capability would not be enhanced, and consequently the gain could not be distributed in full whilst still maintaining the operating capability at the level which existed at the beginning of the period. Illustrations given in the Exposure Draft and by Gynther (1976, p. 58) revealed the absence of any cash flow to the entity resulting from the depreciation of the purchasing power of loan capital.

The new proposals ignored the conclusions of a study published by the AARF in a year prior to the issue of the Exposure Draft. In this paper, the authors Henderson and Peirson (1977, p. 31), had criticised Gynther's interpretation of operating capability stating that the arguments to exclude purchasing power gains on long-term debt applied equally to purchasing power gains on current monetary liabilities and consequently the proposal to differentiate between liabilities was flawed.[13] While Gynther may well have argued that his notion of a working capital pool was an attempt to measure the physical units of cash required to maintain the volume of transactions on a day-to-day basis, a sizeable minority of the submissions on the Draft rejected the Gynther concept and supported the notion of showing the gains on holding long-term liabilities in income. A majority of commentators on the Exposure Draft, however, approved of its general thrust.

The AARF attempted to reconcile the two positions in a new exposure draft *The Recognition of Gains and Losses on Holding Monetary Items in the Context of Current Cost Accounting* issued in August 1979. In doing this, it brought the Australian position much closer to the UK position of *ED24*, issued in April of the same year, which contained both gearing and monetary working capital adjustments. Whilst maintaining the overall entity view adopted in the 1978 AARF draft, gains and losses on *all* monetary assets and liabilities (including loan capital) were now to be brought into account in arriving at 'profit and gearing gain attributable to shareholders', by adjusting both the profit and loss account and the current cost adjustment account. Thereafter, any gains or losses on loan capital[14] previously included in income were to be removed from or added to 'profit and gearing gain attributable to shareholders' and taken to a 'gearing gains reserve account' in order to arrive at 'entity net profit'. This profit figure would be identical to the current cost profit proposed in the 1978 Exposure Draft. Similarly, equity funds in current cost terms would be identical in total although the current cost adjustment account would be reduced by the amount shown in the gearing gains reserve account.

The AARF admitted in the Exposure Draft that the gains or losses on holding loan capital were shown in 'profit and gearing gains attributable to shareholders' because many people believed that shareholders wished to see an indication of the extent to which the proportionate share of resources financed by shareholders had increased or diminished. The Foundation, however, was not prepared to compromise the capital maintenance concept outlined in the 1978 Exposure Draft and reiterated the point made a year earlier, that distributions based on gains on holding loan capital (i.e. distributions from the gearing gains reserve account) would constitute a reduction in the operating capability of the entity unless replaced by additional equity funds or loan capital.

Few submissions were received by the AARF in response to the 1979 Exposure Draft and a section on monetary items based on the Draft was included in a proposed new CCA standard, selectively exposed in 1982, and which emerged the following year not as a standard but as a recommendation – Statement of Accounting Practice No. 1 *Current Cost Accounting*. This put the adjustment for the gain on long-term loans

201

'below the line', as a note which does not affect the profit figure, which is struck after making the working capital adjustment. Thus, the profit figure shows the effects of gains or losses on monetary working capital, but not the gain on long-term borrowing, although the latter can be discovered from the supplementary notes. The gains on long-term loans, calculated as before by means of a general price index, were transferred to a gain on loan capital reserve. The change, in essence, was only one of presentation; the resulting CCA entity net profit figure and the balance sheet would be virtually identical to those resulting from the application of the 1979 Exposure Draft.

(v) Development of the full CCA systems

The third phase of the Australian CCA programme commenced with the issue in March 1980 of an AARF exposure draft, *Current Cost Accounting – Omnibus Exposure Draft* which sought to extend the provisional accounting Standard 'to cover those other areas necessary for CCA to be implemented in a balanced and reasonably comprehensive manner'.[15] This ambitious project proposed *inter alia* accounting treatments for non-monetary assets bought and sold on the same market, investments, decreases in current cost, foreign currency translation, goodwill, and non-monetary liabilities. Some of these proposals were controversial and could well have ramifications in the ultimate form of accounting for price-level changes in Australia. For example, in the case of commodities and trading and portfolio shares where current costs are virtually identical with selling prices it was proposed the *real* gain or loss on these assets should be taken to profit, i.e. the operating capability of the entity was assumed to be its 're-investment ability' in 'real (general price-level) terms'. In effect, this approach is of a proprietary nature, albeit disguised in operating capacity terms. It is obviously only a small step from using a proprietary approach for certain assets to considering an entity as holding a portfolio of assets and measuring real gains or losses on the holding of all assets.

A further crack in the entity façade occurred with the proposed treatment of decreases in current cost, e.g. where a rapid change in technology occurs or the markets on which the entity buys and sells collapse. Under the existing Provisional Standard, profits would have been boosted initially by the reduced depreciation and cost of sales charges. The Exposure Draft, however, proposed that the loss in value should not be offset against previous gains in the current cost adjustment account but should be taken straight to profit thereby negating the concept of preserving the operating capability of assets and once more moving to a position of preserving reinvestment ability.

In late 1983, as a result of the waning interest in CCA, the ASA and ICAA issued, not as had initially been expected, a comprehensive CCA standard, but a non-mandatory recommendation, Statement of Accounting Practice No. 1, *Current Cost Accounting. SAP1* was virtually identical to the previously selectively exposed Draft Standard of 1982, but whereas the 1982 proposal was intended to require major entities to produce supplementary current cost accounts, *SAP1* merely 'strongly recommended' that all entities produce such supplementary statements. The recommendation drew together the proposals of the Provisional Standard and the three Exposure Drafts issued since 1976. The same ambiguity over the proprietary and entity concepts appearing in the 1980 *Omnibus Exposure Draft* remained. In certain circumstances, the guidance notes stated, decreases in current cost 'can mark a permanent impairment [of operating capability], in that the ability of the entity to carry out its activities on the scale which applied at the beginning of the period has been undermined. In this context, scale has to be considered in financial as well as volume terms'.

As for assets bought and sold on the same market (which now specifically included investment properties) the recommendation and its related guidance notes moved away from the use of a general index to record the real gain on the buying and selling of such assets. Instead it introduced the amorphous concept of 'the relevant index' based on the movement in the current costs of assets which the entity could have held in its normal dealing operations during the period. Where, however, the range of assets likely to be held was broad a general price index was to be used. Either of these indices were to be used to adjust the original current cost of the asset to ascertain the gain or loss in terms of 'reinvestment ability'.

Few other changes were introduced in *SAP1*. The proposals of the Provisional Standard amended in 1978 and the thrust of the 1978 and 1979 monetary items exposure drafts were retained, historical cost profit being adjusted by depreciation and cost of sales charges in current terms and by gains or losses on holding monetary items to arrive at 'CCA entity profit'. A note to the CCA profit and loss account added the gain/loss on loan capital to entity per profit for 'those readers who wish to see a proprietary result'. Once again, however, a warning was given (in the guidance notes) that distribution of the gains on long-term borrowings would, unless replaced by additional funding, reduce the entity's operating capability – despite the ambiguities, in the treatment of certain situations, the entity orientation of *SAP1* was clear.

Part I The debate

The debate in Australia is obviously far from being over. A particular problem for the accountancy bodies is the considerable resistance to the introduction of current value accounting standards from businessmen, many of whom seek valuation adjustments for tax purposes while simultaneously opposing them for purposes of reporting business income to shareholders or investors (Mathews, 1980, pp. 268–9). A survey of the annual reports of 130 leading Australian companies[16] during 1980 showed that 91 of these companies were still producing only traditional historical cost accounts (i.e. with occasional partial revaluations), whereas only five were producing main or supplementary current cost accounts, in accordance with the Provisional Standard then in force.

Part of the resistance to the CVA proposals may have been the Australian Government's failure to implement the Corporate Taxation proposals of the Mathews Committee, although Mathews himself argued that the Government could hardly be blamed for shelving further actions until the accounting profession and the business community could agree on standards which could be applied consistently in the three areas of accounting measurement, business policy and taxation policy. It would seem that agreement is unlikely to be immediate. Progress in Australia will, it would seem, have to await such agreement unless other international developments force the pace of change:

> It is generally felt that inflation accounting will not be implemented until there is clear support from industry and Government, or other international developments force its implementation in Australia. (Davison and Westwick, 1981, p. 10)

Thus, despite Australia's undoubted contribution to ideas in the field, and its early development of current cost proposals, the environment has not yet favoured the adoption of a compulsory standard.

3 New Zealand

(i) The CPP and CCA Exposure Drafts by the New Zealand Society of Accountants, 1975 and 1976

In New Zealand, official publications dealing with the effect of price-level changes of financial reporting came later than in Australia or in the UK. Overseas pronouncements, however, were closely watched by New Zealand accountants and several major companies experimented with various methods of inflation accounting using CPP techniques, revaluations at replacement cost or Chambers' CoCoA system. The experiments, however, were generally of a partial nature, being restricted to the provision of supplementary data in additional accounts or to comments in the Chairman's or Directors' Report (see Hopkins and Robb, 1975).

In March 1975, the first official paper, the NZSA's Exposure Draft *Accounting for Changes in the Purchasing Power of Money*, was published. The Exposure Draft was based on the UK's *PSAAP7*, adopting, like the UK's Provisional Standard (as opposed to the Australian CPP Exposure Draft), a purchasing power index related to the expenditure of the individual citizen, the Consumer Price Index.

The Exposure Draft's proposals, however, were quickly overtaken by events overseas. The publication of the Mathews Report, the Australian CCA Exposure Draft and the Sandilands Report a few months after the issue of the New Zealand Exposure Draft, clearly indicated the likelihood of an international trend towards a form of CCA. Moreover, the New Zealand Government instituted its own enquiry in December 1975, and this too adopted a CCA approach.[17] This trend was reflected by the NZSA's first CCA Exposure Draft *Accounting in Terms of Current Costs and Values*, published in August 1976. The Society stated in the introduction of the Exposure Draft that its preparation was assisted by both the Australian current value Exposure Draft and the Sandilands Report. Indeed, the income measurement proposals in the New Zealand Exposure Draft were identical to those of the two foreign publications. The method proposed in the Exposure Draft sought to maintain the operating capacity of the business by advocating a form of physical capital maintenance, charging historical cost profit with additional depreciation based on the current costs of fixed assets and a cost of sales adjustment based on replacement cost.[18] In the preparation of the Exposure Draft, a choice had to be made between the Australian and British asset valuation proposals. While the Exposure Draft ostensibly adopted the value to business criterion using the deprival value of the asset as the underlying principle of valuation, it specifically rejected the use of present value estimates of asset values stating that these values were insufficiently objective to be applied in external financial statements. Consequently, the Sandilands proposals were rejected in favour of the contemporary Australian approach which utilised only replacement cost and net realisable value. While the criteria to be used in choosing between the two values was to be the *impairment of operating capacity*, rather than the Australian *essential to the continuance of operations*, both systems would provide identical results. The NZSA proposed that where the loss of the asset would materially impair the operating capacity of the business, its value would be replacement cost, since continuing replacement of its operating capacity was implied. Where operating capacity would not be impaired by the loss of the asset, replacement cost was not considered relevant since the business could continue its operations without the asset in question. Net realisable value was then considered to be the most appropriate and objective valuation since the value of the asset was in no way dependent on its ownership by the particular business.

(ii) The Richardson Report

CCA took an important step forward in New Zealand when the Government, like its counterparts in Australia and the UK, appointed in December 1975 a Committee of Inquiry into Inflation Accounting under the chairmanship of Dr I. L. M. Richardson. The Committee's terms of reference required it, *inter alia*, to examine the purposes served by accounts and their adequacy to meet these aims; to recommend the accounting method best suited to the needs of New Zealand; and to report on the nature and extent of any changes in taxation policy that might be desirable having regard to the Government's need to maintain an adequate level of revenue.

Some 60 submissions were received including some from Australia and the United Kingdom. In addition, there was a considerable flow of information to the Committee from professional accounting bodies in many countries, including those who were actively considering methods of accounting for price-level changes such as Australia, Canada, The Netherlands, the UK and the USA. Not surprisingly, however, the Committee drew heavily on the Reports of the Mathews and Sandilands Committees and the views of the NZSA in framing its own conclusions.

The Committee's Report (September 1976) rejected the Sandilands proposals for asset valuation. Deprival value was rejected on both practical and theoretical grounds. Two practical reasons for the rejection were given, namely:
(1) the expense and time involved in considering the three bases of valuation when only one was to be used; and
(2) the subjectivity involved in estimating both future receipt flows and the appropriate discount rate.
The theoretical argument concerned the whole basis of the deprival value concept but had strong practical overtones. The Committee did not accept that the asset's value should be equivalent to the maximum theoretical loss sustainable by the entity. Instead it argued (like Chambers) that 'one of the purposes of the accounting system should be

to evaluate the activities of the enterprise in financial terms, giving an account of what it does with the resources at its disposal' (p. 92).

Where PV > RC > NRV the Committee commented that the entity may not wish to replace the asset and accordingly the RC valuation derived from the deprival value system would be inappropriate. Similarly it was argued that where NRV > RC > PV the appropriate amount the enterprise would lose if deprived of the asset would be its net realisable value not its replacement cost:

> To argue that the loss is only the depreciated current replacement cost, on the grounds that the enterprise is able to replace the asset and thus regain the ability to sell for net realisable value, ignores the fact that all the values relate to the age of an existing asset, whereas what the enterprise would pay for replacement would almost certainly be the new price of a similar asset. Thus the concept has doubtful relevance to the real world in which businesses operate.

Instead of the deprival value approach, the Committee recommended the criteria used in both the Australian and New Zealand current cost Exposure Drafts and adopted the Australian 'essential to the business' basis of valuation. Assets which were essential to the business were to be valued at replacement cost. Where the enterprise had made a firm decision to dispose of an asset, and not to replace it with an asset of the same or greater operating capacity, the asset would be regarded as not being essential to the business, and it would then be valued at net realisable value.

As far as income measurement was concerned, the Committee recommended the use of a two-stage profit and loss account. First *current cost operating profit* would be calculated. This profit figure, after taking into account the liability for tax, represented the amount which could be paid to the providers of debt and equity capital without impairing the operations of the enterprise. Second, the profit attributable to the owners was struck, being the amount which could be distributed to the owners without impairing the operating capability of the owners' investment in the enterprise, i.e. maintaining that portion of operating capability which was financed by equity capital.

Current cost operating profit required three current cost adjustments to historical cost profit. Two of these adjustments, the current cost of sales and depreciation based on current costs, had already been proposed in several countries overseas. With the third adjustment, that reflecting the 'change in the value of the operating capacity of the circulating monetary assets', however, the Committee broke new ground. In doing so the Committee specifically rejected the assertion that no gains or losses could arise through holding monetary units.

> We feel sure that the average business man believes that if his firm has held a cash balance through a period of inflation then there has been a loss in value to the business as a consequence of holding cash during that period. (p. 123)

It was argued that a monetary asset had an operating capacity of its own. Consequently, 'if because of inflation the monetary assets are not able to do their job as effectively as before, or the enterprise has to carry more monetary assets to maintain the same level of operating capacity, then this should be recognised in arriving at the current cost profit' (p. 124). A charge against profit in terms of a general purchasing power index[19] was to be made, however, only for those monetary assets (normally cash and debtors) termed 'circulating monetary assets', required to service the normal operations of the business. No loss was to be recorded on 'fixed monetary assets' such as investments.[20] Consequently, changes in the value of fixed monetary assets would be reflected in reserves (the capital maintenance reserve) but would not affect profit. Losses in the purchasing power of these monetary items were considered to be avoidable and to have no effect upon the trading operations of the enterprise.

Attacks on this form of proposal have come from two quarters. One group (Stamp, 1971; Bourn, 1976; Henderson and Peirson, 1977) appeared to agree with Keynes (1936) that cash is held basically for three reasons:

(1) for *transactions purposes* as part of the operations of the entity;
(2) for *precautionary purposes* to meet contingencies; *and*
(3) for *speculative purposes* to the advantage of unexpected investment opportunities.

A loss in the purchasing power of fixed monetary assets consequently reduces an enterprise's scope for action or, as the Australian 1980 Exposure Draft would term it, its 'reinvestment ability'. The authors mentioned above consequently have proposed that the loss on all monetary assets should be charged against profit.

Others (including Gynther, 1966) have argued that a net monetary capital pool should be considered, i.e. the loss on holding monetary assets should be offset by the gain on current (and, on occasion, all) liabilities, and indeed this practice has been followed in recent proposals in most of the industrialised nations (for example, Australia, Canada, South Africa, the UK and the USA). This view was emphatically rejected by the Committee (p. 130).

In our view an enterprise is concerned with maintaining the operating capacity of its assets. The current cost operating profit should therefore be measured in terms of the return the enterprise derives from the employment of those assets in the enterprise's operations. As far as the enterprise is concerned the monetary liabilities are part of the total financing of the whole enterprise. We do not believe that it is relevant or feasible to relate particular liabilities to particular assets or that there has been a gain (or loss) in respect of liabilities insofar as the enterprise is concerned. It can be argued that trade accounts payable relate to stock and trade accounts receivable, and that secured liabilities to the assets over which they are secured. The suggestion that trade accounts payable should be taken into account in the monetary asset adjustment recognises the fact that it is normal for these items to move in direct relation to cost of goods sold. However, this does not necessarily follow and the same argument could apply equally to the movements in bank overdraft. The enterprise may be in a position where it decides to reduce its trade accounts payable by increasing its bank overdraft or reduce its bank overdraft by increasing them. As far as the enterprise is concerned there is a total pool of finance from both equity and borrowings and the operating capacity of the enterprise's assets is not affected by the changes in the method of financing of those assets. In this sense we regard trade accounts payable as borrowing just as much as other outside liabilities. Accordingly, we reject the argument that current monetary assets and current monetary liabilities should be netted off. Nevertheless, we recognise that while the gains (or losses) in respect of borrowings are not relevant as far as the enterprise is concerned, they are relevant as far as the equity owners are concerned.

The Committee's way of reflecting these gains or losses on borrowing was to introduce a gearing adjustment, the inspiration for which had come from the UK debate on gearing in the national press and the publications of Martin Gibbs.[21] The Committee argued (p. 134) that 'if the distributions to the owners (after tax) and to lenders by way of interest are limited to the current cost operating profit of the enterprise and the operating capacity is simply maintained, the debt/equity ratio will be progressively reduced towards zero if there is continued inflation. Such a policy pursued over a long period of time would, we believe, be taking financial conservation to extreme levels'.[22]

The gain on borrowing was to be based on the realised and unrealised gains on holding assets (in practice being based on movements in the capital maintenance reserve). Consequently, a gain on borrowings would not arise unless the enterprise's resources were invested in assets which appreciated in value. CPP methods of showing gains on borrowing were criticised on the grounds that such gains were shown even when assets had fallen in value. Under the Richardson proposals, a loss on borrowings would have been shown in these circumstances.

The adjustment to current cost operating profit was calculated by the formula

$$\frac{\text{average borrowings}}{\text{average total assets}} \times \text{movement in capital maintenance reserve}$$

This approach differed markedly from the two forms of gearing adjustment under discussion internationally at the time. It differed from the Gibbs system in that it was concerned with all borrowings whether short or long term. The Gibbs adjustment was concerned only with bank overdraft and longer-term borrowing – short-term financing such as trade creditors was deemed to be part of working capital and incorporated in a *net* working capital adjustment. (This approach, as mentioned earlier, had been rejected by the Richardson Committee.) It was in even more marked contrast to the 1975 proposals of the German Institut der Wirtschaftsprüfer, which reduced the current cost adjustments made to historical cost profit by the proportion of total non-monetary assets financed by non-equity funds, i.e. an adjustment was made only in respect of *realised* gains or cost savings. (No adjustment for monetary items was made to historical cost profit under the German system.) The concept of profit attributable to the owners, resulting from the adjustment to current cost operating profit to take account of gearing, was, in 1976, a novel approach in an official publication but one which has subsequently been adopted, albeit in different forms, by standard setters in other countries.[23]

(iii) The aftermath of the Richardson Proposals

The proposals of the Richardson Committee were adopted by the NZSA in its next publication on the subject of CCA, *CCA Guidelines* (December 1978). A proposed standard was not issued, since consultation with Society members and the business community had revealed that a dramatic change from HC to CCA within a short space of time would not be acceptable. The Society, however, believed that there was a need for supplementary accounts in terms of current costs and values, and accordingly it proposed that the Guidelines should apply to the financial statements of all listed public companies, for financial periods beginning on or after 1 April 1979.

Profit was to be measured in a manner similar to that proposed in the Richardson Report, although the Guidelines appeared to advocate the use of monetary assets and gearing adjustments somewhat half-heartedly, suggesting that the Richardson method was being adopted as a 'first step' since 'no clearly acceptable method' had yet been evolved. Asset valuation too was to be similar to that favoured by the Report of the Committee of Inquiry, although the Society used its former 'impairment of the entity's operating capacity' criterion for asset valuation, rather than the Australian 'essential to the continued operation of the business' criterion adopted by the Richardson Committee.

Given the apparent lack of enthusiasm for the Richardson Report in the Guidelines, it was perhaps not surprising that in 1981 the Society once more looked overseas for assistance and introduced an exposure draft, *Current Cost Accounting*, intended to apply to listed companies, which moved away from several of the earlier views expressed in New Zealand, being based on the UK's *SSAP16*. As in the UK Standard, four adjustments, namely depreciation, cost of sales, monetary working capital and gearing, were to be made to historical cost profit. Current cost operating profit which, in general terms, was derived by the deduction of the first three adjustments from historical cost profit, and which was intended to allow for the impact of price changes on the *funds* needed to maintain operating capability, would be identical to that obtained by using the principles enunciated in *SSAP16*. In other words, the distinctive monetary asset adjustment advocated in the Richardson Report was replaced by an adjustment which was concerned with net monetary assets (consisting of debtors, less creditors including bank balances and overdrafts, so far as they related to the day-to-day operating activities of the business) identical to that of the UK Standard. Since a portion of borrowings was now included in the monetary working capital, the proposed gearing ratio involved only longer-term borrowings and not *all* borrowings as had been proposed by the Richardson Report. The UK proposal to deduct monetary assets in excess of those needed for working capital from longer-term borrowings (thereby assuming that the longer-term borrowings financed these assets before non-monetary assets) was also adopted. Any excess of these assets over the longer-term borrowings was not covered by the current cost framework, this excess being considered to represent assets held for investment. While the method of dealing with such assets (and the effect) differed between the proposals of the Exposure Draft and those of the Richardson Report, the principle of excluding the effect of holding non-operating monetary assets from current cost operating profit was common to both.

A further feature common both to the new Exposure Draft and the Richardson Report was the calculation of the gearing adjustment based on both realised and unrealised holding gains. In this respect the Exposure Draft broke significantly with the then proposals of the UK and of Canada, New Zealand remaining the only country continuing to incorporate in the profit attributable to shareholders the latter's share of all holding gains financed by long-term borrowing.[24]

As far as the valuation of assets was concerned, the Exposure Draft broke with the NZSA's previously favoured 'impairment of the entity's operating capacity' criterion and adopted *SSAP16*'s value to the business criterion which, in turn, had been derived from the 1976 Australian Provisional Standard. Consequently, the recoverable amount concept was introduced into a New Zealand CCA pronouncement for the first time.

By 1981, therefore, New Zealand had largely fallen in line with UK proposals, with the one major difference that the gearing adjustment was not restricted to realised gains. The proposals of the 1981 Exposure Draft were embodied, without serious modification, in the *Current Cost Accounting Standard No.1, Information Reflecting the Effects of Changing Prices*, issued by the NZSA in March 1982. However, the Introduction to the Standard (para. 1.4) emphasised its experimental nature and that the method it recommended was 'the preferred method' rather than compulsory.

The Standard recognised that the 'preferred method' did not deal with the maintenance of shareholders' funds in general purchasing power terms. Two alternatives were proposed:
(1) an additional statement disclosing the change in the shareholder's equity interest after allowing for the change in the general purchasing power of money; or
(2) the current cost accounts could be prepared using the proprietary approach.

As far as the proprietary approach was concerned, a 'real terms' solution was recommended. All entities coming within the scope of the Standard had to show current cost depreciation and cost of sales adjustments to historical cost profit but monetary working capital and gearing adjustments were not mandatory. Instead of the latter adjustments, the requirement simply stated that 'adjustments relating to monetary items, the effect of borrowing, or equity interests' together with 'any other items reflecting the effect of changing prices' were to be shown in the profit and loss account.

The Guidance Notes to the Standard illustrated two methods of reporting using the financial capital (proprietary) concept. The first, the simplified method, added holding gains to current cost operating profit (historical cost profit less depreciation and cost of sales adjustments) and then deducted an adjustment to maintain the purchasing power of owners' equity. The second, the comprehensive method, added real holding gains on assets to current cost operating profit and then adjusted for the CPP gain or loss on monetary items. The balance sheet in both cases was on a current cost basis.

The New Zealand Standard is, therefore, of an experimental nature, the proposals enabling preparers to model their current cost accounts on the differing proposals in countries overseas. If an international consensus emerges, further changes in standard practice in New Zealand are probably inevitable.

4 Conclusion

In this chapter, we have seen that, in the period 1974 to 1983, both the Australian and the New Zealand standard-setting bodies have gone through the cycle, familiar in the UK and the USA, of initial preference for CPP (albeit with clear reservations), followed by Government intervention which favoured CCA, followed by a period of debate in which the form of CCA, particularly with respect to the treatment of monetary items and the valuation of non-monetary items, was modified. Finally, new current cost proposals emerged. Both used the Australian approach to asset valuation, which was similar in concept to that adopted in the UK (initially) and the USA, but which substituted 'recoverable amount' for discounted net present values. The main differences were in the treatment of long-term monetary items. Short-term monetary items were dealt with, in both Australia and New Zealand, by a monetary working capital adjustment similar, in principle, to that adopted in the UK (*SSAP16*, 1980a), rather than the general index approach adopted in the USA (*FAS33*, 1979b).[25] Long-term monetary liabilities were dealt with in Australia by a general index calculation of the gain on borrowing, similar to that in the USA, whereas New Zealand adopted a gearing adjustment based upon specific price changes, as in the UK. However, the New Zealand gearing adjustment applied to unrealised, as well as realised, gains on non-monetary assets, whereas the UK adjustment was restricted to realised gains.[26]

Part I The debate

Despite the parallels between developments in Australia and New Zealand and those in the UK and the USA, it is clear that there has been a distinctive Australasian contribution to the debate. The most important Australian contribution to the standard practice ultimately adopted was the modification of the pure deprival value method of asset valuation. Rather than using and sometimes reporting highly subjective discounted net present values, the Australian approach uses the criterion of whether the asset is to continue in use in the business to determine its valuation basis and the concept of 'the recoverable amount' to assess value in cases where neither replacement cost nor net realisable value is appropriate. The most important New Zealand contribution was in the treatment of monetary assets. The Richardson Report, with its adjustment for 'circulating monetary assets' and its gearing adjustment, was the first official pronouncement in the world to adopt these approaches. The 'circulating monetary assets' adjustment has since been modified to resemble the net monetary working capital adjustments adopted, subsequently to the Richardson Report, in Australia and the UK, but the gearing adjustment still retains its distinctive character of embracing unrealised gains, as advocated by the original authors of the gearing adjustment (Godley and Cripps, 1975; Gibbs 1976; Kennedy, 1978b). This aspect of the current New Zealand system may point the way for the future development of the UK gearing adjustment. The alternative direction for development is indicated by the Australian system, which, like that of the USA, uses a general index to calculate the gain on borrowing.

The similarities between developments in Australasia and the rest of the English-speaking world are, however, more striking than the differences, and this affords some insight into the factors which have encouraged these developments. Clearly, one factor is a common language and culture, as testified by the distinguished contribution to the international debate by Australasian scholars, described earlier. However, a common set of ideas is not, of itself, sufficient, because the ideas embrace a variety of solutions and also the existence of ideas is not sufficient to guarantee their adoption in practice. The practical developments were prompted in part by the need for harmonisation resulting from close economic ties with the other countries. This can be seen particularly in the late, and rather unenthusiastic, CPP proposals made in both Australia and New Zealand, which were designed to match proposals already made in the USA and the UK. Another obvious factor prompting practical developments was the similarity of inflation rates, reported in Table 8.1; clearly, the inflationary pressures for practical reform arose at similar times and to a similar extent in each of

214

the English-speaking countries. Finally, there were similarities in the other problems of economic policy, particularly between the UK, Australia and New Zealand, each of which was wrestling with the problems of running a mixed economy in the wake of the world oil crisis, and experimenting with such devices as incomes policies to alleviate the trade-off between inflation and full-employment. This is most obvious in the government intervention in each country, the terms of reference of each committee (Sandilands, Mathews and Richardson) showing a concern with wider economic issues.

9

Inflation accounting in other countries

1 Introduction

Previous chapters have dealt in some detail with recent developments in inflation accounting in the UK, USA and Australasia. In this chapter, we shall consider recent developments in those other countries which have made significant advances towards inflation accounting. It is convenient to divide these countries into three broad groups, each of which is dealt with in a separate section of the chapter.

The three groups of countries represent three distinct traditions, although there is considerable diversity within the groups, especially the continental European group. The first group, Canada and South Africa, represent the residue of the Anglo-Saxon tradition previously described in the context of the UK, USA and Australasia, and, not surprisingly, they have followed a similar course to that followed in the other countries, with some distinctive local variations and innovations. The second group, continental Europe, has a distinctive tradition containing three separate strands in varying degrees: the business economics tradition (dominant in The Netherlands), the emphasis on compliance with codified company law (dominant in the Federal Republic of Germany) and the influence of tax law (predominant in France). Finally, but by no means last, we consider Latin America, which is the only region in which Constant Purchasing Power (CPP) accounting has achieved practical acceptance, usually under the pressure of double- or triple-digit annual inflation rates. However, in Latin America also there is considerable diversity, many countries (mainly those with relatively low inflation rates) having taken no steps towards inflation accounting.

2 Canada and South Africa

There are three important factors which help to explain why both Canada and South Africa should have followed the pattern of development observed in the other English-speaking countries, support for CPP in the early 1970s, followed by a switch to CCA, followed by a period in which an attempt is made to adapt CCA to deal with the problems of monetary assets and liabilities which had been addressed by CPP.

Firstly, both countries developed their financial institutions whilst under British rule: both (like Australia and New Zealand) were once Colonies of the United Kingdom and subsequently moved through Dominion status to independence within the Commonwealth (South Africa having subsequently left the Commonwealth). Thus, the company law, financial markets and accountancy professions of these countries have a family resemblance to those of the United Kingdom (and in Canada's case, the USA also, because of geographical proximity), so that new developments which are successful in the United Kingdom (and Australasia) are also likely to be successful in the similar institutional environments of Canada and South Africa.

Secondly, there are close economic ties, not only of trade but also of transnational ownership of assets, between South Africa and the United Kingdom and between Canada and both the USA and the United Kingdom. This makes standard accounting practice across these countries very desirable and reinforces the first factor in encouraging international transplantation of new developments.

Thirdly, as Table 9.1 shows, the inflationary experience of Canada and South Africa during the past two decades has been broadly similar to that of the other countries in what could be broadly described as the English-speaking[1] group: low single-digit annual inflation in the 1960s, accelerating to low double-digit rates in 1974 and 1975 following the oil crisis of the early 1970s and subsequently falling but not back to the lower levels of the 1960s. Thus, the internal pressure of inflation encouraged the adoption of inflation accounting measures at the same time in all of these countries, thus further encouraging international co-ordination of developments.

We shall now consider the broad pattern of developments in Canada and South Africa, in turn, discussing the distinctive developments in these countries, as well as similarities with developments elsewhere in the English-speaking world.

(i) Canada

The first Canadian pronouncement on inflation accounting was *Accounting for the Effects of Changes in the Purchasing Power of Money*, published by CICA (the Canadian Institute of Chartered Accountants) in 1974. This was an accounting guideline, and was not mandatory. It provided guidance on the method of producing sup-

Part I The debate

Table 9.1. *Annual inflation rates in Canada and South Africa, 1961–80*

Year	Canada %	South Africa %	UK %	USA %
1961	1.1	2.0	2.7	1.1
1962	1.1	1.2	4.0	1.1
1963	1.6	1.4	2.0	1.2
1964	2.0	2.5	3.2	1.2
1965	2.3	4.0	4.6	1.7
1966	3.8	3.7	3.9	3.1
1967	3.6	3.4	2.7	2.6
1968	4.0	2.1	4.8	4.2
1969	4.5	3.2	5.4	5.4
1970	3.4	4.2	6.3	5.9
1971	2.8	5.6	9.4	4.3
1972	4.8	6.5	7.3	3.3
1973	7.5	9.4	9.1	6.3
1974	10.9	11.7	16.0	10.9
1975	10.7	13.5	24.2	9.2
1976	7.5	11.2	16.5	5.8
1977	8.0	11.2	15.9	6.5
1978	9.0	10.2	8.3	7.5
1979	9.2	13.1	13.4	11.3
1980	10.1	13.8	18.0	13.5

Source: International Financial Statistics, Supplement on Price Statistics, Supplement Series No. 2, International Monetary Fund, Washington, 1981, pp. 4–5.
Note: Inflation rates are the per cent increase in the average consumer price index for the year over that for the previous year.

plementary CPP information on similar lines to the professional pro-nouncements already published in the UK and the USA (i.e. using an historical cost base), but indicated that other methods of accounting for price-level changes existed, including a system based on current values[2] although 'a number of issues and practical matters would have to be settled before a current value system could become part of generally accepted accounting principles'. In July 1975, CICA published an exposure draft, *Accounting for Changes in the General Purchasing Power of Money*, which again adopted the CPP-adjusted historical cost basis but explicitly stated that it did not preclude consideration of current value or real terms accounting. By this time, the Mathews Report in Australia had already advocated replacement cost accounting, and the SEC in the United States and the Sandilands Committee in

Britain were also about to make replacement cost or current cost proposals, with no CPP requirement.

CICA responded to this changed climate of opinion by issuing a Discussion Paper, *Current Value Accounting*, prepared by its Research Committee, in August 1976. This discussed alternative methods of asset valuation (including those currently being considered for implementation in Australia and the UK) and capital maintenance concepts. Final recommendations on general price-level adjustment were to be deferred pending the receipt of comments on the Discussion Paper.

The Discussion Paper took a 'preliminary position' on valuation methods and income measurement. It advocated a variety of current value methods, the choice depending upon the type of asset: in general, fixed assets, stocks and long-term investments were to be valued at replacement cost, marketable securities at net realisable value, and monetary assets and liabilities at the discounted present value of their future cash flows. Choice of valuation by type of asset was preferred to the Australian 'essential to the business' criterion or the British 'value to the firm' concept.

A real terms measure of income, incorporating holding gains, was proposed. The preferred capital maintenance concept for measuring operating profit was an entity one, based on physical assets, but ultimately income was measured overall by maintaining proprietary capital, defined as the real purchasing power of shareholders' equity: a concept which had been supported by the CCAB in its *Initial Reactions* to the Sandilands Report (1975), and which later found a place in the USA's first inflation accounting Standard (*FAS33*, 1979b).

The next important event in Canada was the publication in June 1977 of the report of the Committee on Inflation Accounting appointed by the provincial Government of Ontario. This Committee was chaired by Mr M. O. Alexander, who later became Director of Research at the United States' FASB.

The Ontario Committee Report rejected the CICA proposal for maintaining the real value of shareholders' financial capital in measuring profit, advocating instead a Statement of the Effects of Inflation based on the 'economic realities of funds available for distribution or expansion'. This was a funds statement adjusted to take account of price-level changes, not a profit and loss account. The aim was to show the effect of inflation on the funds by the business, not to measure income. The proposal was based on the concept of maintaining operating capacity. It sought to maintain physical assets (fixed assets and stock) in measuring 'distributable funds' and it also made an allowance for the effects of the firm's financial structure by means of a gearing adjustment. The latter adjustment abated the depreciation and cost of sales adjustments, so that the charge against funds available for distribution was limited to the proportion which would normally be financed by shareholders, as indicated by the opening ratio of equity to non-equity capital. To our knowledge, this was the first time that a major government or professional pronouncement in the English-speaking world advocated a gearing adjustment based only on realised holding gains, a practice which was subsequently adopted, later in the same year, by the Hyde Committee in the UK, and in the UK's first accounting Standard on the subject (*SSAP16*, 1980a).[3]

The Ontario Committee acknowledged the influence of the New Zealand Richardson Committee in shaping its concept of distributable funds, based on maintaining operating capacity and gearing, but the Richardson approach applied the gearing adjustment to *all* holding gains, not merely *realised* gains (the cost of sales and depreciation adjustments). The Ontario Committee justified its different, more restricted approach, on two grounds: firstly, that unrealised gains could not be realised without impairing the firm's ability to maintain its existing operations, and secondly, that it was not possible to distribute these gains without realisation because it was not certain that they would serve as collateral security for a loan.[4] Thus, the Ontario Committee's recommendation was based upon a mixture of conservatism and concern with distributability.

The Ontario Government took no action on the basis of the Report, but the next pronouncement on the subject by CICA, the Exposure Draft *Current Cost Accounting* (December 1979) did involve a gearing adjustment applied to realised gains only, and might therefore have been influenced by the Ontario Report. However, the 1979 Exposure Draft bore a close resemblance to the UK's *ED24*, published earlier in the same year (April 1979), so it is likely that this also had an important influence.[5] In particular, the Canadian Exposure Draft incorporated a monetary working capital adjustment (rejected by the Ontario Committee) so that, as in the UK, three adjustments to HC operating profit were required to arrive at current cost income:[6] additional current cost of depreciation, cost of sales and cost of net productive monetary items (measured by reference to specific price changes). Current cost income attributable to shareholders was then calculated by deducting interest paid and adding back the 'financing adjustment', i.e. the geared portion of the three earlier adjustments. The asset valuation basis was similar to those advocated in the UK's *ED24* and the USA's *FAS33*. As in *FAS33*, no balance sheet was required, the current values of fixed assets and stock being shown by way of note.

Inflation accounting in other countries

The 1979 Exposure Draft followed the UK's *ED24* with a lag and was published two months after the USA's *FAS33* which, it will be recalled (from Chapter 7), did not make any provision for gearing or monetary working capital adjustments, preferring capital maintenance concepts based upon shareholders' funds adjusted by a general price index to allow for inflation, an approach more consistent with the earlier Canadian *Discussion Paper* (1976). In view of the strong professional and economic ties between Canada and the USA, it is not surprising that, following the publication of *FAS33*, CICA reconsidered its position and in 1981 issued a revised exposure draft, *Reporting the Effects of Changing Prices*. The latter moved towards the *FAS33* position by requiring that a general index be used to calculate the purchasing power gain or loss on monetary items, and the real gain or loss on non-monetary items. Both items were to be disclosed as additional information. Two of the earlier exposure drafts' similarities with *FAS33* were retained, namely the valuation system (which was closer to the *FAS33* system than the British 'value to the owner' rule, although the conceptual basis of both approaches is similar), and the requirement to disclose the current cost of only physical assets rather than a full current cost balance sheet. However, two important differences from *FAS33* remained: firstly, the 'financing adjustment' (gearing adjustment) was retained, in calculating current cost profits attributable to shareholders, although the 'net productive monetary items adjustment' was abandoned to reduce the complexity of the proposals. Secondly, the CICA proposals did not follow *FAS33* in requiring that income from continuing operations should be adjusted for changes in the general price level.

In October 1982, the CICA's first inflation accounting Standard *Reporting the Effects of Changing Prices*, moved Canadian practice closer to the American 'information set' style of reporting, but enabled readers of the accounts to calculate income on either an operating capacity or on a financial concept of capital measured in constant dollars (the proprietary approach).

All the information required by *FAS33* was to be shown,[7] with the exception of CPP income from continuing operations. In addition, however, two gearing (or 'financing' as they were termed) adjustments were to be disclosed (not necessarily in income): one, as before, calculated by reference to the current cost adjustments to 'income on a current basis' (namely the current cost depreciation and cost of sales adjustments); the other, like the New Zealand Standard published earlier in the same year, based on realisable holding gains.[8]

The form of the gearing adjustment has been an issue in the Canadian

221

debate for many years, and it was interesting to note its appearance for the first time in the realisable holding gains form, the advocates of a prudent approach to the measurement of income having succeeded in preventing this form of adjustment being a feature of previous Canadian proposals.

The rationale for the new style of gearing adjustment appeared to be that it enabled users of the accounts to ascertain the amount of increases in current cost during a period which did not need to be met out of present *and future* revenues. The information set approach did, however, facilitate the disclosure of both forms of gearing adjustment, enabling the user to adopt whatever adjustment was considered by him to be most suitable – the absence of a need for the CICA to choose between the two approaches probably resulted in the opposition to the realisable holding gains form of the gearing adjustment being reduced.

Thus, the present Canadian position is intermediate between those of the UK and the USA. The pattern of events in recent years has closely followed those in the rest of the English-speaking world, with many imported ideas, blended and adapted to meet local requirements.

(ii) South Africa

The South African National Council of Chartered Accountants made its first step towards inflation accounting in 1975 with the Discussion Paper, *Accounting for Inflation and Other Changes in the Price Level.* This was a response to two years of inflation at unprecedented rates, and to developments in other countries with strong economic links with South Africa. In accordance with the international climate of opinion at the time when it was written, the Discussion Paper concentrated upon a CPP approach but, as its title suggests, it also addressed the problem of relative price changes and actually proposed the incorporation of current values into the CPP system. Income was to be calculated on a CPP basis by adding to historical cost profit the increase in the purchasing power of the capital invested in non-monetary assets (measured by applying a general index to book value) and deducting the amount required to maintain the purchasing power of shareholders' equity (again, applying a general index to book value). At their simplest, these adjustments amount to the same thing as adding to historical profit a gain on net borrowing, calculated on a CPP basis.[9] However, an important variation was introduced by substituting the current value of non-monetary assets for indexed book value, where the former was materially different. In such cases, if current value was lower than indexed book value, the credit to income was to be limited to the difference between the current value and book value. If the current value were higher than indexed book value, the excess was to be credited to a non-distributable capital reserve. In other words, real holding losses were to be debited to profit but real holding gains were to be credited to reserves: an essentially conservative approach.

The proposal to incorporate current values was probably due to the fact that the Discussion Paper appeared rather late in the CPP stage of the international debate, before, but in the same year as, the USA (through the SEC requirements) and the UK (through the Sandilands Report) made important steps away from CPP and towards current cost accounting. This, together with the fact that the Discussion Paper did not purport to be an exposure draft, also probably explains why the CPP ideas of the Discussion Paper were not developed further in South Africa. The next development was the publication in August 1978, of the *Guideline on Disclosure of Effects of Changing Prices on Financial Results.*

The Guideline was a proposal for CCA adjustments very similar to those proposed by the Hyde Guidelines in the UK in the previous year. It recommended supplementary adjustments to the income statement, with no corresponding balance sheet adjustments. As in the Hyde Guidelines,[10] there were three adjustments to historical cost operating profit, a depreciation adjustment and a cost of sales adjustment, to give a measure of current cost operating profit, and a gearing adjustment. This adjustment abated the two former adjustments to give a measure of current cost attributable to shareholders, thus recognising only the realised holding gains financed by borrowing, or, like the Hyde Guidelines, when monetary assets exceeded liabilities, resulted in a charge against profits.[11]

No further developments have appeared between the publication of the Guideline and the present time (1983). The 1978 Guideline has not been widely followed: Davison and Westwick (1981) reveal that, in a survey of the reports of 528 listed companies, only eleven included supplementary current cost income statements. This reluctance to report on a CCA basis may be due to lack of fiscal incentives to do so, since current cost adjustments are not allowed for tax purposes, and it may also be due to the relative weakness in South Africa of some of the other incentives (such as the need to justify profits in the context of prices and income policies and monopolies legislation) which have been important elsewhere. The experimental nature of the accounting standards in the USA and the UK, and the striking differences between them, must also be relevant, since South Africa has tended to follow, rather than lead, the example of the rest of the English-speaking world, and the precise nature of that example is neither clear nor certain at present (although we try to interpret the important trends in Chapter 10).

3 Continental Europe

It has already been indicated that there are at least three separate factors (business economics, codified company law and tax law) which are present in various degrees in the various continental European countries and have helped to shape their attitudes to inflation accounting. It is not possible here to do justice to the variety of practice and the complex history of accounting in these countries: we can merely hope to outline the more important facts about some of the countries which are, or have been in the past, particularly influential in the international development of inflation accounting. The three countries which are selected for special attention are The Netherlands, West Germany and France. The Netherlands has the strongest business economics tradition, arising from the ideas and influence of Limperg. West Germany's financial reporting rules are enshrined in statute law tradition. In France, the accounts used for financial reporting are also used for tax purposes, so that, for example, asset revaluations in the accounts could lead to increased tax liabilities. France, therefore, represents the tax law tradition.

One country which has not been singled out for special attention, but which deserves reference, is Sweden, whose accounting institute, FAR (Förenigen Auktoriserade Revisorer) produced an exposure draft on Current Cost Accounting in 1980. This bore many similarities to the CICA 'preliminary position' of 1976, described earlier in this chapter and to NIVRA's pronouncement of the same year, discussed below, recommending a 'real terms' measure of income, combining a current cost valuation method with the maintenance of the real purchasing power of shareholders' equity (based on a general purchasing power index) for income measurement. The ideas of Edwards and Bell were influential in the framing of the Exposure Draft. If this becomes standard practice, Sweden could claim to be a world leader in inflation accounting practice.

Under the proposals of the Swedish Exposure Draft, the non-monetary assets in the balance sheet were to be valued at the lower of net current replacement cost and its recoverable amount (the, by now, traditional CCA valuation method in the English-speaking world). Three different versions of the income statement were suggested. The first would show revenue charged with the current cost of depreciation and cost of sales to arrive at current cost operating profit. Realised and unrealised gains/losses on non-monetary assets were then to be added to arrive at 'current cost profit'.

If companies wished, an inflation adjustment could be deducted from income to extend the basic version of the profit and loss account to strike 'real profit'. This adjustment was to be incorporated in the second and third versions of the income statement, either by deducting from current cost profit an amount equal to that necessary to maintain the shareholders' stake in the business over the year in real terms (the consumer price index was to be used), version 2, or by showing real gains/losses on non-monetary items as opposed to nominal gains in the income statement and including an adjustment for the gains/losses on holding monetary items (which could be set off against interest charges), version 3. The latter proposal is very similar to *FAS33*, although instead of the 'building blocks' approach of the American Standard the Swedish version produces an overall income figure.

Few other countries in Europe have been concerned with accounting for inflation, although revaluations of assets were permitted in certain countries (for example, in Belgium by virtue of a Royal Decree published in 1976). Our survey of The Netherlands, West Germany and France will show that even in these countries, progress in inflation accounting practice has been slow in recent years, relative to that in the English-speaking world. Even in The Netherlands, which is well known for replacement cost theories, replacement cost is still not predominant practice. In West Germany, there has been a conscious fear of repeating the disastrous inflation rates of the 1920s, and forms of inflation accounting have been regarded with caution as potential vehicles of inflation. West Germany has enjoyed relatively low inflation rates, as Table 9.2 shows. Thus, inflation accounting practice has not developed to any significant extent. The same is true of France, although for the different reasons, already referred to, that there are potential fiscal disincentives to changing existing accounting practice. Nevertheless, developments in both The Netherlands and West Germany have been influential in the debate on inflation accounting in the English-speaking countries. Moreover, the development of the EC legislation may bring inflation accounting practices in the member countries closer together in the future.

(i) The Netherlands

Traditionally, financial reporting in The Netherlands has been based upon 'sound business practice', as interpreted by the reporting accoun-

Table 9.2. *Annual inflation rates in various Western European countries,*
1961–80

Year	France	Germany	The Netherlands	United Kingdom
	%	%	%	%
1961	2.5	2.1	−0.7	2.7
1962	5.1	3.1	2.3	4.0
1963	5.3	3.0	3.3	2.0
1964	3.0	1.8	5.8	3.2
1965	2.7	3.8	5.9	4.6
1966	2.7	3.5	5.7	3.9
1967	2.8	1.6	3.4	2.7
1968	4.5	1.7	3.9	4.8
1969	6.2	1.8	7.3	5.4
1970	5.8	3.3	3.8	6.3
1971	5.5	5.3	7.4	9.4
1972	6.2	5.6	7.9	7.3
1973	7.4	6.9	8.0	9.1
1974	13.7	7.0	9.6	16.0
1975	11.7	5.9	10.5	24.2
1976	9.6	4.3	8.8	16.5
1977	9.4	3.6	6.4	15.9
1978	9.1	2.8	4.1	8.3
1979	10.7	4.1	4.2	13.4
1980	13.3	5.5	6.5	18.0

Note: The source and methods of calculation are the same as for Table 9.1.

tant. The Act on Annual Accounts of Enterprises, 1971, largely
reaffirmed this approach by stipulating that accounts were to comply
with 'standards that are regarded as being acceptable in economic and
social life'.[12] Thus, the reporting accountant is allowed discretion in
choosing, from the broad range which are currently acceptable, those
accounting policies which he considers particularly appropriate to the
type of business and circumstances being reported. The range of
acceptable standards has been influenced by the close relationship of the
accounting profession with university economics.

Both of the above features (the discretion of the reporting accountant
and the influence of economic ideas) owe a great deal to the influence of
Limperg on the development of the Dutch accounting profession during
the first half of the twentieth century, and together they explain the

evolution of replacement cost accounting in The Netherlands. The discretionary nature of financial reporting practice, together with the influence of the replacement cost ideas of Limperg (derived from business economics) has enabled certain leading companies, notably Philips, to adopt replacement cost methods in their financial reports, in the period following the end of the Second World War. On the other hand, the flexibility which allowed this development to take place has meant that there has been great diversity in the form and the extent of replacement cost accounting, and a majority of companies has retained the historical cost basis. A 1979 survey of accounts, the results of which were reported to us by NIVRA (Nederlands Instituut van Register-accountants) revealed that, out of 120 companies surveyed, 52 per cent gave historical cost accounts (although almost half of these gave some form of current cost information by way of note), and only 7 per cent gave full current (or replacement) cost balance sheets and profit and loss accounts, while the remaining 41 per cent used partial applications of current values in their financial statements.

The only official guidance as to acceptable practice in this area is a 1976 pronouncement by NIVRA,[13] which was illustrative rather than obligatory and has not made a major impact on reporting practice. It proposed (Table 9.3) that income should be reported on both the historical cost and current value bases, and that an indication should be given of the amount necessary to maintain shareholders' wealth in real (general purchasing power) terms. This proposal was similar in principle to the UK's earlier CCAB *Initial Reactions* to the Sandilands Report, although it cannot be claimed that the Dutch were influenced by the CCAB: the Dutch had suggested this approach to the UK bodies in 1974 when the CPP Standard, *PSSAP7*, was under consideration.

Since the 1976 NIVRA statement, there have been two significant developments in The Netherlands. Firstly, the Hofstra Report (1978) on the taxation of personal and corporate income proposed indexation of incomes on a general index basis for tax purposes, broadly consistent with a CPP adjustment of historical costs. However, the proposals of this report have not been implemented and seem unlikely to influence the future development of financial reporting in The Netherlands. The second development is likely to be more significant in this context. The Government's draft legislation to implement the EEC's Fourth Directive permits, as before, both current value and historical cost information. Unlike the old law, however, the proposed legislation sets forth explicit valuation rules as required by the Directive.

The Hofstra Report, although not implemented, is of some interest because it rejected the current value basis in determining income for tax

Table 9.3 *NIVRA's proposals for accounts incorporating specific and general price changes*

Net income on current value basis	*a*
Add: Excess of replacement cost over historical depreciation and cost of goods sold in the reporting period (realised holding gains)	*b*
Net income on historical cost basis	*c*
Add: Excess of replacement cost over historical cost of non-monetary assets held at the balance sheet date (unrealised holding gains)	*d*
Increase in shareholders' equity as recorded	*e*
Equity in prior year's balance sheet	*f*
Change in the index of general prices	*g%*
Increase needed to maintain equity in terms of general purchasing power	*h*
Surplus or deficit	*i*

purposes. There were two main reasons: the subjectivity of current value, and the complexity of applying it, particularly in small businesses. This echoes some of the objections made to current cost accounting in the United Kingdom, particularly in the responses to *ED18* (1976), and it also anticipates the subsequent response of the UK Government to current cost accounting, in preferring a general index for its revised Stock Relief (1981), and in the criticisms of current cost accounting as a basis for taxation in the *Green Paper on Corporation Tax* (1982).

The Report was intended to appeal to the taxation authorities by suggesting a simple and objective method of accounting for inflation. Only two adjustments to historical cost profit were proposed, namely a CPP depreciation adjustment based on a general index revaluation of fixed assets and a cost of sales adjustment also based on a general index – opening stock was simply to be increased, in times of inflation, by the rise in the general level of prices. Hofstra also proposed the use of a gearing adjustment in suggesting that the inflationary gains made on borrowed funds should also be reflected in taxable profit by confining the revaluation of assets (and therefore the adjustment to profit) to those financed by the shaeholders' equity.[14]

The legislation based on the Fourth Directive, has raised the issue of whether or not current values should supplement historical costs in the statutory accounts. During the preparation of the legislation, the Minister of Justice emphasised that valuation in the balance sheet and profit and loss account on a current value basis might be necessary in certain circumstances in order to enable a reasonable judgement to be formed on the financial position and results. Under pressure during the debate on the proposed Act, however, this concept has not emerged explicitly in the legislation – the courts (in the form of the Enterprise Chamber) are to be left to decide the issue. Current cost accounting has by no means superseded the traditional historical cost accounts in The Netherlands.

(ii) West Germany

As we saw in Chapter 2, Germany was a world leader in inflation accounting theory and practice during the period following the First World War. In sharp contrast to this, although Germany had suffered a high rate of inflation during the Second World War,[15] culminating in the post-war 1948 currency reform in West Germany, the new Federal Republic of West Germany saw no significant developments in inflation accounting practice, even during the relatively inflationary period of the mid-1970s. Moreover, the inflation rate in West Germany during this period was one of the lowest of those in advanced economies (see Table 9.2).

These two features, the low inflation rate and the lack of development in inflation accounting practice are related directly to one another, insofar as relatively low inflation rates create relatively little pressure for inflation accounting reforms, but also indirectly, because of their mutual relationship with a third factor, the fear of repetition of the disastrous hyper-inflation which followed the First World War. Because inflation accounting in the 1920s was associated with hyper-inflation, there has been a fear that inflation accounting might encourage inflation, rather than, or in addition to, the reverse relationship, that inflation encourages the development of inflation accounting. Thus, successive West German Governments, supported by the business community have opposed the development of inflation accounting, as part of their counter-inflation strategy, to such an extent that the West German Government was, at one time, reluctant to allow the EEC directives to contain any provision for member states to use inflation accounting systems.[16] Thus, Germany's world leadership in inflation accounting in

229

the 1920s is directly connected with the lack of such developments in West Germany in the past three decades.

Even if the business community, or some members of it, had wished to introduce inflation accounting methods, two powerful legislative factors would have intervened to prevent such methods from being applied in the main accounts. These are the company law requirements, which lay down strict valuation rules, and the tax law, which insists that most tax allowances (such as those for depreciation)[17] be incorporated in the main accounts, as a condition of eligibility. The valuation rules, imposed by company law, are conservative, the overriding legal rule being that no asset value should be overstated. Upward revaluation of fixed assets is not permitted, and downward revaluation of current assets is mandatory where market value is below cost.

It would, however, be possible to introduce inflation accounting reforms by means of supplementary disclosure, and a proposal of this type was made by the West German professional accountancy body (Institut der Wirtschaftsprüfer, IdW) in 1975. This proposal was made at a time when, following the 1973 oil crisis, inflation rates were high in West Germany relative to that country's own experience over the previous two decades, although they were still low in comparison with the contemporary inflation rates of the other industrialised countries of Western Europe. The prevailing climate of opinion in the West German business community is demonstrated by the fact that the 1975 IdW proposal had a negligible influence on financial reporting practice.[18] Only a few large companies have disclosed inflationary profit corrections in their Directors' Reports, as recommended. The main impact of the proposal was probably in its impact on the debate abroad, insofar as it distilled some of the ideas derived from the work of German theorists from the 1920s onwards, making them available in a concise form to overseas standard-setters in the form of a set of fairly simple practical proposals, with the authority of a professional body.

It is therefore worth briefly outlining the proposals of the 1975 IdW recommendation which was entitled *Maintaining the 'Substantialistic Value' of an Enterprise when Determining the Annual Profit*. The central ideas were derived from those of Schmidt rather than Schmalenbach,[19] i.e. they were of a replacement cost valuation basis combined with an entity view of capital, and they therefore envisaged no rôle for general price-level adjustments. Thus, it was proposed to disclose adjustments to profit which would charge the replacement cost of physical assets (stocks and fixed assets) used up in the period. These adjustments alone would have yielded something akin to the Sandilands operating profit,[20] but a form of gearing adjustment was also proposed. This restricted the

230

other adjustments (for replacement cost of goods sold and depreciation) to the proportion of the assets financed by equity capital. In calculating this gearing adjustment, it was to be assumed that equity capital was applied primarily to financing fixed assets and any surplus was applied to financing stocks.[21] Because of the legal restrictions on the form and context of the main accounts, these adjustments were to be made in a supplementary statement (in the Directors' Report for certain companies), and no corresponding replacement cost balance sheet data were to be given.

The resemblance of these proposals to the subsequent (1977) Hyde Guidelines in the UK is very clear. There are differences, in that the IdW proposal was based on replacement cost rather than value to the firm, and the gearing adjustment made a different financing assumption (see note 21), but the basic concept of both sets of proposals is for depreciation and cost of sales adjustments, abated by a gearing adjustment, with no recognition of unrealised holding gains, no current cost balance sheet, and no use of general indices, although specific indices could be used as surrogates for specific prices.

It is extremely difficult to assess precisely the impact of the IdW proposals on subsequent developments in the English-speaking world. Certainly both the Inflation Accounting Steering Group in the UK[22] and the Richardson Committee in New Zealand were aware of them. On the other hand, there was clearly an independent development of the gearing adjustment in the UK, since Godley and Cripps (1975) developed gearing concepts before the German proposals were published (see Chapter 6). However, it seems likely that the German proposals had some impact on standard-setting in the English-speaking world. For reasons which have already been discussed, they had little impact in West Germany itself, and further developments are unlikely unless there is a drastic change in government policy, the business community and the economic environment.

(iii) France

In France, during the period following the Second World War, inflation accounting practice has been confined to pragmatic adjustments, which have typically taken the form of asset revaluations made for the purpose of securing tax reliefs. Recently (March 1981), however, the professional accountancy body (Ordre des Experts Contables et des Comptables Agréés) have made a step towards a more comprehensive approach to accounting for price-level changes, by publishing its non-mandatory

Opinion on the Establishment of Certain Data Adjusted for the Effects of Changing Prices.

From the end of the Second World War (1945) to the currency reform of 1959, when the New Franc was introduced, France suffered spasmodic periods of high inflation, so that the Wholesale Price Index rose from 100 in 1945 to 841 in 1958. During this period, companies were encouraged to revalue their fixed assets, since the revaluation was not subject to tax, but the resulting higher depreciation reported in subsequent accounting periods was allowable for tax purposes. The only exception to this rule was assets whose purchase was financed by loans, revaluations of which were subject to a 5 per cent tax: a primitive form of taxation of the gain on borrowing. Revaluations were subject to an upper limit determined by changes in a price index relating to a large number of commodities.

The tax allowance for enhanced depreciation was complemented by an allowance for stock appreciation. The details of this relief changed during the period, but it was based upon applying annual changes in a wholesale price index to an average stock holding.[23] The index used was therefore similar in concept to that used in the current (1981) UK stock relief scheme.

Following the 1959 currency reform, all large businesses were required to revalue their fixed assets by 1962, and smaller businesses were allowed to do so. Any subsequent revaluations would be treated as trading profit, so after 1962 there was a disincentive to revalue except for those businesses which had accumulated tax losses.[24] The tax allowance for stock appreciation was also withdrawn at this time.

Thus, in the period since 1959, fiscal considerations have inhibited even piecemeal revaluations in accounts. As a result of the high inflation rates of the mid-1970s, revaluations of fixed assets were required, without tax penalty, for listed companies, in 1976–77. All long-term assets had to be valued at their value in use on 31 December 1976. This yielded more relevant balance sheet information, without incurring a tax penalty. There was no subsequent tax benefit because the additional depreciation on revaluation of fixed assets was offset by a revaluation surplus equal to the extra depreciation, in the latter part of the income statement.[25]

The most recent development, the non-mandatory *Opinion* published by the Ordre in 1981, is too recent for its full impact to be assessed at present. It reaffirmed the importance of the historical cost system, but pointed out that both relative price changes and the declining value of the currency unit have eroded the significance of historical cost accounts and that occasional revaluations of fixed assets, as practised recently in

France, have not dealt adequately with the problem. It therefore proposed a more comprehensive system of supplementary disclosure of three adjustments to profit: depreciation to be based on historical cost adjusted by a general index (on grounds of simplicity and objectivity), cost of goods sold to be based on replacement cost, and a financial structure adjustment, preferably reflecting the purchasing power gain or loss on net monetary items. This system was therefore a mixture of a CPP (general index) and CCA (specific price change) approach. It was intended to be experimental and a variety of detailed methods were suggested, particularly in assessing the cost of sales and financial structure adjustments. The latter adjustment could, for example, be based either on a gearing adjustment method (similar to that in the UK) or on a CPP method (similar to that in the USA). Balance sheet valuations were to reflect the methods used in the income statement.

Thus, the Ordre's proposal was eclectic and it was also pragmatic, containing little theoretical discussion or justification for the specified adjustments. It was essentially an attempt to encourage experimentation and open a debate on inflation accounting, rather than presenting an ultimate solution to the problem. Whether it will be widely supported, in the absence of fiscal incentives, remains to be seen.

(iv) Conclusion

The development of inflation accounting in Europe exhibits considerable variety. Only The Netherlands can claim to be in the forefront of world developments, and it seems likely that current value accounting will develop further there in the future. West Germany, on the other hand, has deliberately avoided developments in inflation accounting in a conscious effort to avoid a repetition of the events of the early 1920s when Germany, of necessity, was a world leader in inflation accounting. Between these two extremes, France and Sweden have recently begun to experiment with inflation accounting, the former with an experimental and pragmatic proposal and the latter with a much more ambitious exposure draft. However, one clear general result emerges from all this variety: in none of these countries has a CPP approach been advocated for asset valuation, and the current proposals in each country contain some attempt to allow for specific price changes in assessing costs. On the other hand, there is no apparent emerging consensus on the capital maintenance concept, for profit measurement, the Dutch, French and Swedish seeming to prefer the proprietary approach, whereas the German tradition is of the entity view, as expressed by an operating capacity concept.[26]

Part I The debate

4 Latin America

(i) The inflationary environment

The historical experience described in earlier chapters suggests, not surprisingly, that interest in, and implementation of, forms of inflation accounting tends to be associated with high rates of inflation. Furthermore, the experience of the hyper-inflation, which followed the First World War in Germany and which, to a lesser extent, affected certain other countries on the continent of Europe, suggested that extremely high rates of inflation tend to focus attention on the problem of stabilising the monetary unit of measurement, and therefore to bring into favour solutions which might broadly be classified as being of the CPP type. One area of the world, which we have hitherto neglected, but which has been associated with high inflation rates, is Latin America, and our hypothesis (high inflation rates bring about CPP solutions) is supported by the fact that certain Latin American countries (in particular Brazil and Chile) which have had high inflation rates have been pioneers of inflation accounting based on the use of general indices.

Before discussing the experience of particular countries, it is necessary to examine the inflationary experience of Latin America and dispel the popular illusion that all of the countries of Latin America typically suffer high inflation rates. Table 9.4 gives details of annual percentage consumer price rises in all of the mainland countries of Latin America during the twenty years ending in 1977. Attention is focussed on the price rises of individual years, rather than on compound rates for the period, in order to demonstrate the experience of the typical year. The experience of the USA, which, by world standards, had low inflation rates during the period, is added for comparative purposes.

It is clear from Table 9.4 that many Latin American countries, particularly those in Central America, did not suffer exceptional inflation during this period, although all achieved double-digit inflation rates in the period following the oil crisis of 1973, and could therefore be described as having an inflation problem at least of the same order as that faced by the USA. The typical experience is, however, of inflation at higher rates than those of the USA, and four countries stand out as having regularly sustained very high levels of inflation (double- or triple-digit rates): Argentina, Brazil, Chile and Uruguay. As Brazil is the most populous country of Latin America (and Argentina the third), there is thus some justification for the popular image of the region as one of endemic high inflation rates. This picture is confirmed by the proportionate consumer price rises from 1970 to 1980, published in the *United Nations Bulletin of Statistics*: Chile (June 1980 index 413,669 with

234

Inflation accounting in other countries

Table 9.4. *Inflation in Latin America, 1958–77*

| Country | Number of years experiencing various ranges | | | | Highest annual rate | |
	Triple-digit	Double-digit	Single-digit	Negative	%	Year
Argentina	4	15	1	–	444.0	1976
Bolivia	–	6	13	1	62.9	1974
Brazil	–	19	1	–	87.1	1964
Chile	4	14	2	–	504.7	1974
Colombia	–	11	9	–	31.9	1963
Costa Rica	–	3	16	1	30.1	1974
Ecuador	–	5	15	–	23.3	1974
El Salvador	–	3	15	2	19.1	1975
Guatemala	–	5	9	6	15.9	1974
Honduras	–	1	18	1	12.9	1974
Mexico	–	6	14	–	29.1	1977
Nicaragua*	–	1	13	3	11.4	1977
Panama	–	1	17	2	16.8	1974
Paraguay	–	4	15	1	26.5	1961
Peru	–	8	12	–	38.1	1977
Uruguay	1	19	—	–	125.4	1968
Venezuela	–	1	17	2	10.2	1975
USA	–	1	19	–	11.0	1974

Notes: The inflation rate is measured as the annual percentage rise in a consumer price index, based on averaging monthly rises. 'Triple digit' means an annual rate ⩾100.0%, etc.
*Data are not available for three years for Nicaragua, so there are only 17 observations in all, as opposed to 20 for other countries.
Source: Chapter 25 of *Statistical Abstract of Latin America*, Volume 20, edited by James W. Wilkie and Peter Reich, UCLA Latin American Center Publications, University of California, Los Angeles, 1980.

1970 = 100) and Argentina (June 1980 index 252,694) had by far the greatest inflation in Latin America over the decade, followed by Uruguay (June 1980 index 11,544) and Brazil (February 1980 index 1,030.8, based on 1972 = 100). The comparable indices for the USA and the UK were 213.1 and 363.5 respectively (June 1980 indices, with 1970 = 100). One other feature worth noting is that inflation reached a peak in Brazil very early, in 1964, Brazil having the highest inflation rate in Latin America for each year from 1961 to 1964. Not surprisingly, this led to Brazil being a pioneer of inflation accounting, and of wider forms of indexation.

(ii) Inflation accounting practice

A convenient and up-to-date international survey of accounting principles and practice is provided by the Price Waterhouse study, 1979. This shows the following position for various forms of inflation accounting in Latin America (i.e. the seventeen countries listed in Table 9.4), as of 1979.

General price-level adjustments were required in the main financial statements in two countries, Brazil and Chile, and supplementary general price-level adjustments were required by the auditing profession in Argentina. A note, appended to historical cost statements, disclosing the effect of changes in the general price level, was minority practice (but not required, either by statute or by auditors' assessment of good practice) in Uruguay. In the remaining countries of Latin America, any form of general price-level adjustment was rarely found in practice, and in many (eight of the seventeen, including Argentina) general price-level adjustments would either not be permitted by statute or not be accepted by auditors if they were to replace traditional historical cost accounts as the main financial statements. It is notable that the four clear leaders in the rate of inflation during the past two decades have been the ones to change over to some degree of general price-level adjustment of accounts, Argentina, Brazil, Chile and Uruguay.

The position with regard to specific price adjustments, such as those embodied in CCA systems, was that such adjustments were found occasionally in Latin America, but mainly as piecemeal variations on what are fundamentally CPP systems. In Brazil and Chile, where general price-level adjustment is compulsory, the law does not permit specific price-level adjustment in the main statements, except in the closely defined areas (such as stock valuation in Chile) described in (iii) and (iv) below. In the other fifteen countries, specific price-level adjustments were permitted by way of note or as supplementary statements, but such adjustments were rarely found in practice. The same applied in seven of these countries (including Uruguay) to making specific price adjustments in the main statements, but in eight countries this practice was either not permitted by law (in four countries, including Argentina) or not accepted by auditors. Thus, at the time of the Price Waterhouse survey (June 1979), no form of current value or

236

current cost accounting had achieved even the status of minority practice in Latin America.[27]

Since the time of the Price Waterhouse survey, CPP adjustments were made compulsory for listed companies in Argentina (from 31 August 1980), and subsequently, by a law published in September 1983, inflation-adjusted financial statements must be published as main accounts by all companies. The Mexican Institute of Public Accountants has required (from January 1980) supplementary adjustments to profit figures which may be on either a general price level or a current value basis. This and other recent developments are surveyed in the *Inter-American Accounting Review*, No. 5 (February–March 1981).

It is apparent from this brief survey that Brazil and Chile are the countries which have led the progress of inflation accounting in Latin America, and we shall now consider each of these in more detail.

(iii) Brazil

Brazil has been a pioneer of inflation accounting during the past two decades. Following four years during which the country had the highest inflation rate in Latin America, and a political revolution, the first stage of inflation accounting was introduced in 1964. This was part of an economy-wide system of indexation or 'monetary correction', whereby most contracts which had previously been made in nominal monetary units now had indexation clauses, requiring monetary payments to be increased in proportion to price indices. Friedman (1974) and others[28] have advocated this type of policy as a means of assisting the stabilisation of the price level, by removing the effect of high inflationary expectations on contracts such as the annual wage bargain. On the other hand, others (including, as we saw earlier, an important body of opinion in West Germany) have feared that indexation policies, by ameliorating some of the inequities resulting from inflation, will make continued inflation more acceptable and will 'institutionalise' it. The Brazilian experience is that inflation has indeed persisted, at double-digit rates, since indexation was introduced, but it has never again reached the peak which it attained prior to the introduction of indexation.

The restatement of fixed asset values, by reference to changes in a general price index, was first permitted in Brazil in 1951. However, depreciation on these enhanced values was not an allowable deduction for tax purposes, and there was typically no fiscal incentive to restate.[29] This was changed in 1964, when annual restatement of fixed asset values by reference to a prescribed general price index, based on wholesale prices, became compulsory. The restated amounts were debited to asset

237

accounts and credited to reserves, and were, until 1967, subject to a 5 per cent tax. However, subsequent depreciation based on the restated amounts could be charged to the profit and loss account and was allowable as a deduction in assessing corporate income tax. This was similar to the pre-1959 French system for loan-financed fixed assets. A second important adjustment introduced later, in 1974, was the provision for the maintenance of the purchasing power of working capital. 'Working capital' is essentially defined as net worth, less fixed assets and investments. The provision was calculated by applying the change in an official general index to the opening amount of working capital. The provision was debited as an adjustment to profit for the year and credited as a reserve in the balance sheet. The provision was allowed as deduction from income for tax purposes, subject to certain important restrictions.[30] In addition, any monetary correction of indexed loans to the company was deductible for tax purposes.[31]

The net effect of this system was to produce something very close to CCP accounting, and most commentators[32] seem to interpret it in this manner. A general index was effectively being applied to equity capital, before profit could be recognised for tax purposes, and this same basis was adopted in the published accounts.[33] Fixed assets were revalued by reference to a general index, which could be regarded as restating them in current monetary units. Current assets and liabilities were not restated, on the ground that they were already expressed in relatively recent currency units. The main differences between this system and the commonly advocated CPP systems are:

(1) That the Brazilian system used separate indices for fixed assets and for net working capital, and these were more closely related to wholesale prices than to retail prices.

(2) Working capital items appearing in the closing balance sheet were not restated in end-of-year currency units, the net working capital adjustment being based solely on opening balance sheet figures.

(3) The fixed asset restatement began only in the second year after acquisition.

(4) Profit and loss account flows were not translated into common monetary units.

It is interesting to observe that the Sandilands Committee[34] did not interpret the Brazilian model as a crude form of CPP, but preferred to regard it as an attempt to implement replacement cost valuation (the official indices being interpreted as surrogates for specific price changes) with a 'purchasing power of the business' concept of capital maintenance (which, of course, makes it sound like an approximation to CCA). The Sandilands Committee pointed out that no attempt was made in Brazil to restate the accounts comprehensively in a CPP unit: in particular, the profit and loss account was not restated in end-of-period units. However, CPP does allow the profit and loss account to be in 'average for the year' units, and the use of a general index (albeit based on wholesale rather than retail prices) for all fixed assets, irrespective of type of industry, and for working capital, whether stocks or trade credit, is surely closer to a CPP adjustment of historical cost than an assessment of the replacement cost of specific assets. Furthermore, although there was no comprehensive restatement in terms of a constant monetary unit based on a single index, the net effect of the adjustments was to produce a balance sheet and profit and loss account which were expressed fairly consistently in recent monetary units, using only two indices. It therefore seems that the Sandilands Committee was indulging in special pleading when it tried to identify the Brazilian system as a crude attempt at replacement cost, and it was most certainly stretching credulity beyond tolerable limits in attempting to draw from the Brazilian experience lessons for the likely effect of applying current cost accounting (CCA) in the UK.[35]

Since the time of the Sandilands Report, the Brazilian system has been reformed in a manner which makes it more consistent with the CPP model. The major reforms introduced in 1978 (and described in more detail, with a numerical example, by Fleming (1979)) involve annual monetary correction, by the use of a general index, of permanent assets and shareholders' equity. These accounts are required to be recorded, in the books of account, in 'treasury bond units', a CPP unit which is then translated, by the use of an index, into current monetary units. The records in 'treasury bond units' are updated either monthly or quarterly, eliminating the lag in adjusting asset values, which was one deficiency of the earlier (1964) system. The restatement of assets is credited and the restatement of equity is debited to the profit and loss account, a net debit (i.e. loss) being deductible from profit for tax purposes and a net credit being taxable on a deferred basis (i.e. the tax is levied only when the relevant gain is realised). Depreciation charged in the profit and loss account is based upon the restated opening value of the relevant assets, and is subject to a further 'correction' adjustment to allow for inflation during the period. Current assets (including stocks) and liabilities are not restated in end-of-year units.

Thus, the Brazilian system which is currently in force incorporates many CPP adjustments to historical cost in the main accounts, although the system is not a pure CPP system in the sense of translating all items in the accounts into monetary units of a strictly equal value (i.e. purchasing power as at the same point in time). A notable feature of the implementation of this system is that it has been enforced by government decree, removing the need to gain the voluntary compliance of various preparers, which has been one of the problems facing the FASB in the United States and the ASC in the United Kingdom. Furthermore, the integration of various CPP adjustments with the tax system has provided an additional incentive to comply with the system. This again is a feature which is notably absent from the American and British situations.

(iv) Chile[36]

Chile has rivalled Brazil as the leading Latin American exponent of inflation accounting. Since the end of 1974, Chile has had a requirement under government decree for company accounts to be drawn up on what might broadly be described as a CPP basis, similar to that subsequently adopted in Brazil. As in Brazil, the same system which is used for financial reporting is also used for tax purposes. The main difference from the Brazilian system is that stocks are revalued annually at replacement cost in Chile. Also, when the new system was introduced (1 January 1975), all non-monetary assets (including fixed assets) were revalued at replacement cost, at the company's option. Subsequent annual restatements of fixed asset values are based on general (consumer price) index adjustment rather than current value, except in the case of assets whose value is determined in foreign currency, which appear at current market value, and 'protected' (i.e. indexed) monetary assets and liabilities, which are reported at their current indexed values. Equity interests are also restated annually using the general index. These restatements are all credited (in the case of increases in assets) or debited (in the case of increased claims, such as the adjustment of equity interest) to a monetary correction account, the balance of which is transferred to profit and loss.

Thus, the Chilean system resembles the later Brazilian system, but has a greater element of replacement cost in asset valuation. However, the use of the consumer price index (rather than a general index of permanent assets and shareholders' equity) for restating equity introduces a stronger CPP (or real terms) element than exists in the Brazilian system: it could not be claimed that the Chilean system was based on maintaining the 'purchasing power of the business'. Thus, if the Chilean model can be regarded as an approximation to a pure theoretical model, that model would be a 'real terms' system based on replacement cost valuation, not a CCA model.

Prior to the 1974 reforms, annual restatements of fixed asset values, using general indices, had been allowed in Chile for many years and became compulsory in 1963, when depreciation based on the restated values became an allowable expense for tax purposes. This (1963) system has much in common with the contemporary (1964) Brazilian system and, like it, failed to give full allowance for the effect of inflation on working capital[37] (introduced in Brazil in 1974). It was inflation rates of 508 per cent in 1973 and 376 per cent in 1974 which gave rise to the urgent need for a more comprehensive system of inflation accounting.[38] The Chilean accountancy profession proposed (May 1974) a comprehensive CPP system, similar to that of the *APB3* in the USA and adopted by the Inter-American Accounting Conference in 1970. This no doubt had some influence on the new laws passed in 1974, but it is interesting to note that the Government introduced replacement cost elements into their legislation, at a time when various government bodies in other countries were also about to favour CCA in preference to CPP.

(v) Other Latin American countries

Brief reference has already been made to the fact that Argentina and Uruguay have also adopted inflation accounting adjustments. It is notable that these two countries, although suffering periods of inflation as serious as those in Brazil and Chile, have progressed more slowly. This was due to lack of government support, either by decree or fiscal incentive: in both Argentina and Uruguay published accounts do not have to report profit as assessed for tax purposes. In Uruguay, inflation accounting disclosure is still voluntary and supplementary, and tax reliefs are not dependent on their being consistent with profit reported in published accounts. The recent developments in Argentina appear to have been due to changes of policy by the Government and by the Stock Exchange, both bodies have previously opposed the profession's proposals for CPP accounting, but having changed their attitude under the pressure of recent triple-digit inflation rates. Argentina now has a national policy of indexation similar to those in Brazil and Chile, and CPP accounting is a natural concomitant of this. The other country which has seen significant developments recently is Mexico where, again, past proposals by the profession have been opposed by the Government.[39]

Other Latin American countries have seen little development in inflation accounting practice. This may be partly due to lower inflation rates, but inflation rates have almost invariably been as high as those in the USA, where, as we saw in Chapter 7, there have been very significant developments. Thus, the attitudes of governments and the institutional structure of the various economies (e.g. the absence of highly developed stock exchanges) must also have been important factors inhibiting development. Certainly the lack of development has not been due to lack of knowledge of available techniques: successive Inter-American Accounting Association conferences (the first being held in 1949) have considered the problem of inflation accounting (notably the 1965 and 1970 conferences) and have recommended inflation adjustment procedures on CPP lines.[40]

Thus, Latin America provides an invaluable demonstration of the evolution of inflation accountancy practice, from at least three points of view. Firstly, it provides notable examples of CPP systems in operation, in Brazil and Chile and, more recently, Argentina. Secondly, it demonstrates the importance of extremely high inflation rates, in bringing about CPP systems in these three countries. Thirdly, it illustrates the importance of the economic and political environment, since, although the countries which have adopted CPP have all suffered extremely high inflation, not all countries which have suffered extremely high inflation have adopted CPP methods as standard practice: the obvious example of this is Uruguay, where inflation accounting has no statutory backing and tax reliefs for inflation are given irrespective of whether the effects of inflation are reported in the accounts.

5 General conclusion

The international development of inflation accounting, surveyed in this chapter, contains such variety that it is inappropriate to attempt to summarise it. However, in later chapters we shall attempt to draw some broad conclusions about the development of inflation accounting practice, and some of the themes of this chapter will support those conclusions. It is in the nature of this type of study that the evidence is suggestive rather than conclusive, but at this stage we would invite the reader to consider the following hypotheses which we believe to be supported, or at least suggested, by the evidence of this chapter:
(1) That ideas about inflation accounting have been transmitted internationally on a large scale, and often to the extent that users of those ideas are unaware of their original sources.
(2) That inflation accounting practice develops as a result of the pressures created by high inflation rates (such as followed the 1973 world oil crisis), rather than the more insidious distortions in accounts resulting from the cumulative effects of lower inflation rates.

(3) That a further condition for the development of inflation accounting practice is an appropriate political and institutional environment. In particular, governments must favour inflation accounting as part of their broad economic strategy (as in Brazil, but not as in West Germany) and as being consistent with their fiscal policy. Furthermore, preparers of accounts must favour inflation accounting, fiscal incentives being the most likely factor to bring this about, and users must demand it, an active stock market being the most likely vehicle for such demands.

(4) The nature of the factors described above is that they do not change rapidly from a situation of extreme rejection of inflation accounting to one of enthusiastic acceptance. It is therefore not surprising that the introduction of inflation accounting everywhere has been evolutionary, either involving piecemeal reforms, or long discussion of proposals and counter-proposals, or both. For example, Professor Baxter (1976) has characterised the development of Latin American inflation accounting systems as having two stages: firstly, fixed assets and depreciation are adjusted by reference to a general index, and, secondly, at a later stage, the 'timelag error' on stocks and monetary working capital is corrected by the application of an index. The result is very close to CPP adjustment of historical cost, although certain current value or replacement cost elements appear, as in the replacement cost valuation of stocks in Chile. Different evolutionary patterns might be detected elsewhere, but if evolution is the order of the day, the academic critic should perhaps take the constructive attitude of pointing the direction of future evolution, rather than condemning the early stages out of hand, for lack of theoretical purity.

10
The present state of inflation accounting throughout the world

1 Introduction

Earlier chapters have described the progress of the international inflation accounting debate from the beginning of the century to the present day with particular emphasis, because of their topical nature, on changing views in the 1970s and early 1980s. Before turning, in the final part of this book, to a more analytical assessment of the arguments on the contentious technical issues, the political influences on the debate and its possible outcome, we now pause to examine broadly the position reached at the time of writing – the base from which future inflation accounting developments will evolve.

Looking back over the debate, it could be said that the development of inflation accounting in the recent past has been conducted in individual countries at one of three levels:
(1) the imperative level;
(2) the innovative (primary) theoretical level; and
(3) the secondary theoretical level.

The debate has undoubtedly been more urgent in times of high and rising inflation, when it had become obvious that historical cost financial statements were failing to reflect the reality of companies' financial performance or position. In Latin America, where, in Argentina, Brazil and Chile, prices doubled or came close to doubling annually, the debate was on the *imperative level* – something simply had to be done to combat the misleading results given by historical cost accounts.[1] Theoretical considerations such as whether accounts should be expressed in current cost monetary units as opposed to current purchasing power units became largely irrelevant as the magnitude of the inflationary forces made the difference between the rise in general and specific prices relatively immaterial.

In other countries, where the inflationary period after the 1973 oil crisis led to renewed interest in price-level adjusted accounts, the rate of inflation, while extremely high in terms of previous experience, was not

244

such that historical cost accounts became virtually meaningless. The debate in these (mainly developed, English-speaking) countries was conducted more at the *innovative theoretical level*. There were, however, major pragmatic intrusions, especially after governments or government agencies in four of the countries (Australia, New Zealand, the UK and the USA) had, in the mid-1970s, rejected CPP accounting as a means of reflecting the effects of changing price levels and had promptly changed the course of the international debate. Common government attitudes were the result of common economic, political and social pressures associated with cost inflation, high relative price changes and government interest in controlling prices and incomes, whilst preserving the tax base in money terms.

As a result of cultural and economic relationships and a shared language,[2] ideas were freely interchanged among the countries involved in the debate at the innovative theoretical level and, in earlier chapters, we have traced some of the more obvious exchanges of theory. Ideas were not necessarily adopted unchanged but affected the course of the debate in other countries by being adapted to suit prevalent national theories.

Other major developed countries were not involved in the primary debate – their rôle was that of interested observers, whose emergence in the debate consisted of adopting a variant of a system proposed in one or more of the countries in the innovative theoretical group. The debate in these countries could therefore be deemed to have been conducted at the *secondary theoretical level*. In these countries, those responsible for developing inflation accounting pronouncements were, in essence, sitting in judgement on the efforts of standard-setters in countries in the primary group, and selecting those proposals which held most appeal.

In the remainder of this chapter we shall consider briefly the current position of the debate in countries in each of the three groups we have identified – commencing with the major countries in the group in which the debate was conducted at the imperative level.[3]

2 The present position in Latin America (the debate at the imperative level)

Discussions on accounting for the effects of inflation in Latin America took place against a background of extremely high rates of inflation. Theoretical elegance, consequently, was not as vital as the derivation of practical measures to combat the increasing irrelevance of historical cost accounts. For this reason, therefore, Latin America's contribution to the debate internationally has been at the practical level of implementation of measures to meet fiscal considerations rather than at the more philosophical level of the improvement of reporting practice.

Two practical lessons are, however, available for the rest of the world from the South American experience. Firstly, unlike the experience in the industrialised countries, acceptance of inflation accounting in Latin America was not a problem: fiscal considerations or statutory authority were the key to obtaining compliance in three of the four countries which experienced the greatest increases in inflation. By way of contrast, in Australia and the UK, expectations, raised by Government Committees of Enquiry in 1975, of taxation being linked to current cost accounts have long since diminished and, as the rate of inflation fell, problems of the acceptability of inflation accounting proposals rose markedly.

Secondly, the general index adjustments employed in Latin America have provided examples of CPP systems in action (see Table 10.1) – systems which were discarded in other parts of the world after the Current Cost Revolution in 1975.

At the level of price rises experienced in several countries in this continent, debates on whether general or specific price indices should be used may well have been futile. Major adjustments had to be made to the historical cost accounts if reasonably realistic measures of performance were to be shown: the effect of using different indices would probably have been relatively immaterial. Moreover, in Brazil and Chile, the acceptance of general index adjustments was made easier by the fact that the indexation of accounts was part of a much wider policy of indexing contracts and the tax base, with the active support of governments. This has more recently become the case in Argentina. A further factor in favour of the more objective general index was undoubtedly the ease of verification of the CPP adjustments for fiscal purposes: a major element in the refusal of governments elsewhere to accept CCA systems as a basis for corporate taxation has been the generally subjective nature of the estimation of specific price change and the corresponding fear of tax evasion.

The influence of Latin America on the discussions in the rest of the world has, despite the above lessons for the other participants in the debate, been negligible. The impetus in the debate has instead come from the accountancy profession, often prompted by the Government, in a few nations with sophisticated financial institutions. It is to the debate in these countries to which we now turn.

Table 10.1. *The present position in South America*

	Argentina	Brazil	Chile	Uruguay
Authority	Government and profession	Government	Government	None
Status of inflation adjusted data	Usually CPP adjustments in main accounts (as from September 1983)	CPP adjustments in main accounts	CPP adjustments in main accounts	Supplementary note – minority practice
CPP Adjustment used for tax	Yes (but independent of accounts)	Yes (on accounts basis)	Yes (on accounts basis)	Yes (but not necessary for tax adjustments to be in accounts)
Specific prices allowed	No	No	Yes – for stock	Yes

3 The present position in the countries leading the theoretical debate (the debate at the innovative theoretical level)

Six developed countries could be said to have led the debate in current cost terms in recent years: two in Europe – The Netherlands and the UK; two in North America – Canada and the USA; and two in Australasia – Australia and New Zealand. Each country has contributed ideas to the recent debate after the initial publication in the mid-1970s of basically similar CCA operating profit proposals (involving current cost depreciation and cost of sales) in Australia, New Zealand, the UK and the USA. Some of these ideas have been adopted elsewhere: others have been rejected.

In Europe, The Netherlands provided a classic example of an RC system in operation (Philips) which undoubtedly disarmed critics of the practicalities of such a system, and NIVRA's 1976 statement outlined a real terms solution to the inflation accounting problem – a solution which appears to be increasingly more popular as the debate continues. The United Kingdom's 1975 Sandilands Report introduced the concept of the value to the business which has been adopted in both Canada and the United States although modified in Britain itself where the Australian version employing the non-discounted recoverable amount concept was adopted.[4]

In Australasia, the 1976 New Zealand Richardson Report, borrowing in part from the internal UK debate, became the first official pronouncement to advocate a monetary asset adjustment to profit and a gearing adjustment based on realised and unrealised holding gains (what we term the realisable cost saving approach).

Australia contributed the recoverable amount valuation system (1976) and, later, in its 1978 Exposure Draft, was the first country to support a current cost monetary working capital adjustment, which reflected gains on liabilities.

In North America, the Canadians, through the medium of the 1977 Ontario Report, rejected the gearing adjustment proposed in New Zealand and advocated for the first time in a pronouncement in an English-speaking country a gearing adjustment based on abating additional current cost charges to income[5] (the realised cost saving approach), a prudent approach adopted in both the United Kingdom (the Hyde Guidelines) the same year (although probably from European and UK origins) and, later, in an exposure draft issued by the Canadian Institute itself (1979).

The United States rejected the articulated profit and loss and balance sheet approach and was the first country to adopt the 'information set' style of reporting price-level adjusted data, enabling the reader of the accounts to obtain information based on differing concepts of income – current purchasing power, current cost and 'real terms' data all being provided. This approach may have proved attractive as a consequence of its sound theoretical base, or more mundanely, may have resulted from the difficulty of obtaining agreement for a single method. It has, however, attracted support recently in Canada (particularly) and in New Zealand where an optional approach involving 'real terms' data has been adopted.

Turning to the present overall position in the six countries, it can be seen (Table 10.2) that in certain areas some form of consensus exists. *Current cost valuation* practices are similar, although not identical, variations of the eclectic value to the business criterion proving to be the acceptable choice in practice. Historical costs updated by a general index are not advocated in any country in this group. The *capital maintenance* issue is, however, a subject of contention. In the mid-1970s, proposals in four of the English-speaking countries advocated the maintenance of the operating capacity of fixed assets and inventories (Canada was the sole exception). At the time of writing, however, only Australia continues to advocate an entity form of income measurement.

Two countries (the UK and New Zealand) have introduced a proprietorial element into the physical capital maintenance approach by giving information enabling the reader to ascertain income after maintaining the portion of operating capacity financed by shareholders (the proprietorial entity approach) by means of a gearing adjustment. Canada too has adopted this approach. Indeed, Canada and New Zealand have gone even further towards a pure proprietary concept by allowing, by way of option (New Zealand) or by the disclosure of additional information (Canada), the measurement of income on a 'real terms' basis. The FASB in the USA has, however, since the issue of its 1978 Exposure Draft, generally remained a supporter of the proprietary approach, confirming its viewpoint in the 1981 conceptual framework Exposure Draft, *Reporting Income, Cash Flows and Financial Position of Business Enterprises*.

A major issue in the late 1970s – *gains and losses on monetary items* – has still not been resolved internationally, mainly because no agreement has been reached on the capital maintenance question. The division of view on the objectives of a business – in the UK and Australia as an entity serving a coalition of different interest groups (shareholders, employees, customers and so on), necessitating the maintenance of the 'business', and in the USA as an organisation seeking to obtain profits for its shareholders necessitating the maintenance of shareholders'

Table 10.2. *The present position in the countries leading the theoretical debate*

Statements	Europe		North America		Australasia	
	The Netherlands Note to IASC E6, 1976	UK SSAP16, 1980	Canada Handbook S4510 1982	USA FAS33, 1979	Australia SAP1, 1983	New Zealand CCA-1, 1982
Valuation	Replacement cost	Value to the business (RC, NRV and recoverable amount)	Value to the business (RC, NRV, economic value (EV))	Value to the business (RC, NRV, EV)	Value to the business (RC, NRV and recoverable amount)	Value to the business (RC, NRV and recoverable amount)
Capital maintenance system	Proprietary	Proprietorial entity	Proprietary, entity and proprietorial entity	Proprietary	Entity	Proprietary and proprietorial entity
Operating capacity (broadly) defined	Fixed assets and inventories (in calculating operating profit)	Proportion of fixed assets, current assets excluding surplus cash, less current liabilities, financed by shareholders	Fixed assets and inventories; and proportion of such assets financed by shareholders	Fixed assets and inventories (in calculating operating profit)	Fixed assets and net current assets	Proportion of fixed assets, current assets excluding surplus cash, less current liabilities, financed by shareholders

Gain on borrowing	Indirectly – CPP gains on liabilities	MWCA and gearing adjustment	Gearing adjustments and CPP gains on liabilities	CPP gains on liabilities	MWCA (gain on long-term borrowing shown in note and as a reserve adjustment)	MWCA and gearing adjustment (1 option); CPP gain on liabilities (alternative)
Loss on holding money	Indirectly CPP loss on monetary assets	MWCA and deduction of surplus cash from long-term liabilities used in calculating gearing adjustment	Monetary assets deducted from liabilities before calculating gearing adjustment and CPP loss on monetary assets	CPP loss on monetary assets	MWCA (loss on holding long-term borrowing shown in note and as a reserve adjustment)	MWCA (1 option): CPP loss on monetary assets (alternative)
Status of price-level adjusted data	Supplementary	Supplementary (generally) but can be used as main accounts	Supplementary	Supplementary	Supplementary (generally) but can be used as main accounts	Supplementary
Presentation	Profit and loss account	Profit and loss account and balance sheet	Components of income and information on asset values	Components of income and information on asset values	Profit and loss account and balance sheet	Profit and loss account and balance sheet

Note: MWCA – Monetary Working Capital Adjustment

capital in 'real terms' – has led to differing measurements of effects of price-level changes on monetary items. Consequently, where the proprietary capital maintenance concept is favoured, general index based CPP gains and losses on monetary items exist; where an entity or proprietorial entity view is taken, monetary working capital adjustments calculated on the basis of specific price change and gearing adjustments (proprietorial entity only) are to be found.

The differing adjustments for monetary items are, as we shall discuss later in Chapter 12, attempting to satisfy different objectives – CPP adjustments reflecting the effect of price changes on the purchasing power of the shareholders' investment and in the enterprise, and adjustments based on specific indices being concerned more with the retention of cash within the business to ensure the maintenance of its operating capability.

One point in common in all six countries is the status of the information supplied – price-level adjusted data is given mainly as supplementary information to the primary historical cost financial statements. At this stage of the debate, no country has produced a current cost accounting standard which proposes the replacement of the traditional HC accounts by price-level adjusted data.[6]

The style of presentation of such data differs considerably among the six countries, although a distinct movement towards an 'information set' approach has become obvious in the last few years. This movement and the apparent direction of the debate will be considered in the next two sections, the first of which deals with four countries, two of which could be said to have observed the arguments and sat in judgement on the various proposals emanating from the debate.

4 The present position in the countries following the theoretical debate (the debate at the secondary theoretical level)

The position in the inflation accounting debate in the four countries which we have deemed to have followed rather than have led the debate is outlined in Table 10.3.

Two of these countries (Germany and South Africa) have made only a minimal contribution to the recent debate although, in 1975, the German Institute (Institut der Wirtschaftsprüfer) issued the world's first official pronouncement incorporating a gearing adjustment (based on the realised cost saving concept). The gearing adjustment, albeit in a different form, was at that time already a matter of contention in the UK, but the ultimate outcome of this aspect of the British debate may well have been influenced by the West German recommendation. Since

1975, however, the German Institute has kept out of the international debate – the West German Government frowning upon the notion of inflation accounting, probably because of the memory of the hyper-inflation in Germany after the First World War. The professional accountancy body in South Africa, too, has remained silent in the recent past on the subject of inflation accounting. No contribution to the international discussion has been made since 1978, when the South African Institute issued a more sophisticated version of the UK's Hyde Guidelines, which did little to advance the international experiment.

By way of contrast, the accountancy societies in the two other countries in this group have both, at the beginning of this present decade, issued their first pronouncements on accounting for the effects of price-level changes and have given an indication of the potential direction of the debate by 'voting' on the various pronouncements of those countries involved in the innovative level of the debate. The French proposal is more eclectic (or pragmatic), allowing depreciation based on historical cost adjusted by a general index as a simplified surrogate for RC depreciation. Additionally, it is difficult to define the capital maintenance objective of the French proposal as the gain on monetary liabilities can be calculated by various means including a gearing adjustment based on realised cost savings or a CPP adjustment. The main feature of the system, however, is its proposal for optional treatments to allow further experimentation – a growing trend in the early 1980s. This approach has also been adopted by the Swedish Institute which allows three approaches with increasing degrees of sophistication to the measurement of income, the most refined of which is virtually identical to the *FAS33* real terms proposals.[7]

5 Summary

The debate on inflation accounting has taken two forms over the last two decades largely due to a higher level of inflation being experienced in Latin America than in other countries interested in the subject of inflation accounting. In Latin America, the extremely high annual inflation rates in certain countries demanded practical action as historical cost accounts become not only misleading but increasingly irrelevant as a tax base. In Brazil and Chile, there was little opposition by preparers to the notion of adjusting HC accounts, as the revised accounts were used for fiscal purposes. Indeed, the possible adjustment of the tax base must have provided a powerful incentive to lobby governments to institute reform and accounting reform seems often to have been a by-product of tax reform. In these countries, there is

Table 10.3. *The present position in the countries following the theoretical debate*

	Sweden Exposure Draft (1980)	France Opinion (1981)	West Germany Recommendation (1975)	South Africa Guideline (1978)
Valuation	Lower of RC and recoverable amount	Eclectic – RC NRV and CPP (as a surrogate for RC)	RC	Value to the business (RC, NRV, and recoverable amount)
Capital maintenance system	Proprietary	Proprietorial entity (under one alternative)	Proprietorial entity	Proprietorial entity
Operating capacity to be maintained	—	Amount of fixed assets and stock financed by shareholders (under one alternative)	Amount of fixed assets and stock financed by shareholders	Amount of fixed assets. stock and monetary assets financed by shareholders

Gain on borrowing	CPP gains on borrowings (under one alternative)	CPP gains on borrowings (under one alternative); or gearing adjustment	Gearing adjustment	Gearing adjustment
Loss on holding money	CPP loss on holding money (under one alternative)	CPP loss on holding money (under one alternative)	Indirect – monetary assets deducted from liabilities in calculating gearing adjustment	MWCA (as an alternative to gearing adjustment)
Status of inflation adjusted data	Supplementary	Supplementary	Supplementary	Supplementary
Presentation	Profit and loss account and balance sheet	Profit and loss account and balance sheet	Statement of effect of inflation on accounts	Profit and loss account

widespread indexation of contracts, and indexation of accounts is seen as a natural consequence. Consequently, general price-level adjustments are required by the Government in the main accounts in Brazil and Chile. Similar requirements are enforced by a recent law in Argentina which also has economy-wide indexation of contracts. In Uruguay, where, unlike Brazil and Chile, there is no statutory requirement that income reported in accounts should correspond with taxable income, no obligation exists to reveal the effect of price-level changes in the accounts or in their accompanying notes.

The case of Uruguay illustrates the importance of government in inducing changes of accounting practice – despite extremely high inflation, inflation accounting has not become a majority practice in the absence of a government decree or incentive in the form of making the tax relief dependent upon reporting practice. Elsewhere, in Latin America, inflation accounting has made little progress despite the fact that the Inter-American Accounting Congress supported a CPP approach as early as 1970.

In the other countries involved in the debate, where inflationary pressures, although severe, did not affect historical cost accounts to the same degree as in Latin America, the discussion on inflation accounting has been more at the theoretical level, albeit with practical overtones. Acceptance, however, has been a major problem as the failure of experimentation to produce a consensus on the ideal method for accounting for price-level changes, the lack of fiscal benefits, and declining levels of inflation have reduced interest in the subject.

The debate in these countries has, however, begun to evolve along distinct lines. Table 10.4 indicates that optional treatments or a variety of data allowing the reader to select the information relevant for his needs has become increasingly popular since the beginning of the 1980s as the standard-setters appear to accept that the emphasis on the single measure of income, the 'bottom line fixation', is not entirely appropriate: the 'information set' and optional approaches developing from the more rigid methods proposed in the earlier years of the Current Cost Revolution. For example, standard-setters in Canada, whose CCA Exposure Draft in 1979 was closely modelled on the UK's *ED24*, and in New Zealand, whose 1981 Exposure Draft was similar to *SSAP16* (except for the style of the gearing adjustment), have both moved away from the UK's position – the former opting for an 'information set' approach; the latter moving towards a method allowing different options.

A related effect of the building blocks/information set or optional approaches has been the movement away from the entity approach as

The present state of inflation accounting

Table 10.4. *Current means of accounting for price-level changes in the countries involved in the theoretical debate*

1 *'Information set'* *approach*: the user selects the information required.	USA (1979)	Canada (1982)	
2 *Articulated accounts* (or profit and loss account and details of the value of assets adjusted for price-level changes) *allowing more than one option in the measurement of profit.*	Sweden (1980)	France (1981)	New Zealand (1982)
3 *Articulated accounts – only one method of measuring final profit allowed.* (Components of income usually reported allowing users to make alternative calculations.)	Australia (1983)	UK (1980)	
4 *Profit and loss account only – no options.* (Components of income usually reported allowing users to make alternative calculations.)	West Germany (1975)	The Netherlands (1976)	South Africa (1978)

favoured by Government Committees of Enquiry (in Australia and the UK) and the SEC in the mid-1970s to more proprietary based approaches (see Table 10.5). Only in Australia, has there been an adherence to the entity concept. The difficulties of defining operating capability, the objectivity of the financial capital concept and the inability of the operating capacity concept to cope with investment orientated enterprises, probably all contributed to its diminishing popularity. In addition, even where an operating capacity concept exists, the view that shareholders are entitled to know the share of profit attributable to them has frequently led to the introduction of a gearing adjustment. The American view of the need to measure profits in terms of the increase in the proprietors' stake in the business appears to be more acceptable in the early 1980s than in the mid-1970s.

257

Table 10.5. *The changing capital maintenance approaches in the countries involved in the theoretical debate*

Innovative Theoretical group	First CCA pronouncement		Latest CCA pronouncement
	Authority		
	By Government agency/committee	By standard-setting body	By standard-setting body
Australia	E (1975)	E (1975)	E (1983)
Canada	—	P (1976)	All (1982)
The Netherlands	—	P (1976)*	P (1976)*
New Zealand	P/E (1976)	E (1976)	P/E or P (1982)
UK	E (1975)	ALL (1976)	P/E (1980)
USA	E (1976)	P (1978)	P (1979 and 1981)
Secondary Theoretical group			
France	—	P/E (1981)*†	P/E (1981)*†
South Africa	—	P/E (1978)*	P/E (1978)*
Sweden	—	P (1980)*	P (1980)*
West Germany	—	P/E (1975)*	P/E (1975)*

Capital Maintenance System proposed
P = proprietary
E = entity
P/E = proprietorial entity (i.e. an entity-based method, which involves the use of a gearing adjustment).
ALL = P or E or P/E above.
* = only one CCA pronouncement by standard-setter.
† = under one alternative. (It is difficult to describe the capital maintenance system under the other alternatives.)

The capital maintenance debate is, of course, only part of the wider issue of the objective of financial reporting. The second part of the book looks more analytically at the international debate, examining the causes and influences on the debate, the rôle of theory and the political process of standard setting. By means of comparative analysis we consider in greater depth competing systems of inflation accounting; international views on the measurement of income (including capital maintenance concepts), and the related subjects of the valuation of assets and gains and losses on monetary items.

PART II

Causes and consequences

11

Competing systems of accounting for price changes

1 Introduction

The first chapter of this book, and the whole of its companion book[1] have outlined the main models which have emerged in the theoretical and practical debates on price change accounting. The term 'price change' is used advisedly in preference to 'inflation', since some of these models eschew any use of general price indices and rely solely on recording the price changes of specific assets held by the firm. The previous chapter has surveyed the current state of both theory and practice throughout the world, and it will be seen in the next chapter that there is an extremely wide variety of models available, with quite subtle gradations between them. Any classification is therefore bound to be arbitrary, but it is possible to identify three pure theoretical models, upon which the discussion will focus and around which the variants and pragmatic compromises will be arranged.

The three pure models are:
(1) Historical cost adjusted by general indices, sometimes known as Constant Purchasing Power, CPP. The Real Terms system, (3) below, also involves a constant purchasing power adjustment, but applied to a current valuation base rather than historical cost.
(2) Current or Replacement Cost accounting, relying solely on the specific price changes of the assets held by the firm, and with no use of general price indices. This will be stylised as CCA for present purposes.
(3) Real Terms accounting, RT, involving specific price adjustments to the assets held and used by the firm (as in CCA), but with a further general index adjustment to this base (as in CPP) to reflect the effect of inflation on the capital base of the firm, and, possibly, on the unit of measurement used in the accounts.

The subsequent discussion, focussing on these three pure models, will attempt to impose a pattern on the welter of detailed historical data provided in the earlier chapters, in order to give the reader an over-view of the subject. However, this is an aid to reading the earlier chapters, rather than a substitute for it: the imposition of any pattern on the material necessarily involves the subjective judgement of the authors, which the reader may not wish to accept.

This chapter focusses on whole systems. Certain themes and problem areas which span systems will be discussed in the next chapter. We shall then move to more speculative, but nonetheless important, themes, in the final two chapters, which will consider the factors which have contributed to the course of the debate, and its likely future course.

2 CPP

Here we shall discuss the evolution of CPP accounting, defined narrowly to confine it to the general index adjustment of the historical cost base. This is, in a sense, pure inflation accounting: it is a logical method of dealing with the effects of inflation when historical cost accounting is found to be otherwise satisfactory, and when all prices have changed in the same proportions so that there is no problem of reporting relative price changes. It is not, therefore, surprising that pure CPP solutions have been favoured when inflation has been at a high rate, so that the rise in the general level of prices has been seen to be large. Equally, doubt has been cast upon the method where there has been concern about relative price changes (as in the UK profits crisis of 1974).

(i) Evolution of theory

We have seen in earlier chapters that the theoretical foundation of CPP accounting was laid by Irving Fisher, in *The Purchasing Power of Money* (1911). Fisher saw indexation throughout the economy as a means of dispelling the money illusion, and CPP accounting is the application of indexation methods to accounts. It is notable that the countries in which forms of CPP have established themselves (notably in Latin America) have wider schemes of indexation of which CPP is merely a part.

The next stage in the development of CPP resulted from the stimulus of the German hyper-inflation, following the First World War. Here, CPP techniques were evolved by translating balance sheets into a currency unit of constant value (the Gold-Mark), so that CPP was seen as a currency translation problem. The writings of Mahlberg and others for the first time developed the detailed technique of CPP accounting, as opposed to the broad principle which had been enunciated by earlier writers. These techniques were further refined by the French writers of the late 1920s, and the entire literature of that time was distilled, synthesised and made available to an English-speaking audience by Sweeney (1936). This work laid down the broad pattern for subsequent CPP proposals, and it is probably fair to say that later work has been a matter of filling in the details. The imprint of Sweeney's work can be seen clearly on the later, influential, publications of the American Accounting Association (Jones, 1955 and 1956; and Mason, 1956), the Research Committee of the American Institute of Certified Public Accountants (1963) and the Research Committee of the Institute of Chartered Accountants in England and Wales (1968), which laid the foundation for the CPP proposals by the standard-setting bodies in the UK and the USA.

In more recent years, theoretical writing on CPP has focussed on two separate types of issue. Firstly there has been debate on the appropriate treatment of the gain on borrowing and loss on holding money; in particular, whether the gain on long-term borrowing should be regarded as income, since it is unrealised, and also how to define precisely the 'monetary' assets and liabilities which give rise to gains and losses. Secondly, and more fundamentally, there has been discussion of the merits of CPP relative to other accounting models: historical cost, CCA and RT. This has been conducted on both the theoretical and the empirical level (e.g. attempting to estimate the effects of CPP information on share prices).

(ii) Evolution of practice

The practical development of CPP has always followed appropriate economic conditions, i.e. rapid inflation, which makes a simple and objective adjustment of accounts, such as CPP, highly desirable, and which tends to push into the background anxieties about the deficiencies of the historical cost base or the inadequacy of general index adjustment in dealing with relative price changes. The first stimulus of this kind came from the European inflation following the First World War, notably in Germany. During the same period, inflation was less in the USA and, despite Irving Fisher's advocacy of general index adjustment, a number of companies experimented with replacement cost adjustments. The depression of the 1930s saw the end of inflation and the end of experiments with inflation accounting until after the Second World War.

In the UK and the USA, the post-Second World War inflation was not severe enough to stimulate practical moves towards the implementation of CPP: the subject was largely a matter for academic writers until the 1960s, when steadily rising inflation led to greater interest by

263

professional bodies (the AICPA's *ARS6*, 1963, and the ICAEW's *Accounting for Stewardship in a Period of Inflation*, 1968). In 1969, the American Accounting Principles Board actually produced a CPP recommendation (*APB3*), but this was not followed: professional interest was still somewhat casual. The British Accounting Standards Committee produced its CPP Exposure Draft in 1973, under the pressure of persistent inflation, but it was the 1973 oil crisis, with the attendant higher inflation rate, which tipped the balance temporarily in favour of CPP in all the English-speaking countries.

We have seen that the period 1973–75 saw something of a CPP revolution in these countries, with CPP proposals appearing in the USA, the UK, Australia, Canada, New Zealand and South Africa. In each of these countries it was professional standard-setters who chose CPP and it seems likely that the motivation behind this preference was that CPP offered a relatively simple and objective solution, which would appeal to the professional auditor, but which might not satisfy users of accounts in periods of significant relative price changes. However, in none of these countries did CPP become standard practice (the nearest being a Provisional Standard, *PSSAP7* in the UK, 1974). The CPP revolution was followed equally suddenly by the Current Cost Revolution. The motivation behind this was a mixture of anxiety by governments concerning the possible destabilising effects of any form of indexation, and an anxiety by firms that CPP did not show the true state of affairs as portrayed by the specific prices which they faced. The latter was partly a selfish objection, fuelled by a wish to minimise the burdens and resist pressures on wage rates and selling prices, but it contained an important element of truth. The period was one of important relative price changes (e.g. wages and fuel costs rising more rapidly than selling prices) which CPP failed to capture. There were two aspects to this: firstly, CPP did not value assets at their current market prices, and secondly, the capital maintenance concept of CPP was a proprietary one, whereas some companies would have preferred an entity approach to capital maintenance. The latter objection underlay the controversy about whether the CPP 'gain on borrowing' should be added to profit: many companies felt that this would lead to the over-statement of their profits in a period of inflation, since the gain to shareholders was a loss to holders of loan stock.

Elsewhere in the world, the notable success of CPP was in Latin America, where double (and even triple) digit inflation forced governments to grant piecemeal tax concessions for inflation (typically allowing inflation-adjusted depreciation, followed by inflation-adjusted cost of goods sold) on an indexed basis. In the manner of the continental

European tradition, tax-deductible expenses are typically required to be reported in the accounts in Latin American countries. These piecemeal adjustments gradually developed into a more comprehensive CPP system, first in Brazil, then in Chile and latterly in Argentina, although the Latin American systems are not faithful reproductions of the Anglo-Saxon models, e.g. the use of wholsesale price indices rather than retail price indices is quite common. In these countries, indexation techniques have been introduced elsewhere in the economy, e.g. in wage bargaining and in the bond market, so that the indexation of the company tax base and CPP adjustment of company accounts have not met with the same political resistance as they met in Anglo-Saxon countries. It is also worth noting that indexation methods were a response to rapid inflation in these countries, not the original cause of inflation, although some might argue[2] that, by alleviating the symptoms, indexation causes inflation to be institutionalised and perpetual.

3 CCA

The model which we have defined above as Current Cost Accounting (CCA) originated as replacement cost accounting (RC). In this form, it has deeper historical roots than CPP, which is not surprising, since it can involve the use of current prices, which are an observable phenomenon, rather than index numbers, which are fundamental to the CPP method and which are an artificial construct developed mainly in the twentieth century. Since the CCA method makes use of current prices, it can be regarded as a method of reporting the effects both of inflation (changes in the value of the monetary unit) and of relative price changes: this point of view was expressed strongly in the Sandilands Report.[3] However, if the method is 'pure' CCA, eschewing entirely the use of general price indices, it must adjust capital, for the purposes of measuring profit, by the specific prices of the assets held by the firm. This involves an entity-oriented capital maintenance concept, aimed at maintaining either physical assets or operating capacity or some related concept. It is this type of model which we shall define as CCA. The alternative type of model which combines current (or replacement) cost as an asset valuation base with general index adjustment of capital for the effects of inflation (a proprietary capital maintenance concept) is classified as a Real Terms (RT) approach, and will be discussed later.

An obvious alternative to current cost is current market value, i.e. selling price. However, the advocates of selling price rather than cost (RC or CC) have preferred to combine this valuation basis with a general index adjustment of capital on the logically consistent argument that valuation at selling price naturally arises from a proprietary view of the firm, which regards the firm as a collection of investments to be managed for the maximum benefit of the proprietor, rather than the entity view which underlies the pure CCA model. The current market value, sometimes known as Net Realisable Value (NRV), model will therefore be discussed later under the Real Terms heading.

(i) Evolution of theory

The earliest systematic published work on replacement cost accounting seems to have appeared in Germany immediately before the First World War. This was subsequently developed by Fritz Schmidt, in a series of books and papers published during the 1920s, into a comprehensive replacement cost system, with a profit measure similar to the operating profit adopted much later by the Sandilands Report. Schmidt regarded all forms of asset appreciation (realised and unrealised holding gains) as part of capital rather than profit, adopting the strong capital mainte- nance assumption associated with the 'pure' current cost approach. His replacement cost concept was not a matter of pure reproduction of the assets: he was more concerned to preserve the operating capacity (or what, in one of his English papers, he described as 'the productive instrumentalities') of the firm. His ideas set the pattern for much subsequent theoretical work and were ultimately influential on practice, but they did not find acceptance in practice at the time. Germany in the early 1920s was in the grip of hyper-inflation and the urgency of this problem led to the adoption of the CPP methods advocated by Mahlberg and Schmalenbach.

Replacement cost ideas were developed elsewhere at this time, notably in the early work of Paton, which made a permanent contribu- tion to the stock of ideas available in the English-speaking world, despite Paton's own subsequent change of views. Paton, unlike Euro- pean writers of the period, was prepared to contemplate including unrealised holding gains in income, and in this sense was a precursor of the Real Terms approach rather than the pure current cost model. However, the most influential theoretician of the period, in terms of his impact on practice, was the Dutchman Limperg, who founded the Dutch replacement cost school. He clearly built on the work of Schmidt, but he took it a stage further in his emphasis on replacement *value* rather than replacement cost. As we have already seen (Chapter 2), this introduced a valuation method close to the eclectic 'value to the owner' method which is used by the current cost accounting models which became fashionable in the 1970s, replacement cost being replaced by recoverable amount (the higher of value in use or re-sale value) where that is below replacement cost.

In the early 1930s, Sweeney, the pioneer of CPP also saw the merits of replacement cost as a valuation base, and integrated it with CPP to produce the Real Terms (RT) system, discussed in a later section of this chapter.

These earlier writers supplied the ideas which were available to the next generation of writers, who emerged in the period following the Second World War. During the latter period, there was considerable interest in replacement cost accounting in Britain, with two influential accountancy bodies, the ICWA (1952) and the ACCA (1952), publishing reports advocating replacement cost methods. However, the most distinct British contribution was the adoption, by two authors associated with the London School of Economics, Baxter and Solomons, of the deprival value or value to the owner method of valuation. They derived this from the American writer Bonbright (1937), in apparent ignorance of Limperg's similar replacement value method. The value to the owner method (now described as value to the business) was subsequently adopted by the Sandilands Committee and became a common feature of current cost accounting standards within the English-speaking world. Another British innovation was the gearing adjustment advocated by Godley and Cripps (1975), Gibbs (1976) and Kennedy (1978a and b), although this also owed something to the continental European tradition, particularly the ideas of Schmidt which influenced the German (IdW) professional recommendation of 1975. The gearing adjustment is a device for reporting the gain on borrowing but measuring it in terms of the specific prices of assets owned and used by the firm, rather than a general price index. It thus avoids a full Real Terms adjustment, and, in particular, avoids reporting a gain on borrowing which is measured in terms of changes in the general price level.

There was a strong theoretical interest in current cost accounting methods in Australia during this period. The pioneering work of Mathews and Grant (1958) advocated a replacement cost approach and attempted to quantify the consequences of this change of method for the apparent profitability of Australian companies: this work is of particular interest because Mathews was subsequently Chairman of the Government Committee of Inquiry (1975), which introduced the current cost revolution in Australia. Another influential Australian writer was Gynther, whose pioneering study (1966) of replacement cost accounting was based mainly on a study of Dutch practice. Gynther developed a strongly entity-orientated view of accounting and was influential in the later development of current cost accounting by the Australian

267

standard-setting body. Australia also produced an independent advocate of value to the owner, Wright (1964), who derived the idea from Canning (1929) and described it as 'opportunity value'.

In the United States too there was development of replacement cost ideas. The work of Edwards and Bell (1961) advocated a replacement cost valuation base and a replacement cost operating profit and attempted to provide a basis for this in the theory of economic valuation and decision-making, although the total system proposed by Edwards and Bell was eclectic and embraced the Real Terms model. Subsequently, Revsine (1970) and others explored the properties of replacement cost models as surrogates for economic income measures, and this type of work still continues (e.g. Samuelson, 1980).

There have also been important discussions and developments of replacement cost ideas in The Netherlands and Germany during this period, although the language barrier has prevented them from being fully absorbed into the Anglo-Saxon debate.

In summary, there has been a steady stream of writing about current cost models by accounting theorists. These have led to some important modifications to simple replacement cost (notably the gearing adjustment and the value to the owner system) which have found their way into practice. At a more abstract level, theoretical writers have, in recent years, attempted to justify replacement cost models as measures of (or proxies for) economic income, but they have achieved only limited success in this respect, finding that the correspondence is achieved only under very restrictive assumptions (Revsine, 1976).

(ii) Evolution of practice

Replacement cost or current cost methods date at least from the latter part of the nineteenth century, when current cost valuations were used as a basis for depreciation charges in rate-regulation cases concerning American railway companies (Boer, 1966).[4] The strength of current cost is that it can be used in a pragmatic manner, e.g. being applied to certain key assets, and does not require access to price indices. Replacement cost methods were applied pragmatically by certain American companies to reduce reported profits during the boom of the 1920s, but interest fell away rapidly when the depression of the 1930s led to low profits under the conventional historical cost method (Sweeney, 1964a).

Apart from isolated applications by individual companies, the first widespread application of replacement cost accounting was by Dutch companies in the 1950s and 1960s, although replacement cost accounting has remained a minority practice in The Netherlands. Despite the interest in replacement cost by two British accountancy bodies, the ACCA and ICWA (1952), such methods never approached widespread implementation until the 'Current Cost Revolution of 1975–76', when official bodies in several English-speaking countries moved towards accepting current cost accounting, under government influence. In the USA, the SEC introduced its *ASR190* replacement cost disclosures for large companies in 1976 (announced in 1975), in Australia the Mathews Report (1975) advocated replacement cost methods for taxation and financial reporting, in the UK the Sandilands Report (1975) recommended current cost accounting (with a value to the business base) for financial reporting, and in New Zealand the Richardson Report (1976) recommended current cost accounting (with a variant of value to the business, and, additionally, forms of monetary working capital and gearing adjustments).

The motivation for government intervention in these countries was clearly a wish to supplant CPP, which, as we have already seen, seemed to be gaining the acceptance of professional standard-setters, for whom it had particular attractions. We suggested earlier that the government antipathy to CPP was probably motivated in part by the needs of counter-inflationary economic policy and a wish to avoid a possible spread of indexation, which might institutionalise inflation. There was also antipathy to CPP by companies which, at a time of considerable relative price change, saw specific price changes, rather than general index changes, as being relevant to their activities: we have documented this in the case of the UK by our analysis of responses to *ED8*, the CPP Exposure Draft.

Subsequent to the 'Current Cost Revolution', professional standard-setting bodies have wrestled with the practical problems of implementing the CCA system, thrust upon them by government intervention. We have traced the course of these struggles in some detail, in the chapters relating to specific countries. Certain general features have emerged:

(1) The valuation base has been subject to much discussion. Some variant of value to the firm has always been adopted, with the subjective assessment of value in use being the main practical problem. The precise definition of the operating capacity which has to be maintained, in defining replacement cost, has also proved elusive, especially under conditions of technical change. This problem will be discussed further in the next chapter. The use of specific indices to approximate replacement cost has also been a matter for debate.

(2) The most difficult area has been the treatment of monetary assets

and liabilities. The complete transition from CPP to 'pure' CCA left an obvious gap in the system if it were regarded as a method of inflation accounting: inflation, as it is conventionally understood, leads to losses on holding assets which are fixed in money value and gains (depreciation in the real liability) on liabilities which are fixed in money terms, and the CPP method measures these losses and gains by the application of general price-level indices. In an attempt to fill this gap, there were experiments in the UK, New Zealand, and Canada with gearing adjustments (to deal with the gain on borrowing) and monetary working capital adjustments (to deal with the loss on holding monetary assets) which were based upon the changes in the prices of the specific assets held by the firm, rather than upon general price-level indices. The USA, by contrast, has preferred to maintain both CCA and CPP elements, reconciling them in a partial Real Terms system (*FAS33*, 1979b).

(3) There has been great anxiety about the novelty and the subjectivity of CCA methods, the accounting profession tending naturally to prefer the more evolutionary and objective (but perhaps less relevant) CPP approach. As a result of this, progress towards adopting new CCA standards has been slow. By the end of 1982, only three countries, the USA, the UK and New Zealand, had adopted standards which contained CCA elements, and each of these were regarded as experimental, subject to review at the end of trial periods. Outside the English-speaking world, Germany had a non-mandatory proposal for supplementary CCA disclosure in 1975, but this had more impact outside Germany than within it. The Dutch also have permitted replacement cost accounts for many years and NIVRA issued non-mandatory guidance on the form of disclosures in 1976, and there is a Swedish exposure draft extant. Both of these are basically 'real terms' proposals. However, none of these countries yet has a mandatory standard requiring a form of current cost accounting.

In summary, CCA received its impetus in practice from government intervention in the mid-1970s. There has been considerable controversy and reluctance within the professional bodies which were asked to implement CCA. As a result, only the UK has, hitherto, issued a pure CCA standard, the USA having adopted a 'real terms' approach, and there is currently controversy in the UK as to whether the CCA experiment should continue and, if so, how it should develop. One possibility, which would resolve the debate over gearing and monetary items, would be to follow the USA in its 'real terms' approach. It is to this model which we now turn.

4 Real Terms (RT)

(i) Evolution of theory

The early writers on inflation accounting were none too clear on the distinction between specific price changes and general price-level changes, or on the relationship between the two. In the 1920s, there was a debate in Germany between adherents of Schmidt's replacement cost school and Schmalenbach's CPP approach, the two approaches being regarded as mutually exclusive rather than complementary. The synthesis between the two approaches, to produce an RT system, with general index adjustment superimposed upon a current replacement cost valuation basis, was achieved by H. W. Sweeney and clearly presented in Chapter 3 of his *Stabilized Accounting* (1936). In this approach, capital, for income measurement purposes, is adjusted by a general price index, to satisfy the proprietary approach, but real assets are valued at replacement cost.

Sweeney's approach remained known in the academic literature without being developed significantly for a quarter of a century. The next important development of the approach was by Edwards and Bell (1961) who proposed a much more elaborate presentation of the income statement. Whereas Sweeney had merely distinguished between realised and unrealised gains in arriving at a figure for real income, Edwards and Bell proposed to make the important distinction between operating gains and holding gains. This enabled them to start with a measure of current operating profit, deducting from revenue the cost of goods sold and depreciation valued at current replacement cost. The various holding gains were then added back and a distinction made between money gains and real gains as well as between realised and unrealised gains. Thus, the Edwards and Bell system embraces the current cost income measures advocated by Schmidt, Mathews and Grant and (later) the Sandilands Report, as well as providing information on total real gains, as in Sweeney's original system. It is also possible to retrieve historical cost income and CPP-adjusted historical cost. Thus, the Edwards and Bell approach provides a broad set of information about the effects of both general and specific price changes. This is consistent with the user-orientated view of accounting which has become fashionable in both theory and practice during the past twenty years, and with the view that there are a variety of uses with a variety of information needs.

Another development of the RT variety was the work of Chambers (1966) which advocated valuation at realisable values (selling prices less any realisation expenses). This valuation base goes naturally with a proprietary approach to capital maintenance, since valuation on the assumption of realisation is inconsistent with the entity (or current cost) view that the operating capability of the business must always be maintained. Chambers was therefore consistent in choosing to adjust proprietors' capital by a general, rather than a specific, index for profit measurement purposes. He views the firm essentially as a fund of resources to be applied in whatever use is of maximum benefit to the shareholders, rather than a store of productive capacity to be maintained in its present activity.

A further variation on the valuation basis of RT was provided by Baxter (1967 and 1975), who suggested value to the owner, rather than replacement cost (Sweeney) or net realisable value (Chambers) as the basis of his RT system. This valuation basis was later adopted by Edwards and Bell (Edwards, Bell and Johnson, 1979) and has also been the valuation basis of the US standard (*FAS33*) which was the first to require real terms information. The valuation question will be discussed further in the next chapter.

A final significant development, on a more abstract theoretical level, is the recognition that, in an uncertain world with imperfect and incomplete markets, the appropriate rôle for the accountant is not to provide economic valuations of the firm, but to provide an information set which assists the user in arriving at his own subjective valuation (Bromwich, 1977; Peasnell, 1977; Beaver and Demski, 1979). This seems to be a realistic assessment of the situation which obtains in practice and it lends force to the eclectic real terms approach as exemplified by Edwards and Bell. A more recent example of this type of system, which even embraces the gearing adjustment, is that by Kennedy (1978a).

(ii) Evolution of practice

The RT model was the last to be clarified in theory and it was the last to be advocated by professional standard-setting bodies. We have already seen that the AICPA's *ARS6* (1963) was a seminal work in spreading Sweeney's CPP ideas. However, it spread his RT ideas at best as an optional extra, regarding CPP adjustment of historical cost as the primary reform required to deal with inflation.[5] The CPP Exposure Drafts which followed, from 1969 onwards, took a similar line, as did the UK's Provisional Standard (*PSSAP7*, 1974).

A strong stimulus towards the RT approach was provided by the Current Cost Revolution of 1974–76, which polarised CCA and CPP and alternatives. RT was an obvious means of reconciling these two systems, and this was proposed by the CCAB in its *Initial Reactions* to the Sandilands Report (1975). However, in the UK, the 'real terms' solution was lost in the fierce debate over *ED18* and substituted by the CCA method using gearing (in the 1977 Hyde Guidelines), which was later supplemented by a monetary working capital adjustment (*ED24*, 1979). The rest of the English-speaking world followed suit with the exception of the USA which, with *FAS33* (1979b) moved towards RT by requiring both CCA and CPP income data, with an element of RT in the reporting of real holding gains and losses. This system reported all the elements of an Edwards and Bell income statement, and companies were allowed to adopt a single-statement format. The *FAS33* system has not yet been followed elsewhere in detail, but steps towards RT have been made in the latest proposals for Australia, New Zealand and Canada, which permit an element of general index adjustment in the assessment of the gain on long-term borrowing, combined with CCA valuation systems. Moreover, the Dutch recommendations of 1976 and the Swedish Exposure Draft of 1980 also proposed RT systems. In the UK, stock relief for business taxation has recently been put on a general index basis, as has the capital gains tax base, and current indications (as of mid-1983) are that *SSAP16* is likely to be replaced by a standard which allows general index adjustment of equity capital. Thus, the period from 1979 onwards may prove to have been the period of the 'real terms revolution'.

Apart from the advantages of RT in combining elements of CPP with CCA, the idea of a general purpose information system, with which RT is consistent, received support from the influential Trueblood Report (1973) in the USA, from *The Corporate Report* (1975) sponsored by the UK's ASC, and from the more recent (1980) report written by Professor Edward Stamp for the Canadian Institute of Chartered Accountants. All of these reports emphasised the variety of user information needs.

5 Concluding comment

This chapter has been highly selective. The serious reader is advised to make his own assessment of the mass of detail presented in earlier chapters. The authors' own view, as presented in this chapter, is that the Real Terms (RT) system appears to be emerging as the generally acceptable system which will combine the merits of CCA (specific price changes) and CPP (general price-level changes). We are also of the opinion that this will be a theoretically sound solution to the problem of accounting for price changes, given the variety of users and uses of accounting information, and the uncertainty of the environment in which accounts are prepared and used. We shall return to this theme in the final chapter. However, this view is presented as an hypothesis which the reader should compare with the facts and with any competing hypotheses of his own, rather than a conclusion which follows inevitably from the facts presented in earlier chapters.

12

Particular issues: valuation, capital maintenance and the gain on borrowing

The preceding chapter focussed on systems of accounting for price changes. In this chapter we consider issues central to the systems examined earlier, namely asset valuation and capital maintenance. Arising from the capital maintenance problem is the question of the gain on borrowing. We shall concentrate in particular on the manner in which these issues have been dealt with by standard-setters in the worldwide debate since the 'Current Cost Revolution' of 1975–76, i.e. in the context of Current Cost Accounting (CCA) or Real Terms Accounting (RT). In a constant purchasing power system, the valuation method and the capital maintenance concept follow a relatively predictable pattern – asset valuation results from the historical cost of the asset being adjusted by general indices and the capital maintenance concept is of a proprietary nature: the shareholders' equity stake in the enterprise being maintained in terms of constant purchasing power before income is earned. The CCA system, on the other hand, has been associated with a variety of valuation formulae, which attempt to deal with the identification of replacement cost and the resolution of situations in which replacement cost differs from realisable value. CCA has also been associated with a wide range of capital maintenance methods, ranging from the proprietary to the entity approaches, with a series of intermediate compromises, particularly those associated with the gearing adjustment.

1 Asset valuation

Chapter 2 indicated that the debate on methods of asset valuation is by no means a phenomenon of the era since the Second World War. Both current cost and CPP methods of asset valuation have histories dating back to before the First World War. The replacement cost debate has been traced by Boer (1966) to the deflation (1865–96) following the American Civil War. Similarly, Fisher's (1911) advocacy of indexation to dispel the money illusion heralded the beginning of the CPP method.

275

The CPP method of adjusting historical cost by a general index was then carried forward in Germany by Schmalenbach (1919) and Mahlberg (1923) in response to the rapid inflation following the First World War. It was more fully developed by Sweeney (1936), the latter's work being used later as the model for the AICPA's *ARS6* on CPP accounting, although replacement cost was his preferred valuation base (Sweeney, 1936, Chapter 3). The case for asset valuation based on replacement cost was initially led during the interval between the World Wars by Schmidt in Germany and Limperg in The Netherlands. During this period, Bonbright (1937) developed the eclectic 'deprival value' or value to the owner system which ultimately appeared in the Sandilands Report and led to the development of the recoverable amount concept used in many current cost systems today. This method was also implicit in the work of Canning (1929), and it resembled the replacement value basis developed by Limperg.

Market values too were advocated at this time, the principal advocate being MacNeal (1939). The case for market selling price was later strongly argued by Chambers (1966) and Sterling (1970). As we have seen in earlier chapters, the period following the Second World War has produced a great deal of theoretical writing on forms of current cost or current value accounting, with notable advocates of replacement cost including Gynther (1966) and Mathews and Grant (1958) and advocates of value to the firm, such as Solomons (1966a and b) and Baxter (1967), producing cases for alternative methods of asset valuation. In this chapter, however, we shall be concentrating on the debate among the standard-setters in the 1970s when accountants throughout the world struggled to find the solution to accounting for price-level changes during the inflationary period resulting from the Middle East War in 1973.

In the early 1970s, the accounting profession throughout the world paid little attention to the problems of asset valuation, although, in certain countries, departures were made from the historical cost concept and fixed assets (primarily land and buildings) were revalued. In addition, replacement cost accounting was practised by a minority of Dutch companies. Generally speaking, however, there was no systematic revaluation, but companies would, periodically, modify the historical cost of their fixed assets, especially in periods of rapid inflation, to disclose balance sheet values more closely related to those of the market.

In the 1970s, the accountancy profession's first attempts systematically to adjust asset carrying values in the accounts did not involve substituting supplementary historical cost financial statements with

276

those based on replacement costs (RC), net realisable value (NRV), present or economic values or even a combination of current values. Instead, its attempts were more concerned with restating historical cost of assets in terms of units of constant purchasing power.

The first CPP pronouncement published in the 1970s (the UK's *ED8*, 1973) outlined the general philosophy behind its proposed non-monetary asset valuation system (para. 18) – the restatement of book values (historical or modified historical cost) by means of a general index.

> Holders of non-monetary assets are assumed neither to gain nor to lose purchasing power by reason only of inflation as changes in the price of these assets will tend to compensate for any changes in the purchasing power of the pound.

The Exposure Draft, however, reminded the reader of the dangers of blindly restating assets and disregarding market forces and consequently a lower of restated historical cost and market value was to be applied, preserving the conservative valuation rule already applied within the traditional historical cost system.

The opposition of the UK's corporate sector to *ED8* (see Chapter 4) led to a revision of the asset valuation proposals in the Provisional Standard of 1974 (*PSSAP7*). While the principles of general index restatement and the lower of restated cost or market rule were still to apply, an appendix to the Provisional Standard stated that the introduction of supplementary CPP financial statements did not preclude the revaluation of fixed assets in the ordinary accounts (and, consequently, by implication, the supplementary accounts) 'in accordance with established practice'. These proposals were followed in the Australian (1974) and New Zealand (1975) Exposure Drafts, both of which were based on *PSSAP7*.

The North American CPP Exposure Drafts (FASB, 1974c and CICA, 1975), while adopting the lower cost and market value rule, did not propose revaluation in excess of the restated figures: non-monetary assets were to record values no higher than the units of current general purchasing power invested in the asset. A different approach, however, was taken in South Africa, where the 1975 CPP Discussion Paper was more favourably inclined towards current value revaluations than any of the other countries' proposals. Unlike *PSSAP7*, where the notion of revaluation was hidden in an appendix, the South African paper required that balance sheet values were checked periodically against current values. The value to be used for comparative purposes was replacement cost 'since the merits of the technique (were) so striking' –

despite the acceptance in the paper that the assumption of continuity in the variable cirumstances of modern business life did not seem to be generally acceptable.

In the same month as the South African pronouncement was published, the Current Cost Revolution began. Within the eighteen-month period commencing with the publication of the Mathews Report in Australia and ending with the issue of *ED18* in the United Kingdom, no fewer than twelve major statements advocating the use of current cost information were issued by Government Committees of Enquiry or by bodies regulating accounting practice in seven of the world's major developed nations (Table 12.1), and the asset valuation procedures now being used in these countries were established.

Four approaches were adopted regarding valuation. The first method to appear was that requiring assets to be valued at *replacement cost* (adopted in the Mathews Report, the West German draft recommendation, NIVRA's note to IASC's *E6* and the SEC's *ASR190*). This is the simplest of the approaches adopted, although it still lends itself to a number of ambiguities and subtle variations of definition, e.g. is it the physical asset or its services which are to be replaced and, if the latter, should we take account of the fact that a technically different asset producing the same services might cause differences in operating costs?

The Australian Exposure Draft issued in June 1975 advocated a second valuation system based on assessment of whether or not an asset was *essential to the continuance of operations*, i.e. the valuation reflected the expected rôle of an asset in the enterprise's operations within the foreseeable future. This system proposed the use of replacement cost when it was assumed that the asset was essential to the continuance of operations (it would then be worth no more than it would cost to replace the operating capacity which it provided) and advocated net realisable value when an asset was surplus to the requirements of the entity's operations. Similar proposals were adopted in the New Zealand Exposure Draft (August 1976) and the same country's Richardson Report (September 1976).

The New Zealand publications had both specifically rejected the third asset valuation approach, which was first advocated during this period by the UK's Sandilands Committee. The Committee had advocated the criterion of the *value to the business* (i.e. Bonbright's deprival value involving the use of replacement costs, net realisable value and present values). Both the relevance of the valuation model and the practical implications of assessing economic value were attacked vigorously by the New Zealand publications[1] – the New Zealand Committee of Inquiry, arguing that the deprival value theory had doubtful relevance to the real

Table 12.1. *The Current Cost Revolution*

Date	Country of origin	Issuing authority	Publication	Brief title
1975				
May	Australia	Government	Report of Committee of Inquiry	Inflation and Taxation (Mathews Report)
June	Australia	ICAA and ASA	Preliminary Exposure Draft	Current Value Accounting
August	USA	SEC	Notice of Proposed Amendment to Regulations S-X	Disclosure of Certain Replacement Cost Data
September	UK	Government	Report of Committee of Enquiry	Inflation Accounting (Sandilands Report)
October	West Germany	IdW	Draft Recommendation	Maintaining the Substantial-istic Value of an Enterprise
1976				
January	The Netherlands	NIVRA	Note to IASC	Accounting for Changing Prices
March	USA	SEC	Exposure Draft Accounting Series Release 190	Disclosure of Certain Replacement Cost Data
August	Canada	CICA	Discussion Paper	Current Value Accounting
August	New Zealand	NZSA	Exposure Draft	Accounting in Terms of Current Cost and Values
September	New Zealand	Government	Committee of Inquiry	Inflation Accounting (Richardson Report)
October	Australia	ICAA and ASA	Provisional Standard	Current Cost Accounting
November	UK	ASC	Exposure Draft	Current Cost Accounting

world in which businesses operate and that enterprises should value assets on the basis of what they intended to do with the resources at their command, i.e. the assets' perceived future rôle not their theoretical, economically justifiable rôle.

The deprival value proposal did, however, find favour in North America and was adopted in both the United States (in the 1978 Exposure Draft and *FAS33*) and in Canada (initially in the 1979 Exposure Draft and ultimately in the 1982 Standard), despite a brief flirtation in Canada (in the Discussion Paper 1976) with a system which involved the three value measures involved in the deprival value system but which suggested a particular measure for each different type of asset.[2]

While the UK's *ED18* adopted the Sandilands' value to the business criterion, the next UK CCA pronouncements (apart from the Hyde Guidelines which did not mention asset valuation), namely *ED24* and *SSAP16*, adopted a fourth method – a system which could be termed the 'Australian compromise', which lay between the proposals of the 1975 Australian Exposure Draft and the Sandilands asset valuation criterion.

This hybrid proposal first emerged in the Australian Provisional Standard of 1976 and countered the criticism that valuing all assets continuing in use at current cost could be imprudent by adopting the concept of 'the recoverable amount'. Where an asset's current cost could not be recovered through charges against revenue from the continued use of the asset and/or by its sale, its value was to be shown at the amount of the replacement cost which could be recovered. This proposal was retained in the 1983 Australian Statement of Accounting Practice. It was also adopted in New Zealand (in the 1981 Exposure Draft and 1982 Standard) and South Africa (1978 Guideline) and has emerged as the alternative to the deprival value (value to the business) concept. It should be noted, however, that the deprival value and Australian compromise concepts are very similar, both requiring the estimation of future cash flows relating to the asset, the only difference between the two concepts being the omission of a discount factor in the latter.

There the debate rests at present with deprival value of the Australian compromise version of the concept being accepted by the present leaders in the debate. Practical difficulties do, however, exist. The problems of changing technology and the estimation of realisable values or recoverable amounts in a time of recession have cast doubts upon the asset values derived under these concepts. Indeed, these difficulties have led some opponents of *SSAP16* in the UK to call for the abolition

of the CCA balance sheet and to question the validity of the depreciation adjustment.

Thus, the recent debate on asset valuations has proceeded largely as a
process of compromise between alternative 'pure' systems, guided by
practical considerations (such as the subjectivity of economic values) as
much as by theory. This is a natural way for a debate about practice to
develop, but the relative neglect of theoretical issues means that there
has been a great deal of 'papering over the cracks', and these cracks are
likely to be revealed once more as practice evolves and the demands
made upon financial reports increase.

Perhaps the largest of these problems is the aggregation problem.[3]
The value to the firm principle, which seems to have emerged as the
currently fashionable compromise, has its theoretical roots in the
valuation of the *individual* asset, not the firm as a whole, but accounts,
whether balance sheets or profit and loss accounts, are aimed at the
assessment of the performance of the business as a whole. Other
important problems include the precise definition of replacement cost
under conditions of economic and technical change: replacement cost is
fundamental to the value to the firm method.

Thus, we see an important rôle for theory in the future development
of current cost accounting practice. This includes not only the application of theoretical insights which are already available, but also the
development of new insights. Our own view of the direction which such
developments should take is that attention should no longer focus upon
a single number which is supposed to be an all-embracing measure of
'profit' or 'value'. Rather, the objective should be to provide a useful set
of information from which users can select that which is more relevant
to their own needs. In the context of asset valuation, this might imply
going beyond the 'value to the firm' compromise, which leads to a single
value, and providing multiple values, either in additional columns or by
way of note, subject, of course, to the constraints of cost (to both
preparers and users) of providing and interpreting additional
information.[4]

2 The capital maintenance debate

Capital maintenance lies at the heart of the inflation accounting debate.
If income is to be measured in terms of the increase or decrease in the
wealth of an enterprise, obviously some definition of that stock of
wealth is required. Three basic measures of wealth are evident from the
literature:

(1) financial capital – the equity stake in an enterprise in money terms;

(2) real financial capital – the equity stake in an enterprise in real terms (the proprietary concept);

(3) operating capacity capital – the ability of the enterprise to maintain its ability to provide goods and services (the entity concept).

Financial capital is the historical cost capital maintenance system and consequently will not be discussed further in this chapter. The inflation accounting debate has centred on the two other measures of capital, neither of which has achieved universal acceptance, but both of which are adjusted to take account of price changes.

Proponents of both sides include distinguished theorists: for the proprietary system Sweeney, Edwards and Bell, Chambers and Baxter and, for the entity system, Schmidt, Limperg, Mathews and Gynther. On the one hand, the proprietary theorists have argued that the wealth to be maintained in real terms before income can be measured is that contributed to the enterprise by the owners, adjusted by a general purchasing power index. Opposing this view, the proponents of the entity concept argue that shareholders do not identify their personal stake in the company as a fund of general purchasing power to be adjusted for general inflation but instead regard their investment as a share in a going concern which has to preserve the means of continuing the production of its goods and services before measuring income. The latter implies that the original capital contributed by shareholders will subsequently be adjusted by a specific price index, reflecting changes in the cost of the specific assets which must be maintained.

More recently the debate has been joined by the standard-setting bodies which have also been divided on the issue. In part, this may have been due to differences in environment: the entity concept might be justified in Europe, for example, where a business is regarded more as a coalition of different interest groups with an implicit goal of securing the continuity of the business. In the USA, however, a proprietary view might be preferred because of the stronger emphasis on the need to obtain profits for the stockholders (see Carsberg, 1982). Financial statements are meant to reflect the achievement of the objectives of the business: hence the difference in viewpoint.

Proprietary capital proposals

The measurement of income after maintaining the shareholders' stake in the enterprise in general purchasing power terms was initially the most popular of the two basic capital measures among the standard-setting bodies, but, after the CPP era of 1973–75, most of the countries at the forefront of the debate initially adopted CCA systems with operating capability as the capital base. Thus, the entity approach was initially favoured as the capital maintenance concept to be implemented with CCA. Subsequently, in Australia and the UK, the CCA proposals have remained firmly based on entity proposals, but in the USA proprietary methods have prevailed: *FAS33* adopts a building block approach with similarities to the Edwards and Bell system which also adopted proprietary capital maintenance, although it also contains information of an 'entity' type in its measure of operating profit. Recently, in its 1981 Exposure Draft, *Reporting Income, Cash Flows and Financial Position of Enterprises*, the FASB affirmed its belief in the proprietary approach, having previously held the view that the two approaches should co-exist.[5]

Other countries have wavered in their earlier support of the entity approach. New Zealand having previously adopted operating capacity capital as its income measurement base now, in its 1982 CCA Standard, allows enterprises, as an alternative to the use of the entity concept, to opt for proprietary capital maintenance systems in calculating current cost profit. In the same year, Canada, in its Standard, proposed that enterprises should provide sufficient information to enable the reader to calculate income on both the proprietary and entity bases. The Canadian experiment had now adopted its third capital maintenance proposal. Previously, a CICA Discussion Paper in 1976 had recommended a proprietary measurement base, only to be followed in 1979 and 1981 by Exposure Drafts espousing an entity concept of capital. However, there was a good reason for a gradual disillusionment with operating capacity maintenance: the difficulty of defining operating capacity itself. This issue is developed below.

Entity concept proposals

While the main debate among advocates of accounting for price-level change is centred around the operating capacity (entity concept) or financial capital (proprietary concept) issue, there is a great measure of dispute among supporters of the operating capacity concept over the definition of capital.

There are two aspects to the definition of operating capacity:
(1) measuring the operating capacity of the individual asset; and
(2) identifying the group of assets (and, on occasion, liabilities) comprising the operating capacity of the enterprise.

(1) The operating capacity of the individual asset
Turning firstly to the measurement of the operating capacity of the

283

individual asset, a question exists as to whether operating capacity is to be measured in terms of:

(a) the physical asset itself; or
(b) the capacity of the asset to produce the same *volume* of goods and services; or
(c) the capacity of the asset to produce the same *value* of goods and services.

While the Sandilands Report and, apparently, the 1978 South African Guideline favoured the physical asset approach as being the most useful for those wishing to accept the operating capacity model, *ED18* and the later British pronouncements adopted a volume concept, concept (b); *SSAP16*, for example, defining operating capability as 'the *amount* of goods and services . . . the business is able to supply with its existing resources'.

This volume concept has generally been accepted elsewhere in the Anglo-Saxon world and would now appear to have become the accepted interpretation of operating capacity. For example, while the first CICA pronouncement of Current Value Accounting (the 1976 Discussion Paper) only vaguely defined operating capability as productive capacity, the 1982 Standard clearly stated the concept in terms of the output of goods and services. In the USA, *FAS33* and its preceding Exposure Draft both considered operating capacity in output terms. The volume concept was consistently employed in New Zealand from the initial 1976 Exposure Draft and Richardson Report to the 1982 CCA Standard. The Australian pronouncements were not quite so clear in their interpretation of operating capacity but the 1983 Statement of Accounting Practice unequivocally adopted the volume definition.

The volume concept avoids both the rigidity of the physical asset approach, which has been often criticised since theoretically a narrow (and perhaps out-dated) asset base would be maintained, and the fluidity of the maintenance of the value of production approach. The volume approach is, however, not immune from criticisms, especially when there is technical progress, or there are large relative price and cost changes, or when enterprises are diversifying or changing their areas of operations and consequently their portfolio of assets. These difficulties, and that to which we turn next – the definition of the group of assets which produce the flow of goods and services – have led to questions being raised as to whether an operating capacity capital base is an appropriate instrument on which to base measures of income and whether the maintenance of operating capability can be manipulated by the management of enterprises to serve their own self-interest, e.g. in retaining funds in the business rather than paying dividends.

284

(2) The assets comprising the operating capability of the enterprise

If a consensus may appear to exist on the question of the operating capability of the individual asset, there is little sign of agreement on the subject of the pool of assets forming the operating capability of the enterprise. Two basic questions have arisen, namely:

(a) Are the assets to be maintained simply the physical assets of the enterprise (i.e. fixed assets and stock) or should, in addition, monetary assets be included in the pool?

(b) Should the pool of resources consist of assets only (the 'gross approach') or should operating capacity be considered in terms of net assets, i.e. assets less certain liabilities (the 'net approach').

Since 1975, it has been possible to identify in the literature, and in practice, no fewer than eight different basic notions of the pool of assets forming an enterprise's operating capability – seven of which have been tried in practice (see Table 12.2).

We shall consider briefly each of the basic notions below.

(i) The maintenance of the operating capacity of physical assets

The early pronouncements in the Current Cost Revolution adopted a fairly simple approach to capital maintenance. Indeed, the first five official publications on current cost (or value) accounting, all of which were published in 1975, adopted this concept. In many respects this was not surprising. The first pronouncement – the Australian Mathews Report – leaned not unnaturally on the earlier work of Mathews (its Chairman) and Grant (1958). The equivalent Government Committee of Enquiry in the United Kingdom (the Sandilands Committee), while failing explicitly to acknowledge the main source of the inspiration for their conclusions, probably drew on the work of Edwards and Bell (1961) in proposing the adoption of the concept of operating profit (and separately a summary statement of total gains). The Sandilands Report dismissed the notion of the need to maintain the operating capacity of monetary assets (or, indeed, to adopt a 'net asset' maintenance approach by recording gains on liabilities):

> Because we are recommending that accounts should continue to be drawn up in terms of monetary units (pounds), it follows that no gains or losses in terms of money can arise solely through holding monetary items when prices are changing. The question of whether such gains should be classed as profit does not therefore arise as it does when accounts are drawn up in terms of current purchasing power units.

285

Part II Causes and consequences

Table 12.2. *Operating capacity – various definitions*

Maintenance of the operating capacity of:

(i) *Physical assets (i.e. fixed assets and stock)*
    1975 Australia – Mathews Report
            Australia – CCA ED (and 1976 CCA Provisional Standard)
            USA – SEC Notice of Proposal
            UK – Sandilands Report
            West Germany – Recommendation
    1976 NIVRA Statement (in regard to income on a current value basis)
            USA – SEC *ASR190*
            New Zealand – CCA ED
    1979 US – *FAS33* (in regard to income from continuing operations)
    1981 Canada – CCA ED*
    1982 Canada – CCA Standard*

(ii) *Physical assets + monetary assets (excluding fixed or long-term monetary assets)*
    1976 New Zealand – Richardson Report*
    1978 New Zealand – *CCA Guidelines**

(iii) *Physical assets + all monetary assets*
    No known trial in practice

(iv) *Physical assets + all monetary assets less all liabilities*
    1977 UK – Hyde Guidelines*
    1978 South Africa – Guideline*
    1979 Australia – CCA (ED revised) – as far as profit attributable to shareholders was concerned

(v) *Physical assets + all monetary assets less liabilities (excluding long-term borrowings)*
    1978 Australia – CCA ED
    1979 Australia – CCA (ED revised) – as far as entity net profit was concerned
    1982 New Zealand – CCA Standard*
    1983 Australia – *SAP1*

(vi) *Physical assets + monetary assets (generally excluding cash) less short-term liabilities (generally excluding bank overdrafts)*
    1979 UK – *ED24**

(vii) *Physical assets + monetary assets (excluding 'non-fluctuating' cash) less short-term liabilities (excluding 'non-fluctuating' bank overdrafts)*
    1979 Canada – CCA ED*
    1980 UK – *SSAP16**
    1981 New Zealand – CCA ED*

(viii) *Physical assets + net monetary assets*
    Philips

*Denotes system which also employed a gearing adjustment.

While other early pronouncements including the 1975 Australian Exposure Draft and the subsequent Provisional Standard (1976) adopted a similar attitude, the Australian publications suggested that the question of gains and losses on monetary items required further study. (See operating capacity maintenance systems (iv) and (v) below.)

Others studying the theories of income measurement, some of whom had possibly been introduced to the notion of gains and losses on monetary items by the worldwide flirtation with CPP accounting from 1973–75, were already convinced that the measurement of income necessitated accounting for the effects of price changes upon monetary items.

The following seven concepts of operating capacity maintenance all involve maintaining the operating capability of monetary assets (less, in some cases, liabilities) invariably using specific rather than general price-level changes (although general indices are occasionally recommended for the sake of convenience).

(ii) The maintenance of the operating capacity of physical assets and monetary assets (excluding fixed or long-term monetary assets)

New Zealand's Richardson Committee Report (discussed in Chapter 8) was the first official publication during the period of the Current Cost Revolution to include monetary assets in an entity's pool of operating assets, thereby rejecting the Sandilands notion that as accounts were drawn up in monetary units no gain or loss could arise simply through holding monetary assets.

The Committee argued:

> A monetary asset has an operating capacity of its own – in other words it has a job to do in enabling the enterprise to operate. If because of inflation the monetary assets are not able to do their job as effectively as before, or the enterprise has to carry more monetary assets to maintain the same level of operating capacity, then this should be recognised in arriving at the current cost operating profit.

Gains on liabilities were not included in operating profit although, as we shall discuss later, a gearing adjustment was introduced at a later stage in the profit and loss account. Additionally, the Committee drew a distinction between 'fixed' and 'circulating' monetary assets. The former were items such as debentures and mortgages in which a company could invest in the same manner as an individual person. Where such items were held no adjustment to current cost profit was to be made, since, it

287

was argued, the enterprise could have avoided the inflationary loss on money tied up in them. On the other hand, losses on items such as bank accounts, cash and trade debts were deemed to be unavoidable, and consequently appropriate charges were to be made against operating profit.

While the Richardson concept was later adopted by the New Zealand Society in its 1978 *CCA Guidelines*, it has not generally been accepted elsewhere and was attacked on the grounds:[6]

(a) that all assets contribute to operating capacity; *and*

(b) that current liabilities should be set off against monetary assets to form a working capital pool.

These views have been adopted in varying degrees in the remaining operating capacity concepts discussed below.

(iii) The maintenance of the operating capacity of physical assets and all monetary assets

The argument underlying this concept states that, since the operating capability of monetary assets lies in their ability to purchase goods and services and as cash can be held not only for transactions purposes (the concept underlying the Richardson concept) but also for precautionary and speculative (the ability to take advantage of investment opportunities) purposes, if the purchasing power of monetary assets is diminished by inflation then the operating capacity of the enterprise must be reduced. A charge to the profit and loss account is, therefore, necessary to maintain operating capacity.

Stamp (1971), Bourn (1976), and Henderson and Pierson (1977), have argued in favour of this concept, principally on the grounds that if the value of money depreciates, the enterprise's scope for action has been reduced. No professional standard-setting body has, however, accepted this approach. In general, they have preferred instead to adopt a 'net' approach, considering that operating capability is based on physical assets and net monetary assets.

Five such approaches are considered next.

(iv) The maintenance of physical assets and all monetary assets less all liabilities

This concept of operating capacity maintains the specific purchasing power of an enterprise's net *assets*; profit being charged not only with the cost of maintaining stock and depreciable assets but also with the fall in the specific purchasing power of the monetary assets, while being credited with the gain on borrowings.[7] The overall charge against profit would therefore reflect the charge required to maintain the shareholders' interests in terms of specific rather than general purchasing power.

Like concept (iii) above, this view of operating capacity maintenance is an 'all or nothing' approach, and does not seek to eliminate any particular assets or liabilities on the grounds that they do not form part of the asset or net asset pool forming the operating capability of the enterprise. All other approaches have had to justify with varying degrees of success and contention the omission of certain items from the asset/liability pool. Despite this, however, no 'pure' version of this maintenance concept has yet emerged. Instead, two quite different forms of this operating capacity concept have appeared in the recent past. The first method was initially revealed in the UK's Hyde Guidelines (1977)[8] and copied by the South African professional society in 1978. A charge was to be made in the income statement to account for the effects of inflation on net monetary assets. Where a surplus of liabilities existed, however, it was proposed that a gearing adjustment should be applied to the depreciation and cost of sales adjustments. In other words, the adjustments for surplus monetary assets and surplus monetary liabilities were not symmetrical but were calculated in entirely different ways.

The second method originated in the 1979 revised Exposure Draft issued by the Australian Accounting Research Foundation, which adopted the maintenance concept discussed here as far as 'profit and gearing gains attributable to shareholders' was concerned. The measurement of gains and losses on most monetary items was based on specific price changes. For loan capital (considered to be part of the permanent capital of the enterprise in the earlier Exposure Draft of 1978 – see concept (v) below) a general price index was to be used. The gains on loan capital, however, were later deducted from profit (and transferred to a gearing gains reserve), on the grounds that distribution of such gains would reduce the enterprise's operating capability, to arrive at entity net profit – a profit identical to that shown under the provisions of the 1978 Exposure Draft outlined in operating capacity concept (v), to which we now turn.

(v) The maintenance of the operating capacity of physical assets and all monetary assets less liabilities (excluding long-term borrowings)

This concept of operating capacity maintenance is concerned with the ability of non-monetary assets and net working capital to maintain the same level of operations of the enterprise. As we described in Chapter 8, the concept has won support in Australasia, being adopted by the

Part II Causes and consequences

New Zealand Society in its 1982 CCA Standard (apparently as a reaction to the problems with these items discussed under concepts (vi) and (vii) below) but originating in Australia. The principle advocate of this system (Gynther)[9] and the Australian Accounting Research Foundation, which in its 1978 Exposure Draft (in the drafting of which Gynther played a major part) adopted a similar system, have been criticised on the grounds that, while the proposal included in profit gains resulting from the loss in the specific purchasing power of current liabilities, it excluded similar gains on long-term borrowings since, it was argued, distribution of such gains would impair the basic assets of the company. Gynther counters the criticism by explaining that, to him, current liabilities form part of the *net* current working monetary *asset* pool which is formed by the permanent capital of the firm (see Gynther 1966): gains or losses on holding monetary items could only occur in relation to monetary resources and not in relation to funds employed which support resources. Long-term liabilities are deemed to be part of permanent capital and are similar in nature to amounts contributed by shareholders. Calculating profit on items of long-term debt would, to Gynther, be as illogical, in times of rising prices, as calculating 'profit' on funds received from shareholders. (The revised 1979 Exposure Draft did, however, as seen above, respond in part to this criticism.)

Some critics (e.g. Henderson and Pierson, 1977) have been unmoved by Gynther's argument and have concluded that the concept is based upon a doubtful interpretation of operating capacity and that the arguments used to exclude purchasing power gains on long-term debts could apply equally to gains on current monetary liabilities. This criticism could also presumably be applied to the model described in concept (vi) below, where a 'working capital pool' concept was also in evidence.

(vi) The maintenance of the operating capacity of physical assets and monetary assets (excluding cash) less creditors

We described Gibbs' proposed modification of the Sandilands system in Chapter 6. It will be recalled that he proposed that adjustments for monetary items sould be incorporated into the basic Sandilands system, in two parts:

(a) the broadening of the cost of sales adjustment to take account of 'working capital' rather than simply stock;

(b) the inclusion in income of the proportion of the net holding gains attributable to borrowed money.[10] (This adjustment was added to post-tax operating profits and will be considered under the gain on borrowing below.)

290

In the Gibbs system, the Sandilands cost of sales adjustment was expanded to take account of working capital appreciation (the increased cost of stock plus debtors less creditors) rather than stock appreciation. For some businesses, such as banks, which had to retain a certain proportion of their funds in liquid form, the working capital adjustment incorporated the effect of inflation upon cash holdings but, for industrial companies, an adjustment for cash was not included.

The proposed working capital adjustment undoubtedly led 'operating profit' to reflect to a greater degree than before an enterprise's inflow and outflow of funds but did not reflect the effect of price-level changes on cash holdings and, consequently, could hardly be said to measure income. Two further criticisms of this system were made. Firstly, the claim that financial institutions needed to keep part of their assets in liquid form whereas industrial companies were not so required, led to charges of inconsistency and to criticism of the practical difficulties in determining whether or not an enterprise needs to hold cash. Secondly, by excluding bank overdrafts from working capital, the adjustment would vary depending on whether the enterprise financed its purchases by overdraft or by creditors. Gibbs' argument in favour of this distinction between creditors and overdraft was that banks had to be persuaded to lend more while, with creditors, the loan was automatic: a somewhat extreme assumption.

The Gibbs scheme had, as discussed in Chapter 6 above, been considered by the UK's Inflation Accounting Steering Group (of which Gibbs was himself a member) in developing *ED18* and could have been adopted if directors had made certain adjustments in appropriation accounts. The UK's second CCA Exposure Draft (*ED24*, 1979), however, adopted the basic Gibbs proposals with certain modifications.[11] As in Gibbs' scheme, cash and bank overdrafts were excluded from the monetary working capital adjustment (MWCA) in order, the Exposure Draft stated, to limit the subjectivity involved in defining items to be included in monetary working capital, although cash and bank overdrafts could be considered part of monetary working capital where their exclusion could be shown to give a misleading calculation of profit. The interchangeability of short-term creditors, bank overdrafts and longer-term creditors on one hand, and between debtors and cash on the other, resulted in the ASC receiving similar criticisms to those raised against the Gibbs system.

Gibbs himself did not approve of the *ED24* system. Apart from his criticism of the gearing adjustment (discussed in the next section of this chapter), he objected to the *ED24* treatment of negative net working capital (including stock): Gibbs felt that this should lead to an addition to operating profits as prices rose, whereas *ED24* made no adjustment in this situation, treating positive and negative net working capital asymmetrically (Gibbs and Seward, 1979).

> *(vii) The maintenance of operating capacity of physical assets and monetary assets (excluding 'non-fluctuating' cash) less short-term liabilities (excluding 'non-fluctuating' bank overdrafts)*

A revision to operating capacity concept (vi) was not long in following the introduction of the UK's *ED24*. The CICA's Exposure Draft, issued some months after *ED24* (in December 1979), was the first to move away from the relatively rigid line of *ED24* in generally excluding cash balances and bank overdrafts. The amount of these two items required for the conduct of day-to-day operating activities was to be included in the monetary working capital adjustment (or the net productive monetary items adjustment, as it was termed in Canada).

The UK's *SSAP16* (published in March 1980) adopted a similar capital maintenance system, the ASC having responded to criticism of the treatment of monetary items in the exposure draft. That part of bank balances or overdrafts arising from fluctuations in the volume of stock, debtors and creditors together with any cash floats required to support the day-to-day operations of the business, were now to be included in monetary working capital for the purposes of the adjustment to operating profit – a notion that was followed in the New Zealand Exposure Draft issued in August 1981. The New Zealand Society, however, abandoned this position in its CCA Standard issued in March 1982 in making a further retreat from the initial Gibbs cash-flow style proposals. Under the requirements of the new Standard, all cash balances and bank overdrafts (except those of a capital nature) would be included in monetary working capital. This simplifying proposal has resulted in the present (1982) New Zealand operating capacity maintenance concept being similar to that of concept (v) above.

> *(viii) The maintenance of the operating capacity of physical assets and net monetary assets*

The concept of operating capacity maintenance discussed in this section was used for many years (until 1971) by the Philips company of The Netherlands and was considered and rejected by the UK's Inflation Accounting Steering Group when the proposed monetary items adjustments for *ED18* was detailed. Philips did not pretend to 'apply replacement value theory in all its details'. As the then Chief Internal Auditor of the Company (Goudeket, 1960) wrote:

Certainly theorists can criticise our application in some
respects. As with all problems, it is not a question of the
application of the theory in all details; it is only a question of a
practical application based on theoretical principles. Then a
need is being fulfilled. In practice, it is not the problem, but its
solution, which counts.

The Philips system involved charging the replacement cost of depreciating assets and stock consumed to the profit and loss account but
additionally charged profit with the loss in the purchasing power of the
shareholders' equity invested in monetary assets. The argument for the
latter charge was that 'part of the shareholders' equity is invested in . . .
monetary assets [and consequently] the purchasing power of that part
[of the equity] will diminish in the case of a decrease in the value of
currency of the country' (Goudeket, 1960). Philips calculated the loss in
purchasing power by deducting liabilities from monetary assets and the
balance, multiplied by the inflation factor based on the cost-of-living
index, was charged to the profit and loss account. It should, however, be
noted that if liabilities exceeded monetary assets, then no part of equity
was considered to be invested in monetary assets and no purchasing
power loss was shown. (No gain on net liabilities was taken to profit –
although there was provision for adding to profit gains on net monetary
assets if purchasing power rose but only to the extent of any reserve for
losses in purchasing power.)

The system, therefore, was a variant of the net working capital
models but, in addition, included long-term liabilities as a deduction
from monetary assets. It was criticised on two counts. Firstly, its
financing model assumed monetary assets are generally financed by
liabilities, and, secondly, it was claimed (by those preferring the
proprietary school of thought) that the model was 'lop-sided' in that it
did not recognise monetary gains. More recently, Philips has changed its
views, abandoned the monetary asset adjustment and applied a gearing
adjustment to the additional current cost charges for depreciation and
cost of sales.[12] In other words, the Philips definition of operating
capability is now similar to concept (i) above.

Conclusion on capital maintenance

We have seen above how varied and complicated have been the various
attempts to provide a measure of 'operating capacity' as the basis of an
entity capital maintenance concept. It is tempting to conclude that the
concept of operating capacity should be abandoned entirely and that the

293

proprietary concept, which is relatively simple, objective and intuitively appealing from the shareholder's point of view, should prevail. Indeed, if it were essential to have a single capital maintenance concept, we should support the latter conclusion.

However, as Edwards and Bell more than two decades ago (1961) and Kennedy more recently (1978a) have demonstrated, it is not essential to have a single capital maintenance concept: it is quite feasible to report a number of profit figures derived from different capital maintenance concepts, within a single income statement. We would advocate such a procedure not for the negative reason that we are unable to choose between a bewildering variety of competing concepts, but for the positive reason that different measures of profit may be useful for different purposes. In our account of the capital maintenance debate, we have tried to show that most of the competing concepts have been supported by some form of theoretical argument. We would not accept all of these arguments, and not all of the competing measures could or should be reported within a single income statement (e.g. some of the cash flow approaches might be better accommodated within a flow of funds statement), but we are persuaded that an eclectic approach to capital maintenance and income measurement is desirable. This view is complementary to our view of the valuation debate, expressed in the previous section of this chapter. It was also expressed in Chapter 1 and in the companion volume (Whittington, 1983a).

In the following section, we deal with the question of the gain on borrowing, which is really an aspect of the capital maintenance issue but which has achieved such importance in the debate that it merits separate treatment.

3 The gain on borrowing

Many accountants were probably first alerted to the concept of a gain on borrowing by the debate on current purchasing power. If monetary assets declined in value during a period of inflation, the obvious corollary of this symptom of rising price levels was that the purchasing power of borrowings would similarly decline. While any organisation which had purchased its assets by means of debt financing would repay its borrowing by parting with the same number of monetary units as it had borrowed, such monetary units, in times of rising price levels, were worth less in terms of purchasing power at the time of repayment than at the time the loan was first made. Consequently, the organisation had gained by financing its assets from sources other than its proprietors. The measure of the gain would depend on the capital maintenance concept, as would the corresponding loss on assets of fixed monetary value.

While there was some nervousness about the inclusion of unrealised CPP gains on long-term liabilities in income,[13] the concept itself was seldom in dispute. In the United Kingdom, however, the gains on borrowing shown by property companies in supplementary CPP accounts in 1974, at a time when the property market was in decline, did lead to distrust of the consequences of the concept (Morpeth, 1981), despite the problem being caused not so much by gains on borrowing in highly geared companies as by unrealistic asset values. This experience could well have led to the initial resistance to the translation of the concept of gains and losses on monetary items to CCA. The CCA gain on borrowing took two forms. Firstly, in those operating capacity models which adopt a 'net' asset approach, it is implicitly assumed that the loss on holding monetary assets is offset by the gain on financing by certain forms of borrowing, generally of a short-term (near to cash) nature. This approach has been criticised as it introduces a financing effect into operating profit. A second approach (which has also frequently been adopted by those advocating a net asset definition of operating capacity) to calculating purchasing power gains (albeit usually of a specific nature) involves calculating the gain on borrowing in relation to the appreciation of the assets financed by such borrowing (the gearing adjustment), thereby avoiding the problems associated, by many accountants, with the CPP gain. These gearing adjustments usually come after the calculation of operating profit.

The gearing adjustment consequently appeared as an antidote to the problems of the CPP gain on borrowing. Gains resulting from financing assets by loans were to be measured in terms of the rise in the money value of the assets themselves. The Godley–Cripps method (later amended by Gibbs and then adopted in modified form by the Richardson Committee), was illustrated in Chapter 1, Section 3, and in Chapter 6, Section 2.

This gearing adjustment, embracing unrealised as well as realised gains, obviously alarmed those who considered income in terms of realised trading or investment income and gains on disposal of assets. Consequently, most gearing proposals have followed the thrust of the version first introduced in recent times by the West German (1975) Statement, reducing the additional current cost charges to income, thereby ensuring that current cost income would never exceed historical cost income. In other words, the emphasis has been on a conservative adjustment based on *realised* rather than on *realisable* cost savings (or holding gains).[14] Such a conservative gearing adjustment was introduced into UK practice by the Hyde Guidelines (1977: see Chapter 6, Section 3).

At this stage, it would probably be beneficial to sum up the differences between the gearing and CPP approaches to borrowing.

The main difference to note is that the gearing adjustment is entity-based, as far as the measurement of shareholders' capital is concerned. A measure of income incorporating a gearing adjustment initially charges historical cost operating profit with the additional amounts required to maintain the operating capability of the entity, as a result of price changes, thereby arriving at some concept of operating profit. The *realised cost saving gearing (West German) approach* reduces these additional charges to the extent that they were financed by lenders to the business. The *realisable cost saving (Godley–Cripps) approach*, on the other hand, also includes in profit the loan-financed proportion of the money appreciation of assets not consumed in operations during the year. The proportion of the monetary appreciation of assets financed by shareholders is not included in profit. This profit could be said to represent the maximum amount relating to the accounting period distributable to shareholders while preserving the operating capability of the enterprise, since shareholders' capital is preserved in terms of the specific assets which it finances.

The CPP gain on borrowing, on the other hand, adopts the financial capital (proprietary) approach, whereby income is measured in terms of the increase in the owner's general command over resources. A historical cost based CPP system does not necessarily reflect fully the owner's increase in wealth, since asset values may well differ from historical cost adjusted by a general index, but a 'real terms' system, combining current valuation of assets and liabilities with general index adjustment of the equity capital base, will avoid this difficulty. The latter approach will show real holding gains where the specific net assets of the business have out-performed the general index and a real holding loss where they have failed to do so. The advocate of the gearing approach will argue that such 'real gains' and 'real losses' are illusory, because the essential requirement of the firm is to maintain its 'operating capability' rather than a fund of general purchasing power. However, we saw in the previous section of this chapter that the concept of operating capability has been translated into a bewildering variety of operational forms. We now turn to the corresponding bewildering variety of operational methods of dealing with the gain on borrowing by means of the gearing adjustment.

As we discussed in the last section, many of the early attempts in the mid-1970s to define operating capacity ignored the question of borrowing and assumed that the capital to be maintained consisted of fixed assets and stock. In particular, the two Government Committees of Enquiry reporting in 1975 (the Mathews and Sandilands Committees) both adopted this approach, being followed in the next year by the SEC's *ASR190*, which made similar proposals. As Table 12.2 indicated, in the first two years of the Current Cost Revolution, only one major pronouncement on the subject, New Zealand's Richardson Report (1976), espoused the notion of gains and losses on monetary items.[15] The Richardson Report proposed a charge against profit to maintain the operating capability of monetary assets and a gearing adjustment to include in income attributable to shareholders the appreciation of assets financed by borrowing. While the Richardson approach was not copied in countries other than New Zealand, it probably assisted the critics of physical asset maintenance to persuade the standard-setting bodies to adopt a 'net assets' approach to operating capacity. However, the liabilities included in the 'net' approaches were, in most cases, of a short-term nature: there was an obvious reluctance to bring gains on long-term liabilities into income.

In Chapter 2, we traced the gearing adjustment back to Schmidt. His original proposal concerned only speculative gains and differed from the subsequent gearing adjustment proposals advocated in the mid-1970s by Godley and Cripps, and, indeed, by the German Institute, whose 1975 Statement[16] was the first official pronouncement to propose the use of a gearing adjustment – an adjustment which became a central feature of the inflation accounting debate in several countries.

Table 12.3 outlines the various forms the adjustment has taken since its recent rebirth, as the standard-setters have sought to reflect the fact that benefits can be obtained in inflationary periods by including in income the gain on long-term borrowing, thereby offsetting the conservative nature of the initial current cost accounts.

The two initial modern versions of the gearing adjustment differed from each other in two important respects. Firstly, as described above, the West German adjustment was concerned solely with the abatement of the additional current cost charges for stock and depreciation in income, whereas the Godley–Cripps gearing adjustment included in income the proportion of holding gains which accrued to the proprietors of a business as a result of their having financed appreciating assets by borrowing.

The question of whether the gearing adjustment should be based on unrealised as well as realised gains, has been a central issue in the debate on the gains on borrowing, particularly in Canada and the UK. However, while Gibbs (1976) refined the Godley–Cripps system, the

Table 12.3. *Gearing adjustments – various international proposals*

A	*Realised and unrealised gains brought into income*
(i)	Adjustment adds to profit (attributable to shareholders) proportion of increase in current cost reserves (i.e. CCA adjustments – depreciation, cost of sales and MWCA – and revaluation gains) financed by borrowing

       1976   New Zealand – Richardson Report
       1978   New Zealand – *CCA Guidelines*
       1981   New Zealand – CCA (ED)
       1982   New Zealand – CCA Standard (preferred method)*

B	*Realised gains only brought into income*
(ii)	Adjustment abates earlier cost of sales adjustment and depreciation (in that order)

       1975   West German recommendation*

(iii)	Adjustment abates earlier depreciation and cost of sales adjustments (in that order)

       1978   Hofstra (The Netherlands)

(iv)	Adjustment abates earlier depreciation and cost of sales adjustment (in proportion to the gearing ratio) but becomes a MWCA when monetary assets are greater than liabilities

       1977   UK – Hyde Guidelines
       1978   South Africa – CCA Guidelines*

(v)	Adjustment abates earlier depreciation and cost of sales adjustments (in proportion to the gearing ratio)

       1977   Canada – Ontario Report
       1981   Canada – CCA ED

(vi)	Adjustment abates earlier depreciation, cost of sales and MWCA adjustments (in proportion to the gearing ratio)

       1979   UK – *ED24*
       1979   Canada – CCA ED
       1980   UK – *SSAP16**

C	*Adjustments (A and B) above both shown*
(vii)	Information is given on two gearing adjustments (based on the gearing ratio)
	(a) the adjustment abates the CCA depreciation and cost of sales adjustments (in proportion to the gearing ratio)
	(b) the adjustment is based on the proportion of revaluation gains financed by borrowing

       1982   Canada – CCA Standard*

*Denotes latest position in country.

main thrust of the former's gearing adjustment proposal being that adopted by New Zealand's Richardson Committee in the same year, the notion of including unrealised holding gains in income has not, until recently, found favour elsewhere. Conservatism has been the principal reason for the rejection of the adjustment based on all holding gains. New Zealand has, however, consistently adopted a gearing adjustment based on all holding gains, the Committee of Inquiry's view being upheld by all of the New Zealand Society of Accountants proposals to date, including its 1982 CCA Standard (Method (i) in Table 12.3). Only recently have other current cost standard-setters followed suit, the Canadians in their 1982 CCA Standard acknowledging the potential merits of such a proposal by encouraging disclosure in the notes to the current cost accounts of both a gearing adjustment of this type, and an adjustment based solely on realised gains (Method (vii)).

A second difference between the Godley–Cripps and West German adjustments was the financing assumption inherent in the adjustments. In the West German proposal, borrowings were assumed to finance firstly stocks and then fixed assets – the cost of sales adjustment being abated before any reduction would be made to the depreciation adjustment (Method (ii)).

The only other similar type of adjustment, that proposed by Hofstra in The Netherlands (Method (iii)), adopted the opposite financing assumption, liabilities being deemed to finance firstly fixed assets and then stocks. This assumption was probably employed because the Hofstra Report was concerned with taxation in times of inflation. Since rising stock prices were deemed to have a greater immediate effect on corporate profitability and liquidity than changes in the cost of fixed assets, the depreciation adjustment was reduced prior to an abatement of the additional charge for cost of sales, thereby allowing companies a greater relief from taxation than if the West German financing assumption had been adopted.

Such financing assumptions, however, have not been followed in the rest of the world. Most gearing adjustments are based on the premise that all assets are financed in equal proportions of equity capital and borrowings (however defined). Operating capacity maintenance proposals advocating a 'net assets' approach, however, inevitably assume that short-term liabilities financed first, monetary assets included in the asset pool, and then stocks, since such liabilities are usually deemed to be part of a monetary working capital pool. The difficulties involved in deciding which assets and liabilities form part of the operating capital base of an enterprise have, as we have seen in the previous section of this chapter, been the subject of much debate. Obviously, the definition of operating capability affects the gearing adjustment, since, if the system proposed makes no separate adjustment to maintain working capital, monetary assets invariably are deducted from borrowings in calculating the gearing ratio. This has led to differences between the current UK (Method (vi)) and Canadian approaches (Method (viia)). Both approaches reveal a basic defect when monetary assets exceed borrowings. Invariably, in such cases, no gearing adjustment is shown and no further adjustment is made for the loss in purchasing power or operating capability of the 'surplus' monetary assets. The Hyde Guidelines, later abandoned by the ASC, and the subsequent South African Guidelines (Method (iv)) took account of this problem by using a gearing adjustment to abate depreciation and cost of sales adjustments when liabilities exceeded monetary assets, but, of more importance to the point under discussion, by employing a form of monetary working capital adjustment when monetary assets were in excess of liabilities.

The debate on the gain on borrowing is consequently far from over. The 'pure' purchasing power gain on liabilities obviously has attractions, firstly in its relative simplicity of calculation in being based on a measure of general price-level change, and, secondly, in its objectivity and consistency in encompassing all borrowings. Its main drawbacks probably stem from two related factors; firstly, the individual may wish to see the gain in cash terms and may ultimately reject the concept of a purchasing power unit as counter-intuitive. Where is the gain? When shall I receive it? Secondly, as mentioned earlier, the lack of confidence in the concept was probably accentuated in the minds of the sceptics by the experience of witnessing asset values – the tangible wealth of the enterprise – declining while accounts were revealing gains from borrowings. The problem, however, lay not so much with the concept of the gain on borrowing as with the failure to measure the fall in asset values. If accounts had measured the fall in property values in real terms, then the nature of the difficulties faced by property companies in 1974 would have become only too obvious.

However, as we have seen, attempts to deal with the gain on borrowing by means of gearing adjustments have led to a bewildering variety of controversial alternatives, and recently several countries have begun to suggest that information be given in the financial statements to enable readers to calculate real-terms proprietary income. The United States' *FAS33* requires not only income from continuing operations (i.e. HC Profit less CC Depreciation and Cost of Sales Adjustments) in current cost terms to be shown, but also the real gain on assets and the gain or loss on monetary items. The 1982 Canadian CCA Standard requested similar information to enable the reader to calculate income on the proprietary basis. (As mentioned earlier, it also requires gearing adjustments to be calculated using both the realised and realisable cost saving approaches.) Finally, New Zealand, in its 1982 Standard, gave the option of calculating current cost income on either the operating capability or financial capital basis.

4 Summary

It is obviously difficult to draw simple conclusions from a wide-ranging survey such as this, and, consequently, this summary will simply outline the themes and trends which seem to be visible at the time of writing and which relate to the views expressed in other chapters.

Firstly, in the area of asset valuation, some consensus does appear to be emerging in the leading countries involved in the debate. An eclectic measurement system has been proposed in North America, in Commonwealth countries and in South Africa. In the USA and Canada, the *deprival value* approach of Bonbright has been adopted. In the other countries (namely Australia, New Zealand, South Africa and the UK) the *Australian Compromise* variant of deprival value, which does not involve the discounting of the recoverable amount, predominates. It would seem that, at present at least, systems based on single valuation approaches for all assets have been rejected. Our own view is that future developments should include the reporting of alternative valuations for certain assets where different valuation bases give materially different results.

Secondly, with regard to capital maintenance, this lies at the heart of the inflation accounting debate and the standard-setters of the 1970s quickly and perhaps too hastily took sides. Initially, at least, it seemed that the entity view would predominate – only the USA consistently supported the proprietary or financial capital approach. More recently, however, other countries have modified their original entity approach by the use of a gearing adjustment – a system which is intended to maintain only the operating capacity of the enterprise financed by its proprietors rather than that of the whole entity. Other countries have gone further and abandoned strict adherence to the entity concept, and are allowing enterprises to use, as an alternative, a proprietary approach to income measurement. The difficulties of defining operating capability and its lack of suitability to all type of businesses would appear to be undermining the former popularity of the entity concept. However, the whole debate on capital maintenance has been unnecessarily polarised, since it is possible, within a single income statement, to show the consequences of alternative capital maintenance concepts. In our view, the advocacy of a single, all-purpose capital maintenance concept, is a consequence of a misguided fixation upon a single all-purpose income measure as 'the bottom line' of the income statement.

Thirdly, the gain on borrowing is obviously related to the capital maintenance debate. If, as appears possible at present, the proprietary concept is preferred to the entity approach, the gearing adjustment will probably also be discarded, since its rôle was to introduce proprietary gains into entity-based systems. Various proposals for the gearing adjustment have been propounded. Arguments have developed over the issues of the financing assumptions, the definition of gearing, and whether the geared portion of realised or realisable holding gains should be included in income. Such arguments, however, will be of little consequence if a proprietary capital maintenance system which would recognise gains on borrowing based on a general index is adopted. The simplicity and objectivity of the CPP borrowing gain undoubtedly have attractions. Adoption of such a proposal would not, however, end the debate on the gain on borrowing. In particular, the controversy still exists over whether gains on long-term liabilities can be included in income before such liabilities are repaid and even whether *any* gain on borrowing should be included in profit or should be shown separately as a different form of gain. The debate on this issue is far from settled.

Finally, the recent debate upon the various aspects of current cost accounting, upon which we have concentrated our attention, has been characterised by a great deal of pragmatism and compromise. Such theoretical argument as has been used has been piecemeal, and this has both encouraged the bewildering variety of solutions offered and made a rational choice between them very difficult.

13
The course of the debate: causes and influences

Introduction

In this chapter, we discuss what is perhaps the most fundamental issue which can be addressed by an historical study of the inflation accounting debate: why did the debate take the course which it did? We would not claim to provide a conclusive answer to this question (if, indeed, such an answer exists) and our narrative in the main body of the book (Chapters 2 to 10 inclusive) has been aimed primarily at providing the reader with a clear account of the relevant facts, upon which he can make his own judgements, rather than imposing our own opinions. Nevertheless, we did start out on this study with certain questions in mind (see Chapter 1), and we have reached speculative conclusions *en route*. It is therefore appropriate to bring these questions and speculative answers together in this chapter, for the reader's benefit.

There is no shortage of hypotheses as to the causes of the course of the inflation accounting debate. We list below the more plausible ones, together with brief elaboration. They will then be discussed, in turn, in subsequent sections of the chapter.

(1) *Economic events*. Put at its simplest, interest in inflation accounting rises when the rate of inflation rises and falls when the rate of inflation falls.

(2) *Self-interest*. Various participants in the debate advance arguments which will favour the adoption of accounting systems which advance their own self-interest. This is connected with (1) insofar as the impact of economic events impinges on the interests of different groups.

(3) *Ideas*. In most areas of scientific and technical activity, the evolution of practice and standards of practice are influenced considerably by new discoveries and ideas. This does not preclude (1) and (2) and, indeed, research questions may be initiated by, and funds provided by, self-interested parties, but we would hope that the discovery of new knowledge would lead to an improvement in the techniques available and a deeper understanding of their implications.

(4) *International influences.* Since both inflation and accounting are international, we would expect some parallel developments between countries. Insofar as there was discovery of new ideas ((3) above), we would expect these to be disseminated rapidly between countries which shared a community of scholars and/or practitioners. Equally, economic events (item (1) above) are often international, notably in the inflations consequent upon major wars and crises (such as the 1973 oil crisis), and the self-interest of different groups is also likely to have parallels across countries.

(5) *Accidents of history.* Despite the possible intervention of deterministic factors such as those outlined above, there are also many individual factors which, taken together, might appear to be random, but which are not necessarily irrational and which can be very important in their aggregate impact. These factors include the individual personalities participating in the debate, their education and preferences, and their relationship to one another and the constitutions with which they are involved. Perhaps the most important of all 'accidents of history', from the points of view of a participant in the inflation accounting debate, is the particular historical situation which he has inherited, i.e. the sum total of individuals, institutions, practices and prejudices, which he inherits from the past but which constrain his future actions.

1 Economic events

The idea that a high rate of inflation stimulates a high level of interest in inflation accounting, and vice versa, is not a new one. It was expressed clearly by Sweeney in the 1930s, and with even more eloquence and conviction in his later retrospective review 'Forty Years After' (Sweeney, 1931 and 1964a). The then chief accountant of the United States Securities and Exchange Commission, J. C. Burton expressed a similar view at the time when the SEC was preparing its replacement cost disclosure requirements (Burton, 1975), and more recently Mumford (1979) has analysed the United Kingdom experience since the Second World War in terms of a cycle of inflation accounting activity lagging behind a cycle of inflation. Mumford's predictions have been fulfilled by recent UK experience: the inflation rate is currently (mid-1983) at an annual rate of less than 5 per cent, and the Accounting Standards Committee is in the process of considering the replacement of its current cost accounting standard, *SSAP16*, by a much less demanding recommendation which would, for example, dispense with current cost balance sheet information.

The historical record of Chapters 2 to 10 is clearly consistent with this view. Interest in inflation accounting in individual countries has tended to follow high rates of inflation, e.g. in continental Europe in the early 1920s, and in most of the countries seriously affected by the inflation following the oil crisis of 1973. Also, the most extreme rates of inflation have led to solutions of the CPP variety, using general indices, notably in Germany during the early 1920s and in Brazil, Chile and Argentina during the past three decades. This can be explained in terms of the imperative nature of the problems created by extreme inflation: some form of adjustment is then perceived as being essential, and CPP offers a relatively simple, speedy and objective solution.

However, the relevant economic events are not merely those reflected in changes in the rate of inflation, as measured by movements in a general price level index. Relative prices are also important, and these can change independently of the general price level. This type of change does, however, have similar consequences, insofar as it can lead to historical cost failing to capture changes in the relative values of assets and the relative income and wealth of different individuals. Inflation, in the sense of an increase in the general price level, reduces the relative value of assets fixed in monetary value and increases the wealth of borrowers relative to lenders. Relative price changes of individual assets can also have effects on the relative values of assets and on the relative wealth of owners of those assets. Thus, we would expect large relative price changes to be an economic event which would lead to pressure to replace historical cost accounting with a system which records specific price changes, such as CCA.

There is some impressionistic evidence for this second hypothesis, in our historical record. The period during which current cost accounting ousted CPP as the preferred inflation accounting technique in the English-speaking world was the mid-1970s. The inflation of this period followed the 1973 world oil crisis, which led to increased costs of energy, in the first instance, followed, as a result of government policies, by restriction of profit margins, and large relative changes in the costs of materials, wages, and finished goods. Evidence of this for the UK was given in Chapter 5, Table 5.1. This environment was one in which relative price changes were unusually severe, and it was associated with support for recording specific prices through the medium of current cost accounting (in what we described earlier as the 'Current Cost Revolution'). The need to report the effect of specific price changes in reducing current cost profit margins was expressed very clearly in the writings of influential contemporary advocates of CCA, such as Merrett and Sykes (1974a).

The pressure to report relative price changes accurately (or differently) is, of course, bound up with our next topic: self-interest. Clearly, pressure for revised methods of reporting is likely to come from those who are affected adversely by the present methods. These adverse effects will also depend upon another type of economic environmental factor, government policy. Such matters as taxation and price control may well be determined by reference to reported profits. Thus, in the mid-1970s, the Merrett and Sykes and Godley and Wood debate (discussed in Chapter 5) was mainly concerned with whether stock appreciation should be subject to taxation. It is also notable that the CPP systems introduced in Latin America derived their initial impetus from their association with tax reliefs, whereas progress in certain continental European countries, notably France and Germany, has been impeded by the fact that any revaluation of assets in the main accounts would give rise to a tax liability. With this in mind, we now turn to the important related topic of self-interest.

2 Self-interest

The rôle of self-interest in the advocacy of alternative systems of accounting has been subject to considerable attention in recent years, particularly in the context of inflation accounting. Writers such as those cited by Zeff (1978) have recognised the economic consequences of accounting methods, and the resulting incentive for self-interested pressure groups who press for the adoption of methods which favour their own interests. Other writers have emphasised the political nature of the accounting standard-setting process. Some, such as Watts and Zimmerman (1978 and 1979) regard this process as merely one of political bargaining in which the accounting theorist is reduced to supplying 'excuses' for the systems advocated by alternative self-interested parties. Others, such as Solomons (1979), regard the true object of standard-setting as being to use theory and empirical evidence to produce solutions which transcend the narrow objectives of self-interested groups (Solomons using the celebrated analogy between accounting and cartography). However, despite the fact that self-interest is a currently fashionable theme amongst accounting writers, it has been recognised for a considerable time in the past, e.g. Sweeney (1931 and 1964a) recognised its rôle in the specific context of inflation accounting, in association with the rôle of economic events, which change the solutions which serve the self-interest of different groups. Moreover, there is considerable evidence from the historical record which is consistent with the view that self-interest has been an important factor in the inflation accounting debate ever since its inception.

The earliest example of self-interest at work in the inflation accounting debate which we have recorded is in the USA rate regulation cases of the late nineteenth and early twentieth century, as documented by Germain Boer (1966). New critical insights into these cases have recently been offered by Clarke (1982), but these are concerned with questioning the precise form of price-adjusted accounting which was involved rather than the fact that the participants in the cases (government agencies and regulated companies) switched allegiance between accounting systems as economic circumstances changed their self-interest.

The influence of governments and government agencies, and the wish of companies to obtain favourable treatment from them, has been pervasive in the debate ever since. Apart from the specialised issue of regulated companies in the USA and nationalised industries in the UK, the general regulation of prices became an important issue in the inflation of the mid-1970s. The desire to avoid price controls, by pleading low profitability, was an important strand in the arguments of Merrett and Sykes (1974a) and others who advocated measuring profit in terms of current (or replacement) cost operating profit, excluding holding gains. Taxation is another important aspect of government policy which has influenced the course of the debate. Again, this was a serious issue in the British debate of the 1970s, and successive Chancellors of the Exchequer treated Stock Relief as a temporary measure, to be amended when the ASC settled upon a final solution to inflation accounting. This must have provided companies with yet another motive for supporting measures of profit which excluded holding gains, such as CCA operating profit. Evidence of this was provided in Chapters 4 to 6. We have also seen that taxation has been an important factor elsewhere, in encouraging forms of CPP accounting in Latin America (where it brings tax reliefs) and discouraging any revision of historical cost in accounts in France and Germany (where reported revaluations would be subject to taxation).

We suggested earlier that the Current Cost Revolution of the mid-1970s was partly motivated by government opposition to forms of indexation, due to fear that indexation would institutionalise and perpetuate inflation. CPP was possibly seen as a form of indexation and was therefore opposed by governments in the leading English-speaking countries: in Germany, which had suffered hyper-inflation and experimented with CPP accounting in the 1920s, the opposition to CPP was shared, apparently, by government, the business community and the accounting profession. In this type of situation, it is perhaps somewhat narrow to describe the motivation as self-interest, since the concern is with the well-being of the whole economy, but, of course, the well-being of the economy is important for the individual firms within it.

So far, we have discussed self-interest factors which arise from the relationship between government and firms. It must also be remembered that, within firms, there may be a conflict of interest between management and shareholders and other providers of finance. When the issue is one of paying less taxes or charging higher prices, both of which will increase post-tax profits, the interests of all groups will be similar. However, when the issue is the payment of dividends or the remuneration of management, potential conflict arises between management and shareholders in particular[1] and also between the various providers of finance (e.g. shareholders will benefit from a dividend payment, which will reduce the security enjoyed by creditors of the firm). Of these potential conflicts, the one which is most likely to be discernible in the historical record is that between companies and their shareholders, arising out of the dividend decision. We would expect companies (particularly those in which management was clearly separate from shareholders) to advocate accounting methods which lowered reported distributable profits, whereas shareholders would advocate the reverse, in the absence of confounding factors. In practice, there are usually confounding factors, insofar as tax payments and price controls are also affected by reported profits, but it is still possible for shareholders to prefer some measure of total gains (operating profit plus holding gains) for distribution purposes, if not for tax purposes, whereas companies might prefer a slimmer measure of profit (such as operating profit) for all purposes. The measure of profit for distribution purposes was certainly an issue in the UK debate on inflation accounting in the 1970s.[2] The Government's interest, in the context of its prices and incomes policies, was to reduce the level of dividends by choosing a restrictive measure of profit for dividend distribution purposes, thus restricting dividends and possibly reducing inflationary demands from other parties, such as wage earners. The measure of distributable operating flow emerging from the government-appointed Sandilands Committee (discussed by Sale and Scapens (1978) in the context of dividend distributions) was such a measure. The support of governments and corporate managements for CCA systems in the 1970s is therefore consistent with a self-interest view of the choice of profit measurement for dividend purposes. However, we would put the evidence no higher than this, since the issue is complicated by other considerations (such as taxation) and the attitudes of shareholders are not discernible, since they do not, typically, make comments on exposure drafts.

Another important interest group, other than governments, companies and the providers of finance, is the accounting profession. We have suggested in earlier chapters (particularly Chapter 4) that the early advocacy of CPP by the accounting profession was due to its desire to avoid putting further responsibility on the professional accountant. CPP preserves the historical cost base and thus avoids the learning costs and the additional subjectivity involved in applying a CCA valuation base. The CPP adjustments are relatively objective and mechanical, being concerned mainly with the application of published index numbers. Of course, even lower learning costs and less exposure to subjective judgements are involved if no adjustments whatsoever are made for inflation, and this was the preferred position of most professional bodies in the English-speaking world until the inflation of the 1970s made some form of inflation accounting seem to be essential. The exception to this rule was apparently the advocacy of replacement cost accounting by the ICWA (now ICMA) and the ACCA in 1952. However, since both of these bodies have a majority of members in industry rather than in public practice, their advocacy of replacement cost is entirely consistent with the view that accountants in public practice, who have the responsibility of auditing published accounts, will tend to oppose replacement cost or CCA systems for self-interested motives.

In recent years, there has been a call for accounting disclosure to a much wider range of members of society who have an interest in accounts (e.g. in *The Corporate Report* in the UK and in the Trueblood Report in the USA). These groups may have an important impact on the future of accounting standards in the future, but most of them have had little obvious impact in the past. The one serious exception to this is the employee group. It seems likely that low reported profits have long been used as a device to keep down wage demands. This relationship has been intensified in recent years by government prices and incomes policies.

So far, we have provided a somewhat speculative argument, supported by examples, rather than a systematic test of a hypothesis. Historical evidence on this subject has been provided also by Boer (1966), Clarke (1982) and Zeff (1976b) amongst others. A more rigorous test has been attempted by Watts and Zimmerman (1978), who use the responses to the FASB's 1974 CPP Exposure Draft to test a quite sophisticated theory about the relative self-interest of large and small firms. Their findings are consistent with the hypothesis, although the data available are limited and a test against the null hypothesis does not necessarily exclude alternative explanations of the results. This is a promising line of research which should be followed up, using more data (much of which has accumulated since 1974) and alternative hypotheses.

We have attempted to provide a broader historical perspective, avoiding commitment to a specific hypothesis, or to a single causal factor such as self-interest. However, as we have already indicated, we did have certain prior beliefs about the probable causal factors at work. Our detailed analysis of the United Kingdom debate in recent years, and particularly of the responses to various inflation accounting exposure drafts (Chapters 4 to 6), supported the view that companies, acting in their own interest of keeping profits as low as possible, tended to prefer CCA operating profit as the main performance measure, whereas professional accounting firms preferred the relative objectivity and simplicity of CCP, although there were, no doubt, other factors also at work.

Of course, the fact that companies tended to favour CCA, whereas accounting firms tended to prefer CPP, is merely consistent with a self-interest explanation: it does not establish a causal relationship. It is therefore desirable to strengthen the test by the application of more rigorous hypotheses. This must largely remain a task for future research, but one small step in this direction can be reported here, in order to illustrate both potential and the difficulties of empirical research. We attempted to follow through the responses of certain individual UK companies to the various inflation accounting Exposure Drafts, in order to establish whether their attitudes seemed to be consistent through time. We hypothesised that inconsistent or changing attitudes would be symptomatic of self-interested behaviour. The study is reported in full in the appendix to this chapter. Our results were consistent with the view that self-interest was one factor at work, but that it was only one factor amongst several others. However, our analysis was so limited that we do not attach any great weight to the conclusions. We regard the limitations of the study, which are discussed in some detail in the Appendix, as being important from two points of view. Firstly, they are warning against deriving facile generalisations and excessively strong conclusions from this type of study. Secondly, they provide a challenge for future research. We certainly regard this type of study as worthy of further development, provided that its limitations are always borne in mind and, where possible, are overcome.

Our general conclusion about self-interest must be that there is some evidence that the behaviour of certain important parties to the inflation accounting debate, notably governments, companies and professional accountants, is consistent with the view that their attitudes reflected an important degree of self-interest. However, this does not preclude alternative explanations of their behaviour and it certainly does not preclude the influence of other factors: there was sufficient variety of behaviour and attitude within each interest group to preclude a simplistic self-interest theory as the sole explanation of behaviour. There is considerable scope for further research in this field, but our preliminary conclusion is that self-interest combines with other factors to determine the attitudes of parties to the inflation accounting debate. These factors (particularly economic events) may sometimes reinforce self-interest, but they may also be competitive with it. We now turn to one of these other factors, the influence of ideas.

3 Ideas

The rôle of ideas in the evolution of accounting practice has been explored recently in a controversial paper by Watts and Zimmerman (1979), who regard the accounting theorist as merely supplying 'excuses' to self-interested parties who will select a theory to support positions which have already been selected to satisfy their self-interest. We would not quarrel with some parts of Watts and Zimmerman's analysis: there is certainly a variety of theories available, supporting a variety of positions, and there is evidence consistent with the view that participants in the inflation accounting debate have naturally espoused theories which advance their own interests. However, we do feel that Watts and Zimmerman's conclusions considerably underrate the rôle of the accounting theorist: he not only provides 'excuses' but he sets limits on those excuses by clarifying their assumptions and logical limitations. In this way the rôle of ideas can be to compete with, or to limit, the effects of self-interest.

With regard to the supply of inflation accounting theories, the volume and variety of these will be apparent from our earlier chapters and from the companion volume (Whittington, 1983a). It is apparent, and not surprising, that theoretical writing on inflation accounting tends to flourish when inflation is seen to be an important problem, e.g. the continental European writers of the 1920s and the contemporary work of Sweeney received their stimulus from the inflation which followed the First World War. However, it is also apparent that some theoretical writing was not stimulated by current problems of the day, e.g. Irving Fisher's work, *The Purchasing Power of Money* (1911), which was fundamental to the subsequent development of the theory of CPP accounting, was the result of a sustained theoretical enquiry into macro-economic theory and, in particular, monetary theory. Equally,

Sweeney continued and completed his classic work, *Stabilized Accounting* (1936) as a contribution to knowledge, despite the fact that the drastic change in the economic environment, from 1929 onwards, meant that the subject was no longer of topical interest.

An interesting aspect of the supply of inflation accounting theories is that the total supply currently available in the literature is apparently far in excess of that available to policy makers and participants in the debate. This is a result of the education (or lack of it) of accountants, and their consequent ignorance of the depth of the literature of the subject. Thus many ideas have been either ignored or transmitted imperfectly. In the course of this study, we have interviewed many leading participants in the debate and have found such ignorance to be the rule rather than the exception, even when (as is again the rule rather than the exception) those concerned are intelligent people with a serious interest in the problems in hand. Thus, we find leading advocates of CPP who have never heard of (let alone read) Sweeney, and pioneers of the British gearing adjustment who have never heard of Schmidt. This is partly due to a serious failure of an educational system which emphasises technical skills at the expense of ideas, but it is probably also due to the nature of the standard-setting process, particularly in the UK, which is typically operated on a part-time basis by busy men who are given inadequate research backing. The United States FASB is an honourable exception to this, and, as a consequence, its exposure drafts and standards are typically better argued and justified than those emanating from other bodies, which is not to say that they leave no further scope for improvement.

Thus, the influence of the accounting theorist on the accounting standard-setter may be characterised in similar terms to Keynes' celebrated view of the influence of the economist on the politician:

> . . . the ideas of economists and philosophers, both when they are right and when they are wrong, are more powerful than is commonly understood. Indeed the world is ruled by little else. Practical men, who believe themselves to be quite exempt from any intellectual influences, are usually the slaves of some defunct economist. Madmen in authority, who hear voices in the air, are distilling their frenzy from some academic scribbler of a few years back. I am sure that the power of vested interests is vastly exaggerated compared with the gradual encroachment of ideas. Not, indeed, immediately, but after a certain interval; for in the field of economic and political philosophy there are not many who are influenced by new theories after they are

twenty-five or thirty years of age, so that the ideas which civil
servants and politicians and even agitators apply to current
events are not likely to be the newest. But, soon or late, it is
ideas, not vested interests, which are dangerous for good or
evil. (Keynes, 1936, pp. 383–4)

Although this is a somewhat extreme statement of belief in the power of
ideas (e.g. we would doubt that 'the world is ruled by little else'), it
deserves respect as coming from possibly the most influential practising
economist of the twentieth century (albeit one who had a vested interest
in persuading his audience to the power of ideas) and some instructive
parallels can be drawn with the rôle of ideas in accounting. 'Practical
men, who believe themselves to be quite exempt from intellectual
influence' abound in the accounting profession and in industry. There
are also an increasing number of 'academic scribblers' and there are
'civil servants' (attached to professional bodies), 'politicians' (elected
members of professional bodies, as well as government ministers who
have intervened on important occasions) and even 'agitators' (such as
Messrs Keymer and Haslam who led the rebellion against CCA in the
UK).

Of course, Keynes' eloquent statement is one of belief, since he
presents no evidence to support his hypothesis. However, he does make
one important empirical prediction, namely that practice will lag
behind ideas. We have found a great deal of evidence of this in the
inflation accounting debate. A notable example is the way in which
Sweeney's CPP system, devised in the 1930s, entered professional
thinking and recommendations in the 1960s and early 1970s. Another
important example is the way in which Limperg's replacement value
theory, devised in the 1920s and 1930s, gradually entered practice in The
Netherlands from the 1950s onwards and then achieved wider international influence, e.g. influencing the views of the United States' SEC and
and the UK's Sandilands Report. An even better example of 'the
academic scribbler of a few years back' is Schmidt, who had proposed a
gearing adjustment by the early 1930s which appeared to have no impact
on practice at the time, but which reappeared in a professional
recommendation in his own country in 1975 and in the UK in 1977.
Limperg and Sweeney were at least widely known and acknowledged in
the literature, but Schmidt seems to have been virtually unknown to
those in the English-speaking world who seized on the gearing adjustment with such alacrity in the 1970s.

If this time-lag between the development of ideas and their implementation is to continue, we might look to the present state of theory to

see what ideas are likely to influence practical men in the future. Our own view is that the idea which is most likely to be fruitful is the de-emphasis of the bottom line of the income statement, due to a realisation that the measurement of a single 'true' profit figure is an unattainable objective in an uncertain world characterised by imperfect and incomplete markets. The best recent theoretical work seems to us to be that which suggests that accounts should provide a useful set of information (rather than a single number encapsulating total performance) which enables the user of accounts to make his own assessment for the particular purpose which he has in mind and takes account of his own subjective expectations about future states of the world. Examples of this type of work are Beaver and Demski (1979) and Beaver's recent book (1981), but we would also regard the earlier work of Edwards and Bell (1961) as being consistent with this theoretical position.

In summary, we would accept the Watts and Zimmerman view that particular accounting theories are often espoused for self-interested motives by those who are seeking an 'excuse' for accounting policies which serve their interests. However, we would not agree that the rôle of the accounting theorist ends here. At a minimum, the theorist's adherence to the standards of logical consistency will rule out any self-interested positions which are obviously self-contradictory. The theorist will also clarify the assumptions necessary to sustain a particular position, and this may clarify the fact that different parties are self-interested, and improve the decisions of those, such as standard-setting bodies, which are required to arbitrate between them. We believe, for example, that the theoretical debate on capital maintenance in recent years (as surveyed by Tweedie, 1979) has served to clarify the self-interest of the parties involved: an 'entity' orientation is natural to managers and employees, whereas an 'equity' orientation is natural to shareholders. Moreover, if the theorist can identify factual assumptions or predictions of theories, these can be tested by empirical research.

Finally, we believe that it is important not to attribute narrow self-interest as the only motive for participants in the inflation accounting debate. In the course of correspondence and interviews with a wide range of influential participants in the debate, we have found a considerable intellectual interest in inflation accounting and a genuine desire to progress towards a more consistent and accurate method of inflation accounting, where accuracy implies 'describing the world as it really is', in accordance with Solomons' map-making analogy. Of course, 'the way the world really is' is partly a subjective matter, coloured by individual experience and self-interest, but this does not prevent individuals from striving to overcome their environmental limitations, and good theory can help them to do this. For example, in an earlier chapter, we described the work of the Sandilands Committee in the UK, and stated our view that Sandilands' adherence to CCA was unsurprising in view of the composition of the Committee. Nevertheless, we do feel that this Committee strove to express a coherent theoretical position in an open and honest manner. As a result of this, not only did it make an influential (and, in our view, necessary) case for introducing current values into accounts, but it raised the theoretical level of the debate and clarified those issues (such as the treatment of monetary items) which stood between its own position and the CPP approach preferred by the professional bodies. This was an important step in the evolution of what will (hopefully) become an inflation accounting system which is acceptable as being theoretically consistent as well as being a politically acceptable compromise between the self-interests of various parties.

Thus, we believe that ideas are important, that they are supplied to some extent independently of self-interest, that the demand for them is not solely a function of the desire for self-interested 'excuses', and that the logic and empirical evidence applied by accounting researchers will restrict the scope of self-interested pleas and will expose them for what they are. Of course, it remains for an extreme cynic, whose only belief is in self-interest, to accuse us of pursuing self-interest in taking this view.

4 International influences

In Chapters 2 to 10 we observed some broad international patterns in the evolution of inflation accounting. Amongst the most obvious of these were the early experiments with CPP methods, using gold currency as the unit of stabilisation, in Germany, France and other continental European countries in the 1920s, followed by a subsequent reluctance by these countries to implement inflation accounting as a response to the inflation of the 1970s (Chapter 9). Another clear pattern (also described in Chapter 9) was the adoption of CPP methods as standard accounting practice in the leading South American countries in the 1960s and 1970s. However, possibly the most striking pattern of all was that established in the English-speaking world in the 1970s where the initial adoption of CPP in the early 1970s was followed by the 'Current Cost Revolution' of the mid- and late 1970s, the latter being initiated typically by some form of government intervention (Chapters 4 to 9 inclusive).

Apart from these striking international patterns there were, of course, more subtle international currents (such as the evolution of

Dutch replacement cost accounting and its subsequent influence on the adoption of CCA in the English-speaking countries), but the more striking patterns serve to illustrate the forces at work in spreading inflation accounting ideas and practice. We would suggest that the following are the main factors:

(1) *Common economic environment*. Continental Europe had a common experience of post-war hyper-inflation in the 1920s, and the leading South American countries all suffered extremely high inflation rates in the 1960s and 1970s: in both instances, forms of CPP emerged as the accounting response. The English-speaking world shared a common experience of inflation (but not hyper-inflation) combined with falling profit rates in the 1970s, and the accounting response was similar in all of these countries (initial interest in CPP followed by a 'Current Cost Revolution'). Thus, a common economic environment has led to a common solution, and this is consistent with the 'economic events' factor in the debate, which was discussed earlier in this chapter.

(2) *Linguistic and cultural linkages*. The spread of ideas is facilitated by a common language, which naturally tends to lead to a shared literature. This is certainly true of the English-speaking world and Latin America (which has two main languages, Spanish and Portuguese, which are closely related), and is true to a lesser extent in continental Europe, where geographical proximity tends to lead to knowledge of the main languages, notably French and German. Apart from shared language, there are shared cultural factors, such as attitudes to business and legal systems. The continental European tradition is, for example, more favourably disposed towards an 'entity' approach to the firm, emphasising the importance of the firm independently of its shareholders (although, as we saw in Chapter 9, there is considerable diversity between countries), whereas the Anglo-Saxon tradition, particularly in the USA which has a highly developed capital market, favours a 'financial' view of the firm, regarding it as an equity fund to be administered for the ultimate benefit of the shareholders.

(3) *Institutional and economic ties*. The spread both of ideas and of practice has beeen aided by international collaboration by professional and standard-setting bodies. For example, the current cost Revolution in the English-speaking world was no doubt aided by the fact that the British Sandilands Committee, the United States' SEC and the Australian Mathews Committee maintained contact with one another. At the highest international level, there is the international standard-setting body, IASC, and a recent important

development in Western Europe has been the European Economic Community's various directives. Underlying these formal institutions is the community of interests created by international trade, transnational businesses (which have an obvious interest in the international standardisation of financial reporting), and international professional accounting firms.

These factors have combined to spread both ideas and practice across countries and this has led to parallel developments in those countries which are closely linked and have had similar economic experiences. Equally, these same factors have led to diversity of experience across countries which are less closely linked.

5 Accidents of history[3]

The four major factors influencing the inflation accounting debate, discussed above, do not provide a complete explanation of the course of the debate. Undoubtedly, many influential individuals (such as Limperg) have imposed their personalities on events and have to some extent altered the course of history. Equally other events (such as those in the political world) have influenced the course of the inflation accounting debate, and the impact of any factor or event is constrained by the environment in which it occurs; this is another 'accident of history', a product of past events.

It is also the case that all of the factors discussed previously will vary in such a way that they themselves might be regarded as the products of 'accidents of history': economic events, the generation and spread of ideas, the interaction of self-interested parties, and the international spread of ideas and practice are really the mechanism through which the debate on inflation accounting has evolved, rather than its ultimate cause. In order to find the ultimate cause (if such a concept has any real meaning or operational validity) we would have to look to the causes of variations in these factors, or, in the absence of such an explanation, we may resort to the catch-all description 'accidents of history'. However, this does not mean that the identification of the mechanism of the inflation accounting debate is unimportant. On the contrary, we feel that it affords valuable insights into the accounting standard-setting process and the contribution of various parties to it, and this is the realistic limit of the ambitions of a study such as this. We hope to afford insights into how accounting thought and practice evolve in response to their environment, but we would not hope to explain the history of the environment itself.

6 Conclusion

In this chapter, we have given our own view of the factors at work in the evolution of the inflation accounting debate, as described in Chapters 2 to 10. We would summarise the implications of our interpretation as follows:

(1) Accounting standard-setting is certainly a political process, responding to pressures from the economic environment and compromising between the conflicting interests of different parties. It is important that standard-setters be aware of this and that they be aware of the specific pressures and interests involved. It would be unrealistic to expect to determine standards without such difficulties, and the best way to deal with them is to admit their existence rather than pretending to ignore them.

(2) Ideas do play an important part in the evolution of accounting practice, and the dissemination of ideas is at least as important as their creation. Thus, research has an important rôle in the creation of ideas and in testing their assumptions and predictions, where possible, but education has an equally important rôle in disseminating the knowledge created by research. Although we subscribe to the view that there is need for much more research in inflation accounting and in other fields of accounting, we would subscribe equally to the view that the education of many accountants is woefully deficient. We have found amongst leaders of the profession and setters of standards, examples of ignorance which, in most professions, would be regarded as appalling. There is widespread ignorance of the work of early writers on inflation accounting, and many of those participating in the debate do not know the origins of the ideas which they are discussing. This is partly because accounting has evolved only recently as an academic discipline, so that many of the leaders of the profession (certainly the majority in the United Kingdom) have not had a university education in the subject, and, it must be admitted, the education offered by universities, although improving, is still not as good as it could or should be.[4]

(3) The factors which have shaped the inflation accounting debate are beyond the control of the accounting profession (and even of politicians) and they are ultimately determined by what we have described as 'accidents of history'. We would judge that these factors will continue to press in the direction of creating a demand for accounting standards in general and inflation accounting standards in particular. Inflation rates may be lower in the future than in

the recent past, but they will still probably be high enough to be important to accountants, and relative price changes will certainly continue. The pressures for wider disclosure of business activities, for international conformity of standards, and for accounting methods to be of use in relation to various government policies (e.g. for taxation and price controls) are likely to continue and to lead to pressures for various (sometimes competing) methods of inflation accounting. We therefore regard recent developments in the UK (a fashion for less stringent accounting standards, and actual proposals for a relaxation of *SSAP16*) as being a temporary lull in evolution, rather than as a reversal of the long-term trend.

Appendix to Chapter 13:
an empirical investigation

The empirical investigation which we report here is an extension of the analysis which we reported in Chapters 4 to 6, which described responses to various exposure drafts in the UK. It is merely illustrative because the sample involved is very small. Furthermore, as we shall see, the analysis ignores some important factors, the neglect of which means that the results are bound to be ambiguous. However, we believe that this approach is worthy of more thorough and sophisticated development. Moreover, some of its limitations are shared by other extant studies (such as that by Watts and Zimmerman, 1978), so that discussion of them is of considerable interest.

The basic objective of the study was to establish the consistency through time of the responses to exposure drafts by various parties. We felt that this might shed some light on whether the respondents were acting according to their perceived self-interest rather than according to a consistent, objective view of how accounts should reflect changing prices. More specifically, if respondents to exposure drafts really believe that their views are logically consistent and correct in some fundamental sense, then we would not expect those views to change rapidly or erratically. If, on the other hand, they were responding in their own self-interest, we would expect fairly large swings of view through time, as circumstances changed.

In the UK in recent years we would expect such changes to be particularly apparent in the case of companies. Between 1972 and the autumn of 1974, the strong inflation with high relative price changes provided a strong incentive for them (in general) to favour CCA (although individual companies, because of special circumstances, might find it in their interests to take a different view). In the Autumn of 1974, the introduction of temporary Stock Relief reduced (but did not eliminate) the potential tax advantages of introducing CCA. After 1975, the inflation rate declined gradually, reducing further the incentive to press for CCA. From 1979 onwards, the Government was no longer committed to a prices and incomes policy, thus further reducing the advantages of CCA as a means of justifying price increases. Finally, in 1981, a new Stock Relief system, based upon general index adjustment, was introduced, and the 1982 *Green Paper on Corporation Tax* rejected the case for CCA profit as a corporation tax base. Thus, the possibility of tax benefits from CCA was virtually eliminated. Thus, if companies were purely self-interested, we would expect a slight decline in their support for CCA between their comments on *ED8* (1973) and their response to *ED18* (1976) (since their self-interest peaked in the summer of 1974), and a much more serious decline in support between *ED18* and *ED24*. We would also expect the decline in support to continue between the response to *ED24* and the period of compliance with *SSAP16*, although compliance was mandatory, so that moderate dissent would not be expected to lead to non-compliance.

However, this simple view must be tempered by the possibility of a learning process, as companies became familiar with CCA, and by a learning process by the ASC, which sought to avoid, in *ED24*, the earlier pitfalls of *ED18*. We would also expect considerable changes of view by individual companies as their relative self-interest changed with circumstance and these might mask the trend of declining support. We might hope that the changes in relative self-interest would average out in a large sample: alternatively, individual companies' self-interest could be identified by introducing relevant variables into the analysis.[1] We have not been able to do this here. However, we do attempt to control in a crude way for the effect of learning processes by comparing the changing responses of companies with those of professional accounting firms, the latter being susceptible to similar learning processes (including the technical implementation improvements which ASC introduced with *ED24*), but not to similar changes in self-interest.

Our study is based upon the 32 companies and 10 professional accounting firms whose responses to *ED24* were analysed in Chapter 6. Table 13.1 shows the changing responses of companies to various exposure drafts, and Table 13.2 shows the responses of leading accounting firms for comparison.

The first section of Table 13.1 is a transition matrix, showing how responses changed between *ED8* and *ED18*. Our *a priori* belief was that companies would tend to favour CCA (*ED18*) rather than CPP (*ED8*), although support for CCA had probably passed its peak by the time *ED18* appeared. The table shows that there was indeed greater support by companies for *ED18*: of eight companies,[2] two are on the principal diagonal of the matrix (stretching from Explicit Opposition (*ED8*)/Explicit Opposition (*ED18*) to Explicit Support (*ED8*)/Explicit Support (*ED18*)), indicating an unchanged reaction, four are above the

Table 13.1. *Changing responses of UK companies to inflation accounting*

ED18 / *ED8*	Explicit opposition	Qualified opposition	Qualified support	Explicit support	Total
Explicit opposition		2	1		3
Qualified opposition	1		1		2
Qualified support			1		1
Explicit support		1		1	2
Total	1	3	3	1	8

ED24 / *ED18*	Explicit opposition	Qualified opposition	Qualified support	Explicit support	Total
Explicit opposition				1	1
Qualified opposition	1	2	6	1	10
Qualified support			2	3	5
Explicit support				2	2
Total	1	2	8	7	18

SSAP16 / *ED24*	Non-compliance	Partial compliance	Compliance	Total
Explicit opposition	1		2	3
Qualified opposition		1	3	4
Qualified support	2		12	14
Explicit support			10	10
Total	3	1	27	31*

*One of the 32 companies in the original sample did not have accounts available for the *SSAP16* compliance period.

diagonal, indicating stronger support for *ED18*, and two are below the diagonal, indicating weaker support for *ED18*. There is little sign, however, that firms had opposite preferences for *ED8* and *ED18* as might have been expected: only one company is on the opposite diagonal (running from Explicit Support/Explicit Opposition to Explicit Opposition/Explicit Support). Thus, although companies preferred

Table 13.2. *Changing responses of leading UK accounting firms to inflation accounting*

ED18 ED8	Explicit opposition	Qualified opposition	Qualified support	Explicit support	Total
Explicit opposition					0
Qualified opposition			1		1
Qualified support		2	2		4
Explicit support		2			2
Total	0	4	3	0	7

ED24 ED18	Explicit opposition	Qualified opposition	Qualified support	Explicit support	Total
Explicit opposition					0
Qualified opposition		1	1	4	6
Qualified support		1	3		4
Explicit support					0
Total	0	2	4	4	10

CCA (*ED18*) to CPP (*ED8*), there seems to have been a tendency within the company group to be either in favour of 'inflation accounting' or against it, irrespective of whether it was of the CCA or the CPP variety. An adherent of the self-interest view might hypothesise that this was because any form of inflation accounting would reduce the reported profits of this group of companies, serving their self-interest.

By way of contrast, the responses of professional accounting firms (Table 13.2) changed from majority support for *ED8* to opposition to *ED18*, four of the seven firms are below the principal diagonal, indicating increased opposition to *ED18*. This has already been documented in Chapters 4 to 6 and is consistent with a self-interest view, since professional firms bore increased responsibility and exposure to risk under the *ED18* proposals. The professional firms, unlike the companies, show a fairly consistent reversal of orderings between *ED8* and *ED18*, being on or parallel with the opposite diagonal rather than the principal diagonal. Thus, their position may be characterised as consistent support for CPP and opposition to CCA over this period.

The second section of Table 13.1 shows how companies' responses to CCA changed between *ED18* and *ED24*. Of the eighteen companies in this sample, six showed absolute consistency in being on the principal diagonal,[3] and eleven were above this diagonal, indicating increased support for *ED24* as opposed to *ED18*. We have suggested that pure self-interest is unlikely to have been the predominant factor at work: the increased technical feasibility of *ED24* and the learning process induced by the Hyde Guidelines must have helped to increase support, outweighing any decline in self-interest.

The second section of Table 13.2 shows the responses of professional accounting firms over the same period. These are similar to those of companies, four of the ten responses showing absolute consistency (on the principal diagonal) and five showing increased support (above the principal diagonal). It would take a far larger sample and a subtler analysis to make any attempt at differentiating the changes in professional firms' responses from those of companies. Thus, the comparison offers no clear support for the self-interest view.

The final section of Table 13.1 shows the extent to which companies implemented *SSAP16*, the Standard which emerged from consideration of the responses to *ED24*. This might be construed as a test of how attitudes changed between the issue of *ED24* and of *SSAP16*, when, as we have shown, the self-interest motive is likely to have declined further. However, the issue is complicated by the fact that *SSAP16* is an obligatory standard. The compliance rate is therefore so high that we cannot make any serious inferences about the consistency of views over the period. However, such evidence as there is does not support the view that support for CCA declined notably or that previous supporters became opponents: none of the explicit supporters of *ED24* failed to comply with *SSAP16*.

Conclusions

Our results are consistent with the self-interest view in the transition from *ED8* to *ED18*, insofar as the latter (CCA) proposal was preferred overall by companies and there is little sign that individual companies had consistent preferences as between CPP (*ED8*) and CCA. However, there was no sign after *ED18* that support declined as the factors conducive to companies' self-interest declined. The predominant factor seems to have been improved support for CCA which, as was suggested earlier, may have been the result of a learning process.

These results are very tentative because of the limitations of the analysis. It is these limitations which are the most interesting aspect of the study, both as a warning against facile generalisation, and as a guide to future research which should seek to overcome the difficulties. Important constraints which need to be considered are:

(1) *Sample size.* We have considered a very small sample of responses here and our conclusions would have been firmer had we drawn a larger sample. However, there would still be important constraints. Firstly, respondents to exposure drafts are a select group who are not necessarily representative of general opinion in the sections of the community to which they belong. Secondly, a more subtle analysis, which would be desirable, might require a very large sample (larger than the numbers responding), in order to capture all of the factors which might potentially influence opinion, e.g. within the company group, we might require a representative range of company sizes, in a variety of different industries, with a variety of gearing and liquidity positions and reported profits, and with the possibility of differentiating shareholder-controlled firms from management-controlled firms. It would be possible to think of even more variables which might be required.

(2) *Measurement of responses.* Our categorisation of responses is extremely crude. Our four simple 'for' and 'against' categories cannot hope to capture the subtleties of various reservations and objections, yet these can be vital, particularly in the context of longitudinal studies, of the type which we have attempted, which trace the evolution of responses through time. Thus, opposition to *ED18* did not necessarily imply opposition to CCA: in many cases, it merely implied opposition to the amount of detail required by *ED18* or to the particular form of CCA which it adopted (e.g. the discretionary nature of the appropriation account, and requiring subjective assessments of 'value to the firm'). Thus, objection to *ED18* coupled with subsequent support for *ED24* did not necessarily imply an inconsistent position or a change of heart, since *ED24* sought to remedy some of the more forceful criticisms to which *ED18* had been exposed.

Apart from this problem of capturing the subtle variations in responses, the assessment of responses is a highly subjective process. We reported our own experience of this in Chapter 4. The essential problem is that most responses are quite complex documents, rehearsing various arguments for and against the proposals. The observer's problem is to attach relative weights to the various arguments, since the respondent rarely does this explicitly. Thus, different observers may attach different weights and will then disagree about the nature of the response.

(3) *Missing explanatory variables.* There are many variables which may determine a respondent's attitude, even if he is motivated only by self-interest. Some of these were indicated in (1) above. Moreover, there are other variables which may be important and these need to be allowed for before we attempt to attribute any change in attitude to a single motive such as self-interest. We have already suggested that there may have been a learning process in the implementation of CCA (which is consistent with the view that increasingly enlightened self-interest was at work). However, all the other factors discussed in Chapter 13, some of which were potentially independent of the self-interest motive (economic events, ideas, international influences, accidents of history), were probably at work and were unlikely to remain constant through time.

The limitations of our empirical study are reported in a positive rather than a negative spirit. They do serve as a warning that existing studies have serious limitations, but they also provide a positive challenge to future research in the field: many of these problems can be overcome and awareness of the remainder will improve interpretation of the results of research. However, they should not be used as an excuse for doing no research or for disbelieving any conclusions derived from research: assertions that results are invalidated by simplifying assumptions should not be accepted unless such assertions are supported by evidence.

14

Accounting standards and the future of the inflation accounting debate

1 Introduction

In this, the last, chapter of the book we consider some further lessons we have drawn from our observation of the inflation accounting debate. We examine firstly the rôle of the standard-setting bodies, the problems they face and the way in which the inflation accounting debate was influenced by these difficulties, particularly in the United Kingdom. Secondly, we study briefly the effect of government intervention on the debate, whether by direct action to change its course or by constraining the freedom of the standard-setter through the medium of restrictive legislation. Finally, to enable the reader to judge our interpretation of the debate in the context of our own opinions, we give our views on what we foresee as a future inflation accounting standard. Such an opinion is obviously of a normative nature and we stress that more research is necessary to determine whether our proposal (which has existed in the literature for many years) would be suited to the needs of a variety of users of financial statements. Firstly, however, the rôle of the standard-setting process in the debate.

2 Accounting standards and inflation accounting

In an ideal world, accounting standards would not be necessary.[1] Towards the end of the 1960s, however, a wave of criticism of corporate financial reporting arose from the problems created by the development of complex and innovative business practices and, increasingly, the growth in corporate mergers. In the United Kingdom, this criticism culminated in 1969 in a famous exchange in the pages of *The Times* between Professor Stamp and Ronald Leach, then President of the Institute of Chartered Accountants in England and Wales, a debate which led ultimately to the formation of the Accounting Standards (Steering) Committee.[2]

In the United States, where the AICPA's Accounting Principles Board was already issuing Standards (or Opinions as they were termed) much of the criticism was focussed on the work of the standard-setting body itself. Responding to this criticism, the AICPA set up two study groups: the first (the Wheat Commission) to study the establishment of accounting principles and to make recommendations for improving that process; the second (the Trueblood Committee) to study the objectives of financial statements. Both study groups were to have a major impact on standard-setting worldwide. The Wheat Report resulted in the formation of the FASB, while the Trueblood Report led ultimately to the FASB's major research study and one which could have a major impact on the inflation accounting debate – the Conceptual Framework Project.

The advent of the standard-setting bodies coincided with the world-wide rise in inflation and provided an institutional means of determining the accountancy profession's reaction to the growing demand for price-level adjusted accounts. The standard-setting bodies were in a unique position to influence the debate. Unlike the professional institutes, which are traditionally concerned with several aspects of the welfare of their members, the *raison d'être* of a standard-setting body is to recommend accounting methods to deal with particular problems.

In an ideal world, each problem would be tackled in the following manner.

The standard-setting body would already have determined the conceptual framework for its decisions. In other words, it would have defined the objectives of financial reporting, including the constituency to be served and the type of information which was deemed to be suitable to meet the needs of the various constituents. Thereafter, the process of selecting the appropriate accounting policy to be followed would involve three stages:

(1) *Identification and assessment of theory.* The various theories underlying alternative accounting methods would be examined for individual merit and internal consistency. In the light of the conceptual framework, the relevance of the alternative methods to the various users of accounts would be assessed.

(2) *Research into the costs and benefits of alternative methods.* The rôle of research would be:

    (a) to examine the realism of the assumptions underlying the various methods;

    (b) to assess, and preferably quantify, the benefits accruing to users resulting from the introduction of each alternative accounting method; and

    (c) to identify the costs and practical difficulties of implementation by field studies.

(3) *Choice between alternative methods.* The final stage of the process involves the exercise of judgement in the selection of an appropriate accounting policy. The standard-setting body is confronted by a social choice problem similar to that faced by a government in deciding how to allocate public expenditure and by which means taxes should be raised to pay for it. A choice may have to be made to favour certain groups of users at the expense of others, as ultimately the amount of information which can be published is limited.

    The decision involves the assessment of the benefits accruing to different users of accounts, and the costs associated with these benefits, bearing in mind that some of the users of accounts bear none of the costs. Ideally, the choice would be made from a 'neutral' viewpoint, but 'neutrality' can be determined in practice only if there exists a social welfare function for comparing various costs and benefits to different parties in a manner which is universally accepted as being 'neutral'. In the absence of such an agreed framework,[3] neutrality is a subjective concept, which is likely to vary between different parties to the standard-setting process.

    It is not surprising that practice has failed to match this ambitious ideal.

(i) Identification and assessment of theory

We have indicated earlier that our evidence indicates that generally the standard-setting process operates by the good offices of busy men, frequently ill-versed in the literature of the subject (in the UK as a result of the traditional inadequacies of British accountants' theoretical education), with inadequate research backing. The complete range of options available from theory are, therefore, unlikely to be presented to those responsible for the production of the Standard and, not surprisingly, some theories do not enter the debate for many years after their conception. Key individuals in a position of influence, however, would be able to propose certain theoretical solutions and in the absence of conflicting theories may well succeed in having their preferences adopted.

    The absence of an agreed set of objectives for financial reporting as a basis for a conceptual framework is a further drawback. In the UK, accounting standards are produced on an *ad hoc* basis or, as Bromwich

(1980) would term it, as a stream of 'partial' standards, since a consensus on the method to be recommended for each discrete problem is easier to obtain than agreement to a more comprehensive framework to tackle accounting problems. A stream of discrete, albeit unrelated pronouncements, gives evidence of activity – the search for a conceptual basis for financial reporting could, as the FASB has proved, be a lengthy and expensive undertaking.

In the United Kingdom, the emphasis in the early years of standard-setting was to stem the tide of criticism with evidence of the eagerness of the accounting profession to eliminate poor practice and to regulate its own affairs. The ASC's study on the objectives of financial reporting (published as *The Corporate Report* in 1975) did not commence until some four years after the creation of the standard-setting body – and was then quietly forgotten (see Tweedie, 1981b).[4]

The position does not seem to have changed materially at the time of writing. Macve's report (1981) for the ICAEW on the possibilities for an agreed conceptual structure, which advocated the monitoring of the FASB project and further research on, *inter alia*, the needs of users of accounts has, as yet, had no obvious effect on standard-setting in the UK.

The inflation accounting debate in the United Kingdom has, consequently, taken place in the absence of a theoretical framework against which proposed pronouncements could be assessed. In the United States, the FASB, too, initially developed its statements without the benefit of a formal framework and in the knowledge that there was considerable opposition from industry to Trueblood's emphasis on the satisfying of users' needs as the main objective of financial reporting (see Peasnell, 1982). The importance of this objective was, however, later confirmed by the FASB in its first *Statement of Financial Concepts* (1978a).

More recently, the 1981 Concepts Exposure Draft *Reporting Income, Cash Flows and Financial Position of Business Enterprises* outlined a possible future direction for the inflation accounting debate in America. The Exposure Draft recognised the historical tendency to focus too much attention on the 'bottom line', earnings per share or other highly simplified condensations. It did not reject these aggregations but emphasised the usefulness of components of comprehensive income in satisfying the information needs of different users, who might place different weight on different components.

In this respect, the Americans appear to be well ahead of the British – a theoretical basis for reporting income exists in embryo (albeit only in exposure draft) form, although important questions concerning the capital maintenance concept and the valuation system have not as yet been answered.[5] While, as the Stamp Report (1980) suggests, there may be a danger that the FASB Conceptual Framework project will become too abstract in its approach, the FASB is attempting to remove many of the potential inconsistencies of the partial approach and most certainly sets out a basis from which the next American contribution to the inflation accounting debate could be derived. No other country leading the debate, apart, perhaps, from The Netherlands with its 'business economics' approach to financial reporting, has such an advantage.

(ii) Research into the costs and benefits of alternative methods

It has been a persistent theme in this book, that current pronouncements on inflation accounting do not represent a major advance on the ideas in existence before the Second World War. The 'golden age' in the history of *a priori* research into accounting (Nelson, 1973) – the 1960s, to which we referred in Chapter 3, represented an advance in the sophistication of existing theories rather than the introduction of revolutionary ideas. This was an age of the grand all-encompassing model, defended by its author against its rivals. The debate was at the theoretical level, but lacked empirical research to assess the costs and benefits of alternative systems of accounting.

The lack of empirical research has continued to be a major disadvantage in the inflation accounting debate. Standard-setters, concerned to base their pronouncements on logical and consistent bases, welcome the supply of theories (or 'excuses' in Watts and Zimmerman terms) percolating down through the years, both to clarify the assumptions on which standards are based and to defend the pronouncements against other theorists with different opinions. Empirical research to date has, however, generally failed to put to the test the assumptions underlying the various theories, or to quantify the benefits and costs to various users and preparers of various methods.

In part, this is due to the lack of available evidence: the inflation accounting experiment is sufficiently recent, and subject to such changes of direction to have resulted to date in a relative paucity of comparable information from those organisations complying with the requirements of the standard-setters. Other forms of research of a behavioural rather than economic nature could, however, have been undertaken: researchers have generally failed to test some of the major assumptions underlying the debate.[6] For example, does society believe that an enterprise should be considered as a coalition of interests seeking maintenance of its 'business' or is it of the opinion that the enterprise

331

should be seeking a return on its owners' investment? Do those with different interests in the enterprise hold different views on this question? Do individuals recognise a gain or loss on monetary items in times of inflation and, if so, what form does that recognition take – a gain or reduction of purchasing power (the CPP adjustment); or recognise the need to retain cash to buy similar but more expensive goods in the future (the monetary working capital adjustment in its loss on monetary assets form); or the opportunity to increase borrowing, offering as security assets now valued more highly in money terms (the gearing adjustment)? This is not to argue that the standard-setting bodies should follow limply the fashions of the times and the expressed needs of users. They should also give a lead to users by demonstrating the benefits of breaking with traditional methods of analysis and of using new disclosures. They therefore have an educational rôle in persuading users and preparers to adopt new practices which are justified on the basis of normative theory, such as would be contained in a conceptual framework. However, the conceptual framework will itself be based upon assumptions which should be consistent with the institutions, objectives and beliefs of the society within which the standard-setting process takes place.

Further research is also required into the costs and benefits of possible accounting policies, in other words, into their economic and social consequences. Would the policies lead to detrimental results for enterprises, their owners, or society in general? Inter-disciplinary research of this nature would be far from simple to undertake but is necessary to enable the standard-setter to make more rational decisions in the interests of society. Special pleading from interest groups could then become an accepted part of this research process, their contribution being judged against the needs of the wider community.

In the preceding chapter we discussed the rôle of ideas in the debate: the effect of the 'academic scribbler', the adoption of the theories and their frequent adaptation for 'political' purposes. The rôle of theory in the debate cannot be denied: the rôle of research has, however, been limited. Its function in the 1980s should be to verify the technical feasibility and materiality of various forms of inflation adjustments and to gauge the underpinning and potential costs and benefits of theories of price-level adjusted accounts to ensure that ensuing inflation accounting pronouncements fulfil user needs.[7] Research evidence must be informative. To affect the standard-setting process it must add to the standard-setter's knowledge. It must possess the capacity to change or reinforce the beliefs of those who select or evaluate accounting alternatives (Griffin, 1982).

(iii) Choice between alternative methods

Unless the standard-setter derives its authority from some agency capable of enforcing its pronouncements, the opportunities for 'political' interference will increase as, in the absence of a conceptual framework and a solid research base, self-interest in the effects of particular proposed standards leads to attempts to move the debate in one direction or another.

The ASC, whose authority, unlike that of the FASB, is not backed by a government agency (the SEC),[8] has witnessed companies flouting its recommendations without penalty. In such a situation, without the benefits of a coherent framework of principles, the ASC has to rely on acceptance of its pronouncements, in other words, on the existence of a consensus of views among practising accountants, industry, commerce, and, on occasion, the Government.

The need for consensus, however, can lead the standard-setting body into many difficulties:

(1) A standard based on intellectual logic may be amended to suit one powerful party leaving the standard-setting body open to charges of inconsistency and lack of rigour. For example, during the UK inflation accounting debate, *ED24* permitted financial institutions to include cash in their monetary working capital adjustments. The definition of monetary working capital for other enterprises, however, omitted cash (except where such an exclusion would have been 'misleading') despite the fact that money held by these other enterprises would obviously lose value in times of inflation.

(2) Some enterprises may be exempted from the provisions of the Standard to prevent their opposition from delaying its introduction. Investment-orientated companies were, for example, excluded from the scope of *SSAP16*, presumably because the operating capacity capital maintenance concept fitted uneasily with the style of business of these companies. As we saw in Chapter 7, several industry groups were exempted from the full requirements of *FAS33* in the USA. Sometimes, such exemptions are justified by the peculiar characteristics of certain industries, but they can also be the result of self-interested political lobbying.

(3) To avoid the alienation of certain groups, a number of treatments may be permitted. This can be useful as an experimental measure when no single theory has gained universal acceptance, for example, the proposals concerning *ED18*'s appropriation account in the UK or the alternative inflation accounting treatments permitted in the 1982 New Zealand CCA Standard. On the other hand, it can

cause difficulties for users of accounts if the treatments are radically different and no means of direct comparison of the two differing approaches exists. In such cases, the information set approach has much to recommend it.

(4) Opposition can, on occasion, be stifled by accepting the case it puts forward even when the case is backed by political rather than logical power. In the inflation accounting debate, consecutive pronouncements have by no means evolved smoothly from their predecessor but have adopted quite different approaches – the differing Canadian pronouncements giving an example of this.

These problems have been exacerbated by the difficulty of reconciling widely conflicting interests within tight deadlines often imposed by government agencies or by the perceived urgency of the inflationary situation. There has been pressure, therefore, to ensure that the inflation accounting project does not stagnate. This has resulted in 'cutting corners' by twisting logic, granting unwarranted exemptions from the scope of the Standard, providing discretionary options, or adopting the information set approach. As will be apparent from other sections of this book, we support the information set approach but not this particular motive for adopting it.

The various pressures exerted on the standard-setters, however, should not always be considered to be in the nature of specific pleading. Sometimes the standard-setter has moved too far from the practical problems of implementation or has failed, through lack of foresight or research, to realise that a particular theory is incompatible with the business objectives of particular organisations. As a consequence of such difficulties, the inflation accounting debate has not only improved the theoretical education of the accounting profession worldwide as it continued, but it has also provided opportunities and stimulus for empirical research on the consequences of alternative methods.

3 The rôle of governments in the standard-setting process

Standard-setters have not only, however, faced pressure from those responsible for implementing their pronouncements. Another complicating factor in the inflation accounting debate is the major rôle which can be played by governments. One form of government influence, direct intervention, has already been chronicled in our discussion of the debate to date and a second, the enforcement of statutory accounting principles, is about to play an increasingly important rôle in the future.

Accounting standards and the future

(i) Direct intervention

In four of the countries in which the debate has been conducted at what we have termed the innovative theoretical level, the intervention in the mid-1970s of government-appointed agencies or Committees of Inquiry altered the course of the debate. These government bodies rejected the accountancy profession's CPP solution to the problems of financial reporting in times of inflation and proposed the use of CCA. Since that period, standard-setters in these countries have been only too aware that if the likely impact on society of a proposed inflation accounting pronouncement runs counter to the Government's own objectives, government intervention and possibly the demise of self-regulation may ensue. Standard-setters, consequently, are constrained by the knowledge that they cannot ignore the wider social and economic ramifications of their proposals. In West Germany, for example, the Government's fear of institutionalising the phenomenon of inflation has meant that the inflation accounting debate in that country has been stifled. Elsewhere in Europe, statutory requirements are now prohibiting certain accounting policies and, increasingly, restricting the scope of the debate in that continent.

(ii) Statutory accounting principles

The effect of legislation on the debate has manifested itself in two forms. Firstly, as we have discussed in Chapter 9, fiscal considerations restricted the debate in France but led to statutory CPP accounting principles in Latin America. Secondly, European accounting practice is going to be severely circumscribed by the enactment in individual countries of the provisions of the EC Fourth Directive. Until the passing of the 1981 Companies Act, financial reporting in the UK, unlike that in much of continental Europe, was virtually unencumbered by statutory accounting principles. Experimental practice in the UK could follow or lead that of the USA – the sole objective, provided basic statutory requirements were met, being to ensure that a true and fair view was shown in the financial statements. The 1981 Act, however, has had a potentially devastating effect on future developments in inflation accounting in the UK. The Act, based on the Fourth Directive, which in turn was initially derived from the prescriptive approach of German law, has introduced prescribed formats for accounts and has placed the emphasis (as does German practice) on prudence, to the extent that only realised profits can be included in the profit and loss account.

The 'real terms' comprehensive income approach of the FASB,

335

incorporating unrealised holding gains, is, consequently, not now an option in statutory accounts in the United Kingdom: potential international harmonisation on this basis of accounting can now only occur at the level of supplementary statements. The European emphasis that the objective of financial reporting is to provide an acceptable basis for 'legal' distributions will conflict with the aim of providing users of accounts with information capable of revealing the 'economic reality' of the operations of an enterprise when price levels are changing. Potentially, the debate on inflation accounting in Europe could, at the level of the statutory accounts, become isolated from that in North America and Australasia.[9]

4 The future of accounting standards

The pressures of sectional interests in the standard-setting process, combined with the somewhat erratic interventions by governments, have led to the debate on inflation accounting following a tortuous and hitherto indecisive course. This inevitably raises the question as to how the accounting standard-setting process might be improved in the future. There are three possible directions:

(1) abolish standard-setting bodies and leave accounting standards to be determined in the market place;
(2) strengthen the private sector standard-setting process; or
(3) abandon private-sector standard-setting and substitute government regulation.

We shall consider each in turn.

(1) Abolition of standard-setting

This approach is favoured by a number of American writers of the Chicago–Rochester school (such as Benston, 1981), who would prefer to see voluntary accounting standards, adherence to which was the result of the perceived demands of shareholders and creditors, expressed in the market for shares and loans. The current attitudes of certain governments, particularly those in the USA and the UK, tend to favour non-intervention in the market, so that this approach must be regarded as a serious possibility. Its potential disadvantages are those associated with market imperfection and failure, and they are made more serious by the fact that accounting information has the characteristics of a 'public good', i.e. the costs of gaining access to it are very low relative to the cost of preparing it, so that it is possible for other users to 'free-ride' on those who pay for it. We would regard the creation of non-voluntary standard-setting bodies in many countries as prima facie evidence that leaving standards to the market place has not worked (see, for example, Leach and Stamp, 1981).

(2) Strengthening the private-sector standard-setting process

The private-sector standard-setting bodies in many countries, including the UK, could be strengthened in at least three ways. Firstly, the standard-setting body could be given a large degree of autonomy from professional institutes and other fora in which pressure groups can exert undue influence. Secondly, the standard-setting body could have better research support and full-time members. Thirdly, the Standards which it produced could have legal backing, releasing them from the need to be acceptable on a voluntary basis to all preparers. The country in which most progress has been made in this direction is the USA, where the FASB has all of these three characteristics to some degree. It is notable that the FASB has always been at the forefront of the inflation accounting debate. It is also the case that the recent weakening of its legal backing, due to the less interventionist attitude of the SEC, has made the FASB's position more difficult.

(3) Government regulation

The fear of greater government regulation of accounting has been a major spur to the development of private standard-setting bodies. This fear may have been due partly to a selfish wish by the accounting profession and others to maintain control of standards, in order to serve their own interests at the expense of a wider constituency. However, there are at least two legitimate anxieties about direct government regulation. The first is that it will be too bureaucratic and insensitive to the varied and changing environment in which accounts are prepared. The second is that government is also subject to political pressures by self-interested groups, and may be more arbitrary and unpredictable in its policy towards accounting, as the nature of governments and their problems change. The history of government intervention in the inflation accounting debate does not inspire confidence in the view that direct government regulation would have given rise to a better solution.

Clearly, these are large issues which require more discussion than we are able to devote to them here. We leave the reader to form his own opinion as to the lessons to be learned from the inflation accounting debate for the future of standard-setting. We would merely make the observation that the inflation accounting debate has been extremely tortuous and that the causes of this include the lack of clarity in the relationship between standard-setting bodies and national governments, and the problems of standard-setting bodies in trying to obtain the acceptance of all their constituents.

We now turn from the future of accounting standards to our central theme, the inflation accounting debate, and a consideration of its future course.

5 The future of inflation accounting

At this stage of the book the reader will almost certainly be aware of our own normative view of the future of inflation accounting. Our opinion, which has been outlined in the opening chapter, will be examined more closely in this, the penultimate, section of the book.

Uniquely perhaps, the authors have, during this research project, been able to participate actively in the continuing debate since, in late 1982, one of us (David Tweedie) was appointed to the ASC's Sub-Committee on Inflation Accounting, which had been given the task of producing the successor to *SSAP16*. Our opinions expressed earlier (Chapter 1) about busy men having but a short time to produce a politically acceptable solution to a complex problem applied to the work of this Sub-Committee. One part of our criticism was, however, not entirely valid in this particular instance. We stated earlier that accountants are generally ill-versed in the literature of their own subject and many of the leading participants in the debate may have been unaware of existing theory. In this case, however, the present authors were asked to prepare summary papers, which were duly presented to the Sub-Committee, outlining various theories, the history of the debate in the UK and the trend of the international debate as we perceived it.[10] We also expressed our own opinions on the form of the successor to *SSAP16*. The final outcome of the Sub-Committee's deliberations is not known at the time of writing. The reader, however, in comparing our view with any solution eventually proposed by the ASC different from our own, will be aware that the Sub-Committee responsible was informed of the salient points of our investigation (albeit in outline which was, of course, an inadequate substitute for thorough study of the original subject matter), but, for theoretical or political reasons, chose to take an alternative course to that suggested by ourselves. The story of this part of the UK debate must await another occasion.

In arriving at our view we have made two basic assumptions. Firstly, the conditions of uncertainty under which accounts are prepared make it unlikely that any single measure of profit or net worth can be precise or objective.

Secondly, we subscribe to the general view expressed in four major professional pronouncements on the objectives for financial reporting published in the last decade,[11] namely that the main aim of external reporting should be to serve the needs of users of accounts and that these needs will differ. These assumptions lead us to two related conclusions:

(1) In a world of uncertainty, where valuation and the assessment of income are matters of estimation rather than precise measurement, the information set approach gives the user of accounts various items of information, which will enable him to use his own judgement in assessing the value of the variables in which he is interested. The bottom line approach, on the other hand, constrains him by incorporating limited information of a summary nature, which is deemed by the reporting accountant to encapsulate all that is important about an enterprise.

(2) The components of comprehensive income would probably be more useful to the reader than an emphasis on a single profit figure, because different readers will have different needs, and, therefore, different definitions of 'profit' in mind. For example, it is well-established in UK practice (and reinforced by the 1982 *Green Paper on Corporation Tax* (Cmnd 8456), which asserted the irrelevance of the *SSAP16* version of CCA as a basis for corporation tax) that the measure of income appropriate for tax purposes is different from that which might be appropriate for shareholders in assesssing the economic performance of the business. Equally, the assessment of profit for the determination of dividend distribution (a definition of which is attempted in the UK's Companies Acts 1980 and 1981, and which is discussed critically in Egginton, 1980) may well differ from the concept of profit, which creditors may use in assessing the security of their loans, and the measure which employees might consider appropriate in wage negotiations or in judging their own job security. It is, of course, possible that none of these measures will conform with the economist's definition of 'income' or 'profit'.

Ideally, to satisfy the needs of different users, we would share the views of others (e.g. Stamp, 1972 and Carrington, 1977) that multiple values should be reported for assets when the differences are material. Similarly, we are aware that several income models used in combination would be more likely to be of greater utility to the many users of accounts as each model would present one facet of the economic reality of the situation – one perspective of events.

The cost of preparing additional valuations and income calculations would, however, be considerable. Further research on user needs will have to be undertaken before such proposals could be justified in cost/benefit terms.

We believe that, to have any chance of success, a proposal for a system of inflation accounting must be *practical*, in other words, feasible for preparers and comprehensible to users. For preparers, it is important that the change from *SSAP16* should, like the Hyde Guidelines, *avoid unnecessary complexity* and in addition be *evolutionary* in its approach – in the UK, utilising the experience accumulated in preparing accounts based on *SSAP16* and its predecessors. An evolutionary approach would also help users in making comparisons with the past, while simplicity would aid interpretation.

Our proposal is not new: it is intended to be a practical evolution of present practice based on sound theory. While the basic elements of the proposal have already appeared piecemeal in inflation accounting pronouncements in the United Kingdom, we have not just been guided solely by domestic considerations. The trend of the international debate as we perceive it, and as we shall discuss below, appears to be moving in the direction which we are advocating.

As stated above, our fundamental belief is that we should provide a set of information useful to a variety of users in a wide range of circumstances. In particular, we assume (given no satisfactory empirical evidence to the contrary) that users would require information not, as at present in the UK, simply about the specific price changes of assets owned by the enterprise but also about the effects of general price change (i.e. the change in the purchasing power of money). The Sandilands Report, to which *SSAP16* owes many of its basic principles, confined current cost accounting to specific price changes, precluding the use of general indices and thereby leading to the present approximations to general price-level adjustments, namely the monetary working capital and gearing adjustments. Our method, to a certain extent, goes back in time and incorporates the essential thrust of the CCAB's *Initial Reactions to Sandilands*, which involved both specific and general price changes.

Table 14.1 outlines our proposed method in its simple form. We start with the historical cost profit (before interest and taxation) derived from a conventional profit and loss account. From this is deducted the additional charges necessary to raise depreciation and cost of goods sold to the current cost level. At this stage the current cost operating profit derived is identical to that required by Sandilands, *ED18* and the Hyde Guidelines: it shows the operating profit after charging the current cost

Table 14.1. *Proposed profit and loss account*

	£	£
Historical cost profit		–
Less Current cost adjustments:		
Depreciation	–	
Cost of sales	–	
	———	
Current cost operating profit		–
Add Holding gains:		
Realised	–	
Unrealised	–	
	———	
Total gains		–
Less Inflation adjustment of equity		–
		———
Total Real Gains		£–

of the assets consumed and therefore shows whether the business is operating profitably in terms of currently prevailing prices.

It will now be clear that our view of the basis for evolution does not begin at 1980 with *SSAP16*, although two of the adjustments to the HC profit proposed above are a feature of the present UK Standard. Instead, we have returned to the period of the Sandilands Report and its immediate aftermath. Our method does not have a place for the two most controversial adjustments in the present Standard – the monetary working capital and gearing adjustments.

The next stage is to add back the holding gains on assets for the period, i.e. the increase in asset values due to specific price changes.[12]

This again is a return to the spirit of the Sandilands Report, which proposed a Statement of Gains containing similar information. The realised holding gains represent the excess of current cost over historical cost depreciation and cost of goods sold (i.e. the realised cost savings, namely the depreciation and cost of sales adjustments) plus the surplus or less the loss on the sale of fixed assets. The unrealised holding gains represent the appreciation in money terms in the current cost of assets held during the period and remaining in the possession of the enterprise

Table 14.2. *Alternative format 1*

	£	£
Historical cost profit		–
Less Current cost adjustments:		
Depreciation	–	
Cost of sales	–	
Current cost operating profit		–
Add/deduct CPP gain/loss on		
borrowing and monetary		
assets		–
Add/deduct Realised real holding		
gains/losses:		
Fixed assets	–	
Stock	–	
		–
Add/deduct Unrealised real holding		
gains/losses:		
Fixed assets	–	
Stock	–	
		–
Total Real Gains		£–

at the end of the period. (This would be net of a deduction for gains accrued in previous periods, but realised in the current period.) Further useful information can be obtained separating the gains by type of asset (a method we illustrate in Table 14.2).

The resulting Total Gains figure shows total operating income plus holding gains for the year where the latter are measured in money terms. On its own this would lead to an exaggerated view of gains in a period of inflation and this is rectified by the next adjustment, a deduction for the effects of inflation (measured by changes in a general price index) on equity (measured in terms of current cost at the start of the year). This gives a figure for Total Real Gains, i.e. total gains after eliminating the effects of inflation. If interest payments had to be made, it would be appropriate to deduct them from total gains before making the equity adjustment to yield Total Gains Attributable to Equity: interest is a payment for the use of money made in order to earn equity's share of the total gains.[13]

The equity inflation adjustment can be implemented in the more informative, but slightly more sophisticated, manner illustrated in Table 14.2. This format has the additional advantage of consistency with the reporting requirements of the United States *FAS33* by including the three elements of 'real terms' income required by the American Standard[14] although *FAS33* itself states expressly that 'the increases or decreases in current cost amounts shall *not* be included in income from continuing operations'.

This more complicated method calculates the equity adjustment from the other side of the balance sheet, i.e. by applying it to all assets and liabilities, so that the real gain (as opposed to the money gain) on each category of asset and liability is calculated, rather than a single overall net real gain. This shows how individual assets and liabilities have changed in price relative to inflation and so makes explicit the gain on borrowing and loss on holding money: clearly, interest payments would be offset against the gain on borrowing in this format. One further advantage of this format is that it avoids reporting an inflated Total Gains figure (before inflation adjustment) which might unduly mislead external parties, such as trade unions and Chancellors of the Exchequer, into making excessive demands on company profits.

Having arrived at a Total Real Gains figure, the remaining appropriations (not shown in our simple illustration) would be conventional: taxation and dividends would be deducted and transfers would be made to reserves. It might be useful to encourage companies to make additional discretionary transfers to reserves at this stage, if they felt that the inflation adjustment of equity did not provide adequately for the maintenance of the substance of the business in a period of changing prices.

The simple format in Table 14.1 represents a basic set of information, which is essential if companies are to report the effects of changes in the general price level and in the specific prices which they face. Companies which wish to provide more sophisticated information could provide more detail using the fundamental frameworks provided in Tables 14.1 and 14.2.

Our proposal is similar to the type of profit and loss account statement pioneered by Edwards and Bell (1961). Like Edwards and Bell we prefer a proprietary capital maintenance measure. We have come to this view for three reasons. Firstly, we believe that, in a capitalist economy, wealth creation should be measured in terms of the accretion of the capital invested by the owner; secondly, we are of the opinion that a proprietary based system provides a practical and relatively objective measure of income; and thirdly, like many participants in the debate, we

Table 14.3. *Alternative format 2*

	£	£
Historical cost profit		–
Less Current cost adjustments:		
Depreciation	–	
Cost of sales	–	
Current cost operating profit		–
Add Geared holding gains:	–	
Current cost profit attributable		
to shareholders		–
Add Ungeared holding gains	–	
Total gains		–
Less Inflation adjustment of equity	–	
Total Real Gains		£–

have become disillusioned with the arbitrary attempts to define operating capability (see Chapter 12), and the need to exempt certain enterprises (such as investment-orientated companies) from the provisions of an entity-based pronouncement when their business objectives conflict with the theory underlying the operating capacity concept.

The proprietary base we have chosen eliminates the need for a gearing adjustment. If, however, a gearing adjustment is deemed to be useful, it too, following a suggestion of Kennedy (1978a), could be included in the statement outlined in Table 14.1 as we have illustrated above (Table 14.3).

The gearing adjustment outlined (here styled Geared Holding Gains) is of the realisable cost saving type, i.e. unlike that proposed in *SSAP16*, it adds back to operating profit the geared proportion of realised and unrealised gains. In Table 14.3, Total Gains are equivalent to those in Table 14.1 and Total Real Gains equate with those in Tables 14.1 and 14.2.[15]

In terms of international comparisons, the Table 14.1 version has been proposed by standard-setters in The Netherlands (1976), in Sweden (1980 as one option) and New Zealand (1982 as one option). The alternative proposal in Table 14.2 can be derived from information required by the American and Canadian Standards (1979 and 1982 respectively) and has been proposed in a similar form to that shown in Table 14.3 as an option in Sweden (1980) and New Zealand (1982). International harmonisation, consequently, would be facilitated by the use of our proposal in the UK – although, as mentioned earlier in this chapter, the inclusion of unrealised gains in income would mean that, for member countries of the EEC (or EC as it is now known), our proposed income statements could probably not form the statutory accounts but would have to be of a supplementary nature.

So far we have ignored the question of the balance sheet. International opinion clearly is divided on the issue of whether or not a current cost balance sheet should be provided or even whether the current costs of non-monetary assets should be given by way of note. We would prefer the publication of a current cost balance sheet articulating with the profit and loss account, although the provision of a partial balance sheet would at least provide a better basis for the calculation of rates of return than a statement based on historical cost. Ultimately, the decision about the balance sheet will depend on evidence of its use to readers of financial statements and on the costs of producing such a statement.[16] Evidence too would be required on the most useful valuation bases. While, theoretically, multiple valuation bases would be most satisfactory for the various user groups, potential problems of information overload and expense would almost certainly prevent the provision of such information in the short term.

At the time of writing, the value to the business concept appears to be widely accepted, at least in the English-speaking world, as the basis of standard practice and would seem to be a sensible pragmatic solution until more research into user requirements and feasibility is undertaken. At present in the UK, there is some opposition to the notion of current cost values being included in the balance sheet, due to the difficulties of calculating recoverable amounts in a time of economic recession. There are undoubtedly genuine practical difficulties here – as there are with *any* useful accounting system: experience and research will perhaps teach us the best way of overcoming the present problems. These difficulties, however, are no reason to call for the abandonment of the attempt to value assets in current cost terms, or, worse, of the entire inflation accounting experiment – the subject to which we turn in the final section of this book.

6 An end to inflation accounting?

In the United Kingdom, as elsewhere, self-interest and short-sightedness is threatening the inflation accounting debate. Falling rates of inflation, the not unnatural unwillingness by the Government to base corporate taxation on current cost accounts, low profits in a period of recession and the absence of statutory price controls have reduced the pressure from industry on the ASC to continue the CCA experiment. Company management for the above reasons and because of the lack of obvious enthusiasm from users of CC accounts have increasingly complied only reluctantly with the provisions of *SSAP16*[17] and several have called for an end to the CCA experiment. This would be to ignore the pressures extant since the early 1970s which initially forced the accounting profession and, later, governments to wrestle with the problems of price-level accounting.

A decision to return to the traditional historical cost accounts would have several ramifications.

(1) The hard won and expensive experience gained would be lost and the profession would be unprepared for the future pressures for change which must inevitably occur. Even at a rate of five per cent per annum, the price level would rise by about half in about eight years and double in under fifteen years: there is little guarantee that higher rates of inflation will not occur in the future. Of equal importance in a time of rapid economic and technical changes is the effect of relative price changes since CCA involves the changing values of the specific assets held by the enterprise. Traditionally in the UK, pressure for the accounting profession to form a committee to provide an accounting method to counteract the deficiencies of the historical cost accounts has increased as prices rose, only to diminish as the rate of inflation fell (see Figure 14.1). History should teach us to continue the experiment when the pressure for an instant answer to the problem of price-level accounting is at its weakest.

(2) There is no evidence that the external pressures, which led to government intervention in the debate in the mid-1970s, would not recur if the accounting profession proves unable (or unwilling) to deal with the problem of inflation accounting.

(3) Accounting for price-level changes has important economic ramifications – those clamouring for the abandonment of CCA at the present time may well regret their present opinion if price or income controls were to be reintroduced or if corporation tax or stock relief became dependent on the reporting practice.

The practical difficulties at present confronting accountants as they

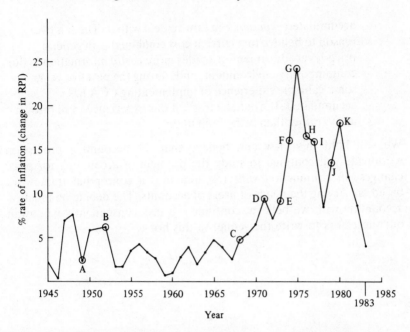

Figure 14.1. The rate of inflation and inflation accounting pronouncements in the UK 1945–83.

Key: A ICAEW Recommendation N12 'Rising Price Levels in Relation to Accounts'; B ICAEW Recommendation N15 'Accounting in Relation to Changes in the Purchasing Power of Money' and Reports by ICWA and ACCA; C ICAEW *Accounting for Stewardship in a Period of Inflation*; D ASSC 'Inflation and Accounts'; E ASSC *ED8*; F ASSC *PSSAP7*; G The Sandilands Report; H ASC *ED18*; I ASC The Hyde Guidelines; J ASC *ED24*; K ASC *SSAP16*.

struggle to implement CCA proposals cannot be ignored. It should be remembered, however, as we stated earlier, that problems can be found in any useful accounting system. As one of us (Whittington, 1983b) wrote on an earlier occasion:

> Certainly, the traditional historical cost basis is not free from practical problems, ambiguities or subjectivity, and one shudders to think of the devastating criticisms which would be poured upon it by Messrs Keymer and Haslam and their supporters, were our traditional method current cost accounting and historical cost the proposed reform. The only reason why historical cost is acceptable is that we have

347

accumulated *experience* in how to deal with it. There is every reason to believe that current cost combined with general price-level adjustment, provides more *useful* information in our contemporary environment, and, during the past five years, some valuable experience of implementing CCA has accumulated. It would be tragic if this experience were thrown away, rather than being built upon.

We still hold this view and believe that the accounting profession worldwide will continue to study the problem of accounting for price changes, in conjunction with research into a conceptual framework based on serving the needs of users of accounts. The debate on inflation accounting will, we believe, continue – a task consequently will await our successors to write the sequel to this book.

Notes

1 Introduction

1 The political nature of accounting standards has been discussed by Solomons (1979) and others.
2 A further discussion of the range of potential users of accounts will be found in *The Corporate Report* (ASSC, 1975).
3 This is adapted from Whittington (1981a). A more sophisticated example, involving purchases and sales as well as simply holding assets, is given in Whittington (1983a).
4 The opening balance sheet is the same, in this example, for all of the alternative techniques illustrated, because we assume that the firm acquired its asset at the beginning of the period, having previously held only cash. Thus, the opening balance sheet shows a single asset, cash £20,000, financed by a £5,000 loan and £15,000 equity. The opening CPP balance sheet would, however, differ if the unit of constant purchasing power were other than the £ current at the balance sheet date.
5 If the opening balance sheet were required to be published together with the closing balance sheet, for comparative purposes, this would have to be translated into 'closing £s' from the 'opening £s' in which it was previously stated.
6 A system based on NRV would be more appropriately described as current value accounting, CVA.
7 A residual problem can arise when an entity holds cash in excess of its borrowing. The monetary working capital adjustment applies only to net trade credit (trade debtors less trade creditors) plus cash (and less bank overdrafts) considered essential for maintaining the day-to-day operations of the business. No adjustment is required for other excess cash balances (*SSAP16*, para. 22).
8 This view is cogently argued by Beaver and Demski (1979).
9 This is discussed in the Meade Committee Report (Meade, 1978), of which one of the present authors was a signatory. Of course, it is not essential to base taxation on profit as reported in the accounts, but, as we shall see in later chapters, the two are tied together by law in many countries, and even when this is not the case, there is a feeling that accounting practices influence tax law (as in the UK debate on stock relief).

2 Inflation accounting before the Second World War

1 Clarke (1982) re-examines these rate regulation cases and suggests that Boer is wrong to emphasise replacement cost, rather than market value (which can imply NRV rather than RC). However, this issue is irrelevant to the central point: that the parties switched sides in pursuit of self-interest.

2 We are grateful to Professor R. H. Parker for this information: it is, of course, probable that further research will unearth earlier contributions. It is notable that Fells, like Middleditch, refers to Fisher (1911).

3 The evolution of Paton's writings on inflation accounting is analysed in Zeff (1979a).

4 Sweeney (1934) provides examples of 'How Inflation Affects Balance Sheets', drawn from a wide range of European countries during this period.

5 Sweeney (1927) provides a detailed account of this.

6 A simple example of such a conflict, which appears in his work, is that he advocated LIFO stock valuation (Schmalenbach, 1959, p. 185). This yields a charge to profit and loss which reflects current cost, but the value of the stock appearing in the balance sheet tends to be out of date. Schmalenbach was prepared to accept the latter deficiency for the former virtue. It is, of course, possible to have the virtue without the deficiency within the framework of current cost accounting, which Schmalenbach rejected.

7 In terms of Hicks' (1946) well-known analysis of income concepts, Schmalenbach would have preferred a 'Hicks number three' (consumption maintenance) measure of income to 'Hicks numbers one and two' (wealth maintenance).

8 One of the present authors advanced this argument more than half a century after Schmalenbach (Whittington, 1974), without being aware of its original source: this probably indicates how the ideas of writers such as Schmalenbach have become absorbed into the way of thinking even of those who have no direct knowledge of them.

9 This argument for historical cost was discussed in Whittington (1983a), Chapter 3, Sections 2, 3 and 4.

10 For example, his discussion of depreciation in Chapter 5 and his discussion of relative price changes in Chapter 6.

11 As will emerge later, the idea of 'speculative' assets was also used by Schmidt and by Limperg.

12 Statistical evidence of this is provided by Fabricant (1936).

13 Canning's work is reviewed at greater length by Chambers (1979) and Whittington (1980).

14 Wright (1964) derived the idea of 'opportunity value', directly from Canning's work, and only subsequently discovered that this was identical with Bonbright's 'value to the owner'. Another author who derived, independently, a similar set of rules was Limperg (see Section 6). The common source of their ideas seems to be the theory of marginal utility (see Mey, 1966).

15 Zeff (1981) has recently explored the background to MacNeal's work and

points out that MacNeal advocated *market* values but did not commit himself as to whether buying prices (RC) or selling prices (NRV) should be the basis of the valuation.

16 It should, however, be noted that books on replacement cost accounting had been published earlier in Germany by Fäs (1912) and Kovero (1912).

17 This theme was subsequently developed by others, such as Schiff (1933), Jones (1935), Haberler (1941), Lacey (1952) and Baxter (1955).

18 Mattessich (1980) has recently related Schmidt's work to that of Edwards and Bell, and to the recent current cost accounting standard (*FAS33*) in the USA.

19 Although Schmidt's valuation basis was replacement cost rather than 'value to the business', as preferred by the Sandilands Committee.

20 This category has recently been used by Merrett and Sykes (1980), who describe it as 'investment assets'.

21 The problem of arbitrary groupings of sources of finance in relation to assets remains a problem of gearing adjustment techniques, even when speculative assets are not selected for special treatment. It is a problem of the systems proposed in recent years in West Germany, the UK, New Zealand and elsewhere. This is discussed further in Chapter 12.

22 The most authoritative account in English of the Philips system is provided by Goudeket (1960). Gynther (1966, Chapter 15) provides a valuable critical discussion. A more recent description of the system, including a discussion of recent changes, is provided by Enthoven (1982).

23 Klaassen (1979) and Burgert (1972) provide statistical surveys of accounting practice in The Netherlands.

24 Limperg's views on economic theory, upon which his accounting theory was based, seem, on superficial inspection, to be dogmatic and ill-justified. This observation is based upon a brief reading of Limperg's collected works (1964) by one of us (Geoffrey Whittington) with the assistance of Professor Willem Buiter. If Limperg's work were translated into English, a more considered evaluation could be made.

25 The Philips system has also provided a stimulus for work by accounting theorists such as Gynther (1966).

26 Sweeney discussed the relationship of his work to *ARS6*, including some points of difference, in Sweeney (1964b).

27 His dis-aggregation of the components of income was not, of course, as detailed as that of Edwards and Bell. In particular, his income statement did not start with a calculation of current cost operating profit and did not provide a statement of both nominal and real holding gains.

28 Baxter (1975) criticises this aspect of his work.

29 But the economist, Irving Fisher (1911 and 1925) was extremely clear on the issue, and Sweeney makes reference to his work on a number of occasions.

30 For example, his depreciation charge to the profit and loss account is based on historic cost adjusted by a general index: in Edwards and Bell's terms, this involves netting off the realised real holding gain on the depreciating assets against full (replacement cost) depreciation.

31 See Clarke (1976) for a discussion of this and a critique of Sweeney's work.
32 See Whittington (1980).

3 Developments in inflation accounting from the Second World War to 1974

1 We would, however, argue that Mumford is incorrect in interpreting the debate as a pure cycle. We would interpret it as a cycle about a trend: each previous cycle has served to advance the debate and this progress has not been entirely lost at the end of the cycle.
2 Tweedie (1979), p. 6, uses this description of the events of 1975 and 1976, and provides a chronological list of the various current cost proposals made during the period. This is also done in Chapter 12 below.
3 Zeff (1976b), p. 136, notes that the SEC Chief Accountant (John C. Burton) published an article on 30 November 1974 (Burton, 1974) indicating his preference for a replacement cost system rather than the CPP proposals of the FASB. Thus the Current Cost Revolution had started in the USA.
4 In Chapter 9 we discuss more recent developments in other West European countries, notably France and Sweden, but these have not yet had a notable impact on practice.
5 Although nowhere has there been a repetition of the German hyper-inflation of 1923.
6 Zeff (1964 and 1976b) has provided excellent and authoritative accounts of this period, upon which this section draws.
7 The acceptance of LIFO stock valuation for reporting purposes, following its acceptance for taxation purposes in 1938, largely resolved the parallel difficulty that historic cost of goods sold might not reflect current replacement cost.
8 The writer of this monograph believes that real income, expressed in terms of current monetary units, will in the future prove the most useful concept both from the standpoint of the individual enterprise and that of the economy as a whole. (May, 1949, p. 80)
9 It will be recalled, from the previous chapter, that Sweeney recognised the loss (or gain) on money held at the end of the year in the unrealised section of his profit and loss account.
10 Furthermore, this company did not follow *APB3* in its treatment of monetary gains and losses.
11 This view is expressed forcefully by Zeff (1976b). The private view of a member of FASB is expressed by Sprouse (1976) in the same volume.
12 A useful account of developments in the UK in this period is Mumford (1979).
13 The Committee on the Taxation of Trading Profits, whose Report was published in 1951.
14 This type of issue is explored further in Chapter 13.
15 In its Report, published in 1951.
16 We owe the information in this paragraph to an interview with the late Sir Edmund Parker in February 1980.

17 The 1968 paper is essentially an elaboration of the ideas contained in the same author's 1962 paper, with the exception that the later paper stabilises the profit and loss account in end-of-year pounds rather than average-for-the-year pounds, for better comparability with the balance sheet.

18 Westwick (1980) gives an authoritative account of the post-war evolution of inflation accounting in the UK: he was a member of the ASSC secretariat particularly responsible for inflation accounting from 1971 onwards.

19 An interesting and important question is 'when, and by whom, was the decision made to make the theme of the Discussion Paper the advocacy of CPP rather than the balanced evaluation of alternatives?'. Westwick (1980), the main author of the 'Tombstone', indicates that the decision to support a CPP solution had already been taken when he joined the ASSC secretariat in April 1971.

20 Later published in *Accountancy* (Parker, 1971).

21 Zeff (1976b) praises the ASSC for its efforts to 'sell' its CPP solution to interested parties, in contrast with the FASB's more passive attitude to its 1974 Exposure Draft.

22 One technical difference between *ED8* and *APB3* was that the former advocated the use of the Consumer Price Index, whereas the latter preferred the GNP Implicit Deflator, which is an index relating to all goods (including capital goods) produced in the economy.

23 The earlier work by R. S. Edwards (1938) also contrasted the approaches of the economist and the accountant.

24 This theme was also developed by Lacey (1952) and by Baxter (1955).

25 Mathews and Grant also provide a useful bibliography.

26 This criticism is developed, in the context of income measurement, in Whittington (1981b).

27 Edwards and Bell describe realised gains *plus* unrealised gains as 'realisable' gains.

28 It will be recalled that the last two of these dichotomies were also made by Sweeney (1936), although Sweeney did not regard nominal gains as being useful information and therefore did not propose that they be reported separately.

29 One fundamental problem is that production is, in its very nature, not instantaneous. It is therefore necessary to hold assets in the course of production, and the allocation of the increment in their value between production ('operating gains') and holding gains is essentially arbitrary, since operating and holding are joint activities.

30 Particularly in his 1970 paper. The general direction has been to harden, rather than soften, his adherence to selling prices and rejection of replacement cost.

31 Here it should be noted that much pioneering work had preceded Chambers, such as Paton and Littleton (1940), which had served to clarify the assumptions and objectives of accounting. Work of this type continues, examples from the 1960s being Ijiri (1967) and Mattessich (1964). Although this type of work is not aimed specifically at inflation accounting, it is

intended to clarify the problems of accounting in general and the level of theoretical debate, and should therefore have an impact on the debate on inflation accounting.

32 Another theorist who developed very similar ideas to those of Chambers at this time is Sterling, whose first major work was published in 1970.

33 Other well-known expositions of the 'value to the owner' rules in this form are Parker and Harcourt (1969), Stamp (1971) and the Sandilands Report (1975).

34 Useful exploration of some of the potential weaknesses of value to the owner, especially as an aggregate concept, are Edey (1974) and Peasnell (1978).

35 Edwards' (1975) rule of valuing assets which will be sold at selling price and those which will be held for use within the firm at replacement cost, is in a similar vein.

36 Stamp (1971) is an exception to this.

37 For example, many of these new ideas were proposed for discussion in *The Corporate Report*, an ASSC discussion document, in 1975, although it must be admitted that the professional response to *The Corporate Report* has been disappointing (this is discussed further in Chapter 14).

4 The contemporary British debate I: the watershed of the CPP experiment, 1973

1 It should be noted that the CCAB and the ASC (formerly ASSC) embrace, *inter alia*, the Chartered Institutes of England and Wales, Scotland and Ireland, so that all the British Isles are affected by this debate: references to 'Britain' or 'the UK' should be interpreted as a rather slipshod shorthand for the British Isles, except in so far as references are made to the UK Government (which appointed the Sandilands Committee) or Inland Revenue (which administered Stock Relief).

2 The Chairman's personal account of the work of the IASG has been published (Morpeth, 1981), as has that of the Secretary of the Group during its formative period (Westwick, 1980).

3 Even advocates of some form of gearing adjustment, such as Kennedy (1978b), objected to the Hyde form, which did not recognise unrealised holding gains. As explained later, where monetary assets exceeded liabilities, the Hyde Guidelines proposed that a charge for the maintenance of working capital was made.

4 This was not to be the case with the profession's first CCA proposals which were, as mentioned in the last section, rejected at a Special Meeting of the Institute of Chartered Accountants in England and Wales (ICAEW).

5 Indeed, the present authors disagreed over the interpretation of several of the responses and had to debate the intention behind each of these responses before the tables shown in this section could be constructed.

6 Some companies, such as Pilkington and Philips, already used a replacement

cost accounting system and were consequently not distinterested in the eventual outcome of the debate. It should, of course, be emphasised that those responding to an accounting standard neither represent a random sample nor necessarily reflect a representative view.

7 The views that accounts should be based on information of use to management is fundamental to the philosophy of Limperg and Schmidt. Philips' accounts have for many years been based on the theories of the former.

8 CPP accounts do use information about the age of assets. An individual's intuitive adjustments for inflation can obviously not make allowance for age without the requisite information.

9 No details of the sample used were given in the published paper.

10 See Aranya (1974).

11 See also McRae and Dobbins (1974) who give confirmatory evidence that civil servants were aware of (and seemed to prefer) current value methods of accounting.

12 See Whittington (1976) pp. 174–5 and Carsberg, Morgan and Parkin (1974) pp. 73–84.

13 Some economists held the contrary view, that indexation could be an important component of stabilisation policy (e.g. see various papers in Liesner and King, 1975).

14 For details of the composition of the Sandilands Committee and the committees of the ASSC dealing with the problem of inflation, see Westwick (1980), pp. 372–3.

15 See for example, *ARS6*, AICPA (1963), pp. 183–93 which discusses and gives an illustration of the Philips' method of financial reporting.

5 The contemporary British debate II: the Sandilands Committee and its Report (1974–75)

1 Evidence for this appears in ASSC's minutes.

2 The general index recommended, however, was changed from the consumer price index to the retail price index, the latter having the convenient property of not being subject to retrospective revision and being available monthly.

3 Both *ED8* and *PSSAP7* explained that the lower of cost (expressed in current purchasing power terms) and net realisable value, for current assets, or 'value to the business' (but not in the form subsequently advocated by the Sandilands Committee) for fixed assets, should be applied in implementing the proposed CPP system.

4 The authors are grateful to Sir Francis Sandilands and Professor Walter Reid for helpful discussions concerning the work of the Sandilands Committee, although neither is responsible for any error of fact or judgement contained in this chapter.

5 Professor Reid, for example, was a specialist in management accounting, at that time.

6 Replacement cost accounting had been advocated many years earlier by the

Research and Technical Committee of the Institute of Cost and Works Accountants (1952).

7 The senior partner of his firm (Coopers and Lybrand), Sir Henry Benson, had been responsible for initiating the ASSC enquiry into inflation accounting. On the other hand, as Stamp (1971) pointed out, the firm was acting as auditor to the UK subsidiaries of Philips Industries, the leading exponent of replacement cost accounting.

8 Although the professional body (the AICPA) and the standard-setting body (the FASB) both favoured CPP at the time. The Chief Accountant of the SEC had made a speech in May 1974 which clearly advocated replacement cost disclosure.

9 The Brazilian system is discussed in Chapter 9.

10 ICAEW, ICAS, ICAI, ACCA and ICMA.

11 It was, however, accepted by the five bodies that in the long run a system of reporting to shareholders could evolve which incorporated the best features of CPP and RC accounting.

12 The submission stated that companies which adopted inflation adjustment procedures prior to the publication of *ED8* tended to use some form of replacement cost accounting. The submission continued 'it is difficult to see what use could be made of CPP data in managerial accounting. As analysts, we would prefer to work with the same figures as management.'

13 The alternative view, 'different measures for different purposes', is succinctly stated by Charles Kennedy (1978a), who also provides an excellent survey of the debate on inflation accounting in the United Kingdom between 1974 and 1978.

14 It should be noted that Professor Merrett was a colleague, at the London Graduate School of Business Studies, of Professor Walter Reid, an active member of the Sandilands Committee, who has acknowledged the influence of Professor Merrett's contribution to the debate.

15 This implies that replacement cost would be used for *valuation* purposes, and a CPP general index method would be used to calculate *capital* to be maintained. A CPP valuation method would, of course, fail to identify the movements of specific prices, so that real holding gains of this type could not be recognised.

16 Merrett and Sykes appeared to use *ex post* income as a proxy for firms' *ex ante* expectations, although they did not make this distinction, or the assumption, very clearly.

17 Kay and King (1978), Chapter 12, provide a good critique of Stock Relief, and empirical evidence of its effect on taxable profits.

18 Capital allowances for most forms of fixed investment were already more generous than replacement cost depreciation: the allowance on plant and machinery allowed immediate write-off of total cost of new investment, irrespective of whether it was a replacement or new investment.

19 Ironically, the modified Stock Relief introduced in 1981 uses a general index, albeit one of wholesale rather than retail prices.

20 A brief summary of the Committee's conclusions was prepared by the Committee itself. See Sandilands Report (1975).

21 For further discussion of this, see Gee and Peasnell (1976). Sweeney (1931) used a similar argument for justifying his advocacy of replacement cost. As was seen earlier (Chapter 2), Limperg's 'replacement value' bore a close resemblance to 'value to the business', and the Sandilands Committee working party had been exposed to his ideas on its visit to The Netherlands.

22 The Committee debated the merits of a depreciation provision based on the average current value to the business of assets held during the year. This was rejected on the grounds that the materiality of the difference between average and year end based provisions was small enough to be outweighed by the practical inconvenience of the average method (see paras. 608–11). The Richardson Committee in New Zealand (1976) came to a similar conclusion (see para. 21.17).

23 The Committee argued that current purchasing power units failed to meet any of the criteria (paras. 409–14). The monetary unit was deemed to meet the first four criteria.

24 The use of general indices is discussed in more detail in the companion volume to this book (Whittington, 1983a, Chapter 4).

25 Although it should be noted that the Report (paras. 760–3) denied that the Brazilian approach was a CPP method, because it did not use a consumer price index to define a constant purchasing power unit.

6 The contemporary British debate III: ED18 to SSAP16 (1976–83)

1 It was recognised that for statutory purposes some historical cost data would probably be required for the indefinite future.

2 See Hamilton (1977).

3 Peasnell and Skerratt showed that the RPI would have been a reasonable proxy for many of the plant and machinery indices (classified by industry) recommended for publication by Sandilands. By way of contrast they found that the US Implicit Price Deflators for Producers' Durable Equipment (which were classified by asset-type rather than by industry) could not be adequately represented by a general index.

4 See appendix to this chapter.

5 These working parties were concerned principally with (1) fixed assets and depreciation; (2) stock and cost of sales; (3) legal implications; (4) the guidance manual; (5) gearing and monetary items; (6) investments. See Morpeth (1981), pp. 48–9.

6 For further discussion of this point, see Lee and Tweedie (1977) and Tweedie (1981a).

7 The latter view was later upheld in the UK by the Companies Act 1981, Schedule 1, para. 12, which states that, unless there are special reasons, only profits realised at the balance sheet date can be included in the profit and loss

account. Only realised profits can now be distributed in the UK – Companies Act 1980, *S39*.

8 A later version of this paper was eventually published in the IASG's *Background Papers to the Exposure Draft on Current Cost Accounting* Tolley (1976b), p. 45.

9 Goudeket (1960), p. 41.

10 The gains/losses on net current monetary items were to be bracketed with income although shown separately. For a simple example see Baxter (1977).

11 Real gains are, as outlined earlier, holding gains or losses greater or less than the change in the historical cost of assets updated by a general price index.

12 In the parlance of the Sandilands Report this reserve would have been termed the Stock Adjustment Reserve.

13 The Godley and Cripps approach would be the same as a 'real terms' approach if specific and general price rises were identical.

14 Gibbs *et al.* (1976), p. 5 – the cash flow approach is obvious in this extract from their paper. This adjustment to profit was to be termed the monetary working capital adjustment (MWCA).

15 Gibbs *et al.* admitted that the gearing adjustment approach was only one way of calculating the gain on borrowed money – another, they stated, and which they previously had supported, was the gain measured by reference to the general rate of inflation. The authors, however, argued against their former views, criticising the CPP method on the basis of the substantial gains on borrowing revealed in the accounts of the companies with large property interests in the early 1970s even when property values were falling. Under the new Gibbs approach, such companies would have shown losses. It should be noted, however, that the companies would also have shown losses if the real loss on property holdings had been shown in the CPP income statement.

16 Until this draft, the surplus on revaluation was added to current cost profit at the foot of the profit and loss account and a transfer to the Capital Maintenance Reserve made out of the combined total, the latter being termed surplus/deficit for the year. Draft 10 formalised the transfer procedure in a separate account.

17 See also *ED18*, para. 258–63 and Appendix 2.

18 The Australian CCA Exposure Draft (ICAA and ASA, 1975) and the New Zealand CCA Exposure Draft (NZSA, 1976) both proposed that backlog depreciation should be charged against retained earnings. The Australian Provisional CCA Standard (ICAA and ASA, 1976), however, proposed that the backlog should be taken to the revaluation reserve (in Australia – the current cost adjustment account).

19 Presumably, the appropriation could be less than the revaluation surplus if general prices rose by less than the rise in the prices of the company's assets.

20 For example, an IASG document analysing the responses to *ED18* reveals that 75 per cent of the 56 questionnaires returned by field testers, who did not submit additional letters of comment on *ED18*, favoured CCA accounts as the main accounts from the commencement of the new standard. Only 25 per cent of the other 638 respondents shared this view.

21 An initial suggestion discussed during a September meeting of the IASG was to base depreciation and the valuation of fixed assets on a simplified replacement cost basis, to use LIFO for the cost of sales and to adjust stock values in the balance sheet to current replacement cost.

22 A more detailed analysis of the 746 responses would undoubtedly be a useful topic for research. Time pressure prevented the present authors from undertaking such an analysis.

23 Yet presumably those responses are included in the ASC's official statistics.

24 As with the responses to *ED8* the authors discussed each response until an agreed interpretation was reached.

25 The IASG data available to us did not include an analysis of these criticisms by different groups of respondents. Westwick (1980, p. 364), however, gives a table which shows this analysis. As his data differs slightly from those available to us, we have not used it in this discussion.

26 It should be remembered that our sample was biased and in particular did not give adequate representation to smaller companies or accounting firms, many of whom traditionally fail to comment on exposure drafts.

27 These were defined as debtors–creditors although 'other items' may have had to be included.

28 This proposal bore a certain resemblance to the conclusions of the 1976 CICA discussion paper on *Current Value Accounting*.

29 See also Morpeth (1981), p. 50.

30 Taken from an IASG secretariat draft paper, May 1977.

31 Hansard, 8 July 1977.

32 ICI was also considering a gearing adjustment during this period. The Finance Director of Ford UK (S. Thomson) and the Deputy Chief Accountant of ICI (J. Pearcy) were both members of the IASG. ICI eventually produced CC accounts in their 1977 annual report using a gearing adjustment which added back to profit the portion of revaluation surpluses financed by borrowings. The ICI accounts, based on the Gibbs approach, unlike those of Ford, charged operating profit with a monetary working capital adjustment (based on debtors less creditors) in addition to a cost of sales adjustment.

33 While the gearing adjustment proposed by the London Society was similar to that adopted by the Hyde Committee, differences were apparent in terms of the definition of liabilities and monetary items. The Hyde Committee considered preference shares to be liabilities and included cash as a monetary asset whereas the London Society considered preference shares to be part of shareholders' funds and, where an organisation had a surplus of cash over liabilities, advocated that no adjustment should be made for that excess cash.

34 *ED18*'s Working Guide, however, provided means of dealing with complexities not mentioned in the Hyde Guidelines.

35 Other commentators later agreed with this view (see for example Baxter, 1978b; Mumford, 1978; and Tweedie, 1978). John Foyle, a former secretary of the IASG informed the present authors that IASG itself realised that the

net monetary assets adjustment was not a natural corollary of the net liabilities gearing adjustment although it was presented as such.

36 *ED18* did not show HC profit in its proposed income statement but commenced with CC operating profit.

37 The *ED24* gearing adjustment differed from the Hyde proposals in that preference shares were now considered to be part of the shareholders' interest in the company rather than liabilities.

38 It should be noted, however, that if CCA were ever used as a tax base, this gearing approach would have an unfavourable effect upon companies.

39 Specific indices were to be used to calculate the amount required to maintain net working capital.

40 These 32 companies consisted of all those of the top 100 companies making a submission.

41 The Hundred Group of Finance Directors, The Midland Industry Group of Finance Directors and The Group of Scottish Finance Directors.

42 Supplementary CCA accounts were required if HC statements were considered to be the main accounts but only 'adequate HC information' was required if CCA accounts were presented as the main statements although companies could produce supplementary HC accounts.

43 *ED24* proposed the inclusion of these items only if their exclusion could be shown to be misleading.

44 41 per cent of the ICAEW's members voted.

45 The stock relief system was, after the 1981 Finance Act, based on a general (single) stock index. Later, the Green Paper *Corporation Tax* (Cmnd 8456) published in January 1982 revealed the Government's doubts that taxation could be based on the proposals of *SSAP16* while the *Finance Act 1982* perhaps gave a further possible pointer to future developments by giving relief from Capital Gains Tax on a general index basis.

46 One of these standards could have called into question the whole basis of the *SSAP16* income model. A draft exposure draft on *Accounting for Changes in Value in Investment-Based Entities* being developed by the ASC in the first half of 1982 (but since dropped from its programme), called for an additional statement in which total gains and losses over the period (realised and unrealised) would be compared with the change in the purchasing power of the shareholders' equity interest as measured by the RPI. This proposal, which borrowed the concept of the Statement of Total Gains and Losses from Sandilands and combined this with a proprietary capital maintenance system, was scarcely consistent with the thrust of the prudent entity based proposals of *SSAP16*. It was, however, compatible with *SSAP16*'s optional disclosure suggestion of a statement of the change in shareholders' equity interest after allowing for the change in the general purchasing power of money.

47 Chaired by Stanley Thomson, Finance Director of Ford UK, whose company it will be remembered pioneered the use of the gearing adjustment in the UK (see note 32).

7 Inflation accounting in the USA (1975–80)

1 The Release also required replacement cost depreciation to be charged on a straight line basis. No justification of this was attempted.
2 Zeff (1979b) provides a useful chronology of relevant events.
3 The Moss and Metcalf Committees reported after *ASR190* was published, but they demonstrate the political environment in which SEC was working.
4 The 'elements' part was the basis of the revised Exposure Draft, *Elements of Financial Statements of Business Enterprises* (FASB, 1979c), which re-titled the central income concept 'comprehensive income' rather than 'earnings'.
5 Specifically, those with *either* inventories and property, plant and equipment (gross of depreciation) amounting to more than $125 million, *or* total assets amounting to more than $1 billion.
6 This included experimentation with format, as well as method. The supplementary data could be presented either as a completely self-contained statement, or in the form of a reconciliation of conventional income (as in the main statements) with price-level adjusted income.
7 RRA is discussed further in a later section of this chapter.
8 *APB3* (1969) was a recommendation rather than a binding standard, and was therefore widely ignored.
9 This hinged on whether exploration costs should be fully capitalised, or whether only that proportion which had led to a successful discovery should be capitalised. The successful efforts approach had been endorsed by the FASB, in *FAS19*, but this was withdrawn following the SEC's intervention.
10 i.e. if supplies were to be maintained in the long term, growers must expect, *ex ante*, to receive an appropriate rate of return on their investment, in addition to recovering the costs of land, labour and other physical factors of production. In the short term, it might be the case that *ex post* returns on investment might be inadequate: in such a situation the value to the firm rules of *FAS33* would imply that current cost be reduced by a lower recoverable amount, which might equal fair value.

8 Inflation accounting in Australasia

1 Since 1977 he has been National Research Partner of Coopers and Lybrand in Australia.
2 There were, of course, many other writers on inflation accounting and related matters in both Australia and New Zealand in the 1960s. Our objective here has been merely to quote a sample of those who have achieved obvious international prominence: it is not intended to be comprehensive.
3 It should be noted that the Australian Companies Acts do not allow any distribution of profit in excess of that reported in the accounts. An increased depreciation charge would accordingly result in lower profits available for distribution.

4 The AASC (Australian Accounting Standards Committee, later the Current Cost Accounting Standards Committee), a committee of the Australian Accounting Research Foundation (AARF) operated under the aegis of the Institute of Chartered Accountants in Australia and the Australian Society of Accountants. The AARF proposes and releases exposure drafts, whilst the two accounting bodies release final statements. For further details of these committees and a contemporary view of the debate in Australia, the USA and the UK from one who has been described as 'the father of CCA in Australia' see Rickard (1978).

5 Namely the UK, the USA and Canada, all of which published CPP statements in 1974.

6 The Sandilands Committee's terms of reference were discussed in Chapter 4. They included 'any implications for the taxation of the profits and capital gains of companies' but their central concern was with the needs of users of financial reports.

7 The proposals for depreciation and cost of sales adjustments were identical to those proposed by Mathews earlier (1955 and 1958, especially p. 141). In those publications Mathews had dismissed the case for adjusting profit to take account of the effect of price-level changes on monetary items on the grounds that (1) it would be difficult to justify the adaptation of the accountant's rôle to preserve the purchasing power of cash resources and money claims rather than simply maintain the value of capital invested in physical assets; and (2) if stock increases were financed by current liabilities the net effect on income would be negligible and little or nothing would have been done to mitigate financial difficulties resulting from the inflation (1955, p. 196 and 1958, pp. 22–3).

8 The note on the status of the Exposure Draft acknowledged that it has been prepared by the AASC with the assistance of 'the wealth of literature which is available on the subject'.

9 This information was given to the authors by the Director of the Australian Accounting Research Foundation.

10 Namely, current costs of fixed assets and inventories, depreciation charges and cost of goods sold. In addition, disclosure of other information, such as the gains and losses on monetary items and the method of their calculation, was encouraged. The SEC's requirements were, of course, on a strict replacement cost basis, whereas the Australian proposals were based on a form of deprival value.

11 Explanatory Statement issued with the Provisional Standard, Appendix 1.

12 The gains and losses on holding monetary items were to be brought into account by a credit/debit to the profit and loss account, with a corresponding debit/credit to the current cost adjustment account. The proposed system now incorporated three adjustments to historic cost profit, namely the current cost depreciation and cost of goods sold adjustments (1976 Provisional Standard) and the new monetary working capital adjustment.

13 Henderson and Pierson did not favour the inclusion of any gains or losses on borrowings. They argued that operating capability should be interpreted as

the operating capability provided by the assets of the entity, i.e. they rejected the net asset approach (assets less certain liabilities).

14 As the intention was 'to assess the extent to which shareholders may be seen to have benefited from gearing', gains or losses on loan capital were to be calculated by means of a general price index (the Consumer Price Index).

15 *A Brief Guide to the CCA Omnibus Exposure Draft* (1980, AARF, p.1).

16 'How Inflation was Reported in 1980' by Elizabeth Kelly, *The Chartered Accountant in Australia*, April 1981.

17 The Richardson Report was published in September 1976, one month after the NZSA's CCA Exposure Draft. It seems highly unlikely that the NZSA had no advance knowledge of the direction of the Richardson Committee's thoughts. The Richardson Report is discussed in more detail in the next section of this chapter.

18 It should be noted that the Exposure Draft also proposed a statement showing the effects of changes in the general price level on shareholders' equity. Equity adjusted in CPP terms was then to be compared with owner's equity stated in current cost terms. The United Kingdom's *ED18*, published three months later (November 1976), also proposed supplementary disclosure of this type of information.

19 The Committee took the view that a specific index was more appropriate theoretically but opted for a general index for practical considerations.

20 'To a significant extent the distinction drawn between circulating monetary assets and fixed monetary assets followed from what are in New Zealand well recognised legal and commercial distinctions between investing on capital account and in trading operations.' Letter from the Right Honourable Mr Justice Richardson to the authors.

21 Information received in a letter from the Committee's Chairman to the authors.

22 Almost identical wording was used by Gibbs *et al.* (1976, p. 6).

23 Professor Mathews (1977, pp. 91–2) later praised the Richardson Committee for its current value adjustments on monetary assets and liabilities. The Mathews Committee raised the issue of gains and losses on monetary items in Appendix A of its Report but did not, in Mathews' words, 'carry through the proposal to its logical conclusion'. Mathews, however, believed that short-term liabilities should have been offset against monetary assets to obtain a measure of net monetary assets, and that the loss on net monetary assets should have been measured by a specific rather than a general price index.

24 The gearing adjustment was calculated as follows:

$$\frac{\text{average long-term borrowing less current assets not included in COSA or MWCA}}{\text{average net operating assets}} \times \text{increase in current cost reserve}$$

25 The financial capital option in the New Zealand Standard does, however, allow the use of the general index approach for monetary items.

26 Gynther (1982) provides a very useful comparison between the US, UK, Australian and New Zealand inflation accounting standards.

9 Inflation accounting in other countries

1 This is merely a convenient category and should not be taken to indicate ignorance of the influence of French-speaking Canadians and Afrikaans-speaking South Africans in their respective countries, or of the existence of English-speaking accountants elsewhere in the world (e.g. the Indian sub-continent and the Far East).

2 In 1972, the CICA had published a sponsored study by Rosen, which had advocated current value accounting, and an opinion survey by the CICA (published in the *CA Magazine*, February 1975, p. 10) revealed that only 15 out of 53 respondents regarded CPP as a completely satisfactory solution to the inflation accounting problem.

3 The Canadian proposal was not, however, identical to these proposals, since it specifically rejected any adjustment for the loss on net monetary working capital (adopted in *SSAP16*'s monetary working capital adjustment, and allowed for by the Hyde Committee when monetary assets exceeded liabilities).

4 The Ontario Committee also differed from the Richardson Committee in rejecting any form of monetary working capital adjustment (see note 3).

5 The preface to the Exposure Draft explicitly acknowledged that the Exposure Draft's recommendations were similar to those of *ED24*. Having outlined the differences between the Canadian Exposure Draft and *FAS33*, the preface expressed the hope that, with the experience of the British, American and Canadian proposals, an international consensus on the most appropriate method would develop.

6 Like the UK's *ED24*, the Exposure Draft required only supplementary disclosure and applied only to large companies.

7 Namely, current cost income; the current cost carrying value of stock and fixed assets; the effect of general inflation during the accounting period on the current cost carrying amounts of fixed assets and stock; and the CPP gain or loss on monetary items.

8 In other words, applying the gearing ratio to the changes during the period in the current cost amounts of stock and fixed assets.

9 Since shareholders' net worth (E) is equal to non-monetary assets (N) plus net monetary assets ($M–L$), where M is equal to monetary assets and L is liabilities, we can calculate the gain on borrowing as $p(M-L)$, where p is the proportionate change in the general price level, or as $p(E-N)$, as in the South African Discussion Paper.

10 There were, of course, differences of detail from the Hyde adjustments, e.g. preference shares were included in proprietors' capital rather than borrowing, for the purposes of calculating gearing, a practice adopted later in *ED24* and *SSAP16* in the UK.

11 The asset valuation system appeared to be derived from the Australian

recoverable amount method. Assets were to be valued at the lower of current cost or recoverable amount/net realisable value.

12 Subsequently, the Government set up a Tripartite Study Group (now the Council for Annual Reporting), representing the accounting profession, employers' organisations and trade unions, to produce an inventory of acceptable standards.

13 Reproduced as an appendix to the IASC Discussion Paper *Treatment of Changing Prices in Financial Statements* (1976). This followed a 1975 exposure draft by the Tripartite Study Group (see note 12) approving both historical and current value accounting methods and recommending disclosure of any significant differences in the results obtained from the two approaches.

14 The financing model chosen for the gearing adjustment was more akin to the 1975 West German proposal (discussed below) in specifying the order in which assets were financed by equity funds than to the British (Hyde) gearing adjustment which assumed that net assets were financed in similar proportions of equity and debt capital. Unlike the German proposal which stated that equity first financed fixed assets and then stocks, the Hofstra adjustment assumed the opposite, i.e. stocks were deemed to be financed by equity capital before fixed assets.

15 The price level by the end of the Second World War was some 300 times above the pre-war level. See Holzer and Schonfeld (1963a, p. 377).

16 See Nobes and Parker (1981, p. 145 and p. 271).

17 Depreciation is based on historical cost and length of asset life for depreciation purposes is specified by the tax authorities.

18 The structure of the capital market, with more emphasis on loan finance by large institutions and less emphasis on equity finance through the stock market than is the case in the English-speaking countries, was also probably an important factor. This system requires less of financial reports, because large lenders can acquire their own information directly, as a condition of lending, without having to rely on published financial reports.

19 The intellectual origins of the recommendation are discussed by Coenenberg and Macharzina (1976).

20 The Sandilands Report was published two or three months before the IdW proposal.

21 This is in contrast with the UK approach of the Hyde Guidelines, *ED24* and *SSAP16*, which assumes that all physical assets are financed in similar proportions by debt and equity, and with the Hofstra proposals which assume that equity capital was applied to the financing firstly of stocks and then of fixed assets.

22 Professor Harold Edey in correspondence, has confirmed that he was aware of the IdW proposals, at the time when he was chairman of the IASG working party on gearing and monetary items, although he finds it difficult to assess their influence on the development of IASG's ideas.

23 Further details of the system will be found in Holzer and Schonfeld (1963b).

24 In such cases, revaluation could be a useful method of carrying forward tax losses beyond the permitted five years, since the depreciation on the

enhanced value would be an allowable tax deduction over the lives of the relevant assets (see Beeny, 1976, pp. 54–6).

25 See Nobes and Parker (1981, p. 272).

26 The 1975 West German proposal, however, involves a gearing adjustment and therefore maintains the operating capability financed by equity. We later term this a proprietorial entity approach.

27 At that time, the progress of current cost accounting was limited to its being minority practice in only two of the countries surveyed worldwide, the Republic of Ireland and the UK (as a result of The Hyde Guidelines). Since then, CCA has, of course, achieved accounting standard status in these two countries and in the USA, New Zealand, and Canada.

28 For a review of some recent work on indexation see Whittington (1976). A notable pioneer of this policy was Irving Fisher, who also wrote a history of the 'stable money movement' (Fisher, 1934).

29 The detailed position, as described by Scapens (1973 and 1975) is that the amount of restatement was taxed at 10 per cent, but the restated amount could then be used as an enlarged base for establishing normal profits for the purpose of excess profits levy. Since these two effects worked in opposite directions, the net effect depended on the precise circumstances of the particular company.

30 See Scapens (1973 and 1975). Altman (1974) and Fleming (1974) provide alternative accounts of the 1964 Brazilian system; Altman gives a numerical illustration.

31 Assets and liabilities subject to monetary correction appear in the balance sheet at their current (corrected) amounts.

32 Altman (1974), Baxter (1976), Fleming (1974), and Scapens (1973 and 1975).

33 Although the detailed provisions and restrictions made the system more complicated in practice.

34 Sandilands Report (1975, Chapter 19).

35 Sandilands Report, para. 763. Current Cost Accounting, as advocated by Sandilands, makes no adjustment for the erosion of working capital, other than stocks, and requires the annual revaluation of specific assets on the 'value to the owner' principle. It specifically rejects the use of general indices.

36 Useful sources of reference on Chile are Baxter (1976), Scapens (1973 and 1975) and Zeff and Ovando (1975).

37 Equity was indexed, the adjustment being offset primarily against the fixed asset adjustment. A surplus (excess of equity adjustment over fixed asset adjustment) could be offset for tax purposes only to the extent of 20 per cent of taxable income.

38 Zeff and Ovando (1975).

39 Professor Zeff, at a seminar given at the London Graduate School of Business in May 1980, attributed the Mexican Government's opposition to the 1977 professional proposal allowing CCA disclosure to fear that inflation would be stimulated by the low profits reported under the CCA method.

40 These are summarised in an appendix to the *Inter-American Accounting Review* No. 5.

10 The present state of inflation accounting throughout the world

1 Although, as was demonstrated by our discussion of Uruguay in Chapter 9, the level at which inflation becomes imperative depends upon the economic and political environment.
2 While The Netherlands is included in this group, the Dutch appear to be well-versed in the accounting theories of the English-speaking nations. However, as we discussed earlier, the latter countries do not have the same understanding of the theories of Limperg.
3 More detailed accounts of the latest pronouncements in any particular country mentioned in this chapter can be found in the preceding chapters.
4 This concept was also adopted in New Zealand.
5 To be precise, in the case of the Ontario Report, the additional charges were deductions from funds available for distribution or expansion from the statement of sources and application of funds.
6 It should not be forgotten, however, that the UK's *ED18* (1976) had recommended that CC accounts replaced the traditional HC financial statements (see Chapter 6).
7 Unlike the Swedish proposal, *FAS33* does not add together the component parts of income.

11 Competing systems of accounting for price changes

1 Whittington (1983a).
2 e.g. Sandilands Report, Chapters 18 and 20, particularly paragraphs 795–6.
3 Sandilands Report, Chapter 1, para. 13.
4 There is, however, some controversy as to whether these were strictly replacement costs or merely current market values (which can include selling prices). This is discussed further by Clarke (1982).
5 Sweeney (1964b) concurred in this view.

12 Particular issues: valuation, capital maintenance and the gain on borrowing

1 Several academics had suggested the abandonment of the PV valuation aspect of the value to the business. See Stamp (1971 and 1975) and Gee and Peasnell (1976).
2 For example, in general, fixed assets, stock (unless obsolete) and long-term inter-company investments would be shown valued at replacement cost; marketable assets would be shown at net realisable values; and monetary assets and liabilities were to be shown at their discounted cash flow value except for short-term items where the time-value of money effect was small.
3 This is discussed in the context of value to the firm by Edey (1974).
4 Stamp (1972 and 1979) explores this possibility.

5 The FASB refers to the proprietary approach as 'financial' capital maintenance and the entity approach as 'physical' capital maintenance. This notation has some advantages, insofar as the entity/proprietary distinction can be interpreted as referring merely to whether the capital concerned is all the long-term capital including loans (the entity capital) or merely that attributable to equity (proprietary capital).

6 See, for example, Henderson and Pierson (1977, p. 28) and Ryan (1978).

7 It should be noted that some protagonists of this method would, for the sake of convenience, use a general index for monetary items.

8 The Hyde Guidelines included preference shares among the company's liabilities.

9 See, for example, Gynther (1976).

10 It may seem that gains on long-term borrowing were being included in income and, therefore, the operating capacity maintenance proposals were similar to concept (iv) (albeit with the exclusion of the maintenance of cash balances and overdrafts.) It should be stressed, however, that it was considered under concept (vi) that when gains on long-term borrowings were distributed, the operating capacity of the enterprise would only be maintained if additional borrowing were to be forthcoming. In other words, the net asset base to be maintained is as stated – physical assets plus monetary assets (less cash) less creditors.

11 The gearing adjustment was quite different from that proposed by Gibbs, excluding unrealised holding gains on assets.

12 Interestingly, Enthoven (1982) attributes this change to high interest rates and high inflation rates making it imperative for Philips to pay attention to these factors as part of its changing financial structure.

13 Baxter (1975), one of the modern proponents of measuring gains on liabilities in CPP terms, expresses a reluctance to include such gains in profit. He is more confident of showing gains of a short-term nature together with (but not included in) other income. We have already seen (Chapter 3, Section 2) that there was uncertainty about this matter in the USA, Sweeney advocating the separation of realised from unrealised gains, but *ARS6* and *APB3* reporting the net gain or loss on all monetary assets and liabilities as a single separate component of the CPP-adjusted profit and loss statement.

14 In the UK, it would now be difficult to incorporate an adjustment based on the realisable cost savings approach in the statutory accounts of a company. The 1981 Companies Act, based on the EC Fourth Directive, only permits realised profits to be included in the profit and loss account, in an apparent effort to equate income with distributable profit. This legal restriction at present bars the way to a more comprehensive approach to the measurement of income in company accounts in the UK. For further discussion on this point, see Tweedie (1983a).

15 While the 1975 West German Statement introduced a gearing adjustment, in practice little attention was paid to its proposals.

16 Coenenberg and Macharzina (1976) trace the influence of Schmidt on the conceptual basis of the 1975 Statement.

13 The course of the debate: causes and influences

1 Watts and Zimmerman (1978) provide a useful analysis of this relationship.
2 This issue has now been foreclosed by the 1980 Companies Act, which, following the EEC Second Directive, provides a definition of distributable profit. Unrealised gains may not now be distributed as dividends, although the definition of realisation leaves some scope for flexibility.
3 The phrase 'accidents or history' was used, in the context of inflation accounting, in an article by Frank Clarke (1980). Although we disagree with him on a number of important issues we would recommend this article and his subsequent book (1982) to the thoughtful reader who wishes to consider alternative interpretations of the events which we have described in Chapters 2 to 10.
4 The Solomons Report (Solomons, 1974) gives a good account of accounting education in Britain in the early 1970s. The lack of action on that report demonstrates the general *malaise* with regard to education.

Appendix to Chapter 13

1 Watts and Zimmerman (1978) use size as a relevant variable of this type. However, it seems likely that there are several other relevant variables, e.g. extent of long-term borrowing, liquidity, profitability and industry (the latter being a proxy for the difference between specific price changes and changes in a general price index).
2 Only a quarter of our *ED24* sample responded to both *ED8* and *ED18*.
3 Seven companies are on the opposite diagonal, indicating a switch of support, but six of these are in one cell, Qualified Opposition/Qualified Support, which does not represent a strong change of view.

14 Accounting standards and the future of the inflation accounting debate

1 For a cogent exposition of the case against accounting standards see Morison (1970).
2 The 'inside' story of the formation of the ASC is to be found in Leach and Stamp (1981).
3 An ambitious conceptual framework might encompass such a social welfare function, and indeed almost any conceptual framework makes some judgements of this type, e.g. by defining the users of accounting information (and implicitly excluding others).
4 By way of illustration, one of us possesses a copy of the *The Corporate Report*, sold as 'surplus to requirements' by the library at the Institute of Chartered Accountants in England and Wales. This copy bears the initials of the former Technical Director of the Institute, who was the Secretary of the Committee which produced the report.
5 The Exposure Draft does, however, advocate that comprehensive income should be based on the financial concept of capital, financial capital being measured in real terms.
6 Gynther (1967) has outlined hypotheses which could be tested.

7 Frishkoff (1982) gives a review of available empirical research. Recent research is reported in the proceedings of a conference on *Research on Financial Reporting and Changing Prices* (FASB, 1983).

8 The support is, of course, not authoritative, as Chapter 7 indicated. The FASB has to steer a difficult course between what the SEC will accept and support as generally accepted accounting principles (GAAP), and what the rest of its constituency will accept, whilst maintaining its own integrity.

9 For further discussion on this point see Tweedie (1983a and 1983b).

10 The papers were skeletal outlines amounting in total to 21 pages, in comparison to the present book and its companion volume which consisted of more than 700 manuscript pages. They were, consequently, by no means a substitute for knowledge of the original sources and the need for a period of reflection on the merits of the respective theories. It should be said, in addition, that papers were also prepared and presented by other members of the committee and its secretary.

11 Namely, the Trueblood Report (1973); *The Corporate Report* (ASSC, 1975); *Statement of Financial Accounting Concepts No. 1* (FASB, 1978a); and the Stamp Report (Stamp, 1980).

12 Table 14.1 shows the holding gains divided into realised and unrealised elements but an even simpler variant could, of course, simply show the total of holding gains.

13 An even simpler variant, which does, however, result in the loss of information on operating profit, would simply involve adding unrealised holding gains to historical cost profit and then deducting the inflation adjustment of equity. Total Real Gains would be identical to those shown in Table 14.1.

14 Namely, current cost income from continuing operations; increases or decreases in the current cost amounts of inventory, property, plant and equipment, net of inflation; and the purchasing power gains or losses on net monetary items.

15 A monetary working capital adjustment could also be included firstly as a current cost adjustment deducted from historical cost profit and then added to holding gains, divided into its geared and ungeared proportions.

16 It is, however, possible to over-estimate the additional cost. The various holding gains and the equity adjustment reported in Tables 14.1 to 14.3 imply that all of the valuations necessary to construct a current cost balance sheet have already been made.

17 A survey commissioned by the ICAEW (Archer and Steele, 1983) reported that only 7 per cent of the 484 listed companies surveyed were happy to comply with *SSAP16*; 11 per cent did not comply with the provisions of the Standard and 60 per cent complied only from obligation.

Bibliography

Accounting Principles Board (1969), *Statement No. 3 (APB3) Financial Statements Restated for General Price-Level Changes*, American Institute of Certified Public Accountants, June 1969.

Accounting Standards Committee (1976), *ED18, Current Cost Accounting*, ASC, London, 30 November 1976.

Accounting Standards Committee (1977), *Inflation Accounting – An Interim Recommendation by the Accounting Standards Committee* (The Hyde Guidelines), ASC, London, 4 November 1977.

Accounting Standards Committee (1979), *ED24, Current Cost Accounting*, ASC, London, 30 April 1979.

Accounting Standards Committee (1980a), *Statement of Standard Accounting Practice No.16, Current Cost Accounting (SSAP16)*, ASC, London, March 1980.

Accounting Standards Committee (1980b), *Submissions on the Accounting Standards Committee's Exposure Draft 24, Current Cost Accounting*, ASC, London.

Accounting Standards Committee (1983), *Report of the Monitoring Working Party* (The Neville Report), ASC, London.

Accounting Standards Steering Committee (1971), 'Inflation and Accounts, Discussion Paper and Fact Sheet', *Accountancy*, London, September 1971.

Accounting Standards Steering Committee (1973), *ED8: Accounting for Changes in the Purchasing Power of Money*, ASSC, London, 17 January 1973.

Accounting Standards Steering Committee (1974), *Provisional Statement of Standard Accounting Practice No. 7 (PSSAP7), Accounting for Changes in the Purchasing Power of Money*, ASSC, London, May 1974.

Accounting Standards Steering Committee (1975), *The Corporate Report*, ASSC, London, July 1975.

AICPA, see American Institute of Certified Public Accountants.

Alexander, S. S. (1950), 'Income Measurement in a Dynamic Economy'. Originally pp. 1–97 of Study Group on Business Income (1950). Revised by David Solomons and reprinted in Baxter and Davidson (1977).

Altman, M. (1974), 'Brazilian Experiment: Accounting for Inflation in Brazil', *The Accountant*, 5 December 1974.

American Institute of Accountants, Committee on Accounting Procedure

(1947), 'Depreciation and High Costs', *Accounting Research Bulletin No. 33*, AIA, New York.

American Institute of Certified Public Accountants, Accounting Research Division (1962), *Accounting Research Study No. 3 (ARS3)*. See Sprouse and Moonitz (1962).

American Institute of Certified Public Accountants, Accounting Research Division (1963), *Accounting Research Study No. 6 (ARS6), Reporting the Financial Effects of Price-Level Changes*, American Institute of Certified Public Accountants, New York.

APB, see Accounting Principles Board.

APB3 (1969), see Accounting Principles Board (1969).

Aranya, N. (1974), 'The Influence of Pressure Groups on Financial Statements in Britain', *Abacus*, June 1974.

Archer, S. and A. Steele (1983), *The Implementation of SSAP16, Current Cost Accounting by Listed Companies*. Unpublished Research Report for the ICAEW, University of Lancaster.

ARS6 (1963), see American Institute of Certified Public Accountants, Accounting Research Division.

ASC, see Accounting Standards Committee.

ASSC, see Accounting Standards Steering Committee.

Association of Certified and Corporate Accountants, Taxation and Research Committee (1952), *Accounting for Inflation, a Study of Techniques under Conditions of Changing Price Levels*, Gee & Co.

Australian Accounting Research Foundation (1978), *Exposure Draft: The Recognition of Gains and Losses on Holding Monetary Resources in the Context of Current Cost Accounting*, July 1978.

Australian Accounting Research Foundation (1979), *Exposure Draft: The Recognition of Gains and Losses on Holding Monetary Items in the Context of Current Cost Accounting*, August 1979.

Australian Accounting Research Foundation (1980), *Current Cost Accounting – Omnibus Exposure Draft*, March 1980.

Australian Accounting Research Foundation (1981), *Proposed Statement of Accounting Standards: Current Cost Accounting*, April 1981.

Barton, A. D. (1974), 'Expectations and Achievements in Income Theory', *The Accounting Review*, October 1974.

Bauer, J. (1919), 'Renewal Costs and Business Profits in Relation to Rising Prices', *Journal of Accountancy*, December 1919.

Baxter, W. T. (1949), 'Accountants and the Inflation', *Proceedings of the Manchester Statistical Society*, 9 February 1949.

Baxter, W. T. (1952), 'Inflation and Accounting Profits', *Westminster Bank Review*, May 1952.

Baxter, W. T. (1955), 'The Accountant's Contribution to the Trade Cycle', *Economica*, May 1955.

Baxter, W. T. (1967), 'Accounting Values: Sale Price Versus Replacement Cost', *Journal of Accounting Research*, Autumn 1967.

Bibliography

Baxter, W. T. (1975), *Accounting Values and Inflation*, McGraw-Hill, New York.

Baxter, W. T. (1976), 'Monetary Correction: Adjustments to inflation in three South American countries', *Bank of London and South America Review*, April 1976.

Baxter, W. T. (1977), 'Brave New Standard: Inflation Accounting, Mark 3', *The Accountant's Magazine*, April 1977.

Baxter, W. T. (1978a), *Collected Papers on Accounting*, Arno Press, New York.

Baxter, W. T. (1978b), 'Are The Hyde Proposals Strictly for Lemmings?', *Financial Times*, 12 April 1978.

Baxter, W. T. and S. Davidson (eds.) (1977), *Studies in Accounting*, 3rd edition. Institute of Chartered Accountants in England and Wales.

Beaver, W. (1981), *Financial Reporting: An Accounting Revolution*, Prentice-Hall, Englewood Cliffs, NJ.

Beaver, W. and J. Demski (1979), 'The Nature of Income Measurement', *The Accounting Review*, 1979.

Beeny, J. H. (1975), *European Financial Reporting, Vol. 1, West Germany*, ICAEW.

Beeny, J. H. (1976), *European Financial Reporting, Vol. II, France*, ICAEW.

Bell, P. W. and L. T. Johnson (1979), 'Current Value Accounting and the Simple Production Case: Edbejo and Other Companies in the Taxi Business', Chapter 5 of Sterling and Thomas (1979).

Benston, G. (1981), 'Are Accounting Standards Necessary?', Chapter 14 of Leach and Stamp (1981).

Boer, G. (1966), 'Replacement Cost: A Historical Look', *The Accounting Review*, January 1966.

Bonbright, J. C. (1937), *Valuation of Property* (2 volumes), McGraw-Hill, New York.

Bourn, M. (1976), 'The Gain on Borrowing', *Journal of Business Finance and Accounting*, Spring 1976.

Bourn, M., P. J. M. Stoney and R. F. Wynn (1976), 'Price Indices for Current Cost Accounting', *Journal of Business Finance and Accounting*, Autumn 1976.

Bromwich, M. (1977), 'The Use of Present Value Valuation Models in Published Accounting Reports', *The Accounting Review*, July 1977.

Bromwich, M. (1980), 'The Possibility of Partial Accounting Standards', *The Accounting Review*, April 1980.

Burgert, R. (1972), 'Reservations about Replacement Value Accounting in The Netherlands', *Abacus*, December 1972.

Burton, J. C. (1974), 'Accounting that Allows for Inflation', *Business Week*, November 1974.

Burton, J. C. (1975), 'Financial Reporting in an Age of Inflation', *Journal of Accountancy*, February 1975.

Canadian Institute of Chartered Accountants (1974), *Accounting for the Effects of Changes in the Purchasing Power of Money*, December 1974.

Bibliography

Canadian Institute of Chartered Accountants (1975), *Exposure Draft: Accounting for Changes in the General Purchasing Power of Money*, July 1975.

Canadian Institute of Chartered Accountants (1976), *Discussion Paper: Current Value Accounting*, August 1976.

Canadian Institute of Chartered Accountants (1979), *Exposure Draft: Current Cost Accounting*, December 1979.

Canadian Institute of Chartered Accountants (1981), *Exposure Draft: Reporting the Effects of Changing Prices*, December 1981.

Canadian Institute of Chartered Accountants (1982), *Reporting the Effects of Changing Prices*, Handbook Section 4510, October 1982.

Canning, J. B. (1929), *The Economics of Accountancy: A Critical Analysis of Accounting Theory*, Ronald Press, New York.

Carrington, A. S. (1977), 'Diversified Models – An Alternative to the Illusion of Certainty in Accounting Reports', in Baxter and Davidson (1977).

Carsberg, B. (1982), 'Reporting the Effects of Changing Prices: the United States Versus the United Kingdom', *Journal of Comparative Corporate Law and Securities Regulation*, 1982.

Carsberg, B., E. V. Morgan and M. Parkin (eds.) (1974), *Indexation and Inflation*, Financial Times Publications.

CCAB (1975), *Initial Reactions to the Report of the Inflation Accounting Committee*, Accounting Standards Committee, London, October 1975.

Chambers, R. J. (1965), 'Edwards and Bell on Business Income', *The Accounting Review*, October 1965.

Chambers, R. J. (1966), *Accounting, Evaluation and Economic Behavior*, Prentice-Hall, Englewood Cliffs, NJ.

Chambers, R. J. (1970), 'Second Thoughts on Continuously Contemporaneous Accounting', *Abacus*, September 1970.

Chambers, R. J. (1977), *An Autobibliography*, ICRA Occasional Paper No. 15, International Centre for Research in Accounting, University of Lancaster.

Chambers, R. J. (1979), 'Canning's *The Economics of Accountancy* – After 50 years', *The Accounting Review*, October 1979.

Chatfield, M. (ed.) (1968), *Contemporary Studies in the Evolution of Accounting Thought*, Dickenson Publishing Company, Belmont, California.

Clarke F. L. (1976), 'A Closer Look at Sweeney's Stabilised Accounting Proposals', *Accounting and Business Research*, Autumn 1976.

Clarke, F. L. (1980), 'Inflation Accounting and the Accidents of History', *Abacus*, December 1980.

Clarke, F. L. (1982), *The Tangled Web of Price Variation Accounting*, Garland, New York.

Coenenberg, A. and K. Macharzina (1976), 'Accounting for Price Changes: An Analysis of Current Developments in Germany', *Journal of Business Finance and Accounting*, Spring 1976.

Committee of Inquiry into Inflation and Taxation (1975), *Report: Inflation and Taxation* (The Mathews Report), Australian Government Publishing Service.

374

Bibliography

Committee on Inflation Accounting, Government of Ontario (1977), *Report* (The Alexander Report), Toronto, June 1977.

Committee on the Taxation of Trading Profits (1951) (The Millard Tucker Committee), *Report*, Cmnd 8189, HMSO, London.

Confederation of British Industry (1973), *Inflation and Company Accounts, an Interim Report for Discussion*, Confederation of British Industry, London.

The Corporate Report, see Accounting Standards Steering Committee, 1975.

Cutler, R. S. and C. A. Westwick (1973), 'The Impact of Inflation Accounting on the Stock Exchange', *Accountancy*, March 1973.

Davison, I. H. and C. A. Westwick (1981), *Inflation Accounting around the World*. Paper presented to the 16th Conference of the International Federation of Surveyors, Montreux, 14 August 1981. Arthur Andersen & Co., London.

Day, A. C. L. (1974). Article in *The Observer*, 3 November 1974.

Dopuch, N. and L. Revsine (eds.) (1973), *Accounting Research 1960–1970: A Critical Evaluation*, Center for International Education and Research in Accounting, University of Illinois.

Drake, D. F. and Dopuch, N. (1965), 'On the Case of Dichotomizing Income', *Journal of Accounting Research*, Autumn 1965.

ED8, see Accounting Standards Steering Committee (1973).

ED18, see Accounting Standards Committee (1976).

ED24, see Accounting Standards Committee (1979).

Edey, H. C. (1974), 'Deprival Value and Financial Accounting', pp. 75–83 of H. C. Edey and B. S. Yamey (eds.), *Debits, Credits, Finance, and Profits*, Sweet & Maxwell, London.

Edwards, E. O. (1975), 'The State of Current Value Accounting', *The Accounting Review*, April 1975.

Edwards, E. O. and P. W. Bell (1961), *The Theory and Measurement of Business Income*, University of California Press.

Edwards, E. O., P. W. Bell and L. T. Johnson (1979), *Accounting for Economic Events*, Scholars Book Co., Houston.

Edwards, R. S. (1938), 'The Nature and Measurement of Income', *The Accountant*, July–October 1938. Revised and reprinted in Baxter and Davidson (1977).

Egginton, D. A. (1980), 'Distributable Profit and the Pursuit of Prudence', *Accounting and Business Research*, No. 41, Winter 1980, pp. 1–14.

Enthoven, A. J. H. (1982), *Current Value Accounting. Its Concepts and Practices at N.V. Philips Industries, The Netherlands*, International Accounting Research Study No. 3. Center for International Accounting Development, University of Texas at Dallas.

Fabricant, S. (1936), 'Revaluations of Fixed Assets, 1925–1934', National Bureau of Economic Research *Bulletin*, 7 December 1936. Reprinted in Zeff (1976a).

FAR (Förenigen Auktoriserade Revisorer) (1980), Exposure Draft on Current Cost Accounting, Sweden.

375

Bibliography

Fäs, E. (1912), *Die Berucksichtigung der Wertminderung des Stehenden Kapitals in der Jahresbilanzen der Erwerbswirtschaften*, H. Laupp, Tübingen.

FAS33 (1979), see FASB (1979b).

FASB (1974a), *Discussion Memorandum: An Analysis of Issues Related to Reporting the Effects of General Price-Level Changes in Financial Statements*, Financial Accounting Standards Board, 15 February 1974.

FASB (1974b), *Discussion Memorandum: Conceptual Framework for Accounting and Reporting: Consideration of the Report of the Study Group on the Objectives of Financial Statements*, Financial Accounting Standards Board, 6 June 1974.

FASB (1974c), *Exposure Draft, Financial Reporting in Units of General Purchasing Power*, Financial Accounting Standards Board, Stamford, Conn., 31 December 1974.

FASB (1976a), *Scope and Implications of the Conceptual Framework Project*, Financial Accounting Standards Board, Stamford, Conn., December 1976.

FASB (1976b), *Tentative Conclusions on Objectives of Financial Statements of Business Enterprises*, Financial Accounting Standards Board, Stamford, Conn., December 1976.

FASB (1976c), *Discussion Memorandum: Elements of Financial Statements and Their Measurement*, Financial Accounting Standards Board, Stamford, Conn., 2 December 1976.

FASB (1977a), *Field Tests of Financial Reporting in Units of General Purchasing Power*, Financial Accounting Standards Board, Stamford, Conn., May 1977.

FASB (1977b), *Proposed Statement of Financial Accounting Concepts. Objectives of Financial Reporting and Elements of Financial Statements of Business Enterprises*, Financial Accounting Standards Board, Stamford, Conn., 29 December 1977.

FASB (1978a), *Statement of Financial Accounting Concepts No. 1: Objectives of Financial Reporting by Business Enterprises*, Financial Accounting Standards Board, Stamford, Conn., November 1978.

FASB (1978b), *Proposed Statement of Financial Accounting Standards. Financial Reporting and Changing Prices*, Financial Accounting Standards Board, Stamford, Conn., 28 December 1978.

FASB (1979a), *Exposure Draft: Constant Dollar Accounting* (Supplement to the 1974 Exposure Draft), Financial Accounting Standards Board, Stamford, Conn., 2 March 1979.

FASB (1979b), *Statement of Financial Accounting Standards No. 33 (FAS33): Financial Reporting and Changing Prices*, Financial Accounting Standards Board, Stamford, Conn., September 1979.

FASB (1979c), *Proposed Statement of Financial Accounting Concepts: Elements of Financial Statements of Business Enterprises*, Revision of Exposure Draft issued 29 December 1977. Financial Accounting Standards Board, Stamford, Conn., 28 December 1979.

FASB (1980a), *Statement of Financial Accounting Concepts No. 2: Qualitative Characteristics of Accounting Information*, Financial Accounting Standards Board, Stamford, Conn., May 1980.

Bibliography

FASB (1980b), *Statement No. 39, Financial Reporting and Changing Prices: Specialized Assets – Mining and Oil and Gas*, Financial Accounting Standards Board, Stamford, Conn., October 1980.

FASB (1980c), *Statement No. 40, Financial Reporting and Changing Prices: Specialized Assets – Timberlands and Growing Timber*, Financial Accounting Standards Board, Stamford, Conn., November 1980.

FASB (1980d), *Statement No. 41, Financial Reporting and Changing Prices: Specialized Assets – Income-Producing Real Estate*, Financial Accounting Standards Board, Stamford, Conn., November 1980.

FASB (1980e), *Statement of Financial Accounting Concepts No. 3, Elements of Financial Statements of Business Enterprises*, Financial Accounting Standards Board, Stamford, Conn., December 1980.

FASB (1981a), *Invitation to Comment on the need for research on Financial Reporting and Changing Prices*, Financial Accounting Standards Board, Stamford, Conn., 15 June 1981.

FASB (1981b), *Proposed Statement of Financial Accounting Concepts: Reporting Income, Cash Flows and Financial Position of Business Enterprises*, Financial Accounting Standards Board, Stamford, Conn., November 1981.

FASB (1981c), *Statement of Financial Accounting Standards No. 46 (FAS46), Financial Reporting and Changing Prices: Motion Picture Films*, Financial Accounting Board, Stamford, Conn., 31 March 1981.

FASB (1982a), *Statement of Financial Accounting Standards No. 54 (FAS54), Financial Reporting and Changing Prices: Investment Companies*, Financial Accounting Standards Board, Stamford, Conn., 27 January 1982.

FASB (1982b), *Statement of Financial Accounting Standards No. 69 (FAS69), Disclosures about Oil and Gas Producing Activities*, Financial Accounting Standards Board, Stamford, Conn., 5 December 1982.

FASB (1982c), *Statement of Financial Accounting Standards No. 70 (FAS70), Financial Reporting and Changing Prices: Foreign Currency Transactions*, Financial Accounting Standards Board, Stamford, Conn., 15 December 1982.

FASB (1983), *Conference: Research on Financial Reporting and Changing Prices*, Financial Accounting Standards Board, Stamford, Conn.

Fells, J. M. (1919), 'Some Principles Governing the Ascertainment of Cost', *Incorporated Accountants' Journal*, November 1919.

Financial Accounting Standards Board, see FASB.

Fisher, I. (1911), *The Purchasing Power of Money*, Macmillan, New York.

Fisher, I. (1925), *The Money Illusion*, Macmillan, New York.

Fisher, I. (1934), *Stable Money: A History of the Movement*, by Irving Fisher, assisted by Hans R. L. Cohrssen, Adelphi, New York.

Fleming, R. (1974), 'Accounting for Inflation in Brazil', *The Accountant's Magazine*, February 1974.

Fleming, R. (1979), 'New Concepts in Brazilian Accounting for Inflation', *The Accountant's Magazine*, April 1979.

Forrester, D. A. R. (1977), *Schmalenbach and After*, Strathclyde Convergencies, Glasgow.

Bibliography

Freeman, R. N. (1983), 'Research Conference Launches FSB Review of Statement 33', *Highlights of Financial Reporting Issues*, FASB, 28 February 1983.

Friedman, M. (1974), *Monetary Correction*, IEA Occasional Paper 41, Institute of Economic Affairs, London.

Frishkoff, P. (1982), *Financial Reporting and Changing Prices: A Review of Empirical Research*, FASB, Stamford, Conn.

Gee, K. and Peasnell, K. V. (1976), 'A Pragmatic Defence of Replacement Cost', *Accounting and Business Research*, Autumn 1976.

Gibbs, M. (1975), 'Why Sandilands is Not the Full Answer', *The Times*, 18 September 1975.

Gibbs, M. (1976), 'A Better Answer to the Problem of Inflation Accounting', *The Times*, 23 February 1976.

Gibbs, M., K. Percy and R. Saville (1976), *Sandilands – The Effect on Dividends*, Phillips and Drew, London.

Gibbs, M. and W. Seward, *ED24 – Morpeth's New Proposals*, Phillips and Drew, London.

Godley, W. and F. Cripps (1975), 'Profits, Stock Appreciation and The Sandilands Report', *The Times*, 1 October 1975.

Godley, W. and A. Wood (1974), 'Stock Appreciation and the Crisis of British Industry', Department of Applied Economics, Cambridge Mimeo, October 1974. Later published in *The Economic Policy Review*, 1975.

Goudeket, A. (1960), 'An Application of Replacement Value Theory', *Journal of Accountancy*, July 1960.

Green Paper on Corporation Tax (1982), Cmnd 8456, HMSO, London.

Griffin, P. A. (1982), *Usefulness to Investors and Creditors of Information Provided by Financial Reporting, A Review of Empirical Accounting Research* FASB, Stamford, Conn.

Gynther, R. S. (1966), *Accounting for Price-Level Changes: Theory and Procedures*, Pergamon, Oxford.

Gynther, R. S. (1967), 'Accounting Concepts and Behavioural Hypotheses', *The Accounting Review*, April 1967.

Gynther, R. S. (1976), 'Some Problems Associated with the Implementation of Current Value Accounting', *The Chartered Accountant in Australia*, July 1976.

Gynther, R. S. (1982), 'Accounting for Changing Prices: Developments in Australia and Overseas', *The Australian Accountant*, August 1982.

Haberler, G. (1941), *Prosperity and Depression*, League of Nations, Geneva.

Hamilton, S. (1977), 'Field Testing ED18: The Practical Reality', *The Accountant's Magazine*, May 1977.

Henderson, S. and G. Pierson (1977), *CCA and Purchasing Power Gains and Losses on Monetary Items*, Australian Accounting Research Foundation.

Hicks, J. R. (1946), *Value and Capital*, Clarendon Press, Oxford. Pp. 171–181 of the second edition (1946) are reprinted in Parker and Harcourt (1969).

Hofstra Report (1978), *An Inflation-Adjusted Tax System*, by H. J. Hofstra, Government Publishing Office, The Hague.

Bibliography

Holzer, P. and H. Schonfeld (1963a), 'The German Solution to the Post-War Price-Level Problem', *The Accounting Review*, April 1963.

Holzer, P. and H. Schonfeld (1963b), 'The French Approach to the Post-War Price-Level Problem', *The Accounting Review*, April 1963.

Hopkins, R. W. and A. J. Robb (1975), 'Inflation Accounting: An Interim Report of Practice', *Accountant's Journal*, February 1975.

Hyde Guidelines, see Accounting Standards Committee (1977).

IASG (Inflation Accounting Steering Group) (1976a) *Guidance Manual on Current Cost Accounting*, Tolley Publishing Co. and The Institute of Chartered Accountants in England and Wales.

IASG (Inflation Accounting Steering Group) (1976b), *Background Papers to the Exposure Draft on Current Cost Accounting*, Tolley Publishing Co. and The Institute of Chartered Accountants in England and Wales.

IASG (Inflation Accounting Steering Group) (1979), *Background Papers to ED24*, Tolley Publishing Co. and The Institute of Chartered Accountants in England and Wales.

IdW (Institut der Wirtschaftsprüfer) (1975), *Maintaining the 'Substantialistic Value' of an Enterprise when Determining the Annual Profit*, Federal Republic of Germany, December 1975.

Ijiri, Y. (1967), *The Foundations of Accounting Measurement: A Mathematical, Economic and Behavioural Inquiry*, Prentice-Hall, Englewood Cliffs, N.J.

Ijiri, Y. (1971), 'A Defence for Historical Cost Accounting', Chapter 1 of Sterling (1971).

Ijiri, Y. (1976), 'The Price-Level Restatement and Its Dual Interpretation', *The Accounting Review*, April 1976.

Institute of Chartered Accountants in Australia and Australian Society of Accountants (1974), *Preliminary Exposure Draft: Accounting for Changes in the Purchasing Power of Money*, December 1974.

Institute of Chartered Accountants in Australia and Australian Society of Accountants (1975), *Preliminary Exposure Draft: A Method of 'Current Value Accounting'*, June 1975.

Institute of Chartered Accountants in Australia and Australian Society of Accountants (1976), *Provisional Accounting Standard: Current Cost Accounting*, October 1976.

Institute of Chartered Accountants in Australia and Australian Society of Accountants (1983), *Statement of Accounting Practice No.1 (SAP1)*, ASA and ICAA.

Institute of Chartered Accountants in England and Wales (1949), 'Rising Price Levels in Relation to Accounts', *Recommendations on Accounting Principles*, N12, 14 January 1949.

Institute of Chartered Accountants in England and Wales (1952), 'Accounting in Relation to Changes in the Purchasing Power of Money', *Recommendations on Accounting Principles*, N15, 30 May 1952.

Institute of Chartered Accountants in England and Wales, Research Committee (1968), *Accounting for Stewardship in a Period of Inflation*, The Research

Bibliography

Foundation of the Institute of Chartered Accountants in England and Wales.

Institute of Chartered Accountants in England and Wales (1974), *A Review of the Relationship between Historical Cost Accounting, Current Purchasing Power Statements, and Replacement Cost Accounting.* A paper prepared for the Inflation Accounting Committee (Sandilands Committee), Accounting Standards Steering Committee, October 1974.

Institute of Cost and Works Accountants, Research and Technical Committee (1952), *The Accountancy of Changing Price Levels*, The Institute of Cost and Works Accountants.

Inter-American Accounting Review (1981), (Revista Interamericana de Contabilidad), No. 5, February–March, 1981, Inter-American Accounting Association, Mexico.

Jones, R. C. (1935), 'Financial Statements and the Uncertain Dollar', *Journal of Accountancy*, September 1935.

Jones, R. C. (1949), 'Effect of Inflation on Capital and Profits: The Record of Nine Steel Companies', *Journal of Accountancy*, January 1949.

Jones, R. C. (1955), *Price-Level Changes and Financial Statements – Case Studies of Four Companies*, American Accounting Association.

Jones, R. C. (1956), *Effects of Price-Level Changes on Business Income, Capital, and Taxes*, American Accounting Association.

Kay, J. A. and M. A. King (1978), *The British System of Taxation*, Oxford University Press.

Kelly, E. (1981), 'How Inflation Was Reported in 1980', *The Chartered Accountant in Australia*, April 1981.

Kennedy, C. (1976), 'Inflation Accounting, Profits, Profitability and Share Valuation', *Journal of Business Finance and Accounting*, Spring 1976.

Kennedy, C. (1978a), 'Inflation Accounting: Retrospect and Prospect', *Cambridge Economic Policy Review*, 1978.

Kennedy, C. (1978b), 'Fixed Assets and the Hyde Gearing Adjustment', *Journal of Business Finance and Accounting*, Winter 1978.

Keynes, J. M. (1936), *The General Theory of Employment, Interest and Money*, Macmillan, London.

Klaassen, J. (1979), 'The Practice of Current Value Accounting in The Netherlands' in Wanless and Forrester (1979).

Kovero, I. (1912), *Die Bewertung der Vermögensgegenstände in den Jahresbilanzen der Privaten Unternehmungen mit Besonderer Berücksichtigung der Nicht Realisierten Verluste und Gewinne*, Berlin.

Lacey, K. (1952), *Profit Measurement and Price Changes*, Pitman, Bath.

Lawson, G. H. (1971), 'Cash Flow Accounting', *The Accountant*, 28 October and 4 November 1971.

Leach, Sir R., and E. Stamp (1981), *British Accounting Standards, the First 10 Years*, Woodhead-Faulkner, Cambridge.

Lee, T. A. (1972), 'A Case for Cash Flow Reporting', *Journal of Business Finance*, Summer 1972.

Bibliography

Lee, T. A. and R. H. Parker (eds.) (1979), *The Evolution of Corporate Financial Reporting*, Nelson, Sunbury-on-Thames.

Lee, T. A. (ed.) (1981), *Developments in Financial Reporting*, Phillip Allan, Deddington, Oxford.

Lee, T. A. and D. P. Tweedie (1977), *The Private Shareholder and The Corporate Report*, The Institute of Chartered Accountants in England and Wales.

Lee, T. A. and D. P. Tweedie (1981), *The Institutional Investor and Financial Information*, The Institute of Chartered Accountants in England and Wales.

Leger, F. (1926), *Le Redressement des Bilans en Francs-papier*, Editions Experta, Paris.

Liesner, T. and M. A. King (Eds.) (1975), *Indexing for Inflation*, IFS/Heinemann, London.

Limperg, T. (1964), *Bedrijfseconomie, Verzameld Werk* (Industrial Economy, Collected Works), Kluwer, Deventer.

London Society of Chartered Accountants (1977), *Submission on ED18*, May 1977.

MacDonald, E. B. (1977), 'Postscript' to Goudeket (1960), in Baxter and Davidson (1977).

MacNeal, K. (1939), *Truth in Accounting*, University of Pennsylvania Press.

McRae, T. W. and R. Dobbins (1974), 'Behavioural Aspects of the Inflation Accounting Controversy', *Accounting and Business Research*, Spring 1974.

Macve, R. (1981), *A Conceptual Framework for Financial Accounting and Reporting. The Possibilities of an Agreed Structure*. A report prepared at the request of the Accounting Standards Committee, ICAEW.

Mahlberg, W. (1923), *Bilanztechnik und Bewertung bei Schwankender Waehrung*, 3rd edition, Kapitel III, Leipzig.

Mason, P. (1956), *Price-Level Changes and Financial Statements, Basic Concepts and Methods*, American Accounting Association.

Mathews Report (1975), see Committee of Inquiry into Inflation and Taxation.

Mathews, R. L. (1955), 'Accounting and Economic Concepts', *The Australian Accountant*, April 1955.

Mathews, R. L. (1965), 'Price-Level Changes and Useless Information', *Journal of Accounting Research*, 1965.

Mathews, R. L. (1977), 'The Shift to Current Values: The Mathews and Richardson Reports', *The Accountant's Journal*, April 1977.

Mathews, R. L. (1980), 'The Mathews Report on Business Taxation: A Reply', *The Economic Record*, September 1980.

Mathews, R. L. and J. McB. Grant (1958), *Inflation and Company Finance*, The Law Book Co., Sydney.

Mattessich, R. (1964), *Accounting and Analytical Methods*, Irwin, Homewood, Illinois.

Mattessich, R. (1980), 'An Evolutionary Survey and Comparison of Current Cost and General Purchasing Power Hypotheses and their Applications'.

381

Bibliography

Unpublished paper read to the International Accounting Historians' Congress.

May, G. O. (1949), *Business Income and Price Levels. An Accounting Study*, Study Group on Business Income, 1 July 1949.

Meade, J. E. (1978), *The Structure and Reform of Direct Taxation*. Report of a Committee chaired by Professor J. E. Meade, Institute for Fiscal Studies, George Allen & Unwin, London.

Meeks, G. (1974), 'Polemics and Policy on Profits under Inflation', *AUTA Review*, Autumn/Winter 1974.

Merrett, A. J. and A. Sykes (1974a), 'The Real Crisis Now Facing Britain's Industry', *Financial Times*, 30 September 1974.

Merrett, A. J. and A. Sykes (1974b), 'Stock Profits: A Business Wonderland?', *The Times*, 7 November 1974.

Merrett, A. J. and A. Sykes (1980), 'Inflation Accounting: How Badly Flawed Is ED24?', *The Times*, 11 February 1980.

Mexican Institute of Public Accountants (1980), *Bulletin on Principles of Accounting, B7: Disclosure of the Effects of Inflation on Financial Information*, Mexico, January 1980.

Mey, A. (1966), 'Theodore Limperg and his Theory of Values and Costs', *Abacus*, September 1966.

Middleditch, L. (1918), 'Should Accounts Reflect the Changing Value of the Dollar?', *Journal of Accountancy*, February 1918. Reprinted in Zeff (1976a).

Moonitz, M. and C. L. Nelson (1960), 'Recent Developments in Accounting Theory', *The Accounting Review*, April 1960.

Morison, A. M. C. (1970), 'The Role of the Reporting Accountant Today', *The Accountant's Magazine*, September and October 1970.

Morpeth, D. S. (1981), 'Developing a Current Cost Accounting Standard', Chapter 4 of Leach and Stamp (1981).

Mumford, M. (1978), 'Indices and the Hyde Gearing Adjustment', *The Accountant's Magazine*, October 1978.

Mumford, M. (1979), 'The End of a Familiar Inflation Accounting Cycle', *Accounting and Business Research*, Spring 1979.

Murphy and Most (1959), see Schmalenbach (1959).

Myddelton, D. R. (1981), 'The Neglected Merits of CPP', Chapter 6 of Leach and Stamp (1981).

National Council of Chartered Accountants (South Africa) (1975), *Accounting for Inflation and Other Changes in the Price Level*, January 1975.

National Council of Chartered Accountants (South Africa) (1978), *Guideline on Disclosure of Effects of Changing Prices on Financial Results*, August 1978.

Nelson, C. L. (1973), 'A Priori Research in Accounting', in Dopuch and Revsine (1973).

New Zealand Society of Accountants (1975), *Exposure Draft: Accounting for Changes in the Purchasing Power of Money*, Wellington, March 1975.

Bibliography

New Zealand Society of Accountants (1976), *Exposure Draft: Accounting in Terms of Current Costs and Values*, Wellington, August 1976.

New Zealand Society of Accountants (1978), *CCA Guidelines*, Wellington, December 1978.

New Zealand Society of Accountants (1981), *Exposure Draft: Current Cost Accounting*, Wellington, August 1981.

New Zealand Society of Accountants (1982), *Current Cost Accounting Standard No.1: Information Reflecting the Effects of Changing Prices*, Wellington, March 1982.

NIVRA (Nederlands Instituut van Registeraccountants) (1976), Addendum to *Exposure Draft No.6, 'Accounting for Changing Prices'*, of the International Accounting Standards Committee.

Nobes, C. and R. H. Parker (eds.) (1981), *Comparative International Accounting*, Phillip Allan, Deddington, Oxford.

Ordre des Experts Contables et des Comptables Agréés (1981), *Opinion on the Establishment of Certain Data Adjusted for the Effects of Changing Prices*, France, March 1981.

Parker, R. H. and G. C. Harcourt (1969), *Readings in the Concept and Measurement of Income*, Cambridge University Press.

Parker, W. E. (1962), 'Changes in Purchasing Power of Money', *The Accountant*, 3 and 10 November 1962.

Parker, W. E. (1971), 'Accounting for Inflation', *Accountancy*, December 1971.

Paton, W. A. (1918), 'The Significance and Treatment of Appreciation in the Accounts', pp. 35–49 of the *Twentieth Annual Report* of the Michigan Academy of Science, Ann Arbor, Michigan. Reprinted in Zeff (1976a).

Paton, W. A. (1920), 'Depreciation, Appreciation and Productive Capacity', *Journal of Accountancy*, July 1920. Reprinted in Zeff (1976a).

Paton, W. A. and A. C. Littleton (1940), *An Introduction to Corporate Accounting Standards*, American Accounting Association.

Peasnell, K. V. (1977), 'A Note on the Discounted Present Value Concept', *The Accounting Review*, January 1977.

Peasnell, K. V. (1978), 'Interaction Effects in CCA Valuation', *Accounting and Business Research*, Spring 1978.

Peasnell, K. V. (1982), 'The Function of a Conceptual Framework for Corporate Financial Reporting', *Accounting and Business Research*, Autumn 1982.

Peasnell, K. V. and L. C. L. Skerratt (1976), *Current Cost Accounting: The Index Number Problem*, International Centre for Research in Accounting, University of Lancaster.

Prest, A. R. (1950), 'Replacement Cost Depreciation', *Accounting Research*, July 1950. Reprinted in Parker and Harcourt (1969).

Price Waterhouse International (1979), *International Survey of Accounting Principles and Reporting Practices*, Price Waterhouse International, New York.

Price Waterhouse (1980), *Disclosure of the Effects of Inflation: An Analysis*, Price Waterhouse & Co., New York.

383

Bibliography

PSSAP7 (1974), see Accounting Standards Steering Committee (1974).

Revsine, L. (1970), 'On the Correspondence Between Replacement Cost Income and Economic Income', *The Accounting Review*, July 1970.

Revsine, L. (1973), *Replacement Cost Accounting*, Prentice-Hall, Englewood Cliffs, NJ.

Revsine, L. (1976), 'Surrogates in Accounting Theory: A Comment', *The Accounting Review*, January 1976.

Richardson Committee Report (1976), *The Report of the Committee of Inquiry into Inflation Accounting*, New Zealand Government Printer, Wellington.

Rickard, D. R. (1978), 'Current Cost Accounting: Update', *The Australian Accountant*, August 1978.

Royal Commission on the Taxation of Profits and Income (1955) (the Radcliffe Committee), *Final Report*, Cmnd. 9474, HMSO, London.

Ryan, J. B. (1978), 'The Theoretical Basis of the Richardson Committee Report', paper presented at the AUTA Conference, University of Exeter, 1978.

Sale, T. and R. Scapens (1978), 'Current Cost Accounting as a Surrogate for Dividend Paying Ability', *Accounting and Business Research*, Summer 1978.

Sampson, C. (1983), 'A Regulator's View of the FASB, the First 10 Years and After', *Journal of Accountancy*, August 1983.

Samuelson, R. A. (1980), 'Should Replacement-Cost Changes Be Included in Income?', *The Accounting Review*, April 1980.

Sandilands, Sir F. (1978), *Inflation and Business Enterprise*, The Stamp Memorial Lecture, 10 October 1978, University of London.

Sandilands Committee (1975), *Inflation Accounting: Report of the Inflation Accounting Committee Under the Chairmanship of F.E.P. Sandilands*, Cmnd 6225, HMSO, September 1975.

Scapens, R. W. (1973 and 1975), *The Treatment of Inflation in the Published Account of Companies in Overseas Countries*, Research Committee Occasional Paper No. 1, The Institute of Chartered Accountants in England and Wales, first edition 1973, second edition 1975.

Schiff, E. (1933), *Kapitalbildung und Kapitalanfzehrung im Konjunkturverlauf*, Vienna.

Schmalenbach, E. (1919), *Dynamische Bilanz* (Dynamic Accounting), Westdeutscher Verlay, GmbH, Koeln and Opladen.

Schmalenbach, E. (1959), *Dynamic Accounting*, 12th edition, translated from the German by G. W. Murphy and K. S. Most, Gee & Co., London.

Schmidt, F. (1921), *Die Organische Bilanz im Rahmen der Wirtschaft*, Gloeckner, Leipzig.

Schmidt, F. (1926), 'Die Bilanzbewertung und der Gewinn' in *Het Internationaal Accountantscongress, Amsterdam, 1926*, J. Muisses, Purmerend (The Netherlands).

Schmidt, F. (1927), *Die Industrienkonjunktur ein Rechenfehler*, Berlin.

Schmidt, F. (1930), 'The Importance of Replacement Value', *The Accounting Review*, Vol. 5. Reprinted in Zeff (1976a).

Bibliography

Schmidt, F. (1931), 'Is Appreciation Profit?', *The Accounting Review*, Vol. 6. Reprinted in Zeff (1976a).

Schmidt, F. (1952), 'The Relative Maintenance of an Enterprise', *Zeitschrift für Betriebswirtschaft*, April 1952.

Schultz, H. E. and others (1976), *Economic Calculation Under Inflation*, The Liberty Press, Indianapolis.

Schwantag, K. (1951), 'Fritz Schmidt's Academic Work', *Zeitschrift für Betriebswirtschaft*, January 1951.

Scott, M. F. G. (1976), *Some Economic Principles of Accounting: A Constructive Critique of the Sandilands Report*, IFS Lecture Series, No.7, The Institute for Fiscal Studies.

SEC (1974), *Accounting Series Release No.151 (ASR151) Disclosure of Inventory Profits Reflected in Income in Periods of Rising Prices*, Washington, 3 January 1974.

SEC (1975a), 'Announcement of Intention to Release a Proposal to Require Replacement Cost Disclosure', *Journal of Accountancy*, June 1975.

SEC (1975b), *Notice of Proposed Amendments to Regulations S–X to Require Disclosure of Certain Replacement Cost Data in Notes to Financial Statements*, SEC, Washington, 21 August 1975.

SEC (1976), *Accounting Series Release No. 190 (ASR190), Amendments to Regulations S–X Requiring Disclosure of Certain Replacement Cost Data*, Washington, 23 March 1976.

SEC (1978), *Accounting Series Release No. 253 (ASR253), Adoption of Requirements for Financial Accounting and Reporting Practices for Oil and Gas Producing Activities*, Washington, August 1978.

SEC (1979), *45th Annual Report of the Securities and Exchange Commission for the Fiscal Year Ended September 30, 1979*, Washington.

SEC (1981), *Accounting Series Release No. 289 (ASR289), Financial Reporting by Oil and Gas Producers*, Washington, 26 February 1981.

Skerratt, L. C. L. (ed.) (1980), *Survey of Published Accounts 1979*, ICAEW, London.

Solomons, D. (1961), 'Economic and Accounting Concepts of Income', *The Accounting Review*, Vol. 36. Reprinted in Parker and Harcourt (1969).

Solomons, D. (1966a), 'Economic and Accounting Concepts of Cost and Value', Chapter 6 of M. Backer (ed.), *Modern Accounting Theory*, Prentice-Hall, Englewood Cliffs, NJ.

Solomons, D. (1966b), 'Review of Chambers (1966)', *Abacus*, December 1966.

Solomons, D. (1974), *Prospectus for a Profession. The Report of the Long Range Enquiry into Education and Training for the Accountancy Profession*, Advisory Board of Accountancy Education (distributed by Gee & Co., London).

Solomons, D. (1979), 'The Politicization of Accounting', pp. 25–39 of Zeff, Demski and Dopuch (1979).

Sprouse, R. (1976), 'Inflation Accounting Principles, and Accounting Profession', Chapter 2 of Schultz (1976).

385

Bibliography

Sprouse, R. and M. Moonitz (1962), *A Tentative Set of Broad Accounting Principles for Business Enterprises*, Accounting Research Study No. 3, American Institute of Certified Public Accountants, New York.

SSAP16, see Accounting Standards Committee (1980a).

Stamp, E. (1971), 'Income and Value Determination and Changing Price Levels: An Essay Towards a Theory', *The Accountant's Magazine*, July 1971.

Stamp, E. (1972), 'R. J. Chambers: Quo Vadis et Cui Bono', *Chartered Accountant in Australia*, August 1972.

Stamp, E. (1975), 'The Valuation of Assets', *CA Magazine*, November 1975.

Stamp, E. (1979), 'Financial Reports on an Entity: Ex Uno Plures', Chapter 8 of Sterling and Thomas (1979).

Stamp, E. (1980), *Corporate Reporting: Its Future Evolution* (the Stamp Report), Canadian Institute of Chartered Accountants, Toronto.

Staubus, G. J. (1971), 'The Relevance of Evidence of Cash Flows', Chapter 3 of Sterling (1971).

Sterling, R. R. (1970), *Theory of the Measurement of Enterprise Income*, University Press of Kansas.

Sterling, R. R. (ed.) (1971), *Asset Valuation and Income Determination, a Consideration of the Alternatives*, Scholars Book Co., Houston, Texas.

Sterling, R. R. and A. L. Thomas (eds.) (1979), *Accounting for a Simplified Firm Owning Depreciable Assets*, Scholars Book Co., Houston, Texas.

Study Group on Business Income (1950), *Five Monographs on Business Income*, American Institute of Accountants, New York.

Study Group on Business Income (1952), *Changing Concepts of Business Income*, American Institute of Accountants, New York.

Study Group on the Objectives of Financial Statements (1973), *Objectives of Financial Statements* (The Trueblood Report), American Institute of Certified Public Accountants, New York, October 1973.

Sweeney, H. W. (1927), 'Effects of Inflation on German Accounting', *Journal of Accountancy*, July 1920. Reprinted in Zeff (1976a).

Sweeney, H. W. (1928), 'German Inflation Accounting', *Journal of Accountancy*, February 1928. Reprinted in Zeff (1976a).

Sweeney, H. W. (1931), 'Stabilized Depreciation', *The Accounting Review*, Vol.6. Reprinted in Zeff (1976a).

Sweeney, H. W. (1933a), 'Capital', *The Accounting Review*, Vol. 8. Reprinted in Zeff (1976a).

Sweeney, H. W. (1933b), 'Income', *The Accounting Review*, September 1933. Reprinted in Zeff (1976a).

Sweeney, H. W. (1934), 'How Inflation Affects Balance Sheets', *The Accounting Review*, December 1934. Reprinted in Zeff (1976a).

Sweeney, H. W. (1935), 'The Technique of Stabilized Accounting', *The Accounting Review*, Vol.10. Reprinted in Zeff (1976a).

Sweeney, H. W. (1936), *Stabilized Accounting*, Harper, New York. Reprinted, 1964, by Holt, Rinehart and Winston, New York, with a new Foreword by

W. A. Paton and an essay 'Forty Years After: Or Stabilized Accounting Revisited', by H. W. Sweeney.

Sweeney, H. W. (1964a), 'Forty Years After: Or Stabilized Accounting Revisited', pp. xvii–xxxix of the 1964 reissue of *Stabilised Accounting*, Holt, Rinehart and Winston, New York.

Sweeney, H. W. (1964b), 'Review Article: Staff of the Accounting Research Division: Reporting the Financial Effects of Price-Level Changes', *The Accounting Review*, October 1964.

Thomas, A. L. (1969), *The Allocation Problem in Financial Accounting Theory*, Studies in Accounting Research 3, American Accounting Association.

Thomas, A. L. (1974), *The Allocation Problem: Part Two*, Studies in Accounting Research 9, American Accounting Association.

Trueblood Committee Report (1973), see Study Group on the Objectives of Financial Statements.

Tweedie, D. P. (1978), 'The Hyde Guidelines – How Are They to be Interpreted?', *The Accountant's Magazine*, April 1978.

Tweedie, D. P. (1979), *Financial Reporting, Inflation, and the Capital Maintenance Concept*, International Centre for Research in Accounting, University of Lancaster.

Tweedie, D. P. (1981a), 'Simplified Financial Statements', in Lee (1981).

Tweedie, D. P. (1981b), 'Standards, Objectives and the Corporate Report' in Leach and Stamp (1981).

Tweedie, D. P. (1983a), 'The ASC in Chains: Whither Self-Regulation Now?', *Accountancy*, March 1983.

Tweedie, D. P. (1983b), 'True and Fair Rules', *The Accountant's Magazine*, November 1983.

Wanless, P. T. and D. A. R. Forrester (eds.) (1979), *Readings in Inflation Accounting*, Wiley.

Wasserman, M. J. (1931), 'Accounting Practice in France during the Period of Monetary Inflation (1919–1927)', *The Accounting Review*, March 1931. Reprinted in Zeff (1976a).

Watts, R. L. and J. L. Zimmerman (1978), 'Towards a Positive Theory of the Determination of Accounting Standards', *The Accounting Review*, January 1978.

Watts, R. L. and J. L. Zimmerman (1979), 'The Demand for and Supply of Accounting Theories: The Market for Excuses', *The Accounting Review*, April 1979.

Westwick, C. A. (1980), 'The Lessons to be Learned from the Development of Inflation Accounting in the UK', *Accounting and Business Research*, Autumn 1980.

Whittington, G. (1974), 'Asset Valuation, Income Measurement and Accounting Income', *Accounting and Business Research*, Spring 1974.

Whittington, G. (1976), 'Indexation: A Review Article', *Accounting and Business Research*, Summer 1976.

Whittington, G. (1980), 'Pioneers of Income Measurement and Price-Level

Bibliography

Accounting: A Review Article', *Accounting and Business Research*, Spring 1980.

Whittington, G. (1981a), 'Inflation Accounting – What Next?', Chapter 5 of Leach and Stamp (1981).

Whittington, G. (1981b), 'The British Contribution to Income Theory', Chapter 1 of *Essays in British Accounting Research*, edited by Michael Bromwich and Anthony Hopwood, Pitman, Bath.

Whittington, G. (1983a), *Inflation Accounting: An Introduction to the Debate*, Cambridge University Press.

Whittington, G. (1983b), 'SSAP16 and the Future', *The Accountant*, April 1983.

Wright, F. K. (1964), 'Towards a General Theory of Depreciation', *Journal of Accounting Research*, Vol. 2. Reprinted in Parker and Harcourt (1969).

Zeff, S. A. (1964), 'Episodes in the Progression of Price-Level Accounting in the US', *The Accountant's Magazine*, 1964. Reprinted in Chatfield (1968).

Zeff, S. A. (ed.) (1976a), *Asset Appreciation, Business Income and Price-Level Accounting, 1918–1935*, Arno Press, New York.

Zeff, S. A. (1976b), 'Response' to Sprouse (1976). In Schultz (1976).

Zeff, S. A. (1978), 'The Rise of Economic Consequences', *Journal of Accountancy*, December 1978.

Zeff, S. A. (1979a), 'Paton on the Effects of Changing Prices', Chapter 7 of Zeff, Demski and Dopuch (1979).

Zeff, S. A. (1979b), 'Chronology–Significant Development in the Establishment of Accounting Principles in the United States, 1936–1978', in Lee and Parker (1979).

Zeff, S. A. (1981), 'The Ordeal of Kenneth MacNeal', *Working Paper No. 8*, Jesse H. Jones Graduate School of Administration, Rice University, Houston.

Zeff, S. A., J. Demski and N. Dopuch (eds.) (1979), *Essays in Honour of William A. Paton*, University of Michigan.

Zeff, S. A. and H. Ovando Z. (1975), 'Inflation Accounting and the Development of Accounting Principles in Chile', *The Accountant's Magazine*, June 1975.

Name index

Name index

Name index

Subject index

Subject index

Subject index

conceptual framework project, *see under* Financial Accounting Standards Board
Confederation of British Industry, 48, 50, 144
constant dollar accounting, *see* constant purchasing power accounting
constant purchasing power accounting, 6, 72, 261–5, 270
  in Argentina, 236–7
  asset valuation, 275, 277, 300
  in Australia, 36, 59, 192–6, 198
  in Brazil, 36, 234–40
  in Canada, 36, 59, 216–18
  and capital maintenance concept, 90, 104, 264, 275
  in Chile, 36, 234–6, 240–3
  developments 1945–74, 36–7, 52–3
  disliked by companies, 68–73, 269
  disliked by governments, 269, 307–8
  example, 6–7
  in France, 20, 233
  gain on borrowing, 63–4, 264, 294–5, 296
  in Germany, 18–20, 102, 262
  high inflation rate leads to CPP solutions, 305, 315–16
  in Latin America, 216, 234–43, 246, 264
  in Mexico, 36
  in The Netherlands, 227–8
  in New Zealand, 36, 59, 204–5, 210, 212, 214
  present position, 58, 248–52, 254–5
  and Schmalenbach, 20–3
  and self-interest, 307, 309–10, 320–6
  in South Africa, 36, 59, 216, 222–3
  supported by profession, 70–2, 309–10
  and Sweeney, 32–4, 263
  in UK, 44–52, 60–83; abandoned by ASC, 142; in *Accounting for Stewardship*, 46–7, 49, 63, 68, 264; advocated in reactions to Sandilands Report, 104; considered by IASG during drafting of *ED18*, 115; in *ED8*, 51, 59, 60, 63–73; failure of general index approach, 87, 88; favoured by ASSC, 50, 103; implications for government policies, 76–7; opposed by industry, commerce and the financial community, 63–4, 68–70, 85, 86–7; opposed by Sandilands Committee, 96–102, 103; in *PSSAP7*, 82–3; in responses to *ED18*, 125, 134; supported by profession, 63, 66–8, 70–2, 86–7; in 'the Tombstone document', 48–50
  in USA, 36, 38–44, 59, 154–89, 263; in

FAS33, 170–9; in FASB's conceptual framework project, 175–9; in FASB's field study, 168–70; and the SEC–FASB relationship, 156–68; and specialised assets, 182, 184
  in Western Europe, 233
Consultative Committee of Accountancy Bodies
  'compromise' system, 113, 115–16, 121–2
  'ideal' system, 113, 115, 121–2
  Initial Reactions to Sandilands Report, 103–6, 109, 112, 121, 147; monetary items, 111, 113, 115–16, 121; RT system, 272–3; supplementary statement of equity interest, 109, 112, 147
continuously contemporary accounting, 191, 198, 204
The Corporate Report, 102–3, 273, 309, 330
cost of sales adjustment
  in Australia, 195, 198, 202
  in Germany, 231
  to include working capital in Gibbs' system, 290–1
  in New Zealand, 205, 207, 211, 220, 223
  in UK, 97, 108, 111, 132–4, 138–40, 149
CPP, *see* constant purchasing power accounting
current cost accounting, 7–8, 59, 261, 265–70
  in Australia, 196–204, 248, 267–9; eclectic valuation approach, 191; monetary items, 199–202; *SAP1*, 203
  basis of opposition, 72, 104
  in Canada, 219–22, 248
  and capital maintenance concept, 90, 104, 275, 281–94
  example, 7
  in France, 233
  gain on borrowing, 295–301, 302
  involves arbitrary allocations, 56
  large relative price changes lead to CCA solutions, 305, 346
  in Latin America, 236–7
  in The Netherlands, 224–9
  in New Zealand, 204–15, 248, 269–70; in the Richardson Report, 206–10
  present position, 248–52, 258
  and Schmalenbach, 21
  and Schmidt, 25–6, 29
  and self-interest, 307, 308–10, 320–6
  in South Africa, 223
  in Sweden, 224–5
  in UK, 95–153, 248, 269–70, 279; considered by IASG during drafting of *ED18*, 107–24; in *The Corporate*

395

Subject index

entity concept of capital maintenance, 91,
249–52, 265, 272, 282–94
advocated by Gynther, 57, 200–1
in Australia, 190–1, 196, 200–3
in CCA, 275
discarded by Sweeney, 24
and gearing adjustment, 296
and Limperg, 31–2, 57
present position, 250–1, 254–5, 257, 258
in retreat because of problems of
defining operating capacity, 301
and Schmidt, 26–7, 57
in UK: characteristic of Merrett and
Sykes' analysis, 90–2, 95; considered
by IASG during drafting of *ED18*,
104, 113–14, 120–4; in *ED24*, 142, 145;
in evidence to Sandilands Committee,
86–7; and ICWA and ACCA, 45–6
in Western Europe, 233, 316
European Community, 225
aids international transmission of ideas,
317
Fourth Directive, 335; effect on UK,
335, 345; in The Netherlands, 227,
229; provided support for ASC, 147
Sandilands Report and EC Directives,
112–13
West Germany and EC Directives, 229

fair value, 17, 180–6
FAR, *see* Förenigen Auktoriserade
Revisorer
FAS33, 40, 155–6, 170–9, 250–1, 270
capital maintenance concept, 167, 178,
283
first standard to require RT data, 272,
273
influence of *ARS6* and Sweeney, 33
influence of conceptual framework
project, 176–9
influence of Edwards and Bell, 54
influenced CICA's 1981 Exposure Draft,
221
monetary items treatment different from
Australasian treatment, 213
operating capacity, 172, 176, 284
permits format preferred by Tweedie
and Whittington, 343
and specialised assets, 179–80, 182–4
valuation, 280
FASB, *see* Financial Accounting Standards
Board
Financial Accounting Standards Board,
154–89, 312, 328–31, 337
conceptual framework project, 163–6,
175–9, 188, 328, 331; CPP proposals of

1974 did not prejudge conceptual
framework project, 43; 'information
set' approach, 54; SEC's attitude, 185
1978 Exposure Draft, 165–8
FAS33, 170–9
field study, 168–70
and the SEC, 156–68, 179–89
and specialised assets, 179–84
valuation, 277–80
financial capital maintenance, 172–3, 186,
281–2
adopted in CPP gain on borrowing, 296
present position, 257
in USA, 164, 167, 316
see also proprietary concept of capital
maintenance
Ford Motor Co., 138
Förenigen Auktoriserade Revisorer, 224
France, 216, 224–5, 231–3
developments to 1975, 36–7
influence on development of inflation
accounting, 20, 262
present position, 253–5, 257, 258

gain on borrowing, 294–302
in *ARS6*, 40–1
in Australia, 200–3
in CCA, 9, 267, 295–301, 302
in CPP, 6, 63–4, 263–4
early form of taxation of gain on
borrowing in France, 232
made explicit in Tweedie and
Whittington's proposed method, 343
present position, 250–1, 254–5
in Richardson Report, 209–10
in RT, 296, 300–1
Schmidt argued against recognising gain
on borrowing, 28
in UK: considered by IASG during
drafting of *ED18*, 116–21, 358n.15; in
ED8, 63–4, 69, 73; excluded from
profit by Merrett and Sykes, 90; in the
Hyde Guidelines, 95; in *PSSAP7*, 83;
and Sandilands, 86–7, 98, 101, 104
gearing adjustment, 9–10, 34, 92–5, 267–9,
295–302
in Australia, 201
in Canada, 219–22, 269
example, 9
in France, 233
in Germany, 252, 295–9
in The Netherlands, 228, 298–9
in New Zealand, 209–12, 214, 248, 270,
295, 297–9
present position, 250–1, 254–5, 257
Schmidt an early advocate of, 28–9

Subject index

Subject index

international harmonisation (*contd*)
  demanded for capital maintenance, 145, 151
  facilitated by use of Tweedie and Whittington's proposed method, 345
  in gearing adjustment, 147
  and multi-nationals, 131, 188
  reason for adoption of CPP in Australasia, 214
  within EC, 225
international transmission of ideas, 36, 242, 245, 304, 315–17

last in, first out, 35, 38, 46, 111
Latin America, 36–7, 216, 234–43, 245–7, 253, 264
  see also under individual countries
LIFO, *see* last in, first out
liquidity, 83, 90, 95, 98, 119–20
London Society of Chartered Accountants, 138

market values, 25, 184, 265, 276
  see also current cost accounting; current value accounting; value to the business
Mathews Committee, 37, 59, 86, 296–7
  see also Mathews Report
Mathews Report, 57, 190, 194–7, 269
  considered by Richardson Committee, 206
  considered by SEC, 159, 161, 188
  operating capacity, 285–7
  valuation, 278
  see also Mathews Committee
Mexico, 36, 237, 241
Millard Tucker Committee, 45
monetary items, 7, 8, 33, 249–52, 269–70
  in Australia, 197, 199–202
  in Canada, 220
  in New Zealand, 207–11, 297
  and operating capacity, 286–94
  research into views on monetary items needed, 332
  in Sweden, 224
  in UK: in *Accounting for Stewardship*, 47; considered by IASG during drafting of *ED18*, 111–24; in *ED8*, 51; in the Hyde Guidelines, 137, 139–40; in reactions to *ED18*, 132–5; in Sandilands Report, 97, 104–5; in *SSAP16*, 146
  in USA, 40–1, 43, 166, 169–70, 171
  see also monetary working capital adjustment
monetary working capital adjustment, 10, 119, 349n.7, 358n.14

in Australia, 191, 201, 213, 248
in Canada, 220, 269, 292
and gearing adjustment, 300
in New Zealand, 211, 213, 269
present position, 250–2, 254–5
in UK, 118–20, 138–46, 269; advocated by ICAEW, 134; in *ED24*, 142–5; in the Gibbs system, 118–20, 291; in the Hyde Guidelines, 138–9, 140, 300; in *SSAP16*, 145–6
money capital, 27, 91–2
multiple profit figures, 69, 103
  see also 'information set' approach
multiple values for assets, 11, 103, 339
MWCA, *see* monetary working capital adjustment

Nederlands Instituut van Registeraccountants, 227–8
  opposed *ED8*, 66
  RT solution, 227, 248, 270, 273
  and Sandilands Committee, 86
  valuation, 278
net realisable value, 266, 271–2
  advocated by Chambers, 55–6
  advocated by Thomas, 56
  considered by AASC, 196–7, 198
  in *FAS33*, 171
  in New Zealand, 205–7
  see also continuously contemporary accounting; value to the business
The Netherlands, 216, 224–9
  developed replacement cost accounting, 36, 225–7
  gearing adjustment, 228, 298–9
  Hofstra Report, 227–8
  influence of Limperg, 226–7
  input to Richardson Report, 206
  move towards RT, 227, 248, 270, 273
  NIVRA's 1976 statement, 227–8
  operating capacity, 292–3
  present position, 248–52, 257, 258, 270
  proposed method of Tweedie and Whittington also proposed in The Netherlands, 344–5
  theoretical framework for standard-setters, 331
  valuation, 278
  visit by Sandilands Committee, 86
Neville Working Party, 149–50
New Zealand, 190–2, 204–15
  calculation of CC income, 301
  capital maintenance concept, 283
  CCA Exposure Draft, 205–6
  CCA after Richardson, 210–13

399

Subject index

Subject index

Subject index

Study Group on Business Income, 38–9, 52
Sweden, 224–5, 253–5, 257, 258, 273, 344–5

taxation, 306, 307
  in Australia, 192, 194–6, 204, 269
  discouraged revision of HC accounting
    in France and Germany, 307, 335
  fears of taxation evasion under CCA, 246
  in France, 224, 231–2
  in Latin America, 237–43, 264, 366n.29
  in The Netherlands, 227–8, 299
  in South Africa, 223
  in terms of reference for Richardson
    Committee, 206
  in UK: CCA basis, 228; effect of stock
    relief, 95–6, 306; effects of inflation
    accounting on the taxation base, 77–9,
    84, 299; encouraged CCA, 307; fiscal
    drag, 77–8; gain on borrowing in the
    taxation base, 73; general index for
    stock relief and capital gains taxation
    base, 273; ICAEW attitude, 45; not
    treated in Sandilands Report, 98; in
    the 'profits crisis', 89–95
  in USA, 162
  in West Germany, 230
Tesco, 126
theory
  capital maintenance concept, 91–2,
    249–52, 271–2, 281–94, 314
  CCA, 7–8, 9–10, 265–70
  CPP, 6–7, 262–3
  developments 1945–74, 52–8
  gain on borrowing, 294–302
  gearing adjustment, 9–10, 295–301
  HC accounting, 5–6
  ignorance of theory among participants
    in debate, 312, 318, 329
  influence on debate, 37, 188, 191, 243,
    303, 311–15
  operating capacity, 283–94
  rôle in standard-setting, 329–30, 332
  RT, 8–9, 271–4
  valuation, 275–81
  see also debate
'the Tombstone document', 48–50
Touche Ross, 161
trade cycle, 26, 53
Trueblood Report, 156–8, 161, 165, 273,
  309, 328
  emphasised needs of users of accounts,
    330

UK, see United Kingdom
uncertainty in income measurement, see
  'information set' approach

United Kingdom, 60–153
  and Australia, 192, 198, 201, 213–15
  and Canada, 216–17
  CCA, 95–153, 248, 269–70
  The Corporate Report, 102–3
  CPP, 44–52, 60–83, 264
  debate 1973–80, 60–3
  developments 1945–74, 44–52
  ED8, 63–73
  ED18 and the IASG, 107–37
  ED24, 140–5
  effect of EC Fourth Directive, 335, 345
  gearing adjustment, 295–6, 298, 300
  government intervention, 74–80
  the Hyde Guidelines, 137–40
  lacks a theoretical framework, 329–30
  move towards RT, 273
  and The Netherlands, 227–8
  and New Zealand, 205, 206, 209, 212–15
  operating capacity, 284–6, 289, 291–2
  present position, 248–52, 257, 258
  the 'profits crisis', 90–5
  PSSAP7, 81–3
  Sandilands, 83–90, 96–102, 103–5, 269
  and South Africa, 216–17
  SSAP16, 145–51
  standard-setting process, 327–8, 329–30
  stock relief, 95–6
  Tweedie and Whittington's proposed
    successor to *SSAP16*, 338–45
  valuation, 277–8
United States of America, 154–89, 263
  and Australasia, 213–14
  and Canada, 217, 220
  capital maintenance concept, 164, 167,
    257, 283
  CCA, 155–6, 165–8, 170–89, 248, 269–70
  CPP, 36, 39, 59, 154–63, 264
  deflation of 1865–96 stimulated debate
    on RC accounting, 17
  developments 1945–74, 38–44
  operating capacity, 159, 172, 176, 284
  present position, 248–52, 257, 258
  proposed method of Tweedie and
    Whittington in use in USA, 344–5
  valuation, 277–80
  visit by Sandilands Committee, 86
  see also Financial Accounting Standards
    Board; Securities and Exchange
    Commission
United States Steel, 38
unrealised gains
  in Canada, 220
  and Edwards and Bell, 54
  inclusion of unrealised gains in income,
    295, 297–8

403

Subject index

in Mathews Report, 195
in The Netherlands, 228
in New Zealand, 210, 212–24, 248
and Paton, 266
and Sweeney, 33, 40–1
in Tweedie and Whittington's proposed
method, 341–2
in UK, 113, 115, 138, 147
in West Germany, 231
Uruguay, 234–6, 241–2
USA, *see* United States of America

valuation, 275–81, 301
in CCA, 269, 275
in CPP, 275
multiple valuation bases in Tweedie and
Whittington's proposed method, 345

present valuation practices, 249–51,
254–5
value to the business, 7–8, 56, 267, 278–81,
301, 345
in Australia, 191, 196, 268
as basis of CC valuation, 11, 249–51, 269
developed by Bonbright, 25, 191, 276
developed by Canning, 25, 268
developed by Limperg, 31, 266
in New Zealand, 205–7, 212
in UK, 96–7, 102, 108, 191, 248
in USA, 168, 171, 177
value to the firm (or owner), *see* value to
the business

West Germany, *see* Germany
Wheat Commission, 328